Building a Web-Based Education System

Colin McCormack
David Jones

WILEY COMPUTER PUBLISHING

John Wiley & Sons, Inc.
New York • Chichester • Weinheim • Brisbane • Singapore • Toronto

Publisher: Robert Ipsen
Editor: Theresa Hudson
Managing Editor: Erin Singletary
Electronic Products/Associate Editor: Mike Green
Text Design & Composition: Benchmark Productions, Boston, MA
Original Artwork: Paul O'Sullivan

This book is printed on acid-free paper. ♾

Published by John Wiley & Sons, Inc.

Published simultaneously in Canada.

Library of Congress Cataloging-in-Publication Data:
McCormack, Colin, 1969-
Building a Web-based education system/Colin McCormack, David Jones.
p. cm.
Includes bibliographical references and index.
ISBN 0-471-19162-0 (pbk. : alk. paper)
1. Internet (Computer network) in education. 2. World Wide Web (Information retrieval system) 3. Computer managed instruction. I. Jones, David, 1968- II. Title.

LB1044, 87.M33 1997 97-33992
025.06'3--dc21 CIP

Printed in the United States of America.
10 9 8 7 6 5 4

Contents

Acknowledgments

I would like to thank all the people who, directly or indirectly, contributed to this book. Deserving of particular mention are Chris Bigum, for his refereeing work, and my sister Kiara who proofread much of the book. My girlfriend Ellen Kelleher helped out by cutting me an enormous amount of slack and acting as my personal librarian. I am also very grateful to the people who agreed to allow their software to be included in the book particularly Martin Holmes and Mark Nottingham. Thanks to all the people on the WWW Course Development mailing list and its host Rik Hall for a lively and useful forum. I'd also like to thank my colleagues and students at U.C.C. who encouraged me and were the subjects of early Web-based classroom systems. Finally, thanks to the folks at Wiley who supported this project.

This book is dedicated to my parents, Anastatia and Matthew, for parenting above and beyond the call of duty.

Colin McCormack (colin@cs.ucc.ie)

To start, let me add my thanks to everyone mentioned by Colin for their contributions. In particular I'd like to again thank Chris Bigum for his insight and suggestions. Like Colin I must also thank my parents, Elwyn and Pam, I owe you a debt I can never repay. On a more original note I'd like to thank the following long list of people who all contributed in various ways to the book or my sanity during the process. Matthew Aldous, Jo Barrie, Doyia Bryson, Renay Buchanan, Scott Bytheway, Pat Cahill, Des Casey, Mary Cranston, Mike Crock, Matthew Harvey, Bruce Jamieson, Kylie Jones, Teresa Lynch, Melinda Midgley, Andrew Newman, Sharonn Stewart, Elizabeth Tansley, Matthew Walker, Andrew Whyte, Judy Yewdale, everyone concerned with CQ-PAN, the members of the Webclass project and the members of the A-Grade, Super League team from ISA. Thanks to the Department of Mathematics and Computing and the Flexible Learning Advisory Group at Central Queensland University for the time and resources to play with the Web and education. A special thanks must go to the hundreds of students who have passed through the classes I have taught, especially those that suffered through my early attempts at Web page design, I only wish I knew then what I know now. Thanks to the people at SIGCSE (**www.acm.org/sigcse/**) for organizing the Barcelona conference at which Colin and I met. Finally I'd like to thank Colin for getting the project started and for putting up with me during the process.

David Jones (d.jones@cqu.edu.au)

And finally thanks to you, the reader, we hope the book helps you and your students.

Preface

Welcome to the wonderful world of the Web-based education system. The World Wide Web has generated a great deal of discussion and is often heralded as providing opportunities for business and as an information and communication resource. The idea of a global information system and the ease with which it can be used means that the 'Web' has captured the imagination of more people than any other computer innovation. The possibility of using the Web for education has generated a great deal of interest among educators throughout the world, a number of whom have taken up the challenge and built their own Web-based classrooms. On the whole however the use of the Web for education is a rarity.

The limited use of the Web in teaching can be attributed to the following factors:

Knowledge. Constructing a Web-based classroom is not a straight forward task and requires knowledge of technical and educational principles. This is a combination that very few educators have.

Reluctance. Some educators are reluctant to adopt new methods, particularly those which involve technology. Some of this reluctance stems from ignorance and misconceptions about the characteristics of new methods and what they have to offer.

Resources. Very few institutions will provide the time, support, training, recognition and infrastructure necessary to implement a Web-based classroom.

The aim of this book is to address these issues and help educators, of all types, use the Web to support their own teaching. We will not show you what you should do but provide you with the knowledge which will enable you to decide what will work in your situation. To help support you each chapter will highlight the principles, positives and problems related to using the Web. In addition each chapter provides practical advice and examples, which when combined with the tools on the accompanying CD-ROM, will help make it possible for you to construct your own Web-based classroom.

Huh?

The fields of computing and education are littered with technical terms and jargon. While the use of jargon has been kept to a minimum you may come across terms with which you are not familiar. To help address this problem the glossary in Appendix B on the CD-ROM provides definitions of many of these terms. A similar glossary can be found on the book's Web site.

WHY WRITE THE BOOK?

The authors, one from Ireland the other from Australia, are University lecturers in computing teaching classes in both on-campus and distance modes. This means that both have expertise in computing, experience with educational principles and classes which were suffering from problems which were impacting the effectiveness and efficiency of the learning experience. This combination provided the motivation and the ability to construct and use a Web-based classroom at a time when other educators without the knowledge or the motivation could not. Having built Web-based classrooms and observed others struggling to do the same identified a need for a book that helps other educators build their own Web-based classrooms.

As time progresses this need is also being addressed by the increasing number of very good tools which can help and support educators involved in this process. People are still making fundamental mistakes, reinventing the wheel and struggling with the issues that others have addressed. It is hoped that this book can help address some of these concerns.

WHO IS THE BOOK WRITTEN FOR?

In writing this book we were attempting to satisfy the requirements of any educator who has an interest in building a Web-based classroom. While our experience in the University sector means much of the terminology and examples we use in the book come from that sector this book is not solely for use by University academics. Any educator, from the primary, secondary, tertiary, vocational or commercial sectors, could take the ideas, approaches and software described here and apply them to their own circumstances.

An educator intending to use this book to construct their own Web-based classroom will need to have some rudimentary computer experience including word processing, file and directory management and use of the World Wide Web. The book and its support tools will provide any other necessary technical knowledge. Those intending to construct more complex Web-based classrooms may need to consult other sources of information mentioned throughout the book.

WHAT WILL I NEED?

The resources you require to build your own Web-based classroom will depend on what you hope to achieve. Many fine systems have been built using a minimum of resources. So don't be put off if your students don't have access to the latest all-singing, all-dancing equipment. By designing the Web-based classroom so that it is appropriate for the characteristics of your students it is possible to implement a useful system.

To construct a Web-based classroom it will be necessary to have access to a collection of raw materials. Those materials fall into four basic categories: networking, hardware, software and educational resources. Most of the software you will require to build your Web-based classroom can be found on the book's CD-ROM or by following pointers from the book's Web site. You may require additional software if you intend building a more advanced Web-based classroom or providing some unique functionality.

On the book's CD-ROM you will find software for three major computer platforms, UNIX, Windows and the Macintosh. Where possible all the software mentioned in this book is available for all three of these platforms. However there are a few cases where software is limited to a particular platform or provides only limited functionality on some platforms.

If you plan to use the software we provide to build your Web-based classroom then you will need either a UNIX, Windows or Macintosh computer. This computer will be used to create your Web-based classroom and to serve your Web-based classroom to your students. It is possible for the development and the hosting of your Web-based classroom to be undertaken on separate computers. This means that you could write all your material on one computer and use another (the server) to distribute it.

The size and speed of the server you will require for your Web-based classroom will depend on several factors including the size of your class, how often the Web-based classroom will be accessed, what features and software you intend to use and what other tasks the server computer must perform. Table 1 provides a list of the minimum specifications we recommend for a computer hosting a single, small Web-based classroom with fairly simple features. If you plan to construct several Web-based classrooms or a single fairly complex one then you should plan to have a larger server computer.

During the development phase it is not necessary for your Web-based classroom to be on a network. It is also possible to distribute your Web-based classroom on disk so that it will not require network access to be used. However, in

TABLE 1

Platform	*CPU*	*RAM*
Windows 95	**486**	**16Mb**
Windows NT	**486**	**32Mb**
Macintosh	**68040, Power PC**	**16Mb**
UNIX	**486 equivalent**	**16-32Mb**

most situations a Web-based classroom must have some form of network connection in order for students to gain access to updates of information and to make use of communication resources. We suggest that a Web-based classroom's network connection should be at least equivalent to that provided by ISDN. A modem connection does not provide sufficient speed. We also suggest that the Web-based classroom be available on the network 24 hours a day. It is not necessary for your Web-based classroom to be on the Internet. A connection via a local area network (intranet) is acceptable if it is sufficient to provide access for all your students.

The final and possibly the most important requirement you will need before you build your Web-based classroom is the educational material it will contain, the concepts, textbooks, tutorial sheets, lesson plans, pedagogy, assignments and exams. Chapter 2 will guide you through a process which will help you identify what resources you have available to you while chapter 4 will provide some pointers on how you can adapt that material for use in your Web-based classroom.

WHAT TYPE OF BOOK IS THIS?

There is no shortage of books written to help people come to grips with Netscape, write HTML, design Web pages, manage a Web server or write Java programs. Similarly there are several theoretical books which examine the possibilities and implications of using the Internet and the Web in learning. Somewhere in the middle of these two book types (the theoretical and the technical) are case studies which describe the experiences of educators using the Internet and the Web. This book aims to show you how to build a Web-based classroom by using an approach that combines the best features of all three book types.

It is unavoidable that in building a Web-based classroom, even with the increasing ease of use of the necessary tools, you will require some technical knowledge. Some of this knowledge will be about computers, software and the Web while other necessary technical knowledge might include knowing how to scan a photo or digitize a piece of video. The book will introduce this knowledge and provide enough understanding for you to construct a Web-based classroom.

It will also provide pointers to other resources, mostly on-line, which can be helpful in gaining a more in-depth understanding.

The foundation of any educational technology project should include a sound understanding of the related educational principles. The book will describe the educational and other non-technical principles that are relevant in the construction of a Web-based classroom. As with the technical knowledge the book will provide a list of pointers to resources which can provide a more in-depth coverage of these topics.

Finally, many chapters provide real-life examples of the processes and decisions made by educators in the building of their own Web-based classrooms. The intention behind the inclusion of these case studies is that they will help to reinforce the principles introduced, provide an opportunity to gather ideas from the experience of others and demonstrate examples of Web-based classrooms in action.

The book provides a very practical and hands on approach to the problem of building a Web-based classroom. The aim is that if you read this book and complete the book's activities then in doing so you will construct your own Web-based classroom.

HOW IS THIS BOOK STRUCTURED?

A project to construct a Web-based classroom can, like any technical or instructional design project, be broken down into five steps, analysis, design, implementation, evaluation and maintenance. As a result we have organized this book so that the chapters follow these steps (see Table 2). These five steps do not necessarily have to be completed one after the other and you may find yourself moving back and forth between steps (and chapters) as you build your Web-based classroom.

The first step in building a Web-based classroom is working out what a Web-based classroom is and why you would want to build one (Chapter 1). Having decided that it is worthwhile for you to build a Web-based classroom it is necessary to analyze the resources and characteristics of the students, staff and raw materials (both educational and equipment) which will be used to build your

Table 2

Task	*Book chapters*
Analysis	**1 & 2**
Planning and Design	**3**
Implementation	**4, 5, 6 & 7**
Testing and evaluation	**10**
Maintenance	**8 & 11**

Web-based classroom and decide what you hope to achieve (Chapter 2). Knowing what you have to work with and what you hope to achieve it is now possible to design the structure and components of your Web-based classroom (Chapter 3).

Having worked out the design you can now carry out the design and construct the various components of your Web-based classroom (Chapters 4 through 7). While in operation the Web-based classroom will require management to ensure that it continues to provide an appropriate learning and administrative environment (Chapter 8). Once the Web based class is built it is necessary to check on its impact and identify areas where improvement can be made. In Chapter 9 we look at some of the software packages which you can use to help you set up and maintain a Web based classroom. Finally we look at the technical details behind setting up a computer to handle a Web based classroom and look at some of the utilities which can add extra features to your systems (Chapter 10).

The CD-ROM

The CD-ROM accompanying this book contains some of the software discussed in the book. The book's Web site contains templates for classrooms and training materials that you may find useful. The design of the CD-ROM means that it should be readable on UNIX, Windows and Macintosh computers. The book's Web site should be readable straight from the CD-ROM or you may wish to install it onto a local hard drive.

On the CD-ROM you will find a list of the software which describes for each individual software package included on the CD-ROM: its purpose, its requirements, whether it is free, shareware or an evaluation copy and the platforms it is available on. The same section on the CD-ROM also describes the process for installing the software onto your system, how to access the nearest Web site and where to go to ask questions if you are having problems.

The best way to use the CD-ROM is through a Web browser. Open the file on the CD-ROM called 'index.htm' for a list of contents. This file will be located in the top directory of the CD-ROM.

The WWW Site

In writing this book there have always been two certainties, it will contain mistakes and by the time it is published some of the methods, tools and procedures discussed will have changed. To address these problems and to also provide a mechanism by which the readers of the book can comment and share ideas there is a Web site for the book. The address for the Web site is

`www.wiley.com/compbooks/mccormack`

The Web site is a much more dynamic source of information and communication than this book can ever be. It provides a number of features including up to date copies of software, a growing list of examples, advice and comments, discussion forums, mechanisms for providing feedback and suggestions and others. Unlike the book the Web site is not intended to be a one-way flow of information. Instead it is hoped that people other than the authors will contribute to the site and the information it presents.

1

What's It All About?

WHAT IS A WEB-BASED CLASSROOM?

The use of computers and communication technologies in learning has a history going back at least 30 years. In that time it has been called by many names, including computer-mediated communication (CMC), computer conferencing, online learning, Internet-based learning, and telematics. The advent of the Web provides a new and interesting environment for CMC that offers a host of new possibilities together with many of the advantages of previous incarnations but without some of the problems that have dogged computer-based learning.

A Web-based classroom is an environment created on the World Wide Web in which students and educators can perform learning-related tasks. A Web-based classroom is not simply a mechanism for distributing information to students; it also performs tasks related to communication, student assessment, and class management. Your imagination and resources are the only limits to how you utilize the Web.

Many of the tools that provide the functionality of the Web-based classroom have very little to do with the Web at all. A Web-based classroom may use Internet applications such as e-mail, Usenet News, FTP, and a variety of other computer applications such as databases. The Web provides the simple, familiar interface by which the students and educators in a class can access and use these applications.

HOW DOES IT WORK?

The following section provides two different explanations of how a Web-based classroom works. The first section presents a hypothetical case study of an educator and a student using a particular Web-based classroom. This case study provides useful insight into how the participants interact with a particular Web-based classroom and gives some idea of what is possible. The second section describes the components that make a Web-based classroom work and how they interact.

A Day in the Life

A Web-based classroom can be used as a supplement to existing teaching methods, currently the most common approach, or as a total replacement for existing methods. The following hypothetical scenarios are based on a Web-based classroom to be used in the second half of 1997. The planning and design of this particular Web-based classroom is used as an example in Chapter 3 of this book. The address of this Web-based classroom can be found on the book's CD-ROM. In the next two sections, we examine the possibilities of a Web-based classroom from the point of view of an educator and a student.

The Educator

Another lecture over. Lectures are definitely shorter now that they concentrate on the difficult concepts. Requiring the students to read the textbook, take part in experiments, and use self-assessment questions also appear to be working. The frequently asked questions page, which contains a list of common questions from last year, definitely helped reduce the number of questions at the start of the semester—though the heavy use of the mailing list by students to ask questions probably makes up for that.

I will have to remember to pick up the video tape of the lecture tomorrow so the audio can be digitized and placed onto the Web with the lecture slides. Some of the distance education students have made some positive comments about being able to listen to a lecture and see the lecture slides. It seems to make them feel more a part of the class. Hearing an explanation of the concepts that is different from the textbook is also helping. In addition, if the analysis of the log files is correct, a number of the on-campus students are also finding the online lectures attractive.

A couple of students have asked about the return of assignment 1 today (they submitted it only last Friday)—best check to see how the graders are doing. The assessment management page (Figure 1.1) reports that most of the assignments have been graded. Best take a final look at the grading and make sure everything is OK before returning the assignments.

Judging by the average grade, it looks like the students ended up grasping the concept of "mutual exclusion." That alternative explanation of the problem that was placed on the Web must have helped. Wouldn't have bothered with it if the records of the self-assessment questions hadn't shown that most students were getting the mutual exclusion questions wrong.

One slight problem the assessment management page shows is that a few students still haven't submitted their first assignments. It might be worthwhile to contact them and see if there are any problems. Playing telephone tag or sending personal e-mail will take too long. A general note to the class mailing list might be a bit too impersonal. The e-mail merge system looks like the best alternative. It provides a simple way to send the same message to all the students, but it will appear to be a personal message. Hopefully, the personal touch will help urge them to reply and let us know whether there is a problem.

It's almost four o'clock, time to go into virtual office mode. Connect to the Web page, log into the interactive chat applet, enter the (virtual) room, and wait for some students to arrive. In the meantime, should probably check some e-mail. Obviously a slow day for students—only two messages, one sent directly to me and the other to the class mailing list. The direct e-mail contains a couple of good questions that will be of interest to the rest of the class. So, a personal reply to the student, which also quietly urges them to use the mailing list next time, and send a section of the reply, without the original sender's name, to the class mailing list. That way the student asking the question gets a personal answer and the other students also see the question and answer, just in case some of them were asking the same question.

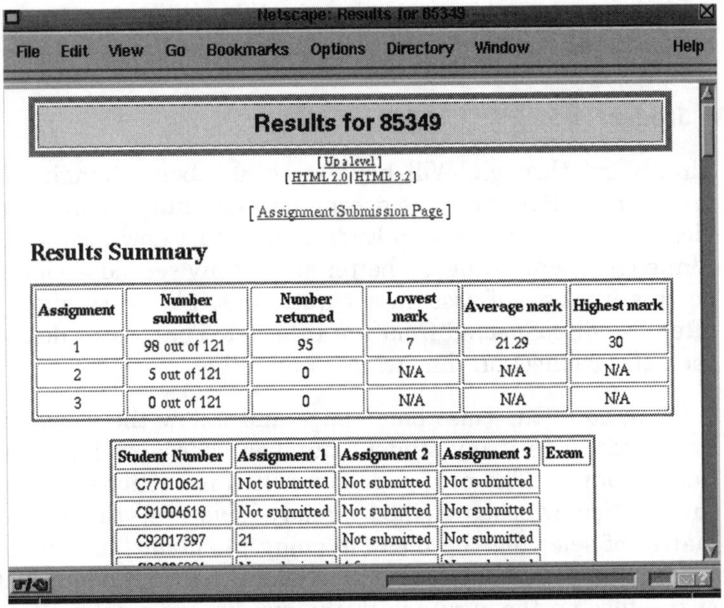

FIGURE 1.1 Assessment summary page.

The message from the mailing list is asking a question about the main concept from last week's lecture, which has already been answered on the mailing list. This student obviously hasn't been taking notice of the mailing list and hasn't checked the Web-based archives. Rather than write another reply, I'll send a reply to the list explaining how to use the Web-based archive and giving the address of the Web page that contains the previous answer. Connect to the Web, go to the mailing list archives, and use the search mechanism to find the actual page. There it is. A couple of the other students on the list added their own comments and pointed to another Web page that offers an alternative explanation; best include those in the reply as well.

Beep! Sounds like someone in the interactive chat room has called me, best see what they want. Having a quick look at the logs of the chat room shows that two or three students have been discussing one of the topics from this week and need another opinion. Actually, the explanation might be helped by a diagram; have to get everyone to open up the shared whiteboard (Figure 1.2) and ask them to put up with my lack of drawing skills. Seems like there were quite a few students interested in this particular conversation, including a couple of lurkers (people who listen to a conversation but don't get involved). Better get a copy of the discussion from the chat room archives and post it to the mailing list. It's directly related to a section in the study guide as well. Might be worthwhile to add the discussion as an annotation to the study guide so they can see the discussion in context.

The Student

Finally got through. Will have to think about changing Internet service providers (ISPs) if this one doesn't do something about improving their service. Oh well, best start up Eudora and start downloading any new e-mail. While it's downloading, I'd better submit my second assignment and maybe do this week's self-assessment questions. I'll worry about reading e-mail after I've disconnected from the Internet. That way I don't have to pay for the extra connection time while I'm reading.

Okay, go to the class home page and follow the assignment submission link. Next, give it my student number, choose assignment 2, and hit the Submit button. The next page gives the instructions on what to submit for this particular assignment. I already have everything ready, so it's just a matter of selecting the files I'm going to submit, hit Submit, and wait for them to be placed onto the server. Okay, that's all done. Just check the size of the files on the server with the size on my machine to make sure that they've been submitted correctly.

While I'm here, I may as well check the results page (Figure 1.1). Will be interesting to see how many students have actually submitted assignment 2 so far. Only five so far, I must be a bit ahead of the others. That's a surprise! It looks like the first assignment has been marked, which means my marked assignment should be in the e-mail that's downloading at the moment. Better write down the highest, lowest, and average marks for the assignment so I can compare how I did.

While I'm here, I'd best head over to the self-assessment center and complete the quiz for this week. Only 10 questions this time, a bit shorter than last week. Okay, all done; hit Submit and wait for the mark—9 out of 10,

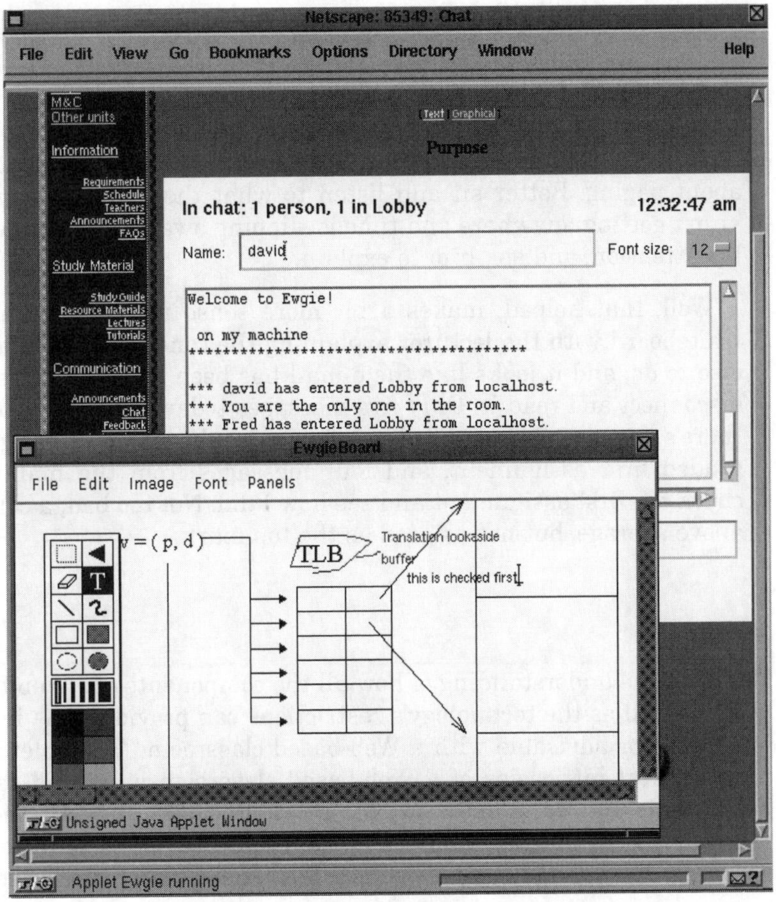

FIGURE 1.2 Chat and shared whiteboard.

which one did I get wrong? Question 5, the question on paging and virtual memory. I'm not sure about that explanation, it seems to contradict what was in the study guide. I'd better check the study guide.

Where is that study guide? Not here, must be in the other room where I left it last night. Too much effort to get up, let's check the Web-based version. Connect to the study material page, there's the study guide; let's check the index for the term "paging." Two entries. Both are a bit vague and don't seem to confirm either answer. I see that there are a couple of annotations; wonder if they will help. Two entries; one is from the lecturer, the other one is from that annoying student who's always asking those stupid questions on the list. Let's leave that one and see what the lecturer had to say; helps a little, but I still think I'm missing something.

I'm going to have to clear this up so I'll have to ask someone. So do I use the mailing list or the chat room? Let's check the chat room first and see if anyone is there. It looks like the lecturer and a couple of students are. The lecturer is away doing something, but it looks like the students are talking about paging. Better sit and listen to what they have to say. They really aren't getting anywhere and time is slipping away. I'll buzz the lecturer, get his attention, and ask him to explain.

Well, that helped, makes a bit more sense now. That diagram on the whiteboard with the lecturer explaining the concepts helped a lot. Nothing else to do, and it looks like the e-mail has been downloaded, so it's time to disconnect and read it. Only five messages today, an all-time low! Let's see, there's the e-mail acknowledgment of my submission of assignment 2, my graded first assignment, and four messages from the mailing list. Let's check the first assignment and see how I did. Not too bad, a couple of points above average, but not as good as the top mark.

How It Works

Having some understanding of how all the components of a Web-based classroom work as well as the technology's restrictions can provide some insight into what is possible or advisable with a Web-based classroom. A complete explanation of the technical intricacies of a Web-based classroom is beyond the scope of this book and is not really necessary for most educators. Instead, the following section and the remaining chapters of the book attempt to provide a basic understanding that can make your use of a Web-based classroom less of a mystery.

The Material for Learning The whole process starts, as most classrooms usually do, with the educator designing the learning experience: preparing the materials, the pedagogy, the outline of the aims of the course, and how to fulfill them.

In the Web-based classroom, this may involve setting up computers for the students to use, preparing Web pages, converting existing computer-based material, creating quizzes, setting up mailing lists, drawing or scanning pictures, digitizing video, and many other tasks. Throughout this book, we try to ease the burden of this process so that you can construct an effective and efficient Web-based classroom.

Many tools can be used to set up the learning experience; these range from large, expensive software packages to a simple programmed tool written by one person. Throughout this book, we will mention software that may be useful and where it can be obtained. We have also tried to include useful programs and raw material on the book's CD-ROM.

The System in Action After you create the learning material, it will be stored on one or more computers. The information can be in a variety of forms such as HTML pages, sound files, pictures, video, or e-mail messages. These computers serve (they are usually called *servers*) as the distribution points for this information. Anyone wanting to access the information will do so from these computers.

Having learning material stored on a computer means that you can search, archive, index, and convert that material easily and very quickly. On many server computers, you will find a variety of applications that enable you to perform these operations very easily. The result of these operations—for example, an index of the learning material—can be made available for people to access via the programs that run on the server.

Client programs are computer programs that ask programs running on a server to perform various tasks (for example, fetch information, send a message). Web browsers such as Netscape and e-mail programs such as Eudora are examples of client programs. In order for the client to make a request to the server, the client and server must observe the same protocol (a set of rules programs have for exchanging information). Each program that runs on the server has its own protocol that lays down the format and order in which communication takes place between it and a client. For example, the POP server has a series of rules on how it sends and receives e-mail.

Programs running on the server provide users with the means of getting at the information stored on the server as well as network services (e-mail, FTP); client programs running on users' individual computers provide the means by which each computer user can access the server. The client program will translate the user's click of the mouse button or sequence of keystrokes into the appropriate server request. For example, clicking on the Check Mail icon of Eudora will cause Eudora to send a request to a POP daemon asking if there is any mail for this user. If there is mail, the server will provide that mail to Eudora. Eudora will then present the arrival of new mail via a sound signal and show the user a list of new mail. Using client programs to access the server means we don't have to know how the client programs or the server programs work to use the system.

An original design aim of the Web was to provide a universal client. This means that by design, Web clients not only access Web servers to get and receive information, they can also access FTP and mail servers. This means that you can use one program, your Web browser, to do everything.

In the past 18 months, companies such as Netscape have extended this concept of the Web browser as a universal client by including programs that handle e-mail and news as built-in parts of the Netscape Web browser. The simplicity of the Web interface and its growing popularity mean that it is becoming easier to train computer users to perform useful tasks. Rather than requiring training on sending e-mail on different types of computers and using different programs, users can now use a browser, a simple all-in-one program that looks the same and works the same, no matter what computer it runs on.

The result: Users can now do just about any task using a Web browser—the universal client. Employing one simple yet powerful program that is widely used in industry and recreation for your classroom helps minimize the new skills you and your students need to learn and helps maximize the possibility of those skills being used outside the classroom.

A Web-based education system is made up of a number of parts: the server, which is used to hold information and direct communication; the client, which students use to ask the server for information; and the network, which teachers and students use to connect to the server.

The server is a computer that not only stores the course material but also contains programs that allow clients on other computers to connect to the server and read information from it or place information on it. The server also allows people using different types of computers to connect to each other so they can have a conversation and share information.

Figure 1.3 shows the series of messages and operations performed when someone uses a server. In the first step, the user creates a message to the server via the browser (perhaps by using a mouse to select a hyperlink or typing some text) or writes some information that will be placed on the server. The browser sends this message over the network to the server in Step 2. In Step 3, the server receives the request from the browser and performs the operations necessary to satisfy it. In step 4, the server returns the information to the browser (client), which will display the information requested for the user.

Once the server is set up to support this model, you can run your class through your browser. Each server has to be set up and looked after by someone. Each server can also be different— each can contain different information, for example. Furthermore, each type of Internet application, such as Usenet, e-mail, FTP, and even the program that allows people to see Web documents (called an HTTP daemon or server) has to be able to run a program on the server that handles them. For example, imagine that you wanted to edit a word processor file; you need to find the word processor that created the file so you can read and edit it.

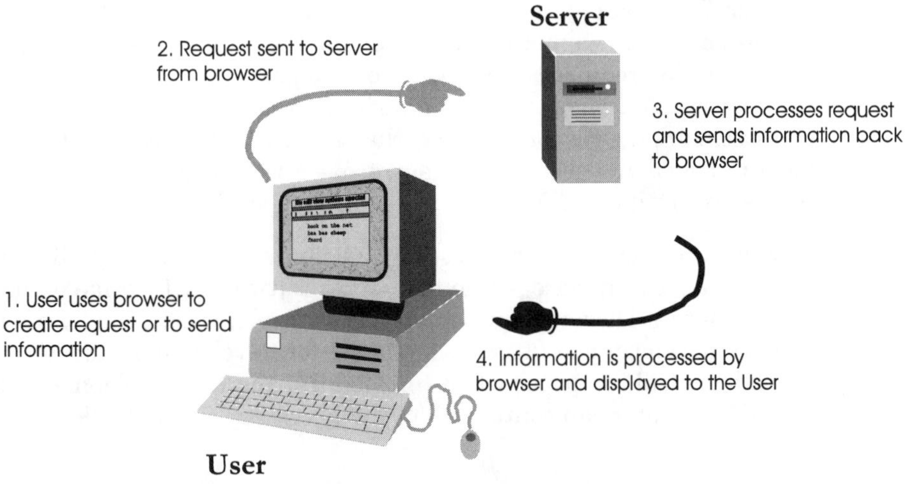
Server
2. Request sent to Server from browser
3. Server processes request and sends information back to browser
1. User uses browser to create request or to send information
4. Information is processed by browser and displayed to the User
User

FIGURE 1.3 Browser server interaction.

It is the same idea with a server: If you want to send and receive e-mail you must find a server that will handle the program in which your incoming and outgoing e-mail was created. There is no need to worry about setting up these programs, because not all of the Web-based classroom facilities depend on them. The most important program to have set up on your server is the HTTP server program that handles requests from clients who need to exchange information with the server.

Client, Server, and Support Software A large collection of software can be used in the development, maintenance, and daily activity of a Web-based classroom. One way of categorizing the software is to use the following three categories:

> **Support.** Software in this category generally has little or no direct connection with the Web. Instead, it is software the participants use to support their activity within the Web-based classroom. Some examples include word processors, graphics programs, and databases.
>
> **Client.** Students and educators participating in a Web-based classroom do so via a computer and a collection of client software. The client software provides the interface to the Web-based classroom that the participants use to perform tasks and interact in the Web-based classroom. Examples of client software include Web browsers such as Netscape, e-mail programs such as Eudora, and programs that provide access to other Internet services such as chats, MUDs, and videoconferencing.

Server. The client software provides the interfaces the participants use, but it does not provide a method for supplying the management and distribution of information required to allow a group of people to communicate and share information. Management and distribution of information in a Web-based classroom are the responsibility of the server software. Each of the major services provided by a Web-based classroom—a Web server, e-mail, mailing lists, interactive chats, and MUDs—all require a specific server.

Typically, the Web-based classroom participants' computers will provide the support and client software, while the server software will reside on one or two central computers. However, this is not always true. It is common for a Web-based classroom's developers to use one computer for development and to move to a server on a central computer when finished. During the development stage, the developer's computer can contain all of the necessary support, client, and server software.

Connections For a Web-based classroom to work, there must be a connection between the client and server software (for example, between a student's browser and the class Web server). Some variation in the types of connections is possible. The following list breaks the possible connections into four broad categories:

LAN and faster. Most university campuses and businesses have some form of local area network (LAN). These connections are among the fastest and most expensive to set up.

Home connections. For most users today, connecting from home means using a modem and a phone line. Although fast enough for most purposes, a modem can be quite slow for the retrieval of large documents or multimedia files (videos and sound clips, for instance). In some parts of the world, ISDN and cable modems are available; these are approaching the speed of some LANs. Although less expensive, these connections are usually paid for by students. In some countries, fees for these connections can be charged on the basis of how long the user is connected.

Hybrid. The slow speed of modem connections has led to the use of hybrid connections. In a hybrid Web-based classroom, a CD-ROM is used to distribute large amounts of information, and a modem connection is used to provide updates and communication. Hybrid connections are a compromise designed to address the problems of current technology, yet they increase development cost due to the need to merge two different environments. As home connection speeds increase, use of hybrid connections will decrease.

None. From one perspective, this connection category is the hybrid approach without the network connection. It is important because, regardless of the hype surrounding the technology, a large proportion of people in the world still cannot gain access to the Internet. Some of these people have access to computers and therefore can still use many of the elements of a Web-based classroom (documents and self tests, for example). However, they will not benefit from the immediate communication and sharing of information possible with one of the other three connection categories.

From the point of view of users, a connection is judged on two essential characteristics: speed and cost. The faster a connection, the less time it takes to retrieve information from servers and the less time the participant has to wait. Generally, the faster the connection, the more expensive it is in purely monetary terms. On the other hand, a slower connection, although financially less expensive, will cost more in time lost waiting for information to download and possibly result in frustration. Another important characteristic is how the cost of the connection is calculated. Construction of a LAN has a large up-front cost, some ongoing maintenance charges, and usually no usage charges; generally the cost is paid by the institution. On the other hand, a modem connection from home might cost less than a few hundred dollars, but it is usually paid for by the student.

Protocols Client and server software use network connections to communicate and share information. However, before they can do so they must agree upon a set of rules that govern how they can communicate; such a set of rules is called a communications protocol. The Internet uses protocols that belong to the TCP/IP protocol stack. The stack is a collection of protocols that each belong to one of four layers. The top layer defines the application protocols that software such as Web browsers and e-mail programs use to communicate with appropriate servers. Table 1.1 summarizes some of the protocols used on the Internet, the programs that use them, and their purpose.

Table 1.1 Clients, Servers, Protocols, and Their Purpose

Client	*Server*	*Protocol*	*Purpose*
Netscape Communicator	Apache	HTTP (HyperText Transport Protocol)	Retrieving Web pages
Eudora	Sendmail	SMTP (Simple Mail Transport Protocol)	Sending e-mail messages
Eudora	A POP daemon	POP (Post Office Protocol) for a user	Retrieving incoming e-mail
Ewgie client (Figure 1.2)	Ewgie server	Ewgie-specific protocol	Interactive chat and a shared white board

HOW CAN YOU USE IT?

What can be done with a Web-based classroom is limited only by the imagination of the educator and the available resources. Because a Web-based classroom is an extension of the educator who built it and designed with a particular situation in mind, the range of possibilities is almost endless. This variety means that we can't describe all the possibilities of a Web-based classroom within this book. Furthermore, only now are people starting to fully understand how to use a Web-based classroom without treating it like a horseless carriage— simply doing electronically what they did physically in the past. The next few years will bring forward Web-based applications that were not even considered yesterday.

The most important thing to remember about a Web-based education system is that, like conventional teaching aids such as videos and slide projectors, it cannot teach the course on its own. It is not intended to replace the role of a teacher but merely to act as a new form of educational tool.

Most types of classes can be put, in whole or in part, on the Web without any great impact on the way the class is taught. Most ideal for the Web are courses that emphasize in-depth coverage and discussion because these can be easily supported, or given entirely, on the Web. Any course that involves extensive writing on the part of the student would also be ideal because the student can share ideas and hand in assignments rapidly using the Web.

It has been found that a Web-based classroom is more suitable in a learner-centered role, meaning that if you make the course information available for the students to go through at their own pace and provide facilities that allow communication between the members of the class or the lecturers, you are encouraging them to take more control of their own education. This approach differs from the traditional method of education, where students sit in a large lecture theater, dutifully write down a lecturer's words, and follow a course of learning suggested by that lecturer. It is worth remembering that students brought up on this force-feeding education method may have difficulty in adapting to any new method of education. With careful design and appreciation of the students difficulties, however, you can introduce students to a more effective and potentially satisfying way of learning using a Web-based education system.

Regarding the substance of a course, most topics can be taught using the Web because all forms of communication and information distribution are supported. In addition, audio, video, and graphical information can be distributed over the Web. For example, students can listen to music in a music course, view a demonstration of a chemistry experiment, or look at slides from a biology lecture. Communication facilities can allow students to "talk" to each other using bulletin boards or live audio links such as telephones.

The following section provides a brief tour of how educators are currently using the Web in education. The tour, like the rest of the book, is structured around four major tasks: information distribution, communication, student assessment, and class management.

Information Distribution

A major task in any classroom is the distribution of information, both administrative and educational. The Web's original purpose was to provide a mechanism by which researchers at CERN (European Particle Physics Center: **www.cern.ch/**) could distribute and access research information, so there is no disputing the observation that in many situations, the Web is an extremely useful tool for the distribution of information.

We can divide information distribution into four separate categories: distribution, conversion, value-added conversion, and creation. This division is based on how the information is created and placed onto the Web. (Chapters 4 and 5 examine the process of distributing information via a Web-based classroom in more detail.)

Distribution Using the Web for distributing information, as a replacement for other media such as disks, CD-ROMs, and print, is the simplest use of the Web. It is also the approach that provides the least benefit. One of its benefits is that it takes advantage of the geographic and temporal independence provided by the Web as a distribution medium. (These advantages are discussed in more detail later in this chapter.)

This approach entails taking existing computer-based material such as files produced with word-processors or presentation programs and placing them on a Web server. Once the materials are on the server, other people can connect to the Web page and retrieve those files. In order for this to be of any use, the users retrieving the information must have stored on their computers appropriate programs that will allow them to view the files.

Examples of this approach include a class in programming offered by Central Queensland University (CQU) where the Powerpoint lecture slides are available from the Web site **mackay.cqu.edu.au/85212/lectures.html**, as shown in Figure 1.4. In a slight modification of the standard practice in many other Web-based classrooms, the files are compressed to make them faster to download.

Another example of this approach is a course in operating systems from Brown University where assignments are made available in both Postscript and Adobe Acrobat format (**www.cs.brown.edu/courses/cs169/asgn.html**).

Conversion The next step up the difficulty level is converting existing paper or computer-based information into a native Web format such as HTML, GIF, or JPEG. The conversion discussed here is automatic conversion performed using another computer program. For example, the latest versions of Microsoft Word provide a facility whereby a Word document can be saved as an HTML document.

The main advantage of this approach is that it places the information in a Web format. This means that the information is platform independent; anyone with a computer that has a Web browser can access the information. There is no longer any need to have a specific program to view the information.

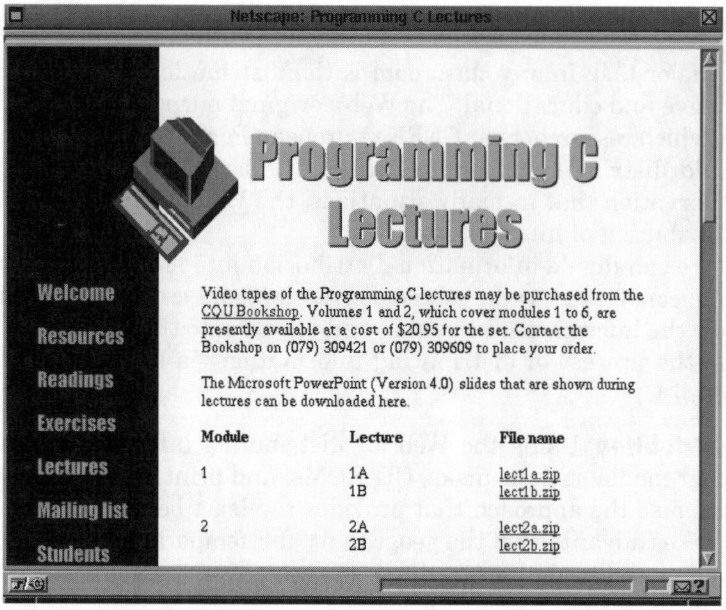

FIGURE 1.4 A sample lecture page.

A drawback of this approach is that the automatic conversions performed by some software can be less than perfect. For example, look at the assignments for the class Quantitative Methods A (Figure 1.5) from a mathematics and computing department. Each of the mathematical symbols contained in an assignment was converted to a GIF image. Given the large number of mathematical symbols in these assignments, the result is a page that takes quite a while to download over a modem.

Value-Added Conversion Value-added conversion takes the conversion process a step further to specifically address the problems of automatic conversion and to use the additional features that the Web provides. The value-added conversion approach enjoys all the benefits of the previous approaches but adds benefits by using the new possibilities that the Web provides. In particular, audio and animation demonstrate the Web's support for media. The major disadvantage of this approach is it requires more work for the developer.

Creation The most difficult and time-consuming of the four categories is creation. With this approach, new material is designed and created specifically for the Web. The design usually employs the special characteristics of the Web to offer new and previously unavailable possibilities. Some examples include a class in screen studies written directly for the Web (**www.arts.cqu.edu.au/candm/scrn_std/ss_home.html**); the Evil Landlady action maze, a collection of Web

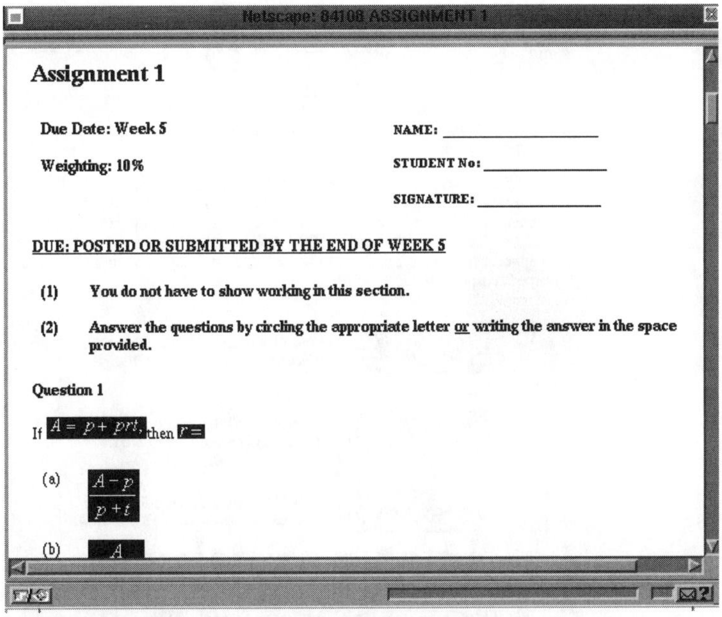

FIGURE 1.5 A complex GIF image for downloading.

pages that use hyperlinks to create a scenario with which students can interact (**web.uvic.ca/hrd/UAP/llady1.htm**); and the Case of the Suspect Water, illustrated in Figure 1.6, a similar use of the Web that introduces students to using the scientific method to manage a project (**www.mib.uga.edu/project/Water-Case/Introduction/Introduction.html**).

Creating material directly for the Web using the Web's special characteristics promises the most benefit and yet is only now being explored as people become comfortable with the environment. The major drawback of this approach is the effort required to produce material that uses the Web's characteristics and users' unfamiliarity with what it is possible to do. Later in this chapter, we'll examine the advantages and new possibilities of this approach in more detail.

Communication

An essential part of any learning experience is communication. A Web-based classroom provides facilities that support a number of types of communication and a number of advantages over traditional face-to-face communication. Chapter 6 discusses the advantages, tools, issues, and approaches to using communication in a Web-based classroom. The following list provides brief descriptions of examples in which communication is currently being enhanced by Web-based classrooms.

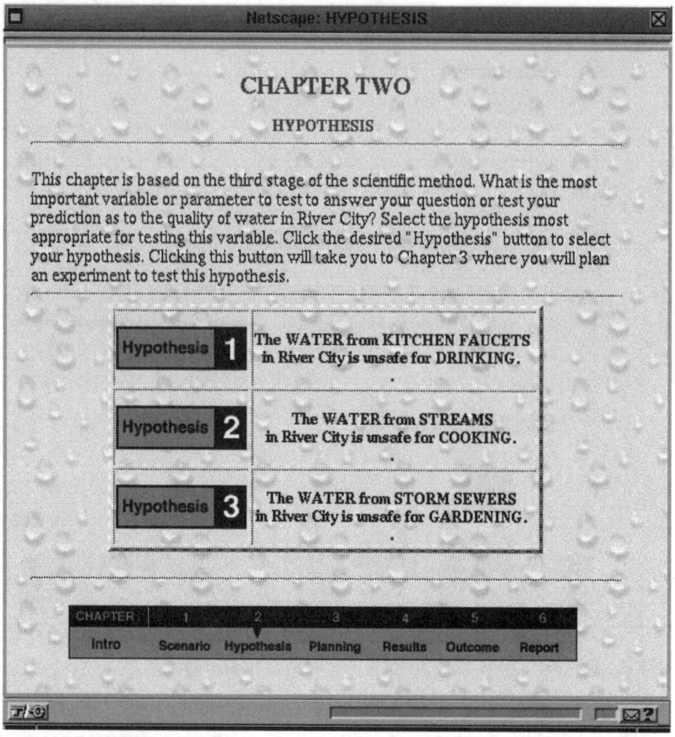

FIGURE 1.6 The Case of the Suspect Water.

In *one-to-one communication*, participants in a Web-based classroom talk privately with other individuals. This discussion can be asynchronous (e-mail), synchronous (interactive chats), text only, or almost face to face (videoconferencing). Using e-mail or other associated communication tools for one-to-one communication in a class is possibly the most widespread use of the medium, which is replacing old methods, such as students asking questions in hallways and is allowing the development of new practices such as the telementoring program at the University of Delaware (**www.asel.udel.edu/sem/programs/telementoring**).

One-to-many communication in a Web-based classroom might include such approaches as online presentations or announcements. Class announcements can be made using Web-based bulletin boards or mailing lists. The distinction between one-to-many communication and information distribution can at times become a bit fuzzy.

Another less well-known example of one-to-many communication is e-mail merge, a process described in the hypothetical scenario earlier in this chapter. E-mail merge is the Internet equivalent to the mail-merge facility provided with most modern word processors. It allows you to combine a list of names, e-mail addresses, and a single message and distribute that message to every e-mail address. The main distinction between e-mail merge and a mailing list is that an e-mail sent via an e-mail merge looks like it is being sent to the recipient and no one else. Some e-mail-merge programs will allow you to customize the message by inserting the name of the person in the message. One application of e-mail merge is to send messages to an entire class, asking each student how he or she is doing. The apparently personal nature of the message helps make the student feel more positive about the class.

Many-to-one communication is the reverse of one-to-many, and the flow of information is from multiple people back to a single person. The most popular use of this approach is to provide feedback, which can take the form of class evaluation forms or direct response.

Last, but by no means least, is *many-to-many communication*. Use of the Web to facilitate many-to-many communication provides a number of benefits over traditional means. (These advantages and the ways in which many-to-many communication can be used are discussed in more detail in Chapter 6.) A number of tools can be used to enable many-to-many communication: mailing lists, interactive chats, and audio- and videoconferencing.

Class Management

Management of the learning process includes tasks such as time tabling, tracking attendance, recording progress, calculating grades, and identifying the learning needs of students. Many educators already use tools such as spreadsheets, databases, and specialized software to perform these tasks. The Web offers an environment that can integrate these separate tools behind a consistent interface and make the whole process of class management more efficient. (Chapter 8 examines class management in more detail.)

WHY BUILD ONE?

The very fact that there is a need for a book about building a Web-based classroom indicates that it is not a quick and simple process. To develop an appropriate Web-based classroom requires a number of skills, a fair amount of time, and a reasonable level of resources. If this is the case, why would you want to expend the effort? Might not that effort be better spent elsewhere? These are the questions that this section attempts to address.

Most educators aim to use a teaching approach that is effective, efficient, and enjoyable. However, many existing approaches suffer from problems that can adversely influence these aims. New approaches, both Web based and not, offer characteristics that make it possible to more easily facilitate these aims. This section describes some of the problems with existing approaches and some of the benefits of using the Web. This list is by no means definitive, but may be familiar to educators who have adopted Web-based classrooms.

Increased Participation

Both the education and training sectors are facing an increase in the number of people needing and wanting to undertake further education. In many cases, this increasing demand on education is outstripping the funding allocated to education. One of the driving forces behind this surge in demand for education and training is the increasing rate of change in work environments brought about by technology and the recognition that most workers will require some form of retraining throughout the course of their working lives.

Increased demand can result in larger class sizes, higher student-to-staff ratios, and a decrease in the interaction between students and staff. This decreased interaction can lead to decreased student motivation and give some students a feeling of isolation. Increased class sizes also put a strain on physical resources. Most university students are familiar with overcrowded lecture halls that force people to sit in the aisles or in other rooms viewing the lecture via closed-circuit television. At some institutions, the inability of physical classrooms to handle the increased class sizes has led to repeat lectures.

Increased Variety

Increased participation in education brings with it an increased variety in the characteristics of students. Educators are now having to face classrooms filled with students with widely different backgrounds, cultures, previous learning experience, preferred learning styles, and personal situations. The assumption that all students come from roughly similar backgrounds is no longer valid.

Need for Increased Flexibility

Among the increasing population of learners is a significant population of mature students who are studying part-time while working and supporting a family. These students must be able to study when and where they can; otherwise, further education is not possible for them. The growing importance of this scenario is evidenced by the increasing interest in distance education methods in which traditional face-to-face communication is not used.

In a commercial training program environment, flexibility is also necessary. Due to pressure of work and personal responsibilities, staff may not be free to attend classes at a fixed time and in a certain location.

Increased Expectations

For most learners today, education represents a considerable investment in time and money, and like most consumers, students are now demanding a service equivalent to the cost. Lawsuits are being lodged by students unhappy with the value of the "product" they have received. As a result, many students want more feedback, more attention, and more resources to help them learn.

The Changing Nature of Knowledge

The amount of new knowledge generated in the last 30 years is greater than that generated during the rest of human history, and new knowledge is being generated at an alarming rate. Along with the rapid growth in knowledge comes the requirement for people to become increasingly specialized in a particular field. As a result, people may need to be retrained more frequently and receive more advanced training in specific areas. Thus the education and training facilities available to these people must maintain contact with current knowledge and be able to adapt to change.

Increased Competition

The education and training sectors are recognized as viable profit-making areas. In the United States alone, commercial organizations spend almost $50 billion a year on education and training. This means that companies such as Disney and other entertainment concerns are moving into the field of "edutainment" (the combination of entertainment and education). Universities are also beginning to see the commercial possibilities of distance education and "franchise" campuses. This increasing competition, in combination with increasing customer expectations, is driving the need for educational institutions to improve the quality of their courses and services.

BENEFITS OF A WEB-BASED CLASSROOM

The belief of many educators that the Web offers a method to address some of these problems comes in part from the Web's particular characteristics. This section examines some of the benefits that the Web offers education.

Computer Mediation

All the information and communication in a Web-based classroom passes through or is stored on a computer. This means it is possible to harness the information processing power of the computer to store, index, search, convert, and distribute information. This ability to use the information processing power of the computer to adapt information to the needs of the learner can remove the rigidity of traditional teaching methods and increase student control over the learning experience.

It can also provide educators with a growing archive of a class because most of the information and communication records are stored on computer for future use. For example, the questions and answers on a class mailing list are usually archived. This resource can be used in following years to form the basis of a collection of frequently asked questions (FAQs). By preempting common student questions using this FAQ list, a teacher may be able to reduce the workload during the initial stages of class.

In order to be able to adapt to the needs of the individual student, it is necessary to be aware of what knowledge they bring to the class and to track their progress through the class. In a traditional situation, tracking a student's progress (using exams and assignments) is difficult, expensive, and requires significant staff time. In a Web-based classroom, not only is the learning material stored on a computer, so is a record of student participation. Using this information and the computer's information processing power, teaching staff can generate student reports, identify problem areas, and even adapt the delivery of material to particular students.

Geographic Independence

In a Web-based classroom, the relative geographic locations of the students and the teacher need not significantly change the quality of the learning experience. Students can study from wherever they happen to be with whatever educational institution best suits their needs. This means that learning is no longer restricted to the physical buildings of the learning institution, and consequently the problems of overcrowding start to disappear. Education can proceed without major reorganization of students' lives, making them feel more in control and hopefully increasing their motivation.

Geographic independence also means that information stored in a Web-based classroom can be changed at any time. There is no longer any delay in distributing material to students; as soon as it is on the Web, students can retrieve it. Information can be corrected, or new and pertinent information can be added. Information can be changed in response to students' requirements or comments, changing management objectives, or a change in the material being taught.

Temporal Independence

The combination of the Web's information distribution possibilities, asynchronous communication, and appropriate pedagogy can free the learning experience from the bounds of time. There is no longer any need for a teacher and 500 students to synchronize their time tables and meet in the same place at the same time. When participation in the learning experience occurs at a time convenient to both the students and the educator, there are a range of advantages. There is no longer any reason for a student (or an educator) to miss a class; the freedom to choose an appropriate time increases students' feelings of control over the learning experience. Students no longer must compete with other students for the educator's limited time, and both student and educator have the time to formulate answers and responses without the pressure of having to provide an immediate reply.

Platform Independence

Many existing applications of computers in education—computer-managed learning (CML), computer-based training (CBT), and CD-ROMs, for example—are specific to a particular computer platform (Windows or Macintosh and so on). This platform specificity means that the producers of these applications must either choose the platform they will support and possibly miss a segment of the market or expend significant extra effort to support multiple platforms. The platform-independent nature of the Web almost totally removes this problem. However, it does still exist if you are planning to use advanced features of the Web that may not be available on all the platforms the students may be using—for example, the Shockwave multimedia system cannot be used on computers running UNIX. The majority of the software needed to access the systems described in this book is available free and can be used on any computer regardless of make or operating system.

A Simple, Familiar, Useful Interface

Many people find learning how to use computers difficult; as a result, they are often reluctant to use them at all. Any use of computers in education should aim to minimize the necessity to learn new skills. Where new skills are required, the instructor should attempt to ensure that those new skills are useful in other arenas. The popularity of the Web means that many students entering a Web-based classroom for the first time may already know how to use the Web. If they do not, the relative simplicity of the tools used to access the Web keeps the effort involved to a minimum. The Web's popularity also means that once a student or teacher knows how to use the Web, that knowledge can be of use in other facets of life apart from education.

Increased Communication

The Web allows students to talk with each other, individually or as a group, and to send questions or hold conversations, oral or electronic, with their educator. Indeed, it is commonly reported that people will talk more electronically (via e-mail or a chat program) than they do in a face-to-face situation.

Increased Learner Control

The combination of computer mediation, platform, and geographic and temporal independence help increase the feeling of control that students have over their learning experience, which is one way to increase student motivation. Increased student control also helps to cope with the increased variety in the backgrounds of students by allowing the students to choose the form of learning activity that is most appropriate for them.

PROBLEMS WITH A WEB-BASED CLASSROOM

The Web-based classroom is not a solution to every problem you may face with your class, nor is it the only solution. Like any medium, it has a number of limitations that must be considered when you are deciding whether or not to build a Web-based classroom.

Access and Resources

Possibly the most-cited problem with using a Web-based classroom is with providing access to the Web and computers to enable that access for both students and educators. In many places around the world, students and educators are struggling to gain access to electricity, let alone computers and the Internet. In these areas, the problem of technology access is a difficult and time-consuming task, often beyond the ability of individual educators to address. On the other hand, in most developed countries, the spread of the Web means that it is increasingly unlikely that students and educators will not have some form of access to computers and computer networks. Whether students have access to the Web and what type of access they have is an important consideration in the design of the Web-based classroom.

Cost

For many traditional, on-campus students, access to the Web is available at no charge via on-campus computer networks. Many commercial companies will provide employees free access to the Web via their LANs. However, for many students based at home, access to the Web costs money, with fees often based on usage. Any form of usage based charging can lead to student anxiety about making extensive use of their Web-based classroom. Anxiety and learning do not make a good combination.

Training

Although the use of the Web is becoming widespread, many students still will require some sort of training on how to use it. It is also important to recognize that for many people, the Web is a very intimidating environment with its own rules and regulations. It is important that both students and staff are comfortable with the new environment of the Web-based classroom.

Adapting to New Methods

The greatest benefits of Web-based classrooms occur via a pedagogy that most effectively uses the characteristics of the technology to increase the quality of the learning experience. The trend in Web-based classrooms is away from the student as a passive recipient of knowledge toward the student involved in the learning process as an active, self-directed participant. Both educators and students with experience only of traditional didactic teaching methods may have problems adapting to this new approach.

Infrastructure, Support, and Administration

The changes brought on by the adoption of a Web-based classroom do not stop with the educator and the student. A Web-based classroom requires infrastructure, support, and administrative procedures that are quite different from those of a traditional classroom. Especially if the move to Web-based classrooms is widespread within an institution, the resource allocation and administrative procedures of an institution must change.

No Uniform Quality

The Web is currently little more than a few years old. As an industry, the Web and associated phenomena are still in their infancy—and it shows. The bandwidth (amount of information a network can carry) available on the Web, while growing, is still limited. This means that in certain areas, the "information superhighway" feels like a dirt track. The reliability of the Internet and its sites can be patchy, so you cannot rely on other Web sites to provide resource material for your students.

In addition, fierce competition between Web browser makers continues to drive nonstandard developments. This means that Web pages written specially for one browser may not work on another. What happens if a student cannot use the browser on his or her computer to read your page? What happens if the company making the browser decides it wants $100 from everyone using it ? In this book we try to follow as closely as possible an agreed-upon, standard way of doing things so that any material you write will be usable for the foreseeable future.

Copyright, Privacy, Security, and Authentication

The issues of copyright, privacy, security, and authentication are all important to consider in any classroom, not just a Web-based classroom. Solutions to these problems are still a long way away for both Web-based and traditional classrooms. Current copyright laws are inconsistent and are still grappling with the demands of long-standing media such as print, painting, and music, so it's difficult to apply them to the fast-moving world of the Web.

Authentication—the question of how you really know the student who turned in an assignment wrote it—is still causing problems in the traditional classroom. The problem has always been with us in one form or another, but the Internet and the Web focus attention on it because access to already existing information can make cheating easier. However, the Web also makes it possible to adopt other assessment methods that increase the difficulty of cheating.

MYTHS

The introduction, by John Perry Barlow, of the idea of "cyberspace natives and immigrants" aptly describes the divide between those people who "grew up" in cyberspace and those who have only recently entered the environment. The natives are comfortable and understand the environment, but many immigrants attempt to understand cyberspace using the terms of reference established in the world they are used to. The misunderstanding of the cyberspace environment by immigrants has led to the development of a number of widely accepted myths and misconceptions. This section examines some myths that surround the Web-based classroom.

It Will Save Money

Many educators believe that the Web can save money if they use it as a replacement information distribution medium for course handouts and lecture notes. At best, this approach reduces the direct cost of production to the institution and redirects it to the student. In many situations, students simply print the material using their own printers or a printer provided in one of the institution's computer labs. This can actually increase the total cost because printing is no longer done by a single, specialized printing/photocopy unit but individually by every student. At its worst, student resentment can grow if they perceive that the institution is more interested in penny-pinching than improving the learning experience. This problem can be addressed if the cost savings made by the institution are put back into the class to provide additional benefits to the student.

It Will Cost Too Much

At the opposite end of the spectrum is the feeling that a Web-based classroom will be too expensive in terms of time, money, and resources and will not offer a sufficient return on that investment. To a large extent, the cost of building a Web-based classroom, just like a normal classroom, depends on the design, features, and implementation of that classroom. Similarly, the extent of the improvement in the learning experience provided by a Web-based classroom depends on the appropriateness of the design to the class, its students, and its teacher. Recent developments, including this book and systems such as Topclass (**www.wbtsystems.com**) and WebCT (**www.webct.com/**) are starting to provide high-level tools that reduce the cost of implementing a Web-based classroom while simultaneously increasing the usefulness of the services offered.

I Can't See Them

Many educators like the ability to look into the eyes of the students as they teach so they can see the gleam of understanding as a student grasps a concept. Many educators see the lack of physical cues in a Web-based classroom as a disadvantage. But is it? How effectively can you gauge the level of understanding in a lecture theater filled with 300 students? Is the ability to see the students an advantage for the students or the lecturer?

Although it is true that the Web-based classroom does not provide the physical cues used by many educators to gauge student understanding, it does provide other capabilities that can perform this task and perhaps do it more effectively. These features, combined with the information processing power of computers, can quickly identify the students who are having difficulty with concepts and discern trends throughout the student body. An educator can also use automation to adapt the format and the order of presentation of information to meet students' needs.

It's Not Interactive

The level of interaction provided in a classroom, Web based or physical, has more to do with the method of teaching than it does with the medium used. A face-to-face lecture can be totally noninteractive if the lecturer's approach discourages student participation. On the other hand, a lecture can provide a great deal of interaction if the lecturer encourages small group discussion and other appropriate behavior. Similarly, a Web-based classroom can be totally interactive or have absolutely no interaction, depending on the educator's approach. However, as described in Chapter 6, the Web-based classroom does provide many characteristics that can make it a more efficient and effective vehicle for interaction.

Education Is More Important than Technology

The educational technology world is full of projects, usually run by people with education backgrounds, in which the educational principles were considered more important than ensuring that the technology was able to make the system work. Many of these projects ended either as expensive white elephants that are too cumbersome to use or were never completed because of implementation difficulties. It is essential to consider the educational principles, but without the appropriate technical knowledge, it can be difficult to implement an effective and efficient Web-based classroom.

Technology Is More Important than Education

At the other end of the spectrum are the projects, normally run by computing people, that have lost sight of the educational principles by focusing on the technical considerations. These types of projects generally end up technically brilliant but fail to serve their educational purpose. In building a Web-based classroom, there should be a balance between educational and technical principles.

It Will Be Just Like the Movies

Motion pictures, overhead projectors, computers, computer-based training, computer-managed learning, and CD-ROMs have all promised to revolutionize education and training. Instead, although proving useful tools for some educators, they have done little to change the shape of education. With this history of failed revolutions, it is no surprise when jaded educators who have seen it all before view the Web-based classroom as just another piece of technology.

The decision about whether the Web-based classroom and its descendants will revolutionize education is largely up to the educators using them and will remain unanswered for several years. However, any prediction of failure ignores the unique characteristics of the Web and the changing face of education. None of the previous technologies has offered an environment in which all aspects of education can take place; none has offered an environment that not only enables interaction but actually offers many advantages over face-to-face communication. With the Web, the learner can be changed from a passive recipient of information to a participant in the learning process.

There Is Only One Way to Do It

The incredible variation of the needs, requirements, and tastes of students and educators means that there is no one correct method for implementing a Web-based classroom. A collection of principles can guide the creation of a Web-based classroom, but not all of them will be applicable in every situation. As mentioned, one of the Web's advantages is that the information-manipulating power of computers means it is no longer necessary for the educator to choose a particular format. The students and educators can mold the Web-based classroom into the shape that best suits them.

It Will Benefit Only Remote Students

A Web-based classroom is not a magic wand that causes benefits to instantly appear. If the design of the Web-based classroom is inappropriate for a particular situation, it may decrease the quality of the learning experience. A Web-based classroom will provide benefits in any situation in which its design attempts to address particular problems with the existing approach. Many Web characteristics make the medium ideal for solving the problems of remote students. However, on-campus education also suffers from several problems, described earlier, which can be addressed with an appropriately designed Web-based classroom.

It's Inhuman

Looking at it one way, a computer-based system of handling communication and information distribution is very impersonal in comparison to a traditional method of education. However, what has been found is quite the opposite. Ordinary lecture-based courses are short in duration and content, and time to communicate with the lecturer is limited and usually discouraged. If online communication is supported, some students feel more comfortable talking to the lecturer and talking to each other.

WHERE DO YOU GO FROM HERE?

This brings the first chapter to a close. Having read it, you should now have some sort of understanding of what a Web-based classroom is, what you might be able to achieve with one, and some of the benefits and disadvantages you have to consider. At this stage, it is likely you have come to one of the following conclusions:

No intention of building a Web-based classroom. For many readers, it may appear that building a Web-based classroom has too many problems, costs too much, and won't provide significant advantage. Please don't use this chapter as the sole guide in making this decision. Before you give up on the idea altogether, look at some of the remaining chapters of the book, some of the resources on the book's Web site, and most important, talk to people who are already using Web-based classrooms in their teaching.

Haven't made a final decision. Because the task is not straightforward, it is important that you be sure before you start. If you're not certain, take the time to explore other sources of information, including the book's remaining chapters. In particular, have a look at Chapters 5, 6, 7, and 8, which discuss what can be done and what is involved. Chapter 9, which describes some of the systems that make building a Web-based classroom simpler, may also be useful.

I want to build a Web-based classroom now. If you are certain you want to build a Web-based classroom, you should start reading the rest of the book. Chapters 2 and 3 discuss in detail the design process for your classroom and will refer you to other chapters in the book when appropriate as well as to other sources of information.

RESOURCES

A number of URLs are listed on the CD-ROM to provide further information and examples on the topics covered in this chapter, which are as follows:

- Conversion of non-Web materials
- Value-added conversion
- Many-to-many and many-to-one communication techniques
- Student assessment of Web-based classrooms
- Class management on the Web

2

Analysis

This is a chapter of questions—questions about the course you are thinking of placing on the Web and questions about its students, educators, materials, and other characteristics that will influence the design of your Web-based classroom. The aim of this chapter is to identify the factors that are likely to influence your Web-based classroom so that they can be taken into account when you start designing and building it. A learning experience, whether Web based or not, works best when the approach taken suits the characteristics of the learners, teachers, and resources that are available. It can fail miserably if it doesn't take these factors into consideration. For example, a Web-based classroom may provide a number of obvious benefits, but there is no point in building one if the majority of your students do not have Web access.

Consequently, your first step in building a Web-based classroom should be to look at the characteristics of the learners and teachers, the available resources, and other factors that will influence the outcome of your course. This chapter aims to help you examine these factors by presenting some stories and asking some questions. This approach will help crystallize in your mind the important factors you must consider when you start planning and designing your Web-based classroom in the next chapter.

While you read through this chapter, you might find it useful to keep notes of the thoughts, observations, and questions that arise. This material will prove useful in the latter stages of your project and may also identify some interesting questions that need further discussion and investigation. If you find you want to ask a question or share an idea, please take the time to drop by the book's Web site and use the forums available there: **www.wiley.com/compbooks/mccormack**.

THE COMPONENTS OF A WEB-BASED CLASSROOM

Many factors can influence the design of a learning experience. To help analyze the particular factors that will influence your Web-based classroom, this chapter divides these factors into five components—outside factors, the subject, teachers, students, and technology—and examines each of these components by providing descriptions of how they can influence your classroom. The effects of these factors will be shown through either a series of questions for you to answer or stories that tell of the experiences of other educators.

The five components this chapter uses to organize the factors that influence a learning experience are as follows:

The outside world. The educational institution, local region, and country in which the learning experience takes place and their associated policies, procedures, laws, and general trends.

The course. The academic program in which the students enroll, including the content, field of knowledge, mode of delivery, and other academic characteristics.

Students. Their age, background, culture, language, and preferred style of learning all influence the design of the classroom.

Educators. The people responsible for creating and teaching the subject also influence the classroom through their background, age, preferred teaching style, experience, and personality.

Technical factors. Computers, software, networks, medium, technical support, and training required to implement the Web-based classroom.

TIP

Stories that describe educators' experiences during the development of their Web-based classrooms are perhaps the most interesting and possibly the most effective methods for learning about the Web-based classroom. Most of the chapters in this book relay stories, mainly from the authors' own experience, but the number and variety of these stories is fairly limited. It would be interesting and useful to collect more of these stories from educators in different situations. In an attempt to do so, the book's Web site includes forums in which you can share stories about your own experience building a Web-based classroom. Please take the time to drop by and share your experience. One idea may be to put together a small journal that summarizes your progress in designing and teaching your Web-based classroom so that other educators can watch a development process unfold. ■

OUTSIDE FACTORS

Any learning experience must take place in a wider context that includes the supporting academic department, institution, culture, society, and government. Each of these outside factors can influence accepted, appropriate educational practice. The outside influences on a Web-based classroom can be placed into two categories:

Educational institution. The school, university, or commercial company that employs the teachers, enrolls the students, and pays the bills. Its policies, procedures, resources, and aims all influence the Web-based classroom.

Society. The culture, form of government policies, and geographical location in which the classroom operates.

Institutional Factors

The existing policies and procedures of the institution in which the Web-based classroom is based can present some of the biggest hurdles in the classroom's development. In fact, the main reason for building many Web-based classrooms (including the authors') was to solve the problems caused by the established policies and procedures of the institution. Although it is possible to implement a Web-based classroom irrespective of the policies and procedures of an institution, it can be a difficult and thankless task. To avoid complications, it is preferable for Web-based classroom development to use the policies, procedures, and support available within the institution.

When constructing your Web-based classroom, it is important that you become aware of, and use to your advantage, the policies and procedures that apply within your institution. Some of the possible institutional influences you should consider include the following:

- Mission statements and directions
- Infrastructure and funding
- Promotion and rewards
- Workload
- Changing teaching methods

Example

During the first part of 1997, Telstra, Australia's main telecommunications carrier, introduced a special scheme for long distance phone calls. After a certain time of night, a long distance phone call cost $3.00, regardless of how long it lasted. This scheme immediately made Internet access more affordable for people, especially students in courses using Web-based classrooms in remote areas of Australia who had relied on long distance phone calls to gain access to the Internet.

- Administrative procedures
- Web publishing policies
- Provision of Internet access and training
- Your colleagues

Mission Statements and Directions

Most institutions have a mission statement that outlines issues the institution considers important and where it sees itself heading in the future. If the Web-based classroom can fit in with the institution's mission statement, you are likely to receive greater support and resources.

Some related questions to consider:

- What is the mission statement for your institution?
- How important is the mission statement to the institution and the people within it? The mission statement's importance can vary widely, from little more than a set of aspirations to the central driving force of the entire institution.
- Which people are most committed to the mission statement? How can they help you? Often, people in different positions will have varying commitment to the mission statement and an interest in seeing that it is advanced.
- What does the institution see as its main business?
- How well does the Web-based classroom fit with that mission?

Infrastructure and Funding

Typically, a direct result of the institution's mission statement will be the level of the infrastructure and funding available for a Web-based classroom. Being familiar with and obtaining a fair share of the available infrastructure and funding provided by your institution can make the construction of your Web-based classroom a more enjoyable and successful project.

Some questions to consider:

- Are there any mechanisms by which you can obtain technical and instructional design assistance?
- Does the institution have any grant or funding mechanism to support new teaching initiatives?
- When do applications for those grants close?
- Who and what projects have previously received funding?
- Was funding provided for equipment, people, or time relief from other obligations? With some grants, you cannot ask for funding for equipment or time relief.
- Is there an institutional mechanism to support subject development?

Promotion and Rewards

Constructing a Web-based classroom, at least initially, requires an investment of considerable time and effort by the educator. Although many universities proclaim the importance of good teaching as a platform for promotion, the reality is that research is usually by far the most important factor. One interesting feature of the world of Web-based classrooms is that many projects, while starting out as efforts to help students, were presented as education research projects and thereby obtained valuable resources. In many situations, there may not be significant tangible rewards, such as promotion, for spending the time required to develop a Web-based classroom.

However, building a Web-based classroom can bring rewards other than promotion: increased job satisfaction, increased interaction with students, happier students, and a more effective learning and instruction environment. It is important that you identify the reasons you are building your Web-based classroom and decide whether it will help you achieve your goals.

Some related questions:

- Why do you want to build a Web-based classroom?
    - Educators want to build Web-based classrooms for many reasons. Some bad reasons include a desire to play with the technology or to hide bad teaching by appearing to be innovative.
- Is what you want to achieve realistic?
- Will a Web-based classroom really achieve these aims?
    - If your aim is to reduce the effort required to teach, the Web, at least initially, may not be the most appropriate approach. In addition, some Web-based classroom designs can result in a greater teaching load because they increase the level of interaction possible and the student's interest in the subject.
- How will you know you have achieved your aims?
- Will the institution's promotion system recognize your work on the Web-based classroom? Is this important?
- What evidence do you need to gather for use in promotion rounds?

Example

In 1996, one of the authors of this book adapted a purely Web-based approach in a subject taken by both on-campus and distance students (about 100 students total). For a normal subject of this size, it is not unusual when marking exams to come across student names that are unfamiliar, especially among distance students. One of the rewards in building the Web-based classroom was that when the author marked exams at the end of the semester, all of the student names triggered memories of conversations that occurred during the semester.

Workload

Most teaching institutions have set methods for calculating the resources required for teaching a class. These resources may include funds for subject development, staff workload calculations, eligibility for teaching support, and conditions of employment. Some approaches used in a Web-based classroom require significantly different resources than traditional approaches. Occasionally, the historical methods for calculating these resources will not adapt to the new requirements.

The tasks, responsibilities, and skills required to teach in a Web-based classroom may be considerably different from those required for a traditional classroom. In the example, the primary educational task changed from that of a verbal information distribution mechanism (giving lectures) to that of a mentor, using personal communication and experience to urge and guide the students to understanding. The employment conditions of some educators are very prescriptive about the educator's tasks, and they may not adapt well to the Web-based classroom.

It is also important to remember that it is likely that, initially, the implementation of a Web-based classroom will require a significant investment of time to adapt to the new environment. However, once the Web-based classroom is complete, the workload in maintaining it can be considerably lower than that involved in a traditional classroom.

Questions to consider include the following:

- How is workload calculated at your institution?
- How will the adoption of the Web-based classroom change your workload during development?
- How will the adoption of the Web-based classroom change your workload during its use?
    - The answer to this question depends on how you plan to use your Web-based classroom. Using it as simply an information distribution mechanism may not increase workload during teaching. However, using a collaborative, highly interactive approach may significantly increase workload.
- Is it possible to modify existing workload calculations to consider the unique requirements of the new medium?
- What assistance are you likely to receive during development of the Web-based classroom?
- What assistance are you likely to receive during use of the Web-based classroom?
- Do the tasks and skills you need for your Web-based classroom fit within your employment conditions? Do you care about this? Does the institution?

Example
At one institution known to the authors, the method for calculating teaching load and eligibility for teaching relief is a spreadsheet using a formula based on the number of lectures, tutorials, and students. In adopting a particular approach to a Web-based classroom, a staff member did away with lectures and replaced them with Web-based study material, with all interaction with students occurring via mailing lists and e-mail. The use of mailing lists increased the interaction between students and the teacher considerably. This is especially true because two-thirds of the students were distance students who previously had limited or no interaction with the staff member. The increase in interaction drastically increased the amount of time required to support the subject. The staff member found that he was spending one or two hours a day, seven days a week, talking with students. However, because the workload allocation formula included no figure for "virtual" interaction and there were no longer any lectures for the subject, the calculated workload for the subject was actually less. A direct result of this situation is that the staff member is receiving less teaching relief at a time when he should be receiving more.

Changing Teaching Methods

At many institutions, any major changes in a subject, including the mode of delivery, content, and forms of assessment, must receive the approval of a committee. Such a procedure is usually in place to ensure the quality and consistency of an institution's offerings. Often, this approval process can add considerable lead-in time to the development of new teaching approaches.

Example
In 1996, the academic department of one of the authors put together a proposal for a coursework masters of information technology degree. Distance students who wanted to upgrade their qualifications were seen as the main market for this degree. The characteristics of the prospective students led to the decision to use the Web as the primary distribution mechanism. During the required approval process, the proposal was rejected due to the lack of standard institutionwide policy on the delivery of subjects via the Web. At this time, that institutionwide policy on Web delivery is still not complete, and the masters proposal remains on hold. Meanwhile, individual lecturers and departments are making significant use of the Web in their teaching, and the institution is promoting this fact in its advertising.

Related questions to consider:

- What formal procedures must be followed to gain approval for a change in teaching method?
- What is the time line for these procedures?
- What information is required?
- What type of proposal has been successful in the past?
- What is the likelihood of success for your proposal?
- Is it possible to bypass this procedure?
- Are there senior people within the committee structure who might champion the Web-based classroom?

Administrative Policies and Procedures

Who can enroll in a subject? How much they must pay? Who looks after them? How is funding for subject development allocated? Answers to these questions are generally found within the institution's administrative policies. Given the history of most institutions, the design of these policies is usually specific to traditional teaching methods and may not adapt well to the Web-based classroom. You may also need to see if you can influence policy in any way; for example, if you want to run a course entirely over the Web, you might like an admissions requirement that the student have access to a computer of reasonable capability and be able to link to your Web system.

Similarly, the administrative procedures of an institution—enrolling students, accepting money, and paying bills—are all tuned to operating in the traditional, paper-based world. The virtual world of the Web-based classroom introduces new participants who want to perform these tasks in different ways.

Questions to consider:

- What is your institution's policy on who can enroll?
- What is the procedure that students must follow to enroll in your class?
- Can they enroll in an individual course? How much will it cost?
- Can payment be made electronically or via credit card?
- Is the procedure (and cost) the same for all courses, despite delivery method?
- Is the procedure (and cost) the same for overseas students?
- How far in advance of the start of a course must students enroll?
- What is the process by which remote students take exams?
- What are the institution's methods for recognition of prior learning?
- What other institutional policies and procedures impact on your classroom?
- Can you influence admission policy?

Web Publishing Access Policies

Many institutions have adopted policies that specify the format and the methods by which official material can be placed on their official Web sites. Some even go to the extent of having all material vetted. Such policies, which aim to promote consistency and quality, may control how you construct your Web-based classroom and what you can do in it. More advanced institutions will support these policies by providing tools and procedures that help staff fulfill the requirements of the policy.

Questions to consider:

- Does your institution have a Web publishing policy?
- What format must material be in before it can be published?
- Must a particular person approve material before it can be placed onto the Web?
- Who controls this policy?
- Can it be changed?
- Are tools available that help people meet the policy's specifications?

Internet Access Policies

Internet access, especially for a large institution, is an expensive and complex undertaking. As a result, most institutions have in place a policy that specifies who can access the Internet, what they can access, and who pays for the service. Institutional policies on providing Internet access to students range from those that provide free access via on-campus local area networks and remotely via modems to those that require students to use and personally pay for commercial Internet service providers (ISPs).

The increasing cost of Internet access and the infrastructure required to support it is forcing some universities to reconsider their policies. Sometimes the lack of funding for Internet access means that the quality of that access is unacceptable. At some institutions, it can be so bad that staff will advise students to gain Internet access via commercial providers.

Example

Many of the current crop of systems designed to make it easier to create Web-based classrooms require the student's PC to be connected to a server in order to participate in the Web-based classroom. In some situations, this means that students must be online for a number of hours a week. This may be quite acceptable if students are gaining Internet access via an on-campus network or in many parts of the United States. However, in many locations—parts of Alaska, most of Australia, and elsewhere—students pay for Internet access based on how long they are connected. This cost can increase drastically if students must rely on long distance phone calls to access the Internet. The longer these students are online, the more anxious they become as they hear that clock ticking.

Related questions to consider:

- Does your institution provide Internet access to students?
- What does it cost?
- What type of access is it?
    - Type of access might include on-campus via a local area network, remotely via modems, via an 800 number, 24 hours a day, or at set times.
- What parts of the Internet can they access?
    - Some institutions restrict students to e-mail or the Web only. Others restrict students to local Internet-based machines without the possibility of accessing sites outside the institution.
- Is the service reliable?
- Is it suitable for a Web-based classroom?
- What alternatives exist for your students?

Colleagues and Superiors

The people you work with and for can offer assistance or act as barriers to the implementation of a Web-based classroom. It is important to be aware of the opinions and ideas of colleagues, especially those who will help or must approve the development of your Web-based classroom. A quotation from Nicolo Machiavelli sums up the problem nicely: "There is nothing more difficult to take in hand, more perilous to conduct, more uncertain in its success, than to take the lead in introducing a new order of things, because the innovator will have for enemies all who have done well under the old conditions, and only lukewarm defenders in those who may do well under the new."

Questions to consider:

- What do your colleagues think about Web-based classrooms?
- What about the people you work for?
- Are any of them likely to be opposed to the adoption of a Web-based classroom in your subject?
- What is the source of these opinions? Is there any chance they may change?
- How will their opposition to the Web-based classroom affect the project?
- Are there any colleagues who are keen to see the implementation of the Web-based classroom?
- Are they in a position to be helpful? How can they be helpful?

The Influence of Society

Society's influences on the Web-based classroom include such factors as varying demand for a course, the tendency toward students with more varied backgrounds, increasing competition for students, communication, power and transport infrastructures, and the laws and regulations governing educational institutions. Other influences on the classroom will include such factors as public holidays, changes in funding, cultural differences, and the level of computer and Internet access.

Questions to consider:

- Are there any cultural influences on your class?
    - Possibilities include public holidays, attitude toward study, the expected relationship between student and teacher, the attitude toward plagiarism, and the ability to understand particular examples.
- What government regulations will impinge on your class?
- What are the enrollment trends for your class: increasing, decreasing, or stable?
- What factors are liable to affect your Web-based classroom?

THE SUBJECT

Whether your Web-based classroom is for an existing subject or a brand-new one, you can draw on existing resources, approaches, and experience to it. This section examines these resources and how their characteristics may affect the implementation of your Web-based classroom.

Subject Type

Subject type refers to such characteristics as the field of study, the mode of delivery, level of offering, and the aim of the subject. These characteristics will help you decide the most appropriate and efficient way of designing the Web-based classroom. For example, a subject that examines 17th-century paintings will have requirements that differ from those of a subject concerned with Java programming.

Questions to ask about the type of subject include the following:

Example
At the start of 1997, telecommunications companies in both Australia and the United States were pushing to implement timed local calls for people connecting to the Internet via the phone and a modem. In Australia, where the charge for a local call is a flat fee (about 25 cents), this is a major change. Such a push, if successful, could drastically affect whether students would be willing to use the Web-based classroom to the full.

> **Example**
> Central Queensland University in Australia has study centers where many of the students are of Chinese origin. In 1997, orientation week for the first semester coincided with Chinese New Year, a major public holiday for these students, so it was necessary to modify the semester schedule for these students.

- What field of study does it cover?
- Are there other Web-based classrooms in this field?
- In what mode is the subject offered (on-campus, distance, part-time, full-time, sandwich course, once a year, flexible delivery, a combination)?

Existing Resources

Adapting existing learning material for use in the Web-based classroom, if done appropriately, can make the development of the Web-based classroom considerably easier. The existing material may be a result of local development or you may use (with the author's permission) resources obtained via the Web. The characteristics of this existing material, including its current format, copyright restrictions, and cost, will determine whether or not you can adapt the material and how to most efficiently do so. (Chapter 4 includes a section that describes the possible methods for converting existing information into a format usable in the Web-based classroom.)

Questions to ask about existing material include the following:

- What format is the material in?
- Can it be converted into a usable Web format (HTML, GIF, JPEG, VRML, PDF)?
- How difficult will that conversion be?
- What tools are available to perform the conversion?
- What is the cost of those tools? Can you gain access to them?
- What tools will be required to use the converted material?

> **Advice**
> Looking at other Web-based classrooms—in particular, classrooms that are in the same general area as yours—is a good way to determine which features work. Other benefits may include the ability to share experiences and approaches with other educators in the same field and possibly even share resources.

Example

Many subjects at Central Queensland University have large numbers of on-campus students (spread among multiple, geographically distributed campuses) and distance students. The traditional approach is for distance students to study using print-based material and on-campus students to receive the traditional lectures. Lectures are usually videotaped and distributed to other campuses for replaying.

The combination of video and Powerpoint slides used for lectures is a significant resource and would be useful for distance students. However, distributing copies of the videotape to every distance student is considered too expensive (using current methods). Before 1997, it was common practice to place the standard Powerpoint slides onto a Web page that the students could download and view with a Powerpoint viewer.

In 1997, new tools meant that the conversion process could go a couple of steps further. By combining images, produced by a tool that converts Powerpoint presentations to a sequence of JPEG images, with streaming audio technology from RealAudio, it was possible to provide a "virtual lecture" experience with little extra effort.

- Will the students need to have access to those tools?
- How much disk space will the converted information require?
- Who owns the copyright on the material?
- Do you have permission to place it on the Web?
- Must the material be password protected?
- Will the combined cost of converting the material and using the material outweigh the benefit gained by the student?

Pedagogy

Many studies have shown that the medium in which learning takes place does not significantly affect the outcome. The approach to using a different medium for learning is often a greater influence on outcome. The chosen pedagogy should be appropriate for the material, the students, the educator, and the medium for the learning experience. The Web-based classroom is a new medium and has its own unique characteristics that contribute to the choice of the appropriate pedagogy.

In designing the pedagogy for the Web-based classroom, lessons from previous offerings of a subject will prove useful. Questions to be considered with respect to previous pedagogy include the following:

- How much of the course content is based on memorizable facts or a core body of information?
- How much of the course relies on activities such as practicing skills, observing a task, demonstrating a correct procedure, and applying information learned in the course?
- What group or individual activities are used within the course?
- What is the primary method of instructing learners in this course?
- What level of interaction occurs between learners and educators?
- How much independent work is required of the learners?
- When and what form of communication takes place among learners as well as between learners and the educator?
- What previous approaches have been used in the course?
- What approaches have other people used in similar courses, especially when using a Web-based classroom?
- What were the outcomes of those approaches?

Experience

For most people, building a Web-based classroom will be an evolutionary process, gradually building on previous experience and becoming more complex as confidence and experience in the new environment grow. It is rare for someone new to the experience to design a completely Web-based classroom on the first attempt. Instead, the design of most Web-based classrooms supplements existing approaches and either accentuates the successful parts or addresses any problems with a subject. You will need to reflect on previous offerings of a subject and identify problems and successes.

Questions to consider include these:

- What percentage of students are passing? Failing?
- Why are they passing/failing?
- How many students are dropping out before the end of the course?
- Why are students dropping out?
  - In distance education, a common reason for students dropping out is the feeling of isolation. In a Web-based classroom, the use of group communication and interaction can help decrease this feeling of isolation.
- Are there particular concepts in a subject that students find difficult to understand?
- Has previous evaluation of the subject identified particular problems with the delivery of the course?
- What are the positive aspects about the subject?
  - Although it may not be possible, or even necessary, to accentuate the positive aspects of a subject, care should be taken so that adopting the Web-based classroom does not decrease or even remove these positive aspects.
- Does the educator teaching the course face any particular problems?

> **Example**
> Many distance education institutions encounter problems with the late delivery of teaching material that prevents distance students from starting on time. With all the necessary material placed on the Web at the outset, distance students can obtain the material when, or even before, they enroll, allowing them to get started while they are waiting for the traditional print package to arrive.

THE TEACHERS

The teaching staff—their characteristics, preferences, and abilities—have a significant impact on the success of a learning experience. The design of any classroom should suit the preferred styles of the teachers who will use it. Possible considerations include the following:

- How long have they been teaching the subject?
  - Attempting to convert a subject into a Web-based classroom without any experience with the subject can prove difficult.
- What is their ability in the subject?
  - In a lecture situation, it is possible to hide a lack of knowledge in a subject area or to keep one step ahead of the class. However, in a Web-based classroom, where the emphasis is on interaction and students working at their own pace, this can be more difficult. Appropriate steps must be taken to ensure that suitably qualified staff are involved in teaching the course.
- How many teaching staff will be involved?
  - Having a team of people involved in developing a Web-based classroom can significantly improve the result and decrease the effort required. On the other hand, if the members of the team do not get along, the opposite can be true.
- How much time can the teaching staff commit to the Web-based classroom?
  - Various approaches to the Web-based classroom can require more or less time. This includes both the development and teaching stages of the Web-based classroom.
- What skills do the teaching staff bring to the classroom? Do they have good interpersonal skills? Can they motivate students? Can they draw? Are they comfortable with technology?
- What are their preferred teaching styles?
  - Teachers have different styles and approaches. It is important that the design of the Web-based classroom reflect those preferences.
- What benefits will the teachers receive from the Web-based classroom? Why are the teachers involved in the Web-based classroom? How will this affect their motivation? Are they involved only to play with the technology?

> **Example**
>
> A common complaint from distance students, including those who have taken traditional print-based distance courses taught by one of the authors, is the sense of isolation they have felt due to the lack of communication. Appropriate use of Internet technologies has helped change many of those complaints into comments like the following: "I think I have gained a lot more from this subject than just UNIX, especially with the interaction for the first time in eight years of external study!" This type of comment, along with the possibility of actually interacting with students, provides all the motivation necessary for some educators to adopt and use these approaches.

THE STUDENTS

Because a primary purpose of a Web-based classroom is to enable students to learn, the classroom's design should reflect the characteristics and needs of the students. What makes this difficult is that students, just like everyone else, have widely different and sometimes competing characteristics. In a perfect world, the design of the Web-based classroom will be flexible enough to adapt to different student characteristics.

Some characteristics of students to consider include these:

- How old are the students?
  - Generally, older students do not feel comfortable with, or take longer to adapt to, technology or teaching methods that differ from what they are familiar with.
- What cultural background do the students have?
  - The global reach of the Web-based classroom increases the likelihood of classes consisting of students from vastly different cultures and leads to many problems due to the widely varying expectations of the learning process and the relationships between students and teacher.
- What language will the students use in the classroom?
- What is their first language?
- What prior educational experience do they have?
  - Students in a modern classroom can have a variety of previous educational experiences, including level achieved and how long ago it was. Often, students are comfortable with approaches that they have seen before and will not adapt easily to new approaches.
- What physical abilities and disabilities do the students have?
  - For example, a certain percentage of the population has some form of color blindness; other disabilities can affect whether or not a student can access or benefit from a Web-based classroom.
- Why are the students studying the subject?
- How motivated are they toward the subject?

    - Students who are not motivated to study or use a Web-based classroom will need special attention and an approach designed specifically to increase their motivation.
- What are the students' preferred learning styles?
    - Students like to learn in a variety of ways, reading material in a different order or using it in different ways.
- What communication skills do the students have?
    - Any Web-based classroom that emphasizes interaction will usually rely heavily on the written word via e-mail or other Web-based communications systems. Some students may not be comfortable with the written word and may require assistance or separate instruction.
- How open are the students to change?
    - Most students are used to the traditional forms of education; adapting to new methods may be a long process that requires significant investment in time and effort.
- What are the benefits to the student of using a Web-based classroom?
    - Students are more likely to feel positive about a new approach if the benefits they receive are significant and they are aware of these benefits.

TECHNOLOGY

All classrooms, traditional or Web based, require the support of technology. Using technology that is inappropriate, unfamiliar, or not quite ready can adversely affect the learning experience. In a traditional classroom, the required technologies—the lights, air conditioning, heating, chalk, white boards, and overhead projectors—usually exist and are familiar to the participants, who are comfortable using them. Their familiarity means that for a normal classroom, the technology considerations, although still essential, are more transparent than the technological considerations associated with a Web-based classroom. It also helps that these technologies—overhead projectors, for example—reinforce the traditional teacher-centered approach of most education.

In a Web-based classroom, the required technologies—Web browsers, Web servers, Internet connections, CD-ROMs, modems, computers, and software—may not be readily available and are, for many participants, new and unfamiliar. The novelty of the technology in a Web-based classroom means that the classroom's design must pay particular attention to the technology, its availability, and its capabilities. If you do not carry out this task, you run the risk that the Web-based classroom will be inappropriate for the available technology. The technology components involved with a Web-based classroom include the following:

Client software and hardware. The client is the collection of hardware and software by which the students and teachers participate in the Web-based classroom.

Server software and hardware. Hosts the Web-based classroom.

Distribution method. The method by which the server and client communicate and share information.

Technical support. The training, problem solving, documentation, and ongoing maintenance that ensure the ongoing operation of the Web-based classroom.

The characteristics of components that we consider here include not only the technical specifications but also the relationship between the participants in the Web-based classroom and the technology. Considerations include how comfortable the students are with their client computers and which department or division owns and controls the server computer. During the lifetime of a Web-based classroom, the technological requirements will evolve. During the classroom's development, the educator may require access to scanners and other production devices that are not required during the operational phase (the two phases may overlap). Similarly, the server computer used during development may differ from that used in the implementation phase.

Client Software and Hardware

Access to the necessary client software and hardware is a requirement that both students and staff must fulfill before they can participate in the Web-based classroom. The characteristics of the client hardware and software have a direct influence on how and what tasks are accomplished within the Web-based classroom. As a result, when planning a Web-based classroom, it is essential to consider the characteristics of the client hardware and software.

Chapters 4, 5, 6, and 7 of this book discuss the systems you may want to implement; these chapters specify the minimum client requirements to use the various systems. To make full use of this information, it is necessary that you answer questions such as these:

- What client operating system is being used?
    - Operating systems support different capabilities. For example, Shockwave is not available for UNIX computers. Java's availability on the Windows 3.1 platform is only recent, and many implementations still suffer from unreliability. Similarly, free viewers for Powerpoint, Microsoft Word, and other applications are available only on certain operating systems.
- What is the minimum client hardware available?
    - Characteristics of the client hardware such as amount and type of memory, CPU, hard disks, CD-ROM, graphics resolution, and the available colors all contribute to what is possible in the Web-based classroom. After all, there is little point in producing scanned photos with 16 million colors if the computers of the students and staff can display only 16 colors.

- What client software is available?
    - This includes Internet software such as Web browsers, mail programs, and traditional software such as word processors and spreadsheets. Distributing Word for Windows files is pointless if some participants do not have access to Word. Similarly, if the only Web browser students can access is Lynx (a text-only browser), there is little point in spending time and energy on graphical design. Most software brings with it standard problems and restrictions. For example, versions of Netscape for the Windows platform have problems printing Web pages with dark backgrounds and light text, and Word for Windows documents can be infected with viruses.
- What other peripherals are available?
    - Is there a printer available? What type of printer—dot matrix, inkjet, or laser? CD-ROM and sound card? Scanner? Video camera? Having access to a particular peripheral may be necessary for certain features of the Web-based classroom.
- What access is there to the client?
    - From where and at what times do the participants have access to the client computers? Can students access the computers only at set times each week or do they have computers at home? What about the educators? If the participants can access the client only at a fixed time in an unfamiliar place, it may adversely affect their participation in the class.
- How competent are participants with using the client hardware and software?
    - Familiar software and hardware will mean less training is needed, and greater participation usually results. Forcing the participants to use new software and hardware increases the cost of adapting to the Web-based classroom. If the participants are new to the technology, you'll need to prepare training materials and documentation.
- Will the students or staff require training in using the computer?
    - Even if the students or teachers have been computer and/or Internet users for many years, they might not have had formal training in using the technology. They may be quite competent in doing basic tasks with the technology, but the lack of formal training may have left them with some fundamental misunderstandings that must be cleared up.

The Server

In most Web-based classrooms, the information and communication that takes place will pass through and possibly be stored on a single server computer or spread among many servers. The server computers supporting a Web-based classroom may provide several services, including mailing lists, Web pages, authentication, and student tracking. Whatever the configuration, the server computers' capabilities have a great deal of influence on what is possible in the Web-based classroom. These questions should be addressed:

- What operating system does the server use?
  - As with the client, the type of operating system on the server will directly affect the software that can be used.
- What are the characteristics of the server's hardware?
  - An under-powered server can result in a less than satisfactory experience. The size and type of CPU, RAM, disk drives, and I/O controllers all contribute to the speed of the server.
- What software is available on the server?
  - Some typical server software includes a Web server, a mailing list manager, an FTP server, a gopher server, or a RealAudio server. Without the appropriate software, it is not possible to offer relevant service.
- What are the capabilities of the software?
  - Not all software is equal. Servers provide different functionality and performance. For example, one particular Web server may be considerably slower than another.
- What else is the server being used for?
  - A busy server will slow any interaction in the Web-based classroom. Is the server being used to perform other tasks not related to the Web-based classroom? Will this affect your classroom?
- How reliable is the server?
  - One of the advantages of the Web-based classroom is that participation can take place at any time. If the server hosting the classroom is unreliable and prone to unavailability, this advantage is removed, and participants can become frustrated.
- What other access do you have to the server?
  - Is the server sitting on your desk or is it hidden away in the bowels of the institution's computer services department? Are you allowed to maintain and modify the machine directly or must you ask other people to perform such tasks?
- What support is available for the server?
  - This question is considered in more detail in the "Technical Support" section of this chapter.

Distribution Methods

An essential part of the Web-based classroom is the distribution of information among students and teachers. In most Web-based classrooms, these connections will occur via a computer network of some description, usually the Internet. However, in some situations, information distribution can be achieved using CD-ROMs (and possibly floppy disks) or even a combination of offline and online methods. The type of distribution method that is appropriate will depend on what the participants have access to and the nature of information being distributed.

Questions to consider about the connection to the Web-based classroom include these:

- What is the most appropriate method—online, offline, or a combination?
    - Factors that influence the answer to this question include to what use the Web-based classroom will be put and to what distribution methods the students have access.
- How fast is that access?
    - Options range from slow modems through ISDN, cable, and local area networks. Offline distribution methods are slow to use initially because they rely on the postal service, but once students have them, access speed is extremely fast.
- How much does the connection cost the student, in both setup and ongoing costs?
    - The costs of most Internet connections via commercial providers are calculated on a time basis. It is also necessary that students have access to a computer, a modem, and a telephone line. Students may also have to purchase and set up these items.
- How much does the connection cost (in terms of setup and ongoing costs) for the teacher and institution?
    - For most institutions, Internet access is charged by the byte transferred. In Australia, this has led to many institutions putting in place restrictions on who can access what on the Internet and implementing other mechanisms such as Web proxy servers and local mirrors of popular sites.

Example

A lecturer in education at Central Queensland University teaching a course in the use of educational technology in schools wants to use a Web-based classroom. There are two major problems:

- A large proportion of the students in this course are studying at a distance, and only a small, though growing, number actually have Internet access.
- An important part of this course is the ability to observe a teacher interacting with a class. For a distance student, the most appropriate method for doing so is some form of video. Given the type of access that most of these students have, distributing video over the Web will be very slow and of questionable quality.

In this situation, one solution is to use a dual distribution method. The Web-based classroom, including the video, is created and placed onto the Web. A version of it is also placed onto a CD-ROM, which is distributed to the students.

- Who pays for the costs involved in information distribution? Does the institution pay for Internet access for the students and the Web-based classroom? Are students responsible for providing their own access?
- How often do students and staff connect?
- Will students connect every day or every week? With an offline Web-based classroom, that connection is with an isolated part of the classroom. This means that interaction with others is not possible.
- When do they connect?
  - Can all students connect simultaneously or will it be at different times? This can influence network and server usage. If all 500 students in a first-year programming course access the server simultaneously, the load can become unacceptably high.

Technical Support

In a traditional classroom, an educator will have the assistance of support staff who may help photocopy material, prepare audio equipment, and maintain lecture theaters and other rooms. A Web-based classroom, on the other hand, doesn't need to be vacuumed, but instead has several other requirements, such as the following:

- Looking after server software and hardware
- Looking after network infrastructure
- Providing training in the use of technology
- Responding to problems and questions

Rather than provide and maintain buildings, in a Web-based classroom the institution must provide and maintain the server hardware, software, and network infrastructure. Most Web-based classrooms will take advantage of the "access anytime" principle, so it may be necessary for the technology to be maintained on an around-the-clock basis.

It is pointless providing and maintaining the technological infrastructure if no one knows how to use it, however. Therefore, the appropriate training and documentation in using the technology must be provided. Equally important is the availability of appropriate assistance with the technology when problems arise.

Some questions to consider regarding technical support include the following:

- Does your institution provide any technical support?
  - Chances are that most institutions already provide some form of technical computing and networking support.
- Will you need to fulfill the technical support role yourself?
  - Many Web-based classrooms, at least in the initial stages, are supported by the academics who developed the classrooms. If you are in this situation, you should ensure that you have the appropriate knowledge and the time to perform support as well as your other tasks.

Advice

In many situations, the institution's level of technical support is not likely to increase sufficiently to offer an appropriate level of support for Web-based classrooms. This is a problem faced by many educators and one that this book is intended to address. Many educators have adopted the use of communities of support that are forming in online forums; these communities discuss everything from particular software or hardware to the use of Web technology in learning. This book's Web site provides pointers to these forums and other online resources that can provide technical support assistance.

- Is the level of support appropriate to the needs of the Web-based classroom?
  - In many cases, technical support staff are seen as overhead, which must be minimized. It is common for institutions to have barely enough technical support staff for existing operations. The addition of a technology-intensive approach such as the Web-based classroom may simply be too much for the existing infrastructure and staff.
- How good is that technical support?
  - The quality of technical support people varies dramatically. A good staffer will have a firm grasp on the technical possibilities and an appreciation and understanding of what people are attempting to achieve with the technology.
- Where is the technical support located?
  - Are all the technical people located centrally or are they distributed into the individual departments that they support? A distributed person is often easier to contact and has a greater appreciation of user's needs.
- When are they available?
- Is technical support available only from 9:00 A.M. to 5:00 P.M. during the week?
- What happens if the server develops a fault on a Friday night?
- Is there a possibility that technical support will be increased to support the Web-based classroom?
- Is there an existing help desk that can support the Web-based classroom?
- Can the students obtain technical support elsewhere?
  - Many students are now getting their Internet access through commercial ISPs. In that case, answers to generic questions and Internet training should be available from this company.

CONCLUSIONS

A range of factors can influence the construction of a Web-based classroom. In this chapter, we have broken these influences into five categories: the outside world, the subject being taught, the students, the educators, and technical issues.

The chapter described each category of influence and how each can affect the design of your Web-based classroom.

You should now be aware of the factors that are likely to influence the design of your Web-based classroom. Taking time now to further consider the possible influences on your plan will help avoid problems and mistakes later. The following chapters—in particular, the planning and design chapter—will draw on the analysis you have performed to aid in the construction of your Web-based classroom.

RESOURCES

You can find pointers to existing Web-based classrooms on the CD-ROM that accompanies this book.

3

Planning and Design

Planning and design are the first steps in implementing your Web-based classroom. Planning helps you decide exactly what you want to do with your Web-based classroom and how you will achieve it. The design of your Web-based classroom helps identify its structure and appearance. This chapter introduces a simple five-step process that can help you plan and design your Web-based classroom. Accompanying each of the five steps is a collection of guidelines, basic concepts, and an example for a real Web-based classroom.

It is strongly recommended that you complete at least Chapter 2 before commencing this chapter. Each of the steps in this chapter require you to make a number of value judgments based on the requirements and characteristics of your Web-based classroom. The analysis described in Chapter 2 will provide much of the information needed to answer these questions. Contrary to the structure of this chapter, planning and design is not a sequential process. You will find yourself moving back and forth between the various steps as you become more comfortable and familiar with the use of a Web-based classroom.

PLANNING

Before starting development on your Web-based classroom, you should perform a planning stage in which you identify exactly what it is you want to achieve and how it can be achieved. You can develop this list in a number of ways. The following section describes one such method, which consists of three steps: develop a list of educational goals, identify how to achieve those goals, and prioritize the list.

Develop a List of Educational Goals

For most people, the primary purpose of building a Web-based classroom is to improve the experience of the students and teachers of a class. The entire development of the Web-based classroom should be directed to this purpose and not others, such as playing with the technology. Your first step is to identify the list of educational goals that will drive the entire design and implementation of your Web-based classroom. Developing this list is a brainstorming exercise. You should forget about the technology and practical considerations. A later step will remove from the list those goals that are not practical. The following suggestions may help you to develop the list of educational goals for your Web-based classroom. See the sidebar for our list.

Strike while the iron is hot. As you teach, you will often see and experience things that you may forget if you don't record or act upon them immediately. One approach is to keep a journal while teaching a subject; in it record the positives and negatives you encounter during the class. Once the class is complete, you can examine and reflect upon the contents of the journal and use it while developing the next offering of the class.

Memory fades. The further removed you are from the offering of a class, the more you will have forgotten about the experience of teaching it. A useful mechanism for refreshing that memory is to review past records of the class. Records might include evaluation or feedback forms completed by students, past assignments and exams or the archives of a class mailing list. Revisiting these records may remind you of aspects of the class that should be addressed.

Don't try to complete this step in one sitting. Spend an afternoon working on it, and then leave it for a week. Then come back, refer to your previous work, and go through the step again. Coming back to the process with a fresh mind can often spark extra ideas.

Ask other people to create lists for your class rather than rely on the list you create yourself. The differences in people's perspectives can be very useful in identifying the negatives and postives of the class. Once finished, collect the lists and combine them. Other people to involve in the process include other staff who have taught the class, students who have taken the class, or colleagues from other institutions who have taught similar subjects.

The Example

The planning and design of a Web-based classroom for the class 85349 Operating Systems (referred to as 85349) will be used throughout this chapter to demonstrate each step. 85349 is a second-year computing class taught at Central

> **Step 1: Develop a List of Educational Goals**
> **Inputs:** An analysis of the current class.
> **Output:** A list of educational goals you want to achieve.
> Write down answers for each of the following questions:
> **What are the problems with your class?** What are the factors that waste time, lessen the effectiveness of learning, make it more difficult for the students to learn, increase the cost of offering the class, and reduce the benefits enjoyed by both the students and the teachers?
> **What are the advantages or positive aspects of your class?** What do the participants most enjoy? What aspects differentiate your class from other classes?
> **What would you most like to do with the class?** Most educators have plans that they would love to implement but can't due to several factors. List yours here. The Web-based classroom and the available tools might make them possible.
> **Develop a list of goals.** Take your answers for the above questions and develop a list of educational goals that will help you address the problems, retain the positives, and achieve your aims. Remember, at this stage you need not worry too much about practical implementation issues. A later step will take care of that.

Queensland University (CQU). A typical 85349 class includes approximately 80 on-campus students and 200 distance students. The following is the output of Step 1 for 85349.

Problems The class is very theoretical. At many universities, this class is the first class of a pair that examine the topic. The first class examines the theory of operating systems; the second concentrates on their practical aspects. Given constraints at CQU, it is not possible to have a second practical class. The emphasis on theory is an added problem because the majority of the computing classes that these students have previously attended are very practical. The change in emphasis is important because many students find it difficult to make the connection between the 85349 theory and the tasks they will face when they are computing professionals. The lack of perceived practical relevance reduces many students' motivation and, consequently, their grades.

The theoretical nature of the class is a particular problem for distance students due to the nature of their study environment. Distance students rely almost totally on a textbook to explain the theories and concepts introduced in the class. This is a problem if the textbook does not meet the student's learning style or prerequisite knowledge or simply does not provide an explanation they can understand. The isolation of distance students makes it difficult for them to receive alternative explanations from staff or other students.

For a number of reasons, many of the 85349 students show very little aptitude for problem solving or a desire for deep learning. Encouraging deep learning is especially difficult given that students do not see the relevance of the material and do not gain feedback on their understanding until at least halfway through the semester.

The field of operating systems is constantly changing as new research develops new insights and as new versions of operating systems are released. The fact that many of the students are familiar with and are using recent operating systems means it is necessary to ensure that the content maintains a connection with their experience. A discussion about an operating system that hasn't been available for a number of years reduces the perceived relevance. For a number of reasons, the class study material has not been updated for at least four years.

The subject is taught in a number of modes, including traditional face-to-face teaching, distance study, and, for the first time in 1997, a remote campus via videoconference. Each of these modes have different requirements, which means that different methods must be used to teach the class. This results in staff duplicating effort to teach the same material in different ways. This is causing significant problems, with increasing pressure on staff to perform research and other professional activities.

It is not unusual for distance students to receive their study materials up to five or six weeks into a semester. This late arrival puts these students at a significant disadvantage. The traditional print-based distance education method also causes a number of other problems, including isolation and slow turnaround time on assignments.

Advantages Because the class is a second-year university course in computing, both students and lecturers are competent computer and Internet users. It also means that most students already have computer and Internet access. Furthermore, students understand how being able to use the Internet will help their job prospects.

The computing emphasis of the class topic means that a significant amount of relevant material is already on the Web. This material includes commercial, professional, and educational resources, including a number of other Web-based classrooms.

The class has used the Internet and the Web for a number of years, so there is a collection of locally developed resource material: Web pages, past student assignments, and archives of mailing lists that can be adapted for use on the Web.

Dreams Central Queensland University's trend toward year-round teaching is increasing pressure on staff to develop "smart" ways of teaching. The ideal situation would see the class and its material designed so that students could start and finish the class whenever they want.

A major aim of this class is understanding the relevance and details of how an operating system works and how it effects the overall operation of a computer system. For most students, the traditional approach of examining theory is too dry and difficult. One solution would be to develop an animated operating system, accessible via the Web, that would allow students to experiment with the workings of the operating system and observe the results.

Goals By examining the problems and advantages of the class, we can identify eight goals to achieve:

1. Ensure that all students receive their study material on time.
2. Design the subject to recognize that reduced time is available to the lecturers.
3. Provide students with early and regular opportunities to test their understanding.
4. Identify early those students having problems with concepts and help them solve these problems.
5. Supplement the theory with a variety of practical tutorials and activities.
6. Reuse material that is already available, including past assignments, previous class material, and material developed by other educators.
7. Increase student-to-student and student-to-educator interaction outside of the lectures.
8. Reduce, and hopefully remove, the distinction between on-campus and distance students.

Deciding How

Now move from the visionary to the practical and think about the approaches you might take to actually achieve the goals you identified in Step 1. Again, this is a brainstorming exercise. The following section gives some advice about how to perform the step. See our list in Step 2 (sidebar).

Don't restrict yourself to existing methods. Become familiar with some of the innovative approaches, both traditional and Web-based, that other people are using. When thinking of Web-based approaches, don't restrict yourself to simply adapting existing practice for the Web. Although adapting existing practice can provide some benefits, significantly greater benefits are possible if you develop new approaches that make full use of the characteristics of the Web. For example, the 85349 course suffers from a common problem of trying to keep the study material not only up to date and relevant, but also supporting the needs of a variety of learners. A typical solution to this problem in print-based distance education is for the teaching staff to expend more effort maintaining the material and providing alternative explanations and examples. The characteristics of the print medium mean that this is the only approach possible. However, the Web and its information distribution advantages make possible alternative approaches. One approach makes maintaining the relevance of the material and providing alternative explanations a responsibility of both students and staff. This could be achieved by implementing an annotation facility, where any visitor to the Web-based classroom could make additions to the teaching material. Such annotations could be made a part of the assessment for the class. The quality of a student's annotation could be judged from the number of visits each annotation receives from other students, votes from other students, and the opinion of a grader.

Remember your class. In the end, some of the approaches you develop will be used by your class. It is important that your approaches are applicable to your class's characteristics. Before developing your list of approaches, it might be useful to review the analysis of the class you produced while reading Chapter 2.

Don't use the Web for everything. When adopting the Web for the first time, it can be tempting to do *everything* on the Web. Even though this is certainly possible, for most educators, building a Web-based classroom is a gradual process that starts small and gradually expands as experience, expertise, and comfort with the environment increase. Very few educators have the time, ability, or support to move directly to a class that is totally Web based. Another important point is that the Web will not always be the most appropriate, effective, or efficient solution to a particular problem. Use a mixture of traditional and Web-based approaches. In doing this, you not only enjoy the advantage of supporting a wider range of students, but you also provide traditional backups in case the technology fails.

For example, using an interactive chat tool for the virtual office could be adapted to support face-to-face discussion as well. A virtual office hour could be held in a student computer lab and students given the choice of participating virtually or physically.

Use multiple approaches. Students have differing learning styles, time constraints, abilities, and learning environments. It is rare to find one approach that suits everyone, so it is a good idea to use multiple approaches to achieve the one goal. For example, if your goal is to increase interaction between students and teachers, you could choose a three-pronged approach: Set up a mailing list for general discussion and announcements, use an anonymous forms page as a feedback mechanism, and employ an interactive chat tool to maintain a virtual office. Each of these approaches have different characteristics that will make them suitable for different students and purposes.

KISS. The KISS maxim ("keep it simple, stupid") is an important one to keep in mind when developing your Web-based classroom. Don't attempt to use complicated technical or educational solutions, especially if you are using a Web-based classroom for the first time or you have limited technical knowledge or support. Nothing discourages students more than technology that fails or doesn't provide significant advantages. Complicated technical or educational solutions always require more time and resources on the part of teaching staff, too. Make sure the cost is worth the benefits. Increased complexity increases the likelihood of failure; it also tends to increase the amount that participants have to learn while not guaranteeing a better outcome.

What are others doing? Although it's certainly possible to develop completely innovative approaches to achieve your goals, the chances are you will end up using an approach that someone else is using. Using another person's approach means you can learn from their experience and hopefully avoid their mistakes. (The book's Web site provides an up to date list of information sources that will help you find out what others are doing.)

The Example

A major influence in identifying approaches for achieving the goals for 85349 was the fact that two-thirds of the students are distance students and that many of the problems with 85349 are a result of the limitations of traditional print-based distance education. As a result, most of the following approaches rely heavily on the Web. Contributing to this is the observation that both the students and staff have access to and are familiar with the Web. This is an example of how the characteristics of a class can strongly influence the approaches that this step develops.

Traditionally, to ensure that all students received study material on time, teachers relied on outside divisions (for example, a mailing service or a student copy center) to make materials available. This meant meeting time lines other than their own, with no guarantee it would make any difference. Via the Web, materials can be placed online weeks before the start of the semester.

In terms of class design, the traditional approach has been the print-based distance education model, in which the only interaction between distance students and lecturer is the occasional phone call and assignment distribution. With a Web-based approach, the lecturer can design the class to recognize the reduced time the lecturers can invest by developing a list of FAQs by going through the archives of

Step 2: Identifying Implementation Methods

Inputs: A list of educational goals you want to achieve and a knowledge of what can be done in a Web-based classroom.

Output: For each goal, a list of non-Web and Web-based methods that can be used to achieve the goal.

For each of the goals from Step 1, perform the following tasks. You may find it useful to make use of tables similar to those used in the following example.

List possible non-Web based methods for achieving the goal.

List possible Web-based methods.

Rule out any of these methods that are obviously not feasible.

mailing lists from previous course offerings and directing the students to always refer to the FAQ list before asking a question. Furthermore, the lecturer can urge students to use e-mail to ask questions either directly to the lecturer or to the class mailing list. Finally, the lecturer can use Web-based assignment submission and automated marking systems to reduce workload and turnaround time.

In the traditional course, class tests are held at random times during each lecture, which cannot be done for distance students who need advanced notice of their required presence in class. In addition, the department has a rule restricting a subject to no more than three assignments due to the time taken to mark and return assignments for distance students. Increasing assignments also increases the workload for both students and instructors. However, in a Web-based version of the course, the lecturer can set up a weekly quiz that is automatically marked. Both distance and local students will benefit from the early and regular opportunities to test their understanding.

In order to identify students who are having problems with the course material, the traditional course lecturer must use assignments, submitted class tests, or interactive tutorials that require students to demonstrate their understanding; however, this approach is problematic for distance students, and it increases the workload. These issues can be resolved via a Web-based approach that allows the lecturer to track student performance in weekly quizzes and automatically flag the names of students having difficulty. In addition, the Web-based lecturer can use small discussion/tutorial groups, with the participation of distance students facilitated by the Internet, and require them to perform an exercise that demonstrates understanding.

In the traditional course, the lecturer can try to liven up lectures with simulations of operating systems, using student participants; however, the lecturer would need to distribute video to distance students, which is not feasible due to cost. The Web-based lecturer can implement Web-based simulations and experiments, ranging from the simple to an animated operating system using Java, that allow students to view and experiment with the concepts at their leisure.

The traditional lecturer attempting to reuse material from previous courses and from other sources must distribute those materials to all distance students via mail. However, the Web-based lecturer can distribute the materials quickly and more cheaply via the Web.

In a traditional class, the lecturer must modify lectures to incorporate more small-group student work and promote interaction with the lecturer, using collaborative approaches for tutorials and labs and possibly organizing "after the lecture" social gatherings. However, all of these activities are limited to on-campus students since distance students may be based as far away as overseas. In a Web-based approach, the lecturer can hold virtual office hours in a chat room or a MUD, have some form of group communication system for announcements, general questions, and discussion and have a page for anonymous feedback benefiting those falling behind or not submitting.

Prioritize the List

In most cases, you will not have the time or resources to implement all of the approaches the previous step identified. It is therefore necessary to rank each approach so that you can make a judgment about which ones you should actually implement. The next step is one approach you can use to prioritize your list. See our list in Step 3 (sidebar).

The method used here, like most ranking methods, requires you to make a value judgment about the relative worth of each possibility. In this step, the worth of each approach is based on its cost-to-benefit ratio. The idea is that the best approaches are relatively inexpensive in terms of time and resources to implement and provide significant benefit to both staff and students. The following step uses six factors as the basis for this comparison.

Benefits. Who does the approach benefit: staff, students, or both? How many students will the approach benefit? Will it help them increase grades, maintain interest, deepen learning, or contribute more to the class?

Hardware costs. Can you implement the approach with existing hardware or will you need to upgrade? (In this case, hardware includes such items as seats in lecture theaters, available rooms, chalk, servers, RAM, and hard disks.)

Software costs. Will the methods you've chosen require the purchase of commercial software or can the participants use software they already have? Is suitable free software available? Will participants need to learn new software?

Network requirements. How fast a network connection do the solutions require? Do students have access to the necessary network connection? Do the staff have access? What will it cost for them to gain the necessary access?

Staff requirements. How much staff time will be required to implement each approach? Will support staff be required? Will staff need to learn new skills?

Student requirements. Will students need to learn new skills? Will students need to perform any unusual tasks they haven't had to perform in the past?

Before completing this process you will need to have some understanding of the relative benefits and costs of each approach you identified in the previous step. If you have no experience with a particular approach or tool, you should make some sort of informed prediction. This can be quite difficult. One approach that may help is to discuss your thoughts with other people who are using the Web. However, you should remember that every situation is different, and an approach that is cost effective in one classroom may not translate well to yours.

Step 3: Prioritize Approaches
Inputs: The output of Step 2. One blank piece of paper or card (about a quarter of page in size) for each approach identified in Step 2.
Output: A prioritized list of approaches.
Prepare the cards. On each card, create a table similar to that shown in the following example.
Fill out a card for each approach. Place the name of the approach on the card. Then for each of the other entries, place a number in the range from 0 to 10. The higher the number, the higher the item's impact or priority. For instance, a 10 beside "benefits" indicates that the particular approach will provide huge benefits to the class. A 10 beside "hardware costs" indicates that the approach does not need any additional hardware requirements. A 0 for "benefits" indicates an approach that provides no benefits. A 0 for "hardware costs" indicates that all class participants will have to spend a lot of money and time obtaining new hardware.
You can modify this approach— for example, you might want to use two numbers for each of the six factors: one number for students and another for staff.
For each card, add the numbers and write the total in the appropriate place.
Sort the cards from the highest total to the lowest. A high total indicates an approach that provides large benefits at a low cost.

The Example

Each table in the following section represents cards that were filled out while performing Step 3 for the 85349 course. Following each table is a short explanation of the numbers assigned to each approach.

Approach: Deliver all material on Web		**Approach:** Design assignments to reduce marking time	
Benefits	8	**Benefits**	7
Hardware Requirements	9	**Hardware Requirements**	10
Software Requirements	9	**Software Requirements**	10
Network Requirements	8	**Network Requirements**	10
Staff Requirements	7	**Staff Requirements**	6
Student Requirements	5	**Student Requirements**	9
Total	46	**Total**	52

For each of the tables, you will notice that the hardware, software, and network requirements for most approaches receives a fairly high mark, indicating that there is little cost involved. This mainly due to the fact that students taking 85349 are expected to have access to computers and to the Internet.

Delivering all material on the Web receives a relatively low mark for student requirements because most students are familiar with the traditional methods for receiving class information. Adopting a Web-based classroom as the primary information distribution medium will require students to change their existing practice and develop new skills.

Approach: Produce a Web-based FAQ		**Approach:** Use e-mail and mailing lists for questions	
Benefits	6	**Benefits**	7
Hardware Requirements	9	**Hardware Requirements**	9
Software Requirements	9	**Software Requirements**	9
Network Requirements	9	**Network Requirements**	9
Staff Requirements	4	**Staff Requirements**	7
Student Requirements	10	**Student Requirements**	9
Total	47	**Total**	50

Developing resources such as a Web-based FAQ and Web-based quizzes requires a significant effort by staff, mainly because the staff must gather the raw material (questions and answers) that will be used to develop these resources. For the FAQ lists, this will involve going back over mailing list archives from previous years and identifying common questions from students, then formulating the questions and answers.

Once the raw material for these resources is available, the actual process of developing the resource is not difficult due to the availability of appropriate tools. In addition, both the FAQ and quiz approaches provide long-term benefits because the resources can be used again and again. This is particularly true if students are urged to contribute additional questions and answers.

The use of e-mail and mailing lists can provide a number of benefits that are explained in more detail in Chapter 6 of this book. A major benefit of having all students on the mailing list is the ability to forward student questions (and answers) to the entire class. This prevents other students asking the same questions and hopefully reduces the workload for staff. One drawback of this approach is that the medium will make it possible for a larger number of students to ask questions, especially in distance education. As a result, staff time spent answering questions may increase.

Approach: Web-based assignment submission		**Approach:** Web-based quizzes	
Benefits	8	**Benefits**	8
Hardware Requirements	9	**Hardware Requirements**	9
Software Requirements	9	**Software Requirements**	7
Network Requirements	9	**Network Requirements**	9
Staff Requirements	7	**Staff Requirements**	2
Student Requirements	9	**Student Requirements**	9
Total	51	**Total**	44

Web-based assignment submission receives a high total mark in our tables due to the fact that a large number of 85349 students are studying at a distance and have access to the Web. Being able to submit assignments via the Web provides a number of significant advantages to these students, including decreasing turnaround time, reducing student concern about assignment delivery, and reducing the amount of effort required to package and submit an assignment. The cost of implementing this approach is quite low because the staff already have access to and experience with a tool that automates many of the tasks involved in managing online submission of assignments. Without this tool, the staff costs are significantly greater.

The high cost of Web-based quizzes, as represented by its score of 2 for staff requirements, is due to two factors. Creating quizzes requires the development of suitable questions and answers, which can take quite some time. Actually delivering the quizzes requires the use of an appropriate tool that is currently not available for the 85349 staff. Adopting Web-based quizzes will require significant effort as the staff develop the questions and find an appropriate tool.

Approach: Discussion groups		**Approach:** Experiments with simulated OS	
Benefits	8	**Benefits**	8
Hardware Requirements	9	**Hardware Requirements**	8
Software Requirements	9	**Software Requirements**	3
Network Requirements	9	**Network Requirements**	10
Staff Requirements	2	**Staff Requirements**	2
Student Requirements	2	**Student Requirements**	5
Total	39	**Total**	36

The idea of small discussion groups facilitated by computer-mediated communications does not score well. This is mainly due to the unfamiliarity of both staff and students with this approach and the resulting effort to become familiar with this approach and getting it to work properly. The cost of this approach is further increased by the nature of the students and of the class. Many of the 85349 students are familiar with traditional computing subjects, in which very little discussion takes place. Changing this way of thinking and convincing students of the benefits of increased discussion can be difficult. To make things more difficult, a large proportion of distance students, due to other commitments, cannot set aside regular time each week to contribute to discussions.

Experiments with a simulated operating system score poorly in the software and staff requirements due to the current state of the tool, which was developed at CQU in the early 1990s. Due to its age, it now suffers from a number of problems that cannot be solved without significant time investment by staff.

Approach: Web-based simulations		**Approach:** Convert Powerpoint slides	
Benefits	8	**Benefits**	5
Hardware Requirements	7	**Hardware Requirements**	9
Software Requirements	5	**Software Requirements**	9
Network Requirements	8	**Network Requirements**	9
Staff Requirements	6	**Staff Requirements**	6
Student Requirements	8	**Student Requirements**	9
Total	42	**Total**	47

A number of available systems could be used to adapt or develop Web-based simulations that could aid students in understanding some of the theoretical concepts of the class. However, developing these simulations will require a significant effort on the part of the staff and may also place some burden on the students.

Converting Powerpoint slides to a Web format is not a difficult job; a number of tools automate the task. Simple conversion will provide some benefits— in particular, distance students will gain an alternate explanation of the concepts. An extension of this approach is to include an audio version of the lecture with the converted Powerpoint slides. This approach requires more effort from the staff because the audio must be converted and placed onto the Web.

Approach	Total Score
Design assignments to reduce marking time	52
Web-based assignment submission	51
Use e-mail and mailing lists for questions	50

Continued

Approach	Total Score
Convert Powerpoint slides	47
Produce a Web-based FAQ	47
Deliver all material on Web	46
Web-based quizzes	44
Web-based simulations	42
Discussion groups	39
Experiments with simulated OS	36

The top three approaches all address one of the major problems of print-based distance education: the isolation of distance students due to the difficulty of communication. The first two approaches deal with assignments, which are the primary mechanism by which students receive feedback. These approaches receive high scores because decreasing the time taken to return assignments should provide a number of significant benefits and can be achieved with limited cost.

The next three approaches all basically deal with distributing information via the Web; all receive almost the same mark. The lower score for the Web-based quiz approach is a result of a suitable tool not being currently available as well as the work involved in identifying and implementing a suitable tool.

Due to the time constraints on the staff and the lower scores of the bottom three approaches, these will not be implemented for the next offering of 85349. They may form part of future offerings of the class.

DESIGN

Armed with a plan that describes what you want to achieve with your Web-based classroom, you now have two tasks to complete: design and implementation. Implementation of your Web-based classroom is associated with the tools you plan to use and is covered in detail in the remaining chapters of this book. The remainder of this chapter examines the design of the structure and presentation of your Web-based classroom. In combination, the structure and design define the interface through which the users of your Web-based classroom will access the information it contains and use its facilities.

Taking the time to do a good job of design will provide many benefits, including the following:

Attract visitors. Given the choice between two Web sites with the same content, people will always choose the site with the more appropriate and appealing design.

Retain interest. A well-designed Web site will be easier for visitors to use and generally provide them with a positive experience. Such positive feelings will increase the likelihood of their continued use of the site.

Prevent the "lost in hyperspace" problem. A structure that is familiar and well organized, combined with a presentation that indicates the visitor's current location, will help visitors know where they are and how to get to their desired destination.

Maximize the audience. A major aim of building a Web-based classroom is to ensure that the largest possible number of people use it. However, some methods restrict the potential audience to those who have a particular browser, physical capability, or network connection. A good design will make it possible for the broadest range of Web users to visit and enjoy your Web-based classroom.

Facilitate expansion. Web-based classrooms tend to grow with time. A Web-based classroom with a poorly designed structure will have to be completely redesigned as it grows, which can significantly increase the amount of work involved.

The Structure

Most Web-based classrooms evolve to provide access to a large amount of information, tasks, and resources. For example, one of the author's Web-based classrooms has more than 10,000 individual Web pages. Any large collection of information must be structured in a logical and familiar manner. If it is not, the users of that information will not be able to perform the necessary tasks or access the required information.

A Web site is actually a combination of two structures: the presentation structure and the storage structure. These structures can be exactly the same, completely different, or any combination in between. The greater the similarity between the two structures, the easier it is to maintain the Web site. The presentation structure is the mental model of the Web-based classroom's structure formed by visitors as they browse through the pages of the site. The storage structure is the hierarchy of files and directories (often called folders) used on the Web server to store the classroom's Web pages and other data.

Figure 3.1 demonstrates the relationship between the presentation and storage structures. The storage structure is created and maintained by the author of the Web site. The presentation structure becomes apparent to Web site visitors as their Web browser and Web server translate the storage structure into the presentation structure. In short, the storage structure is how the material (Web pages, files, and so on) is actually stored on disk, and the presentation structure is the collection of hyperlinks that ties the material together.

The Presentation Structure

The combination of the "look and feel" of the pages in a Web-based classroom and the navigation paths the visitor can take through the site form the presentation

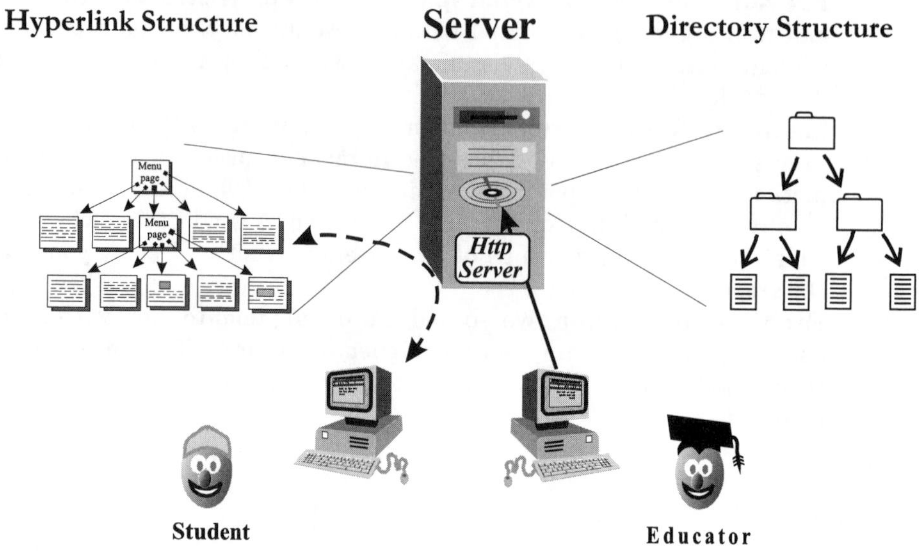

FIGURE 3.1 The relationship between presentation and storage structures.

structure of a site. The presentation structure defines how a visitor to the site can access and traverse the Web-based classroom. The quality of the presentation structure will influence whether or not visitors can find what they are looking for. If the presentation structure does not make sense to the visitor, is too complex to grasp, or is not complete, it will limit the visitor's ability to accomplish a required task.

Types of Presentation Structure There are three common types of presentation structure: hierarchical, sequential, and hypermedia. Each type of structure has its advantages and problems. The one you use will depend on the purpose of the pages you are designing and the tasks people want to do with those pages.

Various sections within a Web-based classroom usually use different presentation structures. To demonstrate each type of presentation structure, this section draws on one Web-based classroom that uses all three. The home page for this Web-based classroom is shown in Figure 3.2.

The Hierarchical Structure Much of the information we are presented with in everyday life uses a hierarchical structure. A hierarchical structure has a group of elements at one level, each of which can lead to other groups of elements. The example Web-based classroom shown in Figure 3.2 uses a hierarchical structure to organize all of the information it contains; this structure is shown in Figure 3.3.

In Figure 3.2, you can see that the page has four main sections: information, assessment, study material, and groups. The titles of these sections are standard

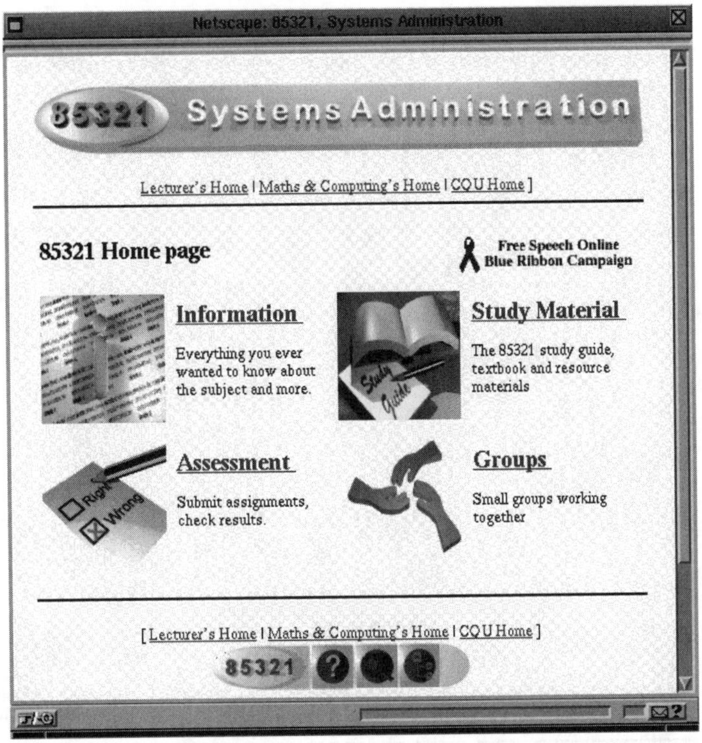

FIGURE 3.2 An example home page.

terms used in a traditional classroom and so should be familiar to the visitors of this Web-based classroom (predominantly students). Each of the links from this page provides access to another page that contains a list of related links. For example, Figure 3.4 shows the Web page that appears if you follow the "Information" link from the page in Figure 3.2. Each of the links on this new page (Figure 3.4) contain information-related links.

Simply creating pages that use a hierarchical structure is not enough. The look and feel of the pages should provide the visitor with hints that the pages are organized in a hierarchical structure. This particular Web-based classroom attempts to do this with the additional navigation bars that appear at the bottom and top of each page.

Figure 3.5 shows these navigation bars in more detail. You can see that the layout of the links on the Web page have been organized in an attempt to represent the hierarchy used by the site.

Sequential Presentation Structure A number of tasks performed in a Web-based classroom suit a more sequential presentation structure. Some examples include pages in a study guide or online text and the slides from an online lecture.

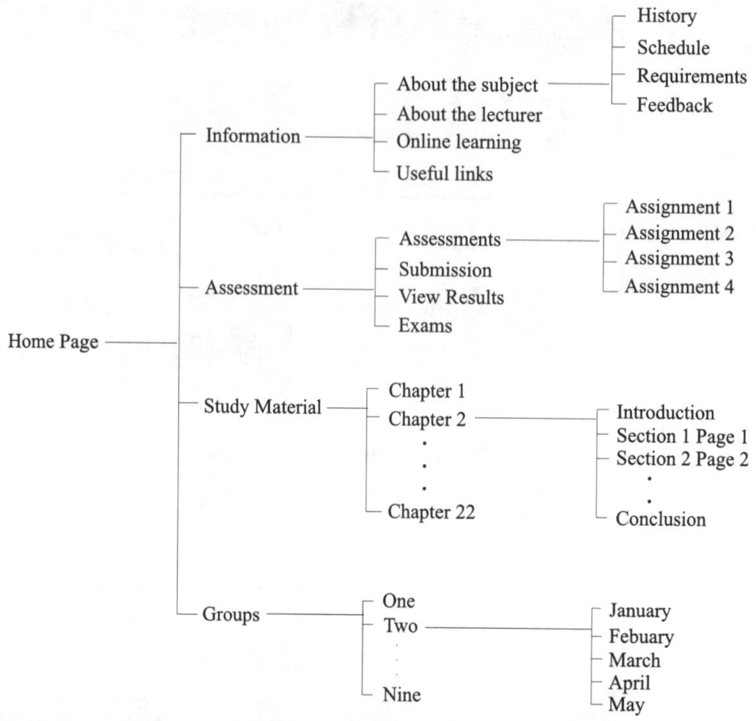

FIGURE 3.3 An example hierarchical structure.

As its name suggests, the sequential presentation structure makes it possible to move through a number of pages, one after the other. This presentation structure closely simulates the operation of a book and is familiar to most people. Figure 3.6 shows an example of one of the pages from the example online study guide.

As with the hierarchical structure, it is important that the look and feel of a page in a sequential presentation structure provide some idea of the valid operations that can be performed. Figure 3.7 shows the navigation bar from one such page. (A similar navigation bar is shown on the pages in Figures 3.2 and 3.4.) The primary difference is that the navigation bar from the page in the sequential presentation structure has two extra icons—the two arrows indicating next and previous page.

Hypermedia Presentation Structure A hypermedia presentation structure takes full advantage of the Web's hypermedia characteristics and allows the visitor to follow links that may lead to a multitude of pages. The advantage of this structure is that it allows more freedom to visitors so they can discover their own

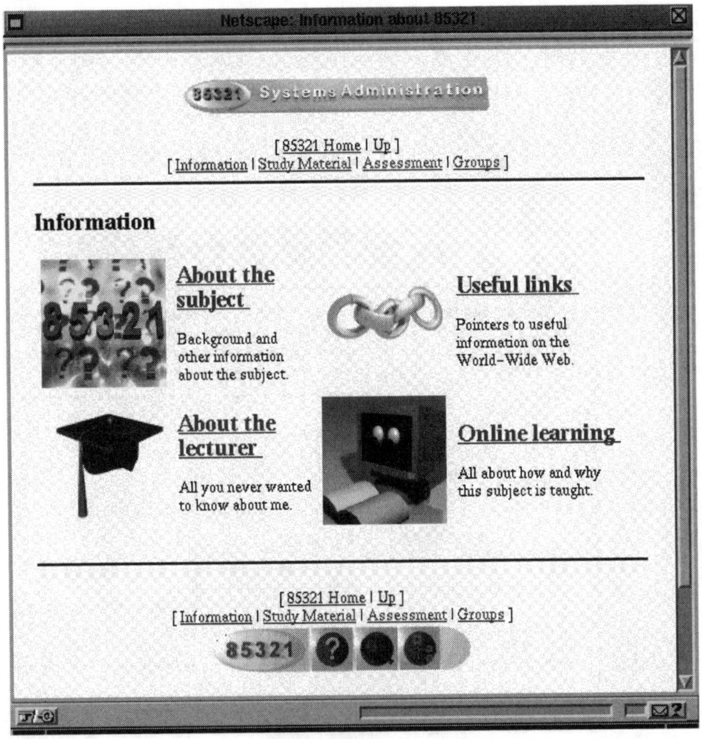

FIGURE 3.4 An information page.

path through the information and make connections that make sense to them. The downside of the hypermedia presentation structure is that visitors can forget where they are and get "lost in hyperspace." This is a problem that you can combat with appropriate structure and a page layout that always provides hints to visitors as to their current location.

The relationship between the presentation structures need not be an exclusive one. One set of pages can actually support multiple presentation structures. For example, the study guide page shown in Figure 3.6 actually supports both the sequential and hypermedia presentation structures. In particular, the links to *vi resources* provide links to other related information that the visitor can follow rather than continue sequential movement through the pages.

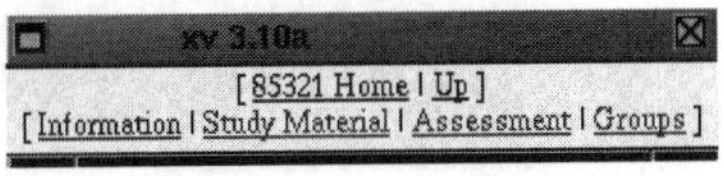

FIGURE 3.5 A hierarchical navigation bar.

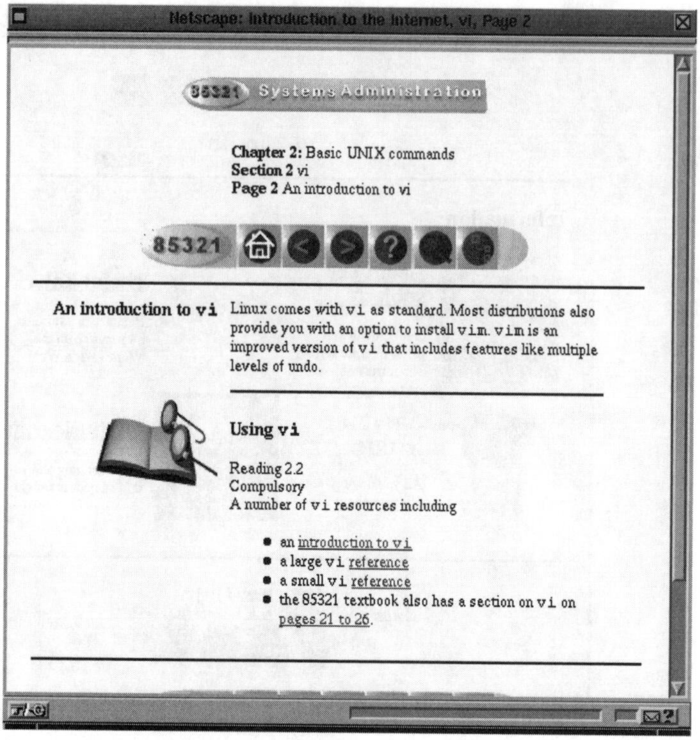

FIGURE 3.6 An example page from a sequential presentation structure.

The Storage Structure

Information on a computer is stored in logical structures called files and directories (sometimes also called folders). All of the HTML pages, images, sounds, movies, and any other data that you distribute via your Web-based classroom must be stored in files on the hard-drive of the computer that acts as the Web server. The storage structure of your Web-based classroom is the structure formed by this collection of files and directories.

In most cases, almost no restrictions are placed on the organization of the storage structure. One extreme is to place all the HTML pages, sound files, and other data for a Web-based classroom into one directory. Although this is possible and

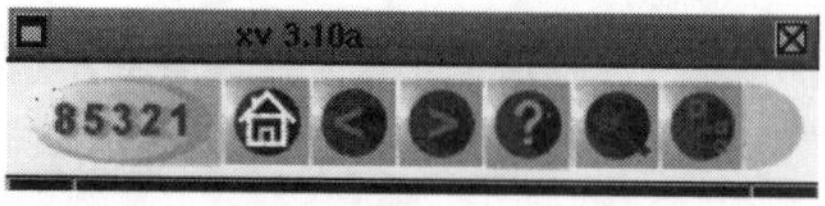

FIGURE 3.7 A sequential navigation bar.

can be quite simple with a small collection of data, it can make maintenance quite difficult as the number of files in a Web-based classroom grows. Maintenance can be considerably easier if directories are used to separate and organize files hierarchically into sections.

It is not necessary for the storage and presentation structures of a Web site to be similar, but it can make maintenance easier if there is some correlation. For example, the Web-based classroom in Figures 3.2 and 3.4 uses a storage structure that strongly resembles its presentation structure. Figure 3.8 is a modification of the class presentation structure illustrated in Figure 3.3; it shows the relationship between this Web-based classroom's storage and presentation structures.

The relationship is shown by adding three extra features to Figure 3.3:

Extra boxes. You will notice that there is an extra box around the entire figure and several additional boxes within it. Each box represents a directory (or folder) on the hard drive of the Web server. The box around the entire figure indicates that all the files for the Web-based classroom are contained within a single directory. As you can see, most of the major pages have been placed in their own directory. By doing this, the presentation and storage structures for this Web-based classroom become very familiar.

Directory names. Each box will have a name, usually in the top left-hand corner, that indicates the name of the directory. In Figure 3.8, the directory names all resemble the presentation names. The exceptions are "study guide" instead of Study Material, "chap2" instead of Chapter 2, and "85321g2" instead of Two.

File names. Every Web page must have HTML stored in a file somewhere. In Figure 3.8, the filename has been added underneath each page name. Many pages are in files called index.html, a common Web filename.

Storage Structure Basics

Figure 3.8 provides a representation of the storage structure for a single Web-based classroom. This section introduces some basic implementation details about storage structures by examining the structure of the entire Web server that hosted this Web-based classroom, which was used during 1996 for the class 85321, Systems Administration, taught by the Department of Mathematics and Computing at Central Queensland University. While in action, the Web-based classroom was hosted on a computer with the host name mc.cqu.edu.au.

The computer mc.cqu.edu.au performed a number of tasks for the department, including hosting the department's Web pages and mailing lists. As with most Web servers, the Web pages for this server were all stored under one directory called the document root (in this case, the document root was a directory called /usr/local/www). To make the Web site easier to maintain, the document root was

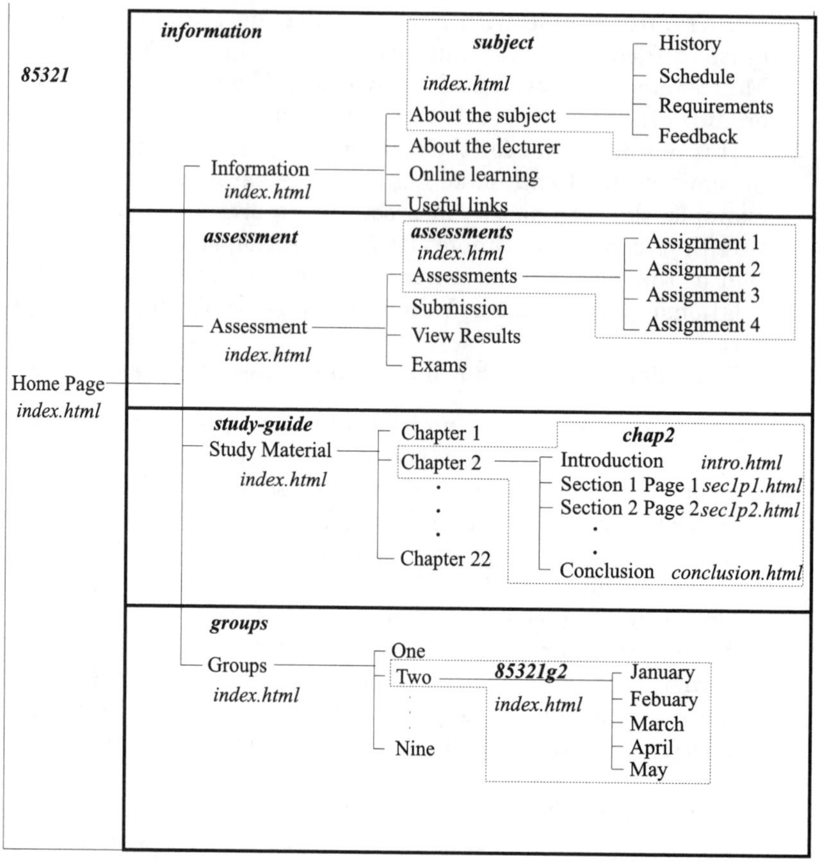

FIGURE 3.8 An example storage structure.

divided into a number of directories, including subjects, information, and staff. The names of these directories provide an indication of the type of information stored in them.

The Web-based classroom for 85321 was stored in a directory called 85321, which was under the subjects directory. As shown in Figure 3.8, the home page for this Web-based classroom was a file called index.html. This information, combined with the host name of the Web server, provides the uniform resource locator for the home page, **mc.cqu.edu.au/subjects/85321/index.html**. (Note that the list of directories does not include the document root directory.)

A uniform resource locator (URL) is simply the address for a piece of information on the Web and is a combination of a protocol, a host name, and a file path. The protocol specifies how the piece of information is to be retrieved. In most cases, Web pages use the HyperText Transport Protocol (HTTP). Other common protocols are gopher and FTP.

The home page for the 85321 Web-based classroom actually has another valid URL apart from the one shown previously. The file path component of a URL usually must include the full directory path and the filename for the page. However, many Web servers have a default filename that is used when a filename is not supplied. The common default value for the filename is index.html. This means that the URLs **mc.qu.edu.au/subjects/85321/** and **mc.cqu.edu.au/subjects/85321/index.html** actually point to the same Web page.

Structure Considerations

The major aim in designing the presentation and storage structures of your Web-based classroom is to reduce the effort required of visitors and the people who have to maintain it. The following are a number of useful guidelines that may help achieve this aim.

Group related elements. Grouping the elements of your Web-based classroom is an essential part of preparing its structure. By grouping the elements in ways that make sense, visitors will be able to predict where a particular piece of information is to be found. If they cannot make these predictions correctly, they will have to hunt around trying to find information.

Provide alternative access methods. Although you might think it makes perfect sense to find a collection of class-related links under a heading "Information," someone else may look for it under "Study Material." One of the advantages of the Web and hypermedia is that, using links, you can provide multiple paths to the same piece of information; in other words, different URLs can lead to the same page.

Include no more than five elements in a page. The short-term memory of most people cannot hold more than five separate pieces of information. The structure of your Web-based classroom should, where possible, recognize this limitation and restrict the number of major choices on one page to no more than five. The page in Figure 3.2 is an example of a good page. The page in Figure 3.9 is an example of a page that contains approximately 20 choices. However, it attempts to meet the "no more than five elements" rule by creating four groups of no more than seven choices in each group.

Balance breadth and depth. Figure 3.10 shows two different structures for the same amount of information. The left-hand structure (a) is a narrow but deep structure; the other structure (b) is a broad but shallow structure. In designing your Web-based classroom, you should aim to achieve a balance that results in a structure that is neither too deep nor too broad. Too deep a structure means that users will have to follow many links to get to the information they want; too broad a structure means a page can become cluttered with a large number of links. A deep structure also complicates navigation.

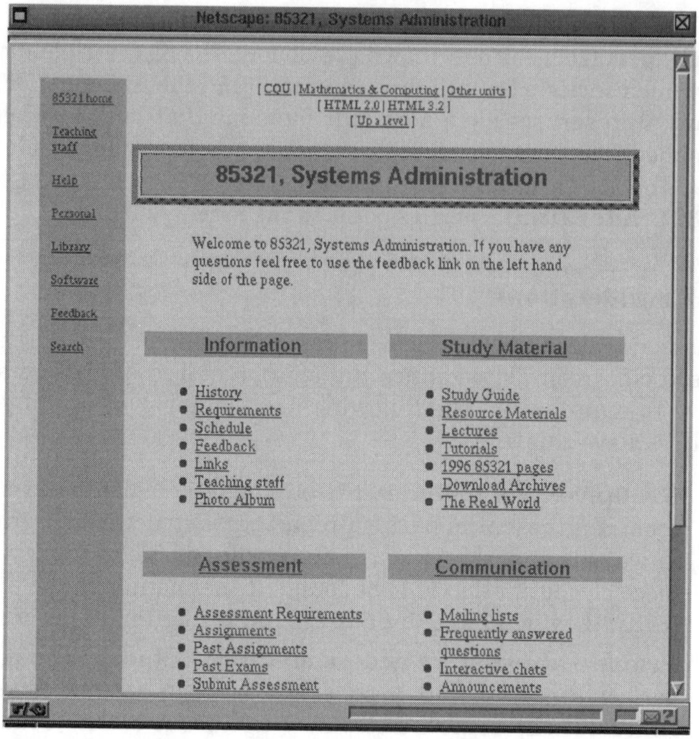

FIGURE 3.9 Four groups of "no more than seven."

Designing the Structure

In Step 4, a process called card sorting is used to organize the information in your Web-based classroom into a structure that seems sensible to a group of people. The structure that this process develops will provide a good indication of the final presentation and storage structure of your site.

The Example

The following section shows the output of Step 3 for the example subject 85349 as well as some of the tasks outlined in Step 4. The test group used in this example was relatively small due to a lack of time and resources. The size of your test group will influence the effectiveness of the process.

Table 3.1 lists a number of the possible tasks that a visitor to the prospective 85349 Web-based classroom may want to perform. For the sake of space, we've limited these tasks to some that are fairly high level; they could be broken down into a number of small tasks.

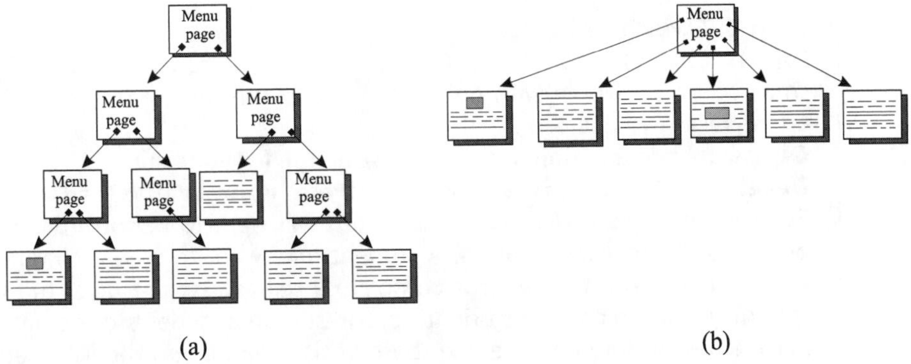

FIGURE 3.10 A deep structure and a shallow structure.

Figure 3.11 shows the initial structure for 85349, which developed after analyzing the results of the card-sorting exercise. Note that the structure is very similar to that in Figure 3.3; this is in part due to the fact that the people involved in the card-sorting exercise are familiar with this structure and naturally gravitated toward it.

Appearance

Designing the appearance of your Web-based classroom serves a much more important purpose than simply making it look pretty. It is the interface through which visitors to your site perform tasks. If that interface is poorly designed, it will make those tasks more difficult to perform. A well-designed appearance will make your site easier to navigate and will motivate and attract students.

Table 3.1 List of Tasks for 85349

Examine administrative information	Check the schedule	Read from the study guide
Examine past exams and solutions	Check the mailing list archives	Look at resource materials
Look at a lecture	Submit an assignment	View results
Read about an assignment	Take a quiz	Use the FAQ
Give some feedback on the unit	Talk to the lecturers	Get some background on the lecturers

Step 4: Structure Design
Inputs: The output of Step 3. A collection of small cards or pieces of paper. A small group of people with different backgrounds, different perspectives, and an interest in your site.
Output: A presentation and storage structure for your site.
Develop a list of tasks available from your Web-based classroom. Each visitor to your Web-based classroom will want to perform different tasks or access different information. A student may want to read a chapter from a study guide, view a lecture, or complete a self-assessment quiz; the teaching staff may want to check a student's progress, add a student to the database, or place a new lecture into the Web-based classroom. Using the list of approaches you identified in Step 3 as a starting point, develop a list of tasks that your Web-based classroom will allow people to perform.
Write one task from your list onto each card. Each card should have a description of one task and a number. The number will be useful when you have to analyze the structures produced by different people.
Give the cards to each person in your test group and ask them to sort the cards into groups. The idea is that each person will sort the tasks you have identified into several related groups. It is likely that some people will want to place one task in more than one group. To support this, it is useful to have duplicate cards.
Ask each person to label his or her groups of tasks. Each individual from your test group should give each collection of tasks a name he or she thinks is meaningful. These names will be used later as either titles for Web pages or as the names of directories.

Designing Web pages is an art that draws on the skills from a variety of fields: computing, graphic design, typography, and multimedia. A look through any good technical book shop or a search on the Web will quickly identify several books and Web sites that provide advice on Web page design. It is beyond the scope of this book to provide an in-depth coverage of design. This section provides a summary of these factors, which have been collected from a variety of sources and personal experience. Pointers to additional sources are provided either in the resources section here or on the book's Web site.

Design, in any field, is a matter of taste and purpose. A design that suits a computing class for distance students will generally not suit an on-campus class in art history. Many of the guidelines below are contradictory or may not be applicable in your situation, and there will always be people who disagree with some or all of them. In the end, it is up to you to make a value judgment about which guidelines apply to your situation.

Ask each person to structure the groups. Each person should organize the groups they have identified into a hierarchy that they think sensible.

Record the groupings and structure. For each person, record the group names, the tasks within each group, and the group hierarchy. Diagrams like those in Figure 3.3 may be useful in this step.

Analyze the results. Examine the structures created by each individual, identify common structures, and try to merge the structures into one.

Test the structure. Prepare a paper-based version of the structure you have developed. Give the mock-up of the structure and a list of tasks to a collection of people. Observe how they perform each of the tasks and record any problems or ways in which the structure can be improved. Make any necessary modifications.

Develop the storage and presentation structures. Once you have developed and tested the final grouping of the cards, it is time to design the storage and presentation structure of your Web-based classroom. A simple approach to this is that each separate group has its own directory; each card with a group name becomes a Web page that is the default page within its directory (for instance, index.html), and each card within a group has its own directory and becomes the default page for that directory.

This approach has the advantage that it is quite simple and straightforward to develop, and the resulting presentation and storage structures are very similar. However, it can result in quite long URLs.

The Limitations of the Technology

All of the many people surfing the Web have varying levels of technology, and much of that technology is very primitive. In designing your Web-based classroom, you must consider at least three common limitations of the technology:

Speed. Do not expect people to wait long periods of time to download those fancy graphics you spent so long creating. This is especially true when the people who visit your Web-based classroom return a number of times. That pretty graphic might be neat the first time, but after waiting for it to download for the thousandth time, it may lose its appeal. Some of the tools mentioned in the resources section below—in particular, Doctor HTML and Bobby—provide feedback on how long it will take to download and display a Web page.

Resolution. Resolution of computer displays range from 640 × 480 to 1,280 × 1,024, with the odd display above or below that range. Producing a design specifically for a high resolution will place people with lower resolutions who visit your Web-based classroom at a disadvantage and may even act as a barrier.

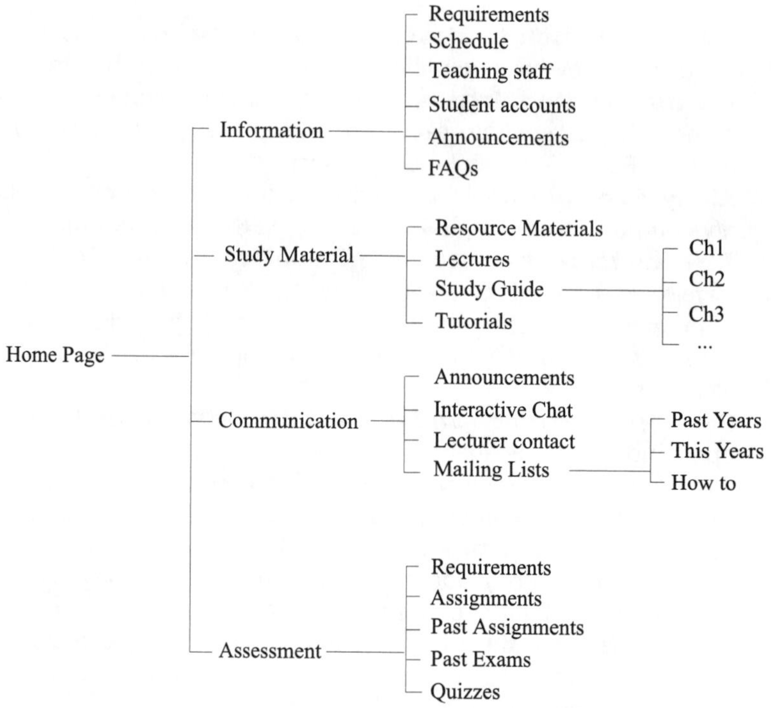

FIGURE 3.11 The structure for 85349.

Colors. The number of colors supported by computers on the Web range from monochrome to 24-bit displays capable of displaying millions of colors. A 24-bit color graphic may look good on an appropriate display, but it may appear totally black on a monochrome screen.

General Considerations Here are some general design considerations that, although not specifically Web related, provide good advice:

Concentrate on the content. The design of your interface should not distract from the content. A common example of this on Web pages is movement. Most Web pages are static; however, the advent of animated GIFs, blinking text, Java applets, and JavaScript has resulted in an explosion of Web pages filled with movement. Movement is particularly useful for getting the reader's attention. However, many Web designers use movement—in particular, animated GIFs—for decoration rather than for content distribution. The result is that the reader's eye is drawn away from the main content of a page toward some relatively unimportant decoration.

A good design is a simple one. Many first-time Web authors overload their pages with graphical dividers, bullets, headings, animated GIFs, and other visual garbage that can prevent the visitor from getting to the content of the page. Keep page layout simple and clean.

Legibility is key. Ask yourself whether people visiting your Web-based classroom can easily read and understand the content of all the pages. You should remember that not everyone has the same equipment or capabilites that you have. What you see on your Web browser is not always what other people will see. Legibility can be reduced by incorrect use of colors, poor choice of fonts and font sizes, overuse of movement, and many other factors. A mistake made by many first-time Web designers is the overuse of background images or badly chosen text colors that can make reading text quite difficult.

Make the prominence of objects on the page suitable to the objects. What is the most important concept or piece of information on your page? Is it obvious? Large size, particular colors, and movement all contribute to make page elements more noticeable and consequently more effective.

Visitors should always know the context in which they are currently operating. On the Web, the page design should provide visitors with information such as where they are in relation to the rest of the Web site, how far are they progressed in completing some task, and the result of the last operation performed.

Consistency means predictability. By being consistent throughout your Web-based classroom, you will make it possible for visitors to become familiar with the "behavior" of your site and be able to predict how to perform tasks and find their way around. Unexpected changes in page layout or the behavior of certain components will only confound and confuse.

Be accurate. One of the most effective methods for decreasing the use of a Web-based classroom is for it to contain mistakes. Common mistakes in a Web-based classroom include invalid HTML, broken images, and links that don't work. A large number of programs will automatically check and notify you of these problems. Pointers to these tools are provided in the resources section of this chapter and in the following chapter.

Be unique. It is not uncommon for institutions to attempt to achieve quality through consistency of appearance. Even though some level of similarity in institutional material helps establish a corporate identity, it can in some cases be counterproductive. When a Web-based classroom has a unique look and feel, it is quite easy for visitors to identify when they enter or leave its domain. In addition, each Web-based classroom has its own requirements. Designing a single appearance that supports the requirements of all Web-based classrooms is very difficult.

The appearance of a Web page must match the purpose of the page. This implies that pages within the same Web-based classroom will have a different page layout. For example, a page containing a self-assessment quiz will have page elements that allow visitors to modify and submit answers. A page containing an online lecture may contain elements that allow the visitor to listen to some audio and to move onto the next slide.

Support a variety of visitors. Some tools are making it easier to support a wider range of visitors by automatically generating different types of page layout. For example, the Web page in Figure 3.12 contains the same information as the page in Figure 3.9. The primary difference is that the pages are written using different versions of HTML to accommodate differences in browsers. Rather than have the page designer produce two versions of the same page, the particular tool used for this classroom, Webfuse (discussed in Chapter 9), did the conversion automatically. By having different page layouts available, you can keep a large number of visitors happy.

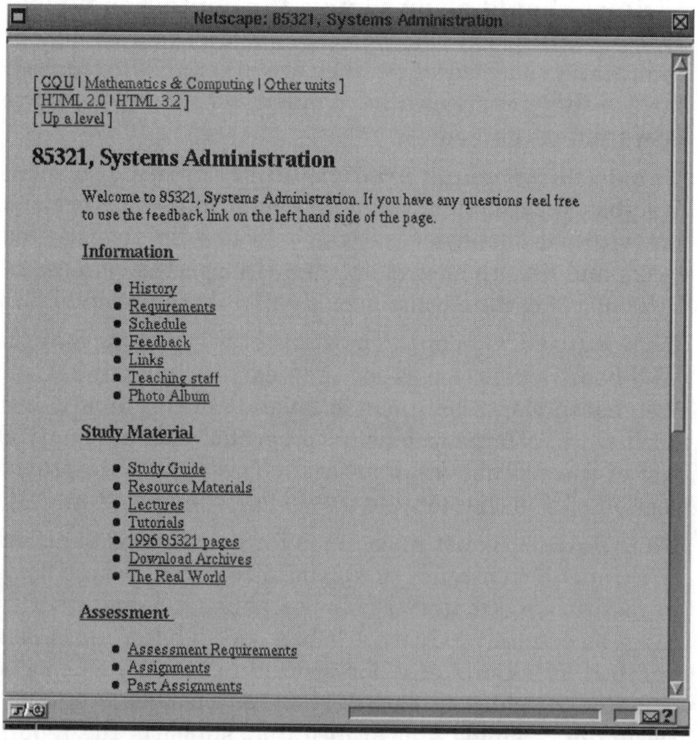

FIGURE 3.12 Same page, different format.

Colors The colors used in a Web-based classroom provide a simple method to either greatly improve the legibility of a site or completely destroy it. The following are some general suggestions for the use of color if you intend to define your own text and link colors:

Use bright colors for links that have not been visited and less bright colors for visited links. The basis for this assertion is the combination of two assumptions: inks that have not been visited are more important than links that have been visited, and bright colors draw the eye more than dull colors.

Don't use color simply for the sake of using color. Instead, color should be used for a specific purpose to indicate a particular task, event, or collection of information. It should be used consistently. If a dark blue background is used to indicate a group of navigation icons, it should not be used for another purpose. Try not to use more than four colors in a single page and no more than seven for an entire site.

Finally, do not use the color combinations shown in Table 3.2. They are unattractive and hard to read.

HTML HyperText Markup Language (HTML) is the basic building block of the design of a Web page. You should be aware of a number of issues and considerations in using HTML to design your Web-based classroom.

Markup versus Page Specification HTML is a markup language designed to allow the author to specify the content of a document as a sequence of sentences, paragraphs, and headings. The purpose of HTML was not to allow the author to control the final presentation of a document. Instead, it was intended that readers of the document would be able to choose the presentation that best suits their preferences and needs. For example, visitors with vision impairments might set their browsers to use very large fonts or use a non-visual HTML browser.

The migration of desktop publishers and graphic designers onto the Web has changed this situation. People who use these packages are accustomed to being able to specify and control the exact look and feel of a document. Their need to do this has led to many tricks, tips, and HTML extensions designed to achieve this

Table 3.2 Color Combinations to Avoid

Yellow on white	Yellow on purple	Green on white
Yellow on green	Magenta on green	Blue on black
Red on black	Magenta on black	Yellow on white
Red and blue	Red and green	Blue and green

goal. Some of the pointers in the resource section of this chapter describe these methods in more detail.

Such methods, although improving the author's control over presentation, generally rely on small tricks or non-standard HTML that are not viewable under all browsers. They also remove the readers' ability to adapt the presentation to their situations and may not adapt well to people without fast Internet connections. For example, these approaches make it possible to specifically set the size of the font used on a Web page. This can cause problems with people with a vision impairment who require a large font.

Standards Competition amongst browser developers has led to a large number of nonstandard extensions to HTML. As a result, you will see many Web pages that include "best viewed with . . ." icons. These icons are indicative of the problem caused by these extensions. Only particular browsers will be able to gain the full benefit from the extensions. Those people without these extensions will not be able to view your pages.

Wherever possible, you should restrict yourself to using standard HTML 2.0 or HTML 3.2 tags to maximize the possible audience for your pages. The definition of these standards can be found on the World Wide Web Consortium's Web page, **www.w3.org**. (For more information on this issue, refer to the Best Viewed with any Browser home page at **server.berkeley.edu/~cdaveb/anybrowser.html**.)

Font Size and Style Recent developments in HTML allow the author to specify the size and type of font to use for text, making it possible to create quite effective, attractive Web pages without the use of graphics. However, the use of fonts—in particular, trying to use different fonts—does lead to problems with portability between platforms. Figure 3.13 shows the same page viewed with the same browser (Netscape Navigator) but on different operating systems. The top image is on a computer running Windows '95; the bottom image is on a computer running Linux.

This problem is a result of the page using a font that is not available under the Linux operating system. A solution to this problem is to specify multiple fonts, with the aim that at least one of those fonts will be available on all computer platforms. For example, the HTML fragment <FONT FACE="Arial, Helvetica, Geneva"> will use a sans serif font on Windows (Arial), UNIX (Helvetica), and Macintosh (Geneva) computers.

Graphics The first components of page layout most people think of are fancy graphical images. Computer graphics, although not necessary to achieve an attractive site, can be used to achieve many interesting effects. The following discusses issues involved with using graphical images:

Obvious meaning. Examine the navigation bar shown in Figure 3.7. Can you describe the purpose of each of the seven icons from this bar? Figure 3.14

FIGURE 3.13 One page, one browser—two operating systems.

describes the intended meaning of each icon. How many of them did you identify correctly?

Trying to develop a presentation that relies solely on image to represent tasks is difficult because of people's different backgrounds and associations. This is especially true given the global nature of the Web and the tendency for different cultures to place different meanings on the same image. To avoid this sort of confusion, a common practice is to associate a small label with each image, as shown in Figure 3.15.

Give visual clues. The appearance of icons and how well they provide visitors with the necessary visual clues directly influences how many people use a particular operation. The designers of Sun's Web interface reported an increase of more than 400 percent over two months due to the redesign of some icons (**www.sun.com/sun-on-net/uidesign/usabilitytest.html**). An example of this can be seen in Figure 3.16, which contains two images designed to perform the same task: to take the visitor to the previous page. One of the images consists of just the text; the other is designed to look like a button. The idea is that the button-like appearance will give visitors clues that indicate that they can press/click on this icon and something will happen.

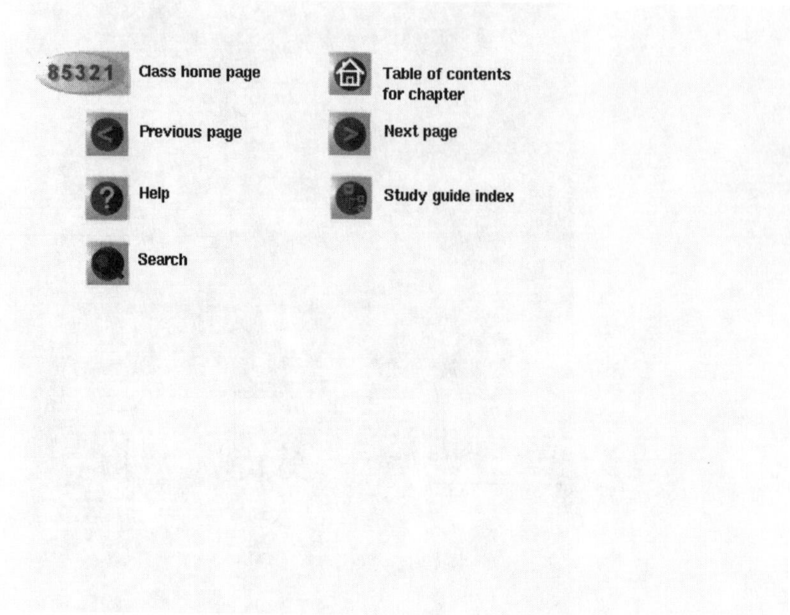

FIGURE 3.14 Icons and meanings.

Layout The layout of a page deals with how its contents are organized. This section describes guidelines and offers suggestions for developing a page layout that is both attractive and helps visitors:

> **Same task, same location.** Building on the suggestion for consistency, it is common for the pages of a Web-based classroom to make use of a single page layout. The page layout may change slightly due to the different requirements of an individual page (such as a lecture slide needing different navigation support than the archive of a mailing list), but they should still be recognizable

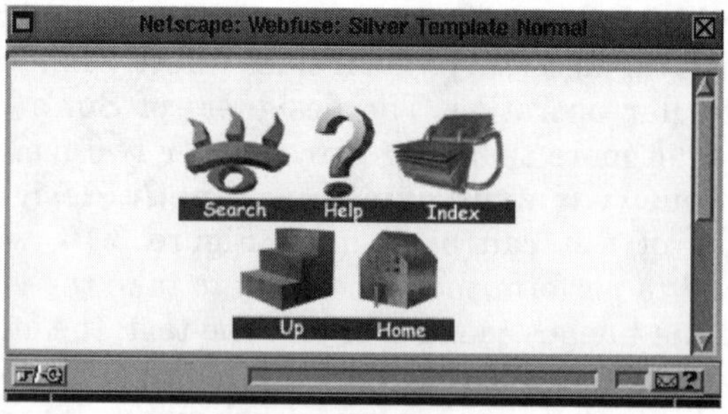

FIGURE 3.15 Navigation bar with labels.

FIGURE 3.16 Two Back buttons.

as belonging to the same classroom. This consistency serves a dual purpose: It allows visitors to predict where particular components will be and what they will do, and it helps visitors recognize when they are in the Web-based classroom. Figures 3.2, 3.4, and 3.6 are examples of pages from a Web-based classroom that use a consistent page layout.

Grouping. Grouping, as shown in Figure 3.9, is a useful mechanism for making it easier for visitors to choose from a wide range of information. The following guidelines provide some guidance in how to group information on a Web page:

1. Group related elements together.
2. A particular type of group should always appear in the same location on a page to ensure consistency.
3. Use white space, color, or graphical images to clearly indicate where groups start and stop.
4. Groups that contain information or tasks that are important or will be used the most often should appear at the top.
5. If the components of a group are used in some order, they should appear in that order.
6. If there is no apparent order for the elements of a group, order them alphabetically or numerically.
7. If two or more groups are related in some way, the representation of those groups should provide some indication of that relationship.

Text layout. With HTML now providing greater support for the use of text with different colors and fonts, you can use just text and still develop an attractive presentation. A major benefit of using straight text is that it significantly reduces the time required to download a page. Another advantage is that the absence of images makes it somewhat easier to design the layout, particularly for those who have limited artistic ability. For example, the 1997 version of the Web-based classroom shown in Figures 3.2 and 3.4 was redesigned to use a text-only layout because some students reported that the pages containing pictures or icons were taking too long to download. One page from this new text-only Web-based classroom is shown in Figure 3.9.

Many commercial Web sites are starting to use a quite effective appearance that is reminiscent of newspapers and magazines. This layout is particularly useful for reasonable amounts of text because the small width of the columns requires less side-to-side eye movement and can reduce fatigue.

Metaphors. The Web-based classrooms shown in Figures 3.2 and 3.9 use a very simple, direct metaphor. In fact, they are little more than pretty menus that structure access to the information and tasks of the Web-based classroom. Although this approach is functional, some may think it a little dry and boring.

One approach that may solve this particular problem is that of "third-generation" Web sites, as described by David Siegel in his book and Web site, *Creating Killer Web Sites* (Hayden, 1996. **www.killersites.com/**). Third-generation Web sites aim to create an entire visual experience for visitors by combining tight control over the visual appearance, a metaphor, and a visual theme.

One problem with this approach is that effective metaphors and visual themes for an entire Web-based classroom are difficult and time-consuming to develop. It is also possible that, given the global nature of the Web, some people may not understand the metaphor. Finally, by using a metaphor, you restrict your Web-based classroom to the actions and ideas that fit within that metaphor.

Page Components and Templates Creating a page template for your Web-based classroom is one approach that can significantly reduce the effort involved in creating a consistent appearance. A page template is a skeleton Web page that contains most of the structure and components that form the presentation you have designed. The idea is that each new page for your Web-based classroom is created by taking an empty template and providing the content for the new page. Many modern Web publishing tools support the concept of page templates; some even supply a collection of example templates you can modify and use.

The common approach with page templates is to divide a page into a number of separate components. Three standard high-level components of a Web page are the header, the body, and the footer. Figure 3.17 shows how a page from one Web-based classroom can be divided into these three components.

The header of a Web page is everything that appears before the main content of the page. It should not be confused with the HTML head component of a page (the section of the page between the <HEAD></HEAD> tags). The header in Figure 3.17 includes the HTML head component but also includes other elements such as the banner graphic, navigation links, and the page title.

The body component of a page normally contains the main content of the page, which is generally unique for each particular page.

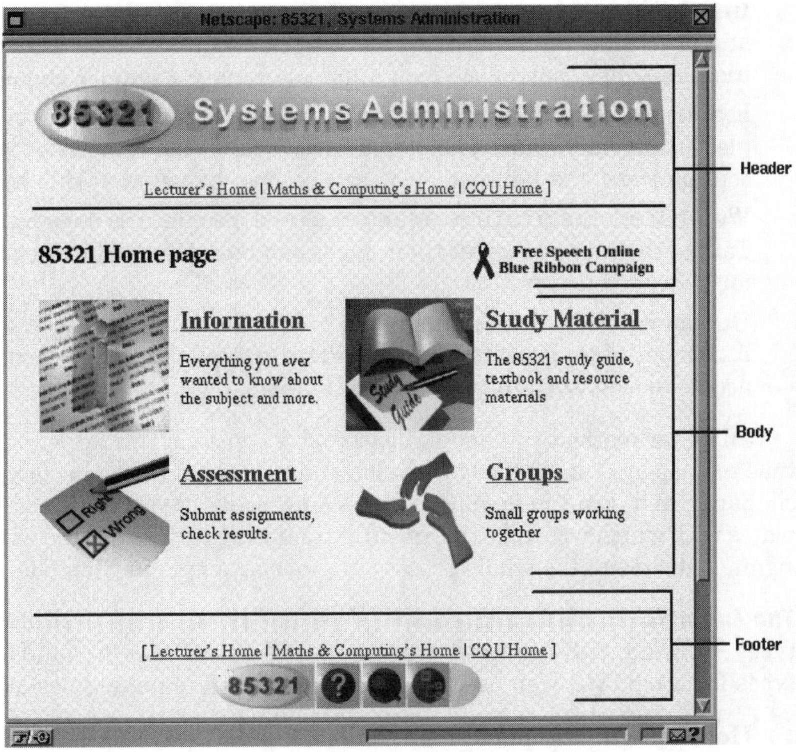

FIGURE 3.17 A page and its components.

The footer can often contain the same information as the header. This is mainly due to the fact that most of the navigation links on a page appear in the header. Replicating these links in the footer helps reduce the amount of movement a visitor to the Web page needs to make. It is also common for the footer of a page to include such information as the name of the author of the page, the date the page was last modified, and the page's URL.

Creating a Look and Feel The discussion in the previous sections of this chapter provides some insight into the issues you need to consider when designing the presentation of your Web-based classroom, but it doesn't answer the big question: How do you do it? Because the process is creative, there is no one answer; everyone will have a style or method that works best for them. The following section provides one set of steps that may help you develop the appearance of your Web-based classroom.

Before starting, you should remember that creating an attractive, usable, and consistent appearance requires considerable time and some artistic ability, especially if you start from scratch. The following list provides suggestions for sources that may help you in developing a look and feel:

Institutional design. Many institutions already have standard templates and icons that can be used in Web pages. Some institutions have strict specifications that control the look and feel of institutional Web pages.

Existing templates. Many modern Web publishing tools provide page templates that can be adapted for your use. A collection of URLs of Web pages that contain icons and templates you can use can be found at this book's Web site.

Web-based inspiration. Many talented people are designing Web pages. Taking the time to look at their pages can be a source of inspiration and ideas for your own design.

Outsource. The final approach is to hire someone to do the design for you. A number of professionals on the Web are available for hire or you may have access to talented students and volunteers.

Whichever method you adopt, don't rush to write HTML. Spend a great deal of time using pencil and paper to develop and experiment with prototypes. With pencil, paper, and some imagination, you can quickly create and modify rough templates with which you can experiment. Attempting to do the same with HTML adds significant time to the whole process. See our attempts in Step 5 (sidebar).

The Example To perform Step 5 for class 85349, we must first identify the page types. Working with the structure shown in Figure 3.11, we can identify five page types for the 85349 Web-based classroom. These five page types are:

Home page. The plan is for the 85349 home page to be different from the other pages in the classroom and hopefully serve as a colorful introduction to the class.

Index pages. The primary purpose of index pages is to create the structure of the 85349 Web-based classroom. These pages contain a number of links to other pages.

Content pages. A content page is used as the standard default page type. If a page isn't one of the other four page types, it will be a content page. A content page simply contains any HTML the author wishes.

Study guide pages. The pages of the study guide for 85349 will be the primary source used by students to progress through the 85349 Web-based classroom. The 85349 study guide will use a sequential presentation structure and so needs extra navigation links to support this structure.

Lecture pages. The online lectures for 85349 will also use a sequential presentation structure but will have one or two other slight differences from a study guide page.

The next step is to identify and group the page elements. In order to help students find their way around the 85349 Web-based classroom, every page, except the 85349 home page, will contain a navigation bar on its left-hand side. This navigation bar will provide links to each of the major pages in the 85349 Web-based classroom.

Table 3.3 provides a summary of the other navigation links that each page type will have. Finally, each page will also have a space for the content of the page.

Next we identified the theme. The planned theme for the 85349 Web-based classroom is fairly simple due to time constraints and author's lack of artistic ability. The theme is to be blue and primarily text based. The intention is to give the impression of water. Blue was chosen mainly because of the author's preference—in particular, a dislike for bright backgrounds. It was also decided that the 85349 Web-based classroom would be available in two formats, graphical and text only. The text-only version is designed to provide access to people with less capable Web browsers and slow network connections.

Step 5: Designing a Page Layout

Inputs: The output of Step 4, a list of the pages and the content likely to be used in the Web-based classroom.

Output: A collection of page layout templates for the pages in your Web-based classroom.

Identify all the page types. Your Web-based classroom will contain a number of page types; develop a list of them.

Identify and group the page elements each page type requires. Different page types will require different page elements. For example, a page from a study guide may need navigation links to the next page, previous page, glossary, and index. Once you've developed the list of elements, try to group them into sensible collections.

Identify the feel or theme you want for your Web-based classroom. The feel or theme for your Web-based classroom can range from something as simple as "everything should be blue" to a full-fledged metaphor that extends through every page in your site.

Combine the elements and the theme. Work out how the groups of page elements you have identified will be placed on the page. Where will the navigation bars go? Where will the links to the home page go? Using the identified theme, design the icons, color, and layout of these elements to fit the theme. The aim of this particular step is to produce a paper-based prototype for each page type you identified in the first step.

Initial testing. Show other people your design. Gather feedback and suggestions and possibly modify your design until people are happy with it.

Produce page templates. Time to implement your paper-based prototypes. Write the HTML and create the graphics necessary to implement your design.

Final testing. Test the implementation of your design under various situations, including different connection speeds, resolutions, color depths, and browsers. Testing should include using automated validation tools such as Doctor HTML and Bobby (mentioned in the Resources section).

Table 3.3 85349 Page Types and Navigation Links

Page Type	*Navigation Links*
Content and index	85349 home page, search, help, index, and up
Study guide	Table of contents, next page, previous page, 85349 home page, search, help, and index
Lecture	Next slide, previous slide, up, and audio

Then we combined the elements and the theme. The presentation of the 85349 Web-based classroom and its components went through a number of paper-based versions. Figure 3.18 shows one of the final paper-based prototypes for the index and content page types.

After producing and showing the paper-based prototypes to a number of people, we converted them into HTML code and images. The icons were produced using a graphic manipulation program for UNIX called GIMP (**www.xcf.berkeley.edu/~gimp/gimp.html**), which provides similar functionality to programs such as Adobe Photoshop and Paintshop Pro. Figure 3.19 shows a final version of the prototype shown in Figure 3.16.

The final testing of the presentation for the 85349 pages involved the following three steps:

Upload. A version of each prototype was placed onto a Web server so it could be available for the following steps.

Bobby. Each page was given to Bobby to receive feedback on the characteristics such as the speed of downloading and any problems the design might cause for people with disabilities. Bobby reported the original design would take about 15 seconds to download over a 14.4K modem, and a number of minor problems with the HTML coding made the pages less accessible to people with disabilities.

HTML validation. Finally, each page was run through the WebTechs validation service, which performs a strict validation of the HTML.

A pointer to the real 85349 Web-based classroom can be found on this book's Web site.

WHERE TO FROM HERE?

If you have completed all of the steps outlined in this chapter, you will now have some idea of what services your Web-based classroom will provide, some possibilities about how you might implement it, how it will be structured, and a collection of templates that specify what it will look like. So, what next?

For most people, the next step in building a Web-based classroom will be to find out more about the medium by reading the rest of the book and perhaps talking with other people. What you find out may result in a return to this process to

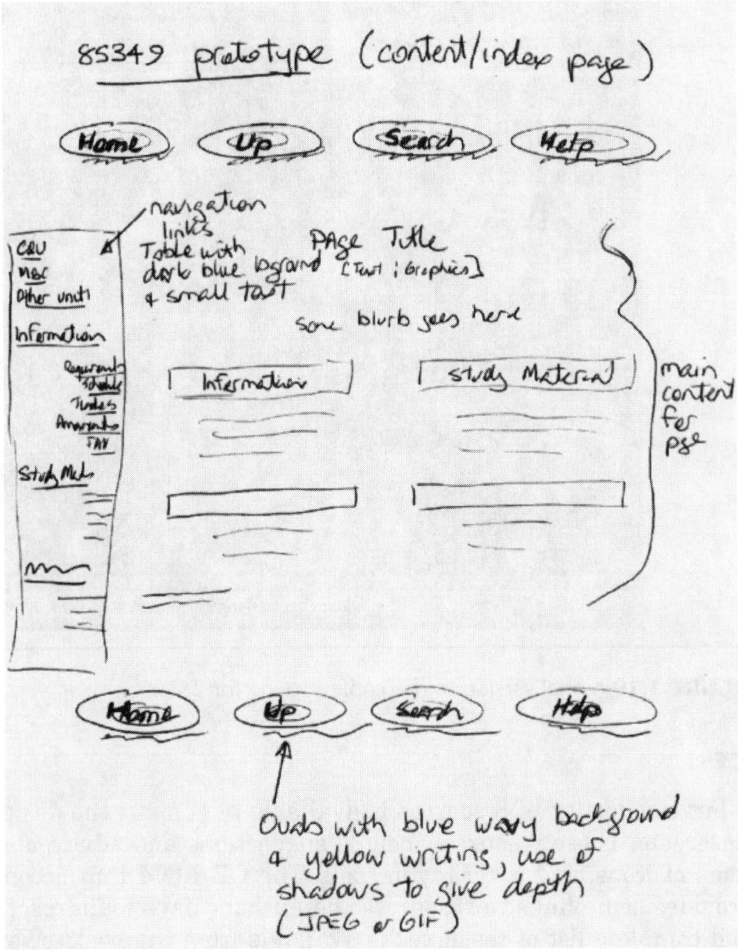

FIGURE 3.18 A paper-based prototype.

make some adjustments. The next step is to identify the tools you will use to implement your Web-based classroom, become familiar with them, and then start construction.

As we've seen, the design of a Web-based classroom must draw on technical, educational, artistic, design factors, and personal preference. There is no one correct design, simply designs that are more appropriate to a given situation or for a particular person. Designing your Web-based classroom must be done with a set of educational goals and the characteristics of your class firmly in mind. The beauty of design is that you are never finished. The more experience you have, the more ideas you will generate for improving the design.

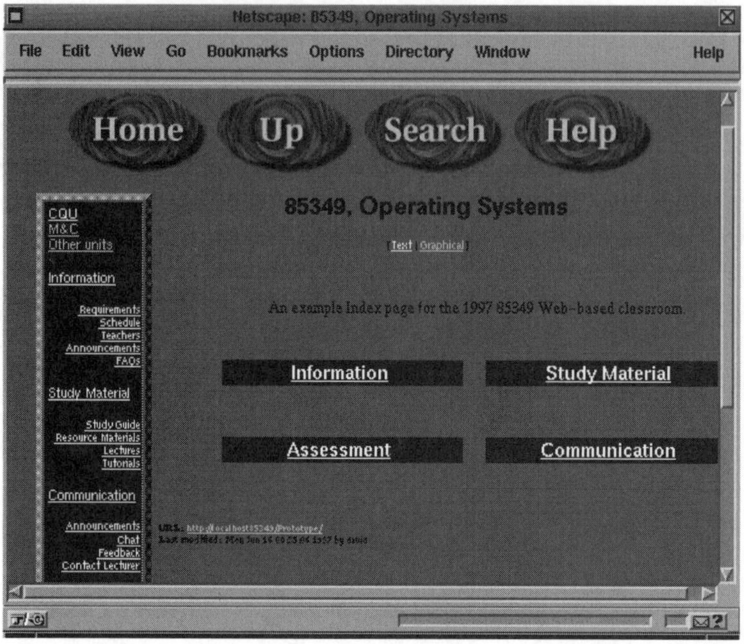

FIGURE 3.19 A final version of the content page for 85349.

RESOURCES

A large collection of resources is available to support the design of a Web-based classroom. These resources include suggestions and advice about design, collections of icons, and a variety of tools. The CD-ROM that accompanies this book provides some links to resources the authors have found useful. A more recent and complete list of resources is available from the book's Web site. Topics covered on the CD-ROM include the following:

- Web site layout (the good, the bad, and the truly terrible)
- Browser compatibility
- Web tools
- Online forums on the Web classroom experience

4

Content Development

This chapter looks at how you select and prepare material (text, sound, and video) for viewing on the Web. The chapter also looks at browsers and how they handle such information. The chapter is divided into the following sections: content preparation, viewing tools, content distribution, and related topics.

CONTENT PREPARATION

In this section, we discuss preparing the content on your Web site and the tools such as HTML that are available. Keep in mind that this is not a guide to writing HTML. Many books and online services, some listed on this book's CD-ROM, do a good job of teaching you how to use HTML.

HTML

HTML is constantly evolving as a language for formatting information. Each version of HTML has its own version number. The first version of HTML was 1.0; the current version of HTML, which most browsers support, is 2.0. There is a specification for HTML 3, but few browsers support it in its entirety. What the various versions mean in real terms is that some formatting operations are possible only in later versions of HTML. Browser makers have also added their own custom extensions to HTML; for example, Netscape added the ability to display tables. Some of these extensions have been incorporated into the general standard for HTML, but some extensions may be viewable only on certain manufacturers' browsers. This should not concern you unless your students are using a very old browser that supports only HTML 1.0 (for example, Netscape 1.0), in which case you should keep in mind that these students might not be able to view any advanced formatting feature that you place in HTML.

Writing HTML You can use a straightforward text editor to write HTML pages. You simply need to include the proper HTML tags so that a browser will recognize your HTML correctly. Some useful text editors are BBEdit (**www.barebones.com/bbedit.html**) for Macintosh users and Textpad (**www.textpad.com**) for Windows users.

What You See Is What You Get (WYSIWYG) editors are one of the most popular ways of creating HTML. Using a WYSIWYG editor means you can write your HTML page as though it were a normal word-processed document; you don't have to worry about inserting all the relevant HTML tags.

A complete list of HTML authoring tools available is on the Web page **homepage.interaccess.com/~cdavis/edit_rev.html**. Some examples of these are found in Table 4.1.

Checking Your HTML A number of utilities are available that will allow you to check your HTML to see if any browser will have a problem with it. The most popular of these is a Perl utility called WebLint; you can find out more about it at **www.cre.canon.co.uk/~neilb/weblint/**.

In addition, a number of online checking services will check the HTML found at a particular URL. Two of those services are HTML Validation Service (**www.hensa.ac.uk/html-val-svc**) and Net Mechanic (**www.netmechanic.com**), which will also rate your server's response time.

Converting Material If you have material in an existing file format, you may be able to find a utility or an add-on for the program that created the file in order to convert the material into HTML. Two translators to look at are **www.w3.org/hypertext/WWW/Tools/Word_proc_filters.html** and **www.yahoo.com/Computers_Internet/Software/Internet/World_Wide_Web/HTML_Converters/**. A brief summary of popular HTML converters is given in Table 4.2.

Table 4.1 HTML Authoring Tools

Package	*Platform*	*Location*
HoTMeTaL	Unix, Macintosh, and Windows	ftp://ftp.ncsa.uiuc.edu/Web/html/hotmetal
HTML Editor	Macintosh	dragon.acadiau.ca/~giles/home.html
Netscape Gold	Unix, Macintosh, and Windows	www.netscape.com/
Claris Homepage	Macintosh and Windows	www.claris.com/products/claris/clarispage/clarispage.html

Adobe has produced a Web site that assists in the creation of HTML versions of PDF documents. See **www.adobe.com/prodindex/acrobat/accessadobe-com.html** for more details.

Using Multimedia on the Web

Basically, multimedia can be broken down into pictures, sound, and video. In this section, we look at the various multimedia elements that you can incorporate into your Web pages, how to create the elements, and instructional purposes for which they are suited. There are a number of packages for creating multimedia that will save you some trouble. Most of them require some sort of plug-in for the student to view them. The most popular multimedia creation package is called Authorware (**www.macromedia.com/software/**).

Table 4.2 HTML Converters

Program Name	*Format Converted*	*Location*
Internet Assistant for Word, Powerpoint, and Excel	Microsoft Word, Powerpoint, and Excel	www.microsoft.com/msdownload/
Rtftohtml	Rich-text format (RTF)	www.sunpack.com/RTF/ rtftohtml_overview.html
Rtftoweb	RTF	ftp://ftp.rrzn.uni-hannover .de/pub/unix-local/misc/ rtftoweb/html/rtftoweb.html
Wp2x	WordPerfect for DOS	journal.biology.carleton.ca/People/ Michael_Richardson/software/ wp2x.html
Wptohml	WordPerfect	ftp://ftp.coast.net/SimTel/msdos/ wordperf/
Latex2html	LaTeX	cbl.leeds.ac.uk/nikos/tex2html/ doc/manual/manual.html
Hyperlatex	LaTeX	graphics.postech.ac.kr/otfried/ html/hyperlatex.html
Qt2www	Macintosh Quark XPress	the-tech.mit.edu/~jeremy/ qt2www.html
Websucker	Macintosh Pagemaker	www.msystems.com/mcohen/ websucker.html
Txt2html	Plain text	www.cs.wustl.edu/~seth/txt2html/
Webify	PostScript	cag-www.lcs.mit.edu:80/ ~ward/webify/

NOTE

Some converters for older versions of word processors will not perform a complete translation into HTML. For example, Internet Assistant for Word 6.0 will not translate tables or graphics included in the word processed document. ■

Using Pictures Pictures can have a powerful impact on your Web pages. You can set the scene for a play by providing a picture of a location, provide a picture of a famous painting for study, include a picture of equipment you are describing—you can even include pictures of images on a computer screen. Pictures can also take on other qualities; you can create an image map that will allow your students to select and click on parts of a picture, which will bring them to other pages or more pictures. For example, they can zoom in on parts of a painting to view it in more detail. We'll discuss this technique in a moment.

Inline Images You can include inline images within your Web page, subject to certain self-imposed limitations. An inline image can be included in your page by writing the following code:

```
<img src = "file.gif">
```

where file.gif is the name of the image. The picture is automatically loaded and displayed in the browser (provided it is of a type the browser can display). They are called inline images because they appear to be part of your HTML text.

One of those self-imposed limitations is to avoid including too many images or images that are very large, because they can cause a page to take a long time to download, frustrating the person waiting to read it. Of course, if visitors get tired of waiting, they can press the Stop button to cancel the image loading and do without it altogether. They can even configure the browser so that it no longer loads images automatically. This means that any images you have included will not be viewed. You should set yourself a per-page limit on the number of images and how large they can be in terms of bytes. This limit will vary depending on how the students are accessing your system. For instance, if they are using a LAN, their browsers will load images more quickly than if they were connecting via modem. You can run tests on various computers and network connections to see how long files take to load, then use these tests to estimate how many images can be comfortably included in a page. You should not abandon large images or multimedia components just because the students have a slow network connection, but provide proper links to all of them so that students have the choice of loading them or not.

If you do not want to have a picture loaded as part of your HTML page, you can provide a proper link to a picture via the following code:

```
<a href="file.ext"> Link to picture, 150k</a>
```

FIGURE 4.1 An icon indicating a GIF file of 102K will be downloaded.

This statement provides a link to a picture called file.ext., When a visitor clicks on the link, the picture will load in the browser window. You can include the size of the picture so the visitor will have an idea of how long it will take for the browser to load the image. For instance, Figure 4.1 includes an icon that indicates that the student is about to download a picture of type GIF, which is 102K in size.

One other approach is to include miniature versions of pictures, called thumbnails. Thumbnails give visitors a rough idea of what the picture looks like and whether it would be of any use to them. A thumbnail picture acts as a link to a larger picture.

Image Format There are numerous ways of storing images, usually dictated by the program used to create them. The best thing to do is to put your images in a form that can be viewed by the majority of browsers. The two most popular forms are GIF and JPEG. GIF files have the extension .gif; JPEG files usually have the extension .jpg. Both GIF and JPEG formats support compression, which reduces the size of your image file.

The GIF format is marginally more popular because it allows effects such as interlacing (the picture is displayed on-screen in stages, with one stage laid over another), transparent background (an image's background can be made to blend in with the background of a page), and animation (combining a number of images in one file and coding them to download at preset intervals to give the illusion of movement).

JPEG supports more colors than GIF and is more suited for photographs. If you have a line drawing or a cartoon, however, GIF is a better format.

Your images could have been created in one of a number of formats. For example, on a Macintosh, they may be in PICT format; on Microsoft Windows, they could be in PCX format. What you need is a utility that will translate your image into a GIF or a JPEG for uploading to your Web site. Many of the programs used to create pictures can export those pictures to other formats. Try to use the export option of your picture-creation program first. If this does not work, you can use a program that will convert from one image type to another. Some shareware programs to do this are shown in Table 4.3.

You can turn portions of your screen into a picture by using a capture utility that will convert the resulting image into a GIF or JPEG file. You can display the material on-screen, do a screen capture of it, then save the screen capture in a

Table 4.3 Shareware Programs That Convert from One Image Type to Another

Package	*Platform*	*Location*
PaintShop	Windows	www.jasc.com/
XV	UNIX	ftp://ftp.cis.upenn.edu/pub/xv
ImageMagick	UNIX,Windows, Macintosh	www.wizards.dupont.com/cristy/ ImageMagick.html
GraphicConverter	Macintosh	members.aol.com/lemkesoft/ gcdownload.html
GifConverter	Macintosh	www.kamit.com/ gifconverter.html

form that a browser can display. PaintShop and XV both have a built-in capture facility. FlashIT is a capture utility available for the Macintosh (**ftp://ftp.zdnet .com/pub/private/sWlIB/graphics_multimedia/graphics_tools/flashi.hqx**).

If your images can't be converted into a form that can be displayed by a browser and it is not possible to do a screen capture, you will have to ensure that students have a utility or a program on their computers that will enable them to see your images. You can set up your Web page so that this utility is automatically started with the image when the student clicks on the link to it (see the "Helper Applications" section later in this chapter for more information). For example, if your image is in PICT format, you can set up the browser so that it starts a program that can display a PICT image.

Image Size Many conversion packages allow you to save JPEG pictures using varying degrees of compression. The higher the compression, the less space the file will take and the faster it will load into a browser. Unfortunately, compressing a graphic means its quality will also be reduced, so it could end up looking a little fuzzy. Another thing you can do to reduce the size of your graphics is to reduce the number of colors used in them, such as reducing a 256-color image to one using a gray scale.

You can use online services such as GifWizard (**www.gifwizard.com/**) to reduce the size of a GIF. Some graphic conversion utilities also incorporate features that allow you to reduce the size of your images. A discussion on tools and techniques available for image compression can be found at **webreference.com/ dev/graphics/**.

Creating or Linking to Images If you want to create your own Web page pictures, you can use the simple drawing packages supplied with the majority of computers. These packages usually save the images in their own special format, but they can be converted using one of the conversion utilities previously mentioned.

With the newer versions of Netscape and Explorer, simply position your mouse pointer over an image displayed in the browser window and click the right mouse button. (If you're using a Macintosh, hold the mouse button down.) This will bring up a menu that will allow you to save a copy of that image on your local machine. This makes copying other people's images very easy. Be careful, though— even though each image doesn't carry a copyright message, you are still obligated to obtain the artist's permission before you use the work. To find resources that provide copyright-free images, see **www.yahoo.com/Computers_and_Internet/Multimedia/Pictures/**.

Instead of using copies of other people's pictures, you can provide a link to them or include their URL as part of an inline reference on your Web site. This can cause problems if the image is stored on a distant machine because it will take longer to access and load than if it were stored on your server. It also means that you must keep an eye on the link to see that the other site stays the same. (For example, if the image were a news photo, it could be removed after a few weeks.)

Using Photographs You can convert photographs into a computer graphic file in two ways. One way is to scan the photographs into the computer using a scanner. The other is to use a Kodak PhotoCD made up from photographic film. The PhotoCD will contain your photos scanned onto a CD-ROM by your local film processor. The results from a PhotoCD are much better than those obtained by scanning in your photos. However, the PhotoCD will store the images in a special file format, so you will need to use a conversion utility (such as PaintShop) to translate them into JPEG form. (For more information on the PhotoCD and a list of associated utilities, see **www.mindspring.com/~cfall/**.) A number of film processors are now offering a service for selecting photos from a negative and scanning them onto a file, which they will place on a floppy disk. This may be worth considering if you want an alternative to the PhotoCD. There may be differences in the quality of the resulting image, so be careful.

Becoming more and more popular now that their prices are dropping are cameras that store the photos they take on a disk or a chip that is built into the camera. These digital cameras store images that can be transferred directly to a computer (if you have the right connector and software) and converted into a form suitable for your Web pages. Visit **www.cnet.com/Content/Reviews/Compare/Digicam/** for a review of some digital cameras and a checklist of what to look for.

Check Your Graphics When you have produced your graphics, whether pictures or photos, you should do a few quick checks. Load the image directly into your browser and check that it will be appropriate for the student. An image is appropriate if it is not too large or too small for the type of screen resolution the students' monitors have. If an image is too large, it will take up a lot of space, and a student will have to use the scroll bar to view all the image. If it is too small, the student won't be able to make out the contents of the image. Another thing you should check is if the image is of the correct brightness. You can adjust the brightness of an image using an image viewing and conversion utility, but the student has no easy way of adjusting an image on a Web page. Images that are too dark will not be discernible and are a waste of space.

Storing Your Pictures in a Central Location If your pictures are used on many Web pages, such as icons, you do not need to store a copy of them in each directory that a Web page uses. The most efficient way of managing Web page images is to create a directory for them, preferably near the start of your root directory. You can then refer to each icon using a URL such as /Icons/icon-name.gif. This means that icons will become stored (or cached) in your browser, speeding up the time it takes to load, for example, a page with a graphical navigation bar. An example can be seen on this book's CD-ROM in the directory /infodist/tutorial; the directory icons contains a set of icons that are used in almost every page in that section of the CD-ROM, and the directory pics will contain a set of pictures that are used on multiple Web pages.

Image Maps An image map is a picture, certain sections of which are defined as pointing to HTML pages. What this means is that you can mark out the outline of countries on a map, for instance, and associate each outline (each section of the picture) with a page that contains information on that country. When the student clicks on the country, the browser can detect on what part of the picture the student clicked and load the appropriate page. Image maps are often used for navigation bars. They work via a set of coordinates for different areas of the picture. When the student clicks on a part of the picture, the browser records the position of the mouse on the picture and tries to match that position with a corresponding set of coordinates. Each of these sets of coordinates has a URL associated with it, which the browser then loads. This idea is illustrated in Figure 4.2.

There are two ways of implementing an image map, the old way (called the client side) and the more up-to-date way (called the server side).

Client-side image maps involve keeping a list of coordinates in a separate file on the server. A reference to this file is contained within the HTML document that contains the image map. When the student clicks on the image map, information on the coordinates is selected and the name of the file that contains the coordinates and their matching URL are sent to the server. The server then fetches the appropriate URL. This is known as server-side image maps and was the technique originally adopted to implement image maps. (Look at **hoohoo.ncsa.uiuc.edu/docs/tutorials/imagemapping.html** for a guide to server-side image maps.)

Most modern browsers will support the newer image map method known as client-side image maps. This means that the HTML page that contains the picture used as an image map will also contain the list of coordinates and the URLs these coordinates will lead to. No server need be involved, and the image map is portable (in other words, you do not need to have access to a server to use it). (A tutorial on client-side image maps is available at **www.spyglass.com/techspec/tutorial/img_maps.html**.)

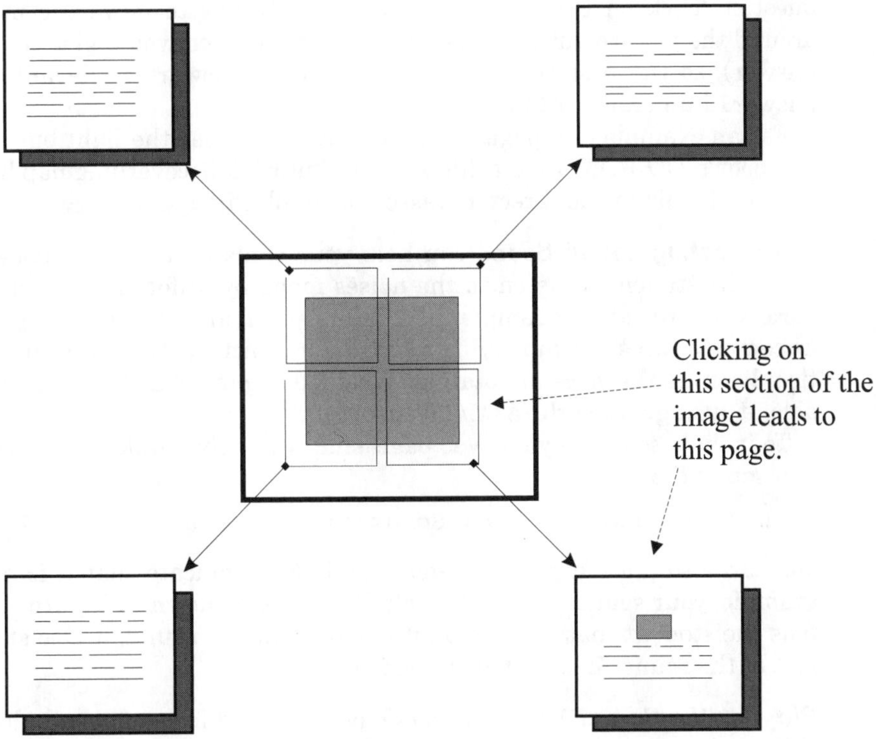
Clicking on
this section of the
image leads to
this page.

FIGURE 4.2 An image map representation.

Web sites on which software for creating client-side and server-side image maps are shown in Table 4.4.

Image maps are ideal for a Web site quiz system, but beware: When the mouse pointer is on a picture, the link associated with that section of the picture is displayed on the bottom bar of your browser. This means for example if I ask the

Table 4.4 Web Sites Containing Software for Creating Client- and Server-Side Image Maps

Package	*Platform*	*Location*
MapEdit	Windows and UNIX	www.boutell.com/mapedit/
WebMap	Macintosh	home.city.net/cnx/software/webmap.html
MapThis	Windows	www.ecaetc.ohio-state.edu/tc/mt
LiveImage	Windows	www.mediatec.com/

question 'click on France' the student merely has to move the mouse button around the picture until they see 'france.html' (which would give the student the answer), so the best thing to do is give your answers irrelevant names, e.g., answer1.html, answer2.html.

For an example of a page using an image map, see the light bulb diagram on the book's CD-ROM in the file /infodist/tutorial/discover/imgmap.htm and the light bulb quiz in the directory /assess/examples/imapq.htm.

Incorporating Sound Sound can help your explanations a great deal. You can allow the student to listen to the noises made by different types of engine, the variety of bird calls, or samples of music. You can also record voice passages such as commentaries accompanying a lecture or a picture. (For an example of narration, listen to the voice annotations included as part of a Netscape tutorial available at **w3.ag.uiuc.edu/AIM/2.0/tutorial/**.)

To include sound in your Web page, simply supply a link such as the following to a sound file:

```
<a href="sound.ext>Bird Song</a>
```

You can also place a picture before the link to indicate that it is a sound—for example, your sound link could look like the one shown in Figure 4.3. This link tells the student that clicking on it will download a sound; it also states the format of the sound file and how large it is.

Playing the Sound Most browsers have a limited form of sound-playing ability built in. Netscape Navigator version 2, for example, comes with a built-in sound player (naplayer) that will play sounds in the AU or AIFF format (provided you have set up the server to tell the browser that the file contains sound; see the "Helper Applications" discussion). If a browser cannot find an application to play the file, it will ask the browser's user to find one for it.

Sometimes the students cannot hear the sound because the sound-playing facility is set up incorrectly on their computers or the sound is indistinct because it was poorly recorded. Remember that when a student clicks on a link to a sound file, the browser downloads and plays it. Once the browser's helper application is finished playing the file, it is usually deleted, so visitors will have to reload it to

FIGURE 4.3 A birdsong sound link.

Table 4.5 Popular Sound File Formats

File Extension	*Usual Platform*
.wav	Windows
.au	Sun
.aiff	Macintosh

listen to it again. (See the "Helper Application" section for advice on how to enable them to download the file, save it, and play it repeatedly.)

Sound File Format and Size Sounds are stored in files that can use a number of formats, the most popular of which are shown in Table 4.5.

There is no clear standard for sound files at the moment. The most popular format tends to be AIFF due to the availability of AIFF players for every platform.

The big problem with sound files is their size, which is usually related to its quality. The clearer the sound produced, the more likely the sound file is of high quality. If you do not adjust the quality of the sound sample when you are recording or storing it, a few seconds of sound will require many hundreds of thousands of kilobytes to store (and many seconds to transmit).

Because files containing voice narration usually take up a lot of space, you should be careful that you make appropriate use of them. You should use them when it is necessary for understanding. For instance, when teaching foreign language pronunciation, a sound file will help the student, who can play the file over and over again. Another example is a sound file of an important explanation of a difficult concept or one that describes the components of a diagram, because having something explained verbally usually makes it easier to understand. You can also use voice narration for added effect, such as playing a famous speech or quotation to help students relate to the material better and provide a richer learning experience.

Two factors affect the size of a sound file: the sampling rate and the resolution. The sampling rate is the number of times per second that the sound being recorded is stored. Not every part of the sound that you are recording can be stored, so the sampling rate dictates the interval at which to record. The rates vary from 8KHz (8,000 times per second) to 48KHz (48,000 times a second). The higher the frequency, the better the quality of the sound, but the bigger the file produced. An 8KHz sampling rate is good enough for most voices, though it may not be good enough to discern subtle differences in pronunciation.

Sound resolution refers to the range of the sound in terms of high and low notes. Resolution is measured in terms of the number of bits used for converting the sound to computer format and whether the sound is in stereo or mono form. For example, you can have 8-bit sound and 16-bit sound. Again, the difference is quality—the higher the resolution, the greater the quality, but the larger the sound file produced.

Most sound files are set at mono, 8 bit, with a 22KHz sampling rate. These settings represent the best compromise between quality and size for most people, but you should experiment with the settings on your sound recording or editing utility to find ones suitable for your particular purpose.

Recording Sound There are a number of ways to get sound into your computer.

One way is to record sound from a CD. If you have a CD-ROM drive, your system should have come supplied with a utility for playing audio CD-ROMs. This CD-playing utility will usually allow you to record some of the audio sound from CD and store it in a sound file. You can then convert this sound into a form that a browser will be able to handle. Ensure that you have permission to use the sound recorded on the CD, which is probably copyrighted. A number of CDs are available with sound effects and samples that allow people to use portions of them, but recording and distributing a copyrighted work can lead to trouble.

To record sound using a microphone, you need a computer capable of recording sound. Most computers equipped with a sound card have a socket for a microphone, so you can connect a microphone to the sound card and use software that will record sound supplied through this microphone connection, thus creating a sound file. Again, this software should have been supplied with your computer or the sound card if you purchased it separately. It is important that you obtain a good-quality microphone for your recording. Microphones supplied with computers are often of poor quality and tend to muffle the sound.

Armed with a good microphone, try to ensure that when recording you follow these guidelines:

- You speak clearly and without an accent that could obscure the meaning. If you haven't got a good speaking voice, persuade someone else to do the narration.
- You don't get too close to the microphone (this causes muffling). Try to keep the microphone to one side of your mouth when speaking.
- You record in a quiet environment so that there is no background noise to distract the listener.
- Keep the narration short and to the point; dramatic pauses or waffling take disk space. However, if you have an editing facility that will enable you to cut out portions of the recording later, you can leave pauses so that it is easier to edit the sound file.

Another approach is to record sound on a cassette tape using the built-in microphone available in most pieces of audio equipment. You can feed the output from your cassette recorder into the computer by connecting the headphone socket from the tape recorder to the microphone socket of your sound card. To do this, you need a two-way jack that you can plug into the headphone socket of your tape

Table 4.6 Web Sites with Sound Utilities

Name	*Platform*	*Location*
CoolEdit	Windows	www.ep.se/cool/
GoldWave	Windows	web.cs.mun.ca/~chris3/goldwave/goldwave.html
Sound Exchange	UNIX, Windows	ftp://oak.oakland.edu/pub/simtelnet/msdos/sound
"SOX" Wavicle	Macintosh	hyperarchive.lcs.mit.edu/HyperArchive/Archive/Graphic_%26_Sound_Tool/snd/sample-editor-103.hqx
SoundHack	Macintosh	hyperarchive.lcs.mit.edu/HyperArchive/Archive/_Graphic_%26_Sound_Tool/snd/sound-hack-0868.hqx

WARNING

> We are not responsible for any damage caused to your equipment if this method goes wrong. Always ensure that the connectors are of a compatible type and that you do not force plugs into the wrong sockets. ■

recorder and into the microphone socket of your sound card. These jacks are available from electronic hobbyist shops. Alternatively, if the speaker system on your computer came with cables, you might be able to use one of these, because most systems use a two-way jack to link the output from the sound card to one of the speakers. Find out if one of the cables has both ends of the same connector type as that used for your headphones, and use it to connect the cassette recorder with the microphone socket of your sound card. You can then use your recording utility to record sound played from your cassette player without having to drag your computer around with you.

Utilities for recording, editing, and converting sounds can be found in Table 4.6.

Incorporating Video Video is extremely useful for detailed demonstrations or experiments and to show real-life situations or examples. Like sound, video clips can be created from existing videotapes or recorded live.

You can include a video clip in a Web page by supplying a link to it, like this:

```
<a href="videoclip.ext">Download a video</a>
```

The students' browsers should be configured to run a helper application that will allow them to play the video as they did a sound clip. Some browsers also have plug-ins that will allow students to display a video clip within the browser

Distillation Experiment (550k, quicktime)

FIGURE 4.4 An icon indicating a video clip will be downloaded (a 550K quicktime file).

window. Again, you can include an icon that indicates the Web page visitor is about to download a video clip, as shown in Figure 4.4.

The problem with including video in your Web page is that video files consume a lot of disk space, so if an animation or a series of photos will do the job, use those instead. For instance, there is no point videotaping a whole lecture, because storing it could easily require hundreds of megabytes; you could just as easily convert the slides displayed during the lecture into pictures and provide a slide show with accompanying narration via a sound file.

Video File Format and Size Like sound, video formats were developed for different computer platforms, as shown in Table 4.7.

For video, as for sound, you should experiment with different compression schemes. You also need to make sure that the format of your video files can be clearly identified—for instance, save Quicktime files with the extension .qt. Make sure your students have the software necessary to play the videos or will have access to instructions telling them where to get such software. One last important point: If you are making video files on a Macintosh, make sure you "flatten" them—in other words, save them in a form that can be viewed on non-Macintoshes.

There is no easy way to decide on a video format. Quicktime is currently the most popular format, with players available for most platforms. You may need to provide your video file in a variety of formats if you are unsure what platform your students will be using. If in doubt, why not investigate converting your video file into an animated GIF that can be displayed by most browsers without a plug-in?

Table 4.7 Video Formats for Various Computer Platforms

Extension	*Format Name*	*Developer*
.mpeg, .mpg	MPEG	Standards body
.qt, .mov	Quicktime	Apple
.avi	Audio/Video Interleave	Microsoft

A Macintosh utility that converts from AVI to Quicktime is available at **hyper-archive.lcs.mit.edu/HyperArchive/Archive/gst/mov/avi-to-qt-kit.hqx**. Intel's SmartVid utility coverts between AVI and Quicktime and works on a Windows platform; find out more about it at **developer.intel.com/pc-supp/multimed/indeo/smartvid.htm**.

Creating a Video File Unlike a sound card, most computer systems will not come complete with facilities that allow you to convert a video signal into a video file. You need to obtain a video-digitizing board to translate the signals from your video equipment into a form the computer can store. With the digitizing board, you should get software that will allow you to record and store video clips. This software may allow you to store your clips in different formats or you may need to obtain other software to do this. You also need a video camera or a VCR to send the picture to your video-digitizing board. It is usually advisable to have a large, fast hard disk to be able to cope with a flood of information from the video digitizing board.

Using a Digital Camera to Create Video Some digital cameras, like the QuickTake digital camera from Apple, not only take digital snapshots, but allow you to take multiple snapshots and put them together to form a quicktime movie. This is by far one of the handiest ways of making a movie; the only drawback is that the camera must be attached to your computer while taking the video pictures. (More details are available at **imaging.apple.com/cameras/cam-main.html**.) Specialized digital video cameras—for example Hitachi's MPEGcam—are also starting to appear on the market; visit **www.mpegcam.net/** for more information.

Streaming Sound and Video The goal behind streaming is to save you having to download an entire video or sound file before you can use it. Because, for example, video is viewed a picture at a time, all you really need is a single picture at any one instant. A streaming system allows a server to send you a sound file, for example, in a form that allows your player to play the information as it receives it. This means that the total amount of information being transferred is the same as if you put the video or sound all in one file; however, because the information is in a format that allows you to play it as you receive it, you can start listening to it as soon as you get the relevant part.

Think of this concept as resembling a TV broadcast. Your TV doesn't have to wait until it loads the entire program; it just displays each sequential picture as it receives it. It's the same way with streaming. Most information sent using streaming is compressed, so it must be uncompressed by your computer before it can be played. This means that your computer must be fast enough to keep up with decompressing each new piece of information it downloads.

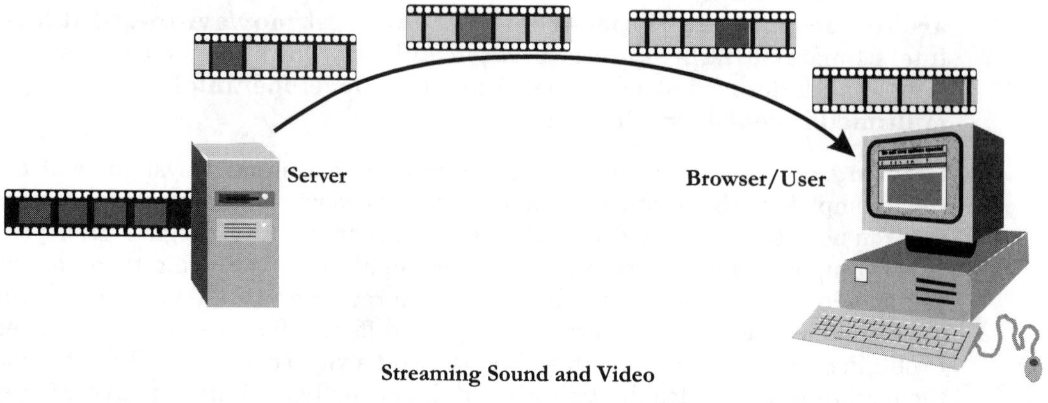

FIGURE 4.5 Streaming over a network.

Currently, there is no standard format for streamed information. The usual standardization method in the case of such a new technology is to wait until competition in the marketplace produces a market leader, which then becomes the standard. You can get a rough idea of what is involved in the streaming process from the diagram in Figure 4.5; it shows the server sending each piece of video file to the browser or helper application, which then displays the portions of the file it has received.

For a sound-streaming system, you will need to buy a special recording utility from the relevant company and use that company's browser plug-in (usually available free) so that your students can listen to the sound. Similarly, you can convert your video files into a form that can be streamed. Some companies that offer facilities for streaming video and sound are listed on the book's CD-ROM.

Animation Animation involves creating or obtaining pictures and putting them together one after another to create the illusion of movement. These pictures are then displayed in sequence in a browser, with one picture replacing another in quick succession. You can draw the pictures using any drawing package, but there are a number of methods for putting them together for display in a Web browser.

One way to create Web animation is using a server-push mechanism. Using this method, at certain intervals the server decides to send the browser a replacement picture for one it is currently displaying. This method works only on Netscape browsers and was rendered obsolete by the GIF89a method of animation, which we'll examine more closely in a moment. The problem was that if the server was slow, the animation "stalled." It also meant that you have to write a program for the server to tell it what images to send and when. Explanations for

Table 4.8 Utilities to Construct Animated GIFs

Package	*Platform*	*Location*
Egor	Windows 95	www.sausage.com/egor.htm
ImageMagick	Windows, Macintosh, UNIX	www.wizards.dupont.com/cristy/ImageMagick.html
Gif Construction Kit	Windows	www.mindworkshop.com/alchemy/gifcon.html

the server-push mechanism and some examples of it can be found at the links listed on the CD-ROM.

The most popular way to animate pictures is client-side animation using the GIF89a graphic file format. The GIF89a format allows you to put pictures inside one GIF file together with control instructions that indicate how long each picture is to be displayed, whether to loop the animation, and so on. The browser will then display the pictures contained in the GIF file, one after another. With this method, you do not need special browser helpers or plug-ins to display the animation in your browser window, because most modern browsers will support this system. You do not need a server to supply new pictures; however, you will need special software to put the images together into one GIF file.

Utilities that can be used to construct animated GIFs are shown in Table 4.8.

You can also use utilities to convert video files to animated GIFs. This has the following advantages:

- With a GIF animation utility, you can vary the amount of time that each frame is displayed. For example, if you made an animated GIF of an experiment, you could lengthen the time that some frames are displayed so that the animated GIF would slow down for an important part of the experiment that students might miss if they were playing an ordinary video.
- The student does not need a plug-in to view the video—just a browser capable of supporting animated GIFs.

A Macintosh utility that will convert Quicktime movies to animated GIFs is GifBuilder (**iawww.epfl.ch/Staff/Yves.Piguet/Clip2gif-home/GifBuilder.html**). Gif Construction Kit can convert AVI movies to animated GIFs. MPEG files can be converted into animated GIFs using MPEG2GIF, available from **www.boxtopsoft.com/MPEG2GIF** (Windows '95 only).

Another alternative is to use a JavaScript utility (Netscape 3.0 or higher) for presenting a video-style interface in which the video is composed of a collection of individual GIF pictures. An example, and its source code, is available at **www.dos-online.de/danger/sss/javascript/demo.htm**.

A number of CD-ROMs that contain images and animations taken from various areas of interest (science, nature, etc.) have been published. For some examples, visit **www.photodisc.com/** Alternatively, you can look at picture libraries available on the Web; many of those also contain animated GIFs.

Virtual Reality Virtual reality is the creation of a reasonable perception of reality using electronic means. You can use virtual reality to construct a 3D display of buildings, environments, or objects in your browser or a helper application.

The most common way of employing virtual reality on the Web is via Virtual Reality Modeling Language, or VRML. VRML allows you to write a description of a "world," the objects it contains, what they look like, and so on. Your students can download this description into a browser that will display the world you've created. Students can navigate through this world using various movement options, such as forward, back, up, and down. With VRML, you could create a complete "virtual university" with a virtual campus, virtual lecture rooms, and virtual meeting places, although this is a bit ambitious for today's system capabilities.

VRML is more commonly used for creating explorable objects, like ships, towns, buildings, or items of machinery. Navigating around 3D worlds can put quite a strain on most computers, and you should be aware that most of the worlds which contain a reasonable level of detail are very large.

A listing of links examining VRML's educational uses can be found on this book's CD-ROM. A number of applications shown in Table 4.9 will help you build a VRML world.

VIEWING TOOLS

In this section, we look at the viewing tools necessary to set up your Web site. These tools include browsers and helper applications that will assist you and your students in getting the most satisfaction from your Web-based classroom.

Browsers

What sort of browser will the student use to view your pages? The two most popular browsers are those written by Netscape (Navigator) and Microsoft (Explorer). The Netscape Navigator browser is currently the most popular and is available for a wider variety of platforms than is the Explorer. You can download

Table 4.9 Applications for Building a VRML World

Package	*Platform*	*Location*
Virtual Home Space Builder	Windows, Macintosh	www.paragraph.com/
Pioneer	Windows	www.caligari.com/

Table 4.10 Older Versions of Netscape Navigator

Browser Version	*Windows*	*Macintosh*
Netscape Navigator Version 1.0	ns16-100.zip	netscape.sea.hqx
Netscape Navigator Version 1.2	n16e122.exe	netscape-1.12.hqx
Netscape Navigator Version 2.0	n16e201.exe	2.01NetscapeInstaller.hqx

Navigator from **www.netscape.com/**; download Explorer from **www.microsoft.com/**.

One thing to note is that companies will generally make only the latest versions of their browsers available. The latest versions always have more features than the previous versions and therefore require more computing power and more space. The older versions of the browsers are available on many mirror sites on the Internet. You might need to use an older version of a browser because of the limitations of your students' equipment. See Table 4.10 for the names of some of the older versions of the Netscape browser. Find out from where you can download these files by searching the archie file location system for the filename (**web.nexor.co.uk/archie.html**).

The earlier the version of the browser, the fewer demands it will make on students' computers. However, the earlier the browser version, the fewer features it will have. You should choose a version equivalent to version 2 of Netscape so that you can use JavaScript. Other browsers besides Netscape will also run JavaScript.

One last, important point. Many companies release beta versions of browsers. These are versions of the browser that the company wants people to test for problems. Beta versions are not suitable for use in an education system, because they have not been perfected. Furthermore, some browsers come with a preset expiration date that causes the browser to stop working after a specified date. Check any browser you intend using to see if it is of sufficient maturity and if it will expire in the middle of your course.

Check also that your students have access to a networked computer that can display graphics. If they don't, you can use the Lynx Web browser, which is a text-only browser (**www.cc.ukans.edu/about_lynx/**).

Offline Browsers Offline browsers are designed to be used without a network connection. This means that they can be very small in terms of size, but are usually a little short on features. Offline browsers can display HTML files in the same manner as Netscape or Explorer, but they are very useful if the student does not have access to a network. Netscape and Explorer can usually be used offline, too, but some reconfiguration of their settings may be required (look in the instructions supplied with the browser for details). I view, a Windows-only browser (**www.talentcom.com/i view/i view.htm**), is one such browser.

Helper Applications

When a browser asks the server for a page of HTML, the browser can display the page on the screen. When a browser asks the server for a file that contains information other than HTML, it may not be able to display the contents of the file itself and will need to call another program on the computer. This other program is called a helper application or plug-in; it helps the browser display the file. For example, you may need a helper application to display a video, to play a sound, or to display a word-processed file. The difference between a helper application and a plug-in is that the helper application is usually independent of the browser—in other words, it will run without the browser. The plug-in, however, is specific for each type of browser. The plug-in will also display the information it receives inside the browser window, whereas a helper application will start up another program to view the information.

The procedure that is followed when the browser loads a non-HTML file is as follows:

1. The user clicks on a link that contains the name of the file.
2. The browser asks the server named in the link (or if no server is named, it asks the server that supplied the page containing the link) to send it that file.
3. The server looks for the file and looks at the file extension to see what sort of data the file contains. For example, if the files extension is .htm or .html, the server knows the file contains HTML; if the extension is .wav, the server knows the file contains sound. The server keeps a list of file extensions and corresponding list describing file contents. This corresponding list contains what is known as the MIME type of the file. A MIME type is a standard way of denoting the type of information a file holds. A MIME type consists of two parts: a general category, such as image, sound, or video, which denotes what sort of information the file contains, and a specific type, such as mpeg, quicktime, or x-msvideo, which indicates the specific file format. This is known as the file's subtype.
4. The server sends the file to the browser along with the MIME type of the file. If the server cannot find the file's extension in its list, it tells the browser it doesn't know what the file is. The browser then tells the user it has got the file, but doesn't know what to do with it.
5. The browser stores the file in memory or on the user's disk. It then looks up its own list of MIME types to see what program it should run to handle the file it has received. If it can handle the file itself, it does; otherwise, it starts the helper application and gives it the file.
6. The helper application starts and displays the file in its own window. When the user exits the helper application, the temporary file the browser created to store the information is deleted.

To configure a computer to run a helper application when it receives a particular file type, you must change two things. You must change the settings on the server so that it recognizes the extension for the file; that way, the server can tell the browser that it is delivering a file of a specific type. You may also need to change the browser settings so that it knows what application to start when it receives a file.

To change the server, you need to find the configuration file for the server. This file is usually called srm.conf and is discussed in more detail in Chapter 10.

In the srm.conf file, you will find headings such as: application/x-abc and xyz. These indicate that the server will tell any browser that requests a file with the extension .xyz that it has a MIME type application/x-abc. You now add your new type to the list by including the file's type, the extension it normally has, and its format. For example, to add the ability to start the Microsoft Word processor when your browser receives a Word document, follow these steps:

1. Decide on the MIME type of the Word documents. A list of standard MIME types is available at **ftp://ftp.isi.edu/in-notes/iana/assignments/media-types/media-types**. Word files have the type application/msword. If the list does not contain a MIME standard for your file format, place an *x* before the format—for example, x-myformat (the *x* denotes it is a provisional standard so you are free to customize).
2. Add this item to the server configuration file with the extension for most Word files: .doc.

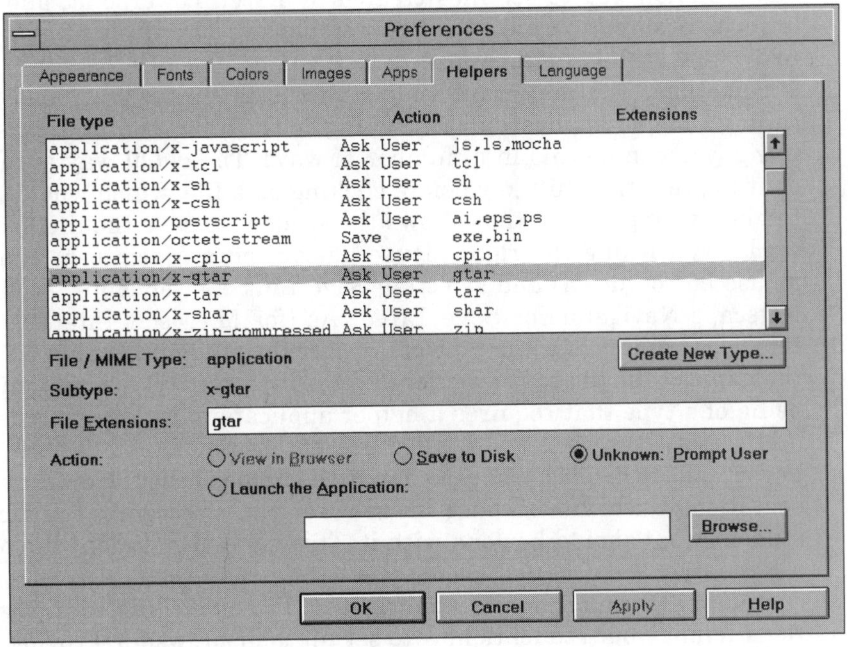

FIGURE 4.6 A MIME configuration window.

3. Restart the server (this is not always necessary, but it's best to be on the safe side). Any browser that asks for a file with the extension .doc will be told it is getting a file of type application/msword.

You also need to tell the browser what to do with files of a certain type. To do this, look under your browser's Options or Preferences menu for a heading called "helper applications" or "MIME types." This listing will look something like Figure 4.6.

You then have to tell the browser what to do with files of a particular type. So for your Word files, you need to add the following:

- Mime type: application
- Subtype: msword
- Extensions: doc

Using the Browse button, you then select the application that is associated with each file of this type and that is started by the browser in order to deal with it—in this case, Word—and click the button that tells the browser to launch the application when it receives a file of this type.

Many software companies provide free viewers for their document format. These viewers allow students to get a program that will view a file created by a specific application, but do not allow them to change their contents. For instance, Adobe Acrobat allows you to see PDF files (**www.adobe.com**), and Microsoft viewers allow you to see files created by Excel, Powerpoint, and Word (**www.microsoft.com/download/**). A comprehensive list of plug-ins is available at: **browserwatch.iworld.com/plug-in.html**.

Sometimes you may want your students to simply download files without calling a helper application. Depending on the browser and the platform you're using, you can do this in a number of ways. The usual way is to tell the student to press the Shift key before clicking on a file, which would normally call the helper application that allows the student to save the file. If this does not work, try clicking the right mouse button (on a Macintosh, simply hold the mouse button down) and selecting Save Link As (for more recent versions of Netscape Navigator) or Save Target As (for Microsoft Internet Explorer). If this does not work for the type of browser the student is using, you can change the name of the file so the server and the browser will not recognize the file as being of a type that requires a helper application. In other words, if you have a Microsoft Powerpoint file called presentation.ppt that the browser will call Powerpoint to display, you can change the name of the file on the server to presentation.pt, which will cause the browser not to recognize the file and ask the student what should be done with it. This gives the student the option of saving the file.

One final note on helper applications: Provide a link to a page of instructions telling your students how to set up their browsers. Provide them with a page of links to helper applications they can obtain if their machine does not contain them.

CONTENT DISTRIBUTION

How do you distribute the information you have prepared? The most common way is by using an HTTP server to distribute the documents or archival files that contain the documents. Alternatively, you can distribute the material on disk or CD-ROM. Setting up an HTTP server is covered in Chapter 10. In this section, we look at some of the problems and issues associated with various ways of distributing material to students.

If you plan to use a server, you may need to set it up yourself (see Chapter 10). Hopefully you can find an existing server that you can use. The server must have sufficient disk space to store your course and have access to a network with a large enough capacity to handle the files related to your course or courses. You must ensure that you have sufficient access to the server to perform updates to the material whenever you want. Certain servers are maintained by system managers who must vet the material in case it contains sensitive information before it is placed online.

Another possibility is to distribute the material in archive form or on floppy disk or CD-ROM. This means students without access to a network can view all the material designed for a browser . This technique, known as offline use, means that the students can keep accesses to a server to a minimum.

Some organizations have not yet set up a machine to act as an HTTP server and because FTP servers are more common and more easily set up, you might want to consider using one. However, FTP servers were not really designed for handling Web activity. You can still use your links, but they all have to be absolute links and start with the URL ftp://.

You also need to have anonymous FTP enabled on the FTP server so that any user can connect to get the files you are distributing (HTML, video, etc.). All UNIX systems come with FTP built in. However, you may need to configure the FTP account or create accounts for your users. Macintosh users can access NetPresenz at **www.share.com/peterlewis/netpresenz**; Windows users can access QVTNet at **www.frontiernet.net/~qpcsoft**.

Getting the Information to Your Server

When you have written your tutorials and pages on your computer, you may need to move them to the server. The easiest way to move whole structures of files is by archiving the structure using an archiving program (see the "Archives" discussion later in this chapter). Ensure that the server has a copy of the archiving program so that it can remove the files from the archive and reconstruct the directory structure.

If you are using a browser that supports uploading (such as Netscape 2.0 or higher), you can use an upload utility (**www.selah.net/udload/udload.cgi** contains such a utility). An upload utility allows you to call a page on the server that will handle the transportation and storage of files. Netscape Navigator Gold allows you to upload using FTP or HTTP. If your server allows FTP and you have an FTP utility for your computer, you can use FTP to transport your files.

Here are some things to remember when uploading files:

- Give files proper names, with no spaces within the filename or strange punctuation.
- Give them proper extensions such as .html or .htm.
- Include all components of an HTML file (the GIFs and the other files to which each HTML file links).
- Maintain the directory structure—for instance, if a link points to a file maindir/file.html, make sure that when the file is loaded onto the server, there is a directory called maindir and it contains the file file.html.
- Watch that the names stay the same. Some platforms will change the names of files they receive. For example, if you uploaded a file called First.html, the server might change it to FIRST.HTML; because all links are case sensitive, this may cause an error.

A utility called Samba allows a UNIX computer to act like a Windows file server, thereby enabling you to copy files from a Windows machine directly to the server (**samba.canberra.edu.au/pub/samba/docs/faq/sambafaq.html**).

If you are using the FrontPage Web creation package from Microsoft, you can obtain a utility program for your server (called a server extension) that will allow your FrontPage program to automatically upload your Web pages to the server (**www.microsoft.com/frontpage/**).

If your server computer and the computer you are using to write the files are of a similar type—for example, both Windows or both Macintosh—you can set up file sharing so that files can be easily copied from one directory to another.

There is one last way to get your files onto the server. UNIX systems support a facility for sharing disks called mounting. This means that a computer can connect to another computer's disk and use it as though the disk belonged to the computer itself. If the computer you are using to write the material and your Web server allow mounting, you can simply mount the root directory and copy the files into it. Mounting is built into most UNIX machines. A mount utility called PC-NFS is available for DOS and Windows (**www.tsoft.net/software/nfs-client.html**); another utility called Omni-NFS (**www.xlink.com/**) works for Windows '95 and NT. Both of these programs enable you to mount a disk on a UNIX machine from a DOS system.

Using Web Files Offline

All your tutorials do not have to be stored on a server and accessed via a network. You can distribute the HTML files on disk. This way, known as offline use, students can access the material while not connected to a network. This will not make any difference to how the material is displayed in the majority of cases, because a browser does not make a distinction between the files on a disk or on a server.

You can distribute the information in a number of formats, the most common being CD-ROM, floppy disk, or archive format. If you are preparing a course and are intending to distribute it in a form that can be viewed offline, you must consider a number of things: how links are represented, which format of distribution to use, and how you can tie offline information with online information.

Links and Offline Viewing First and foremost is the question of links. If you do not intend using a server, all your links should be implicit ones. This means that you do not mention the server's name or any absolute paths when writing your HTML code. This enables you to use your HTML files with their associated links in any subdirectory and on any medium. For example, if you placed the following link in a file:

```
<a href="X">Menu</a>
```

the URL X should be of the form path/filename, not of the form http://machine/path/filename. You should also assume that there is no root directory—for example, a reference to /Icons on a local file system could search on that disk for the directory located at the root called Icons or it could search in the directory of the document you are currently viewing. Therefore, you must keep more rigid control of all your link references if you intend distributing material on disk or in archive form.

Remember too that if students are viewing the information stored on a computer that is not connected to a network, they may encounter links that were set up to point to outside resources they may not be able to access from their computer.

CD-ROMs and Floppy Disks Two common forms of disk are used for offline viewing: a CD-ROM and a floppy disk. Each has different formats. For instance a floppy disk could be initialized to be suitable for a Macintosh or a PC. Note that most Macintoshes can read disks that have been initialized for a PC, but very few PCs can read disks initialized for the Macintosh. CD-ROMs can be created in a format that allows any machine to read them.

If the material in your information distribution system is large, such as video clips or sound files, it can represent an enormous saving to students in terms of time spent downloading the files from the Internet if the information is stored on their computers. Ideally, you should combine material on students' local computers with the course components on the server; this is known as a hybrid system, which we discuss later in this chapter.

If your students are quite a distance away, they may have to wait a considerable time for their disks, which may even arrive damaged, to arrive by mail. Downloading all the information in archive form means students don't have to wait for postal delivery, but they may expend considerable expense downloading a large archive.

If your students have been sent information on disk, it is impossible to change that information, whereas information that is incorrect and incomplete and stored on a server can be changed in an instant. Students who have received incomplete information on their disks most be notified and instructed how to obtain new copies of the information.

Distributing your material on floppy disk means you may have to provide different sets of disks for different computers. CD-ROMs have become very popular because the disks can be produced in a standard format that many different types of computer can use. CD-ROMs are also less prone to damage during transit. Another big advantage of CD-ROMs is that they can store about 650MB of information per disk, whereas the average floppy can store only 1.44MB.

On the plus side, floppy disks are extremely cheap, whereas as CD-ROMs can cost up to $30 each and require a special and costly device to create them.

Note that not all computers have built-in CD-ROM drives, so if you plan to distribute your material on CD-ROM, check that all students have access to a CD-ROM drive. Only in the last few years have CD-ROMs come as standard on computers, and computers sold in bulk lots still tend not to have them.

You could adopt an approach in which you distribute information in a number of ways—floppy disk, CD-ROM, and archive—but this could be costly and difficult to manage.

Archives Another distribution method to enable local access is to place all your files in one large archive file and make this available for downloading. This means, for example, that students can get a copy of their course as soon as they sign up, the files can be downloaded in the correct format for their computers, and they can try to download again if they receive a faulty copy. Sections of the course can also be changed, and students can replace their copies of the section on their own computers.

However, this approach has a number of disadvantages. One is that students need a storage area on disk big enough to hold the archive file and the uncompressed files the archive contains. This is usually only a problem if the archive is of considerable size. With a CD-ROM, students need no extra space on their disk drives. Another problem with archiving is that the download time could be long—for example, if you make a 650MB CD-ROM of information available as an archive, and the download rate via modem is 28K per second, it would take about seven hours to download the file. (However, you could reduce the amount of space needed for the archive file using compression.)

A Hybrid System The best of both worlds would be if you could combine pages on your server with information students have on CD-ROM or their local disk drives. In other words, the page on the server would instruct the browser to load sound, video, and picture files located on the local disk. This hybrid system enables you to distribute core material and use it in pages on the server, which you are free to change at any time.

The problem with a hybrid system is phrasing the links on the pages contained on the server so that they point to the local disk. The server does not know that students' CD-ROMs are located, for example, on drive f or that the files are located in the subdirectory /courses on students' machines. This information is needed to include the material in the page on the server. What you need is a method of handling references to the local storage on the computer. We'll do this using the JavaScript language.

To set up a hybrid system, you need to do two things. First, you need to tell the browser to make a note of the disk drive and directory where the local information is stored. The browser can use this information to handle requests from the server to display the local information. You tell the browser where the local information is by loading an HTML page that will register its location on students' disks. This page should be contained on the CD-ROM you send students and should be loaded by them into their browsers before they start to use the server.

The page will contain a link to a page on the server. This page will contain a JavaScript program that places the location of the page into the browser's memory. This information will be saved when the student exits the browser and loaded again when the student restarts the browser. So, for example, if a student loads the page start.html from the directory f:\course\, this page would call a JavaScript program on the server, which would store the information that the local directory was d:\course. The JavaScript program puts the information into what is known as a cookie.

The second step is to access the files by using the information the browser "remembers" about where the files are kept. Now that the browser contains the location of the files on CD-ROM in its memory, you need to find a way for the pages on the server to find where the files are located on students' computers. You put some JavaScript code on each of the pages that will use the files on students' computers. This JavaScript code will ask the browser where the files are located and alter the links on the page it receives from the server to point to the files on the local disk.

Let's look at an example. Your page on the server points to a file called videos/video.mov, so the JavaScript program contained in this page will ask the browser where it keeps the files on its local disk. They are contained in f:\courses. The JavaScript program then adds this information to the link so that the link now points to f:\courses\videos\video.mov. Any time a student clicks on this link, the file will be loaded from the CD-ROM. Another student could have copied all his files to the directory c:\mycourse. He will have started the page that will have created a cookie containing c:\mycourse. If he receives a page from the server that contains the link videos/video.mov, it will be translated into c:\mycourse\videos\video.mov.

To sum up, the advantages of a hybrid system are threefold: It enables you to distribute information on CD-ROM to reduce the amount of time the student spends downloading. It also keeps all the advantages of using a server and locally stored resources. Furthermore, it works for all platforms—UNIX, Macintosh, and Windows. The disadvantage of a hybrid system is straightforward: You need to use a JavaScript program for every page in which you want to make a reference to the local information on a CD-ROM or hard disk.

The following two files will perform the tasks necessary to initialize the hybrid system. You should put the following HTML code into the page that the student will load to initialize the system:

```
<html>
<head>
<meta http-equiv="refresh" content="0;url=
http://server.name/path/setlocn.htm">
</head>
If your browser does not transfer to another page please
click on this link:
<a href="http://server.name/path/setlocn.htm">Set local disk
location</a>
</html>
```

Change the address **http://server.name/path/** to point to the location where you have stored the JavaScript HTML file called setlocn.htm (shown here). This file is stored on the CD-ROM as /content/hybrid/start.htm.

Here are the contents of the page setlocn.htm. When this piece of JavaScript is loaded into the browser, it sets a variable in the browser that indicates that the directory in which the code was run is the root directory of the course material stored on the computer. This file is contained on the CD-ROM in the /content/hybrid/setlocn.htm.

```
<html>
<head>
<title>Setting location of local files</title>
<script LANGUAGE="JavaScript">
var loc=document.referrer;
var slashposition=loc.lastIndexOf( '/' );
if(slashposition==-1)
 slashposition=loc.lastIndexOf( '\\' );
var path=loc.substring(0,slashposition);
```

```
var expires=new Date();
expires.setTime (expires.getTime() + 1000*24*60*60*365);
document.cookie="flocation="+path+";expires="+expires.toGMTSt
ring();
</script>
</head>
<body>
This page has set the location of your files for use by the
server.
</body>
</html>
```

The next piece of JavaScript code needs to be placed inside each page on the server that attempts to access the local disk or CD-ROM. It will read the cookie value to obtain the location of the root directory and attach the URL referenced to it. To do this, you need to phrase your links differently.

If you want to provide a reference to a local HTML file, your code should look like this:

```
<script LANGUAGE="JavaScript">
Href("Link","Description");
</script>
```

where Link is the path to the file and Description is the description that will accompany the link. This is equivalent to

```
<a href="link">Description</a>
```

If you want to provide a reference to a local image, your code should look like this:

```
<script LANGUAGE="JavaScript">
ImgSrc("Link");
</script>
```

where Link is the path of the image you want to include. This is equivalent to

```
<img src="Link">
```

The paths of the images and HTML files can be worked out from the local copy of the course material file; if the copy of the course file had an image in the directory /Icons, you could tell the students' browsers to look in the directory Icons stored on the local disk with the code

```
ImgSrc("/Icons/image.gif");
```

The full code can be found on the CD-ROM as /content/hybrid/hybrid.htm): It needs to be placed inside each page that refers to a CD-ROM or local disk.

Table 4.11 Archiving Utility Resources

Archive Type	*Platforms*	*Software Location*
ZIP	UNIX	www.c3.lanl.gov:8075/zipinstallunix.html
	Macintosh	www.awa.com/softlock/zipit/zipit.html
	Windows	www.winzip.com/
	Windows/DOS	www.pkware.com/
TAR	UNIX	Built into UNIX systems
	Windows	www.winzip.com/
	Macintosh	hyperarchive.lcs.mit.edu/HyperArchive/Abstracts/cmp/HyperArchive.html
STUFFIT	Macintosh, Windows	www.aladdinsys.com/consumer/expander1.html

If you are worried that students may have problems using this system, you can provide backup links to the material stored on the server.

Archiving Utilities An archiving program allows you to place a large number of files into one file, which makes them easier to transport. It also allows you to maintain the directory structure you have built for these files. One of the most popular archiving programs is PKZIP, which is available for most platforms. The archiving program TAR, also very popular, is the main archiver used on UNIX systems. For the Macintosh, the STUFFIT archive format is usually the most popular. See Table 4.11 for resources.

A number of utilities can create executable archive files that will unpack themselves once run, making it easier for your users because they do not have to run an unarchiving utility. However, this means that they must all have a platform similar to the one on which you created the self-extracting file. Examples of programs that can create self-extracting ZIP files are zip2exe (**www.pkware.com/**) and the Windows-based ZIP utilities referred to above (**www.winzip.com**).

Web Page Length

A common question asked by new Web page designers is, "Should I try to fit all the text in one page or break it up into different pages?" Each approach has its advantages and disadvantages. The approach you follow depends to a large extent on the content of your page. For instance, if the page forms a large block naturally—for instance, a scene from a play—there may be no way you could break the page up that would not interfere with the presentation of the material. If the piece of text naturally contains sections or forms its own hierarchy—for example, a description of the parts of a computer—maybe it is more appropriate to break up the material into separate pages. If the page consists of a list of terms and creating a new page for each term would result in pages that contain only a few lines, this new arrangement could confuse readers, so the information would be best left all in one page.

When is a page too long? Again, it depends on content. Three to four pages are considered long enough for a student to read without interruption. Remember that when students view a page that cannot all fit into their browser window at the same time, they must use a scroll bar (or the arrow keys) to move up and down the page. Using this method, it is easy to lose your place in the text. Another problem with scrolling is that students might never get to the end of the material; they might assume they are on the last section of the page when another part lurks unread. (Using a navigation bar to mark the end of each page helps solve that problem, though.) Certain approaches favor the creation of a "mind map" of the material, showing how each element relates to another. Breaking up a page into a series of structures that have links between related pieces of information facilitates this learning approach very well. It is unusual to break up items that are generally printed out anyway, such as reports or academic papers.

In summary, we give the advantages and disadvantages of each approach and leave you to make up your own mind. The advantages to keeping all the material on one page are as follows:

It's easy to prepare and update. You can write a long page without having to create any links to subsections. You can easily alter any information in the section by editing the whole page.

It's easy for the student to print. Students have all the material in one block, so they need to print only that page.

It's more difficult to get "lost." Having subsections and sub-subsections of a page can cause the reader to get disoriented if the structure is not clear or if proper navigation facilities have not been provided.

It's easy to search using the built-in find feature available in most browsers. Most browsers have a search facility that allows you to search for keywords in the current page (i.e., "Find" in Netscape). With one large page, you can search for all the relevant terms. With a series of subpages, you must either load each subpage individually and then search it or use a search facility program on the server which will search the pages for you (see Chapter 10).

Disadvantages of including all content on one page include the following:

It's difficult to keep your place. You must scroll down the document using the scroll bar.

There's no logical decomposition. If you break a page up, you can structure it so that each component is in its correct section. This helps the student understand the place of a section in a structure.

It can take longer for the student to load the page into the browser. Longer pages contain more information and can thus take longer to access and load. This can be annoying if the student wants just one part of the page.

Advantages of maintaining multiple pages are:

The topic can be divided into relevant sections. This gives a student an idea of how each relates to the others.

It makes it difficult for the student to print a document. This can be an advantage if you don't want the student wasting resources.

It's easier to get an overview of the structure of the material.

Smaller pages mean faster loading times.

Disadvantages of multiple pages include these:

Students can get lost if the structure is confusing.

It is difficult to print the whole document if it is broken up into many pages.

There are compromise ways to get the best of both long and short pages. One method of making a long page easier to handle is to break it up into segments using location tags to create an overview at the start of the document and have the overview elements link to later sections on the page.

For example, a long page could consist of a menu at the start:

Topic 1
- Subsection 1.1
- Subsection 1.2

Topic 2
- Subsection 2.1

Each of these menus would contain a link that, when clicked on, would lead the student to the relevant section later in the page. For example:

```
<a href="#Topic2">Topic 2</a>
```

At each subsequent section on the page, the tag that is associated with that part of the page is attached to the relevant section. These tags are called anchors. For the long page in the previous example, go to the section of the page that deals with Topic 2 and add the HTML code:

```
<a name="Topic2">Topic 2 </a>
```

This scheme makes it easier to manage long pages. It's not ideal for all situations, but it is an acceptable compromise if you want to create a navigable long page. (A utility, written in Perl, that will automatically create a table of contents all items in header tags (<h1>,<h2>, etc.) in a document or series of documents can be found at **www.oac.uci.edu/indiv/ehood/htmltoc.doc.html**.)

If you are running a Web server that supports a system known as Server Side Includes, you can break your page into a number of pages and "stick" them together to form a large single page. For example, if your group of pages consisted of the following:

```
section1.html, section1-1.html, section1-2.html,
section2.html, section2-1.html
```

each HTML page you want to include a single one of these pages would contain a directive of the form:

```
<!--#include file="section.html"-->
```

If you wanted to give Server Side Includes to include all the files in your HTML document, the code would look like this:

```
<!--#include file="section1.html"-->
<!--#include file="section1-1.html"-->
<!--#include file="section1-2.html"-->
<!--#include file="section2.html"-->
<!--#include file="section2-1.html"-->
```

The server will take the contents of each file in quotes and send it into the browser. The browser will receive the contents of the files section1.html, section1-1.html, and so on and load them all into the one page for display. (Server Side Includes is described in more detail in Chapter 10.)

Printing the Material

We have three considerations related to printing material. The first is helping the students print; the second is printing a record of the course for students; and the third is stopping the students from printing.

Helping the Students Print When we talked about page length, we found that it is much easier to print a long page than a series of hyperlinked pages. You saw that it was possible to have both systems if you could use Server Side Includes; however, this is not always possible, so you should perhaps provide two versions of any material that you think the students may need to print. One version would be hyperlinked to reflect the topic's nature, the other version would be a collection of the hyperlinked pages all rolled into one.

If you intend for students to print the material, you should try to ensure that the page's background colors are amenable to printing—for instance, black on white. You should also try and keep the pictures to a minimum because printing pictures slows up many printers. One option is to provide a summary page and encourage students to print that page instead of trying to print the whole document.

Printing a Course Record Something instructors often forget when presenting a course electronically is that in a "normal" course, students finish the year with a set of paper notes and a set of marked assignments. Many students use these notes again to review the course at a later stage. With an electronic system, the notes are all stored online, so it may be difficult for students to make a copy of them and to refer back to them in subsequent years. You should therefore consider printing the notes and tutorials you have written and giving these to the student. It is no harm to also print the assignments and the suggested solutions to these assignments.

One policy you can adopt is to inform the students that you will distribute printed copies of course material at the end of the course, preceding the exams. This means you can incorporate any updates you've made to material during the course and discourage students from trying to print their own individual copies of the material.

Remember that printing material that has been designed for a hypertext structure can lead to notes that are difficult to follow. To overcome this, you can provide a map of the structure and the position of the relevant pages to give the students a point of reference.

What Can Stop Students from Printing? It is not unknown for students to access online material and attempt to print it as opposed to reading it on-screen. Printing material intended for electronic viewing wastes valuable time and resource, particularly because most printers were not designed to perform large-scale printing tasks. Therefore, educators typically look for a way to stop students from printing the tutorials. However, the simple rule is, if students can read it, they can print it. You can do a number of things to make it more difficult for students to print material.

You can divide the tutorial into a large number of small pages (making sure the division is justified and not contrived). This means that the students are more likely to read the material online because it is faster to read it than to print it.

Another thing you can do is to change the background color to a dark color and the text to a light color (white or yellow) by putting

```
<BODY bgcolor="#10299C" text="#ffffff" >
```

at the start of your documents, which gives you white text on a blue background. This text is still readable, but most printers will print a blank page. The problem with this is that students can easily change the default text color for their browser, which will display the page in a form that can be easily printed. Finally, you can encourage students not to print the material by telling them that the information on the system is constantly changing and any document they print may be out of date tomorrow. You could also promise to distribute copies of the material at the end of each course, as suggested previously.

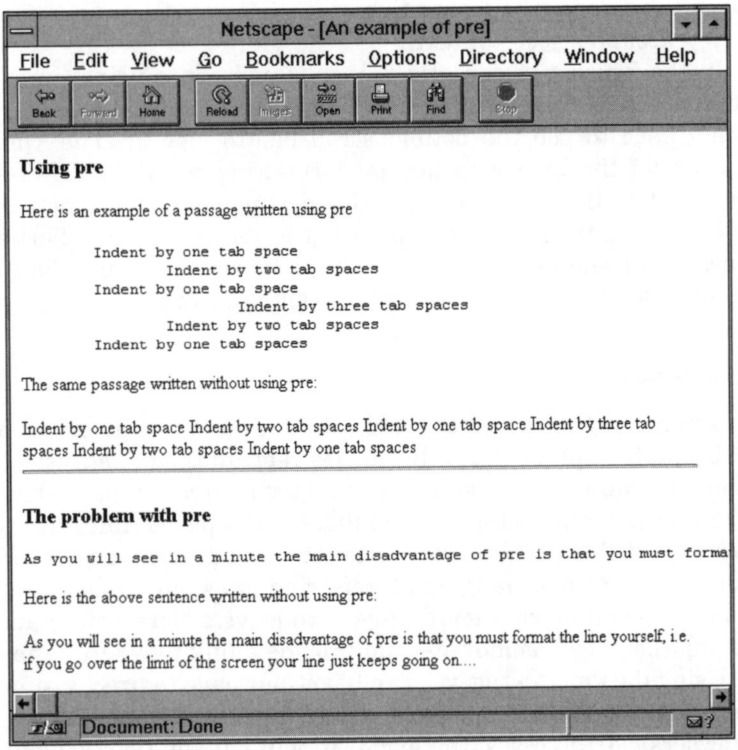

FIGURE 4.7 An example of <pre>.

You should also consider the possibility that there is another reason behind a desire to print material other than to have a personal copy of it. Students may have difficulty reading the text on the screens or obtaining sufficient access time on the computer facilities to peruse the material at their leisure. Many students also want to have a printout as a "security blanket" in case anything happens to the system. In this case, they need to be assured that they are guaranteed access and that a backup is made of the information regularly.

Preventing the Browser from Formatting Your Text

HTML tends to take certain liberties with any text you give it. For example, if you indent your text by a few spaces or include a tab character, this will not normally appear when you convert your material into HTML. There are numerous tricks to overcome this anomaly (visit **www.killersites.com/1-design/single_pixel.html**); one of the easiest is to place the <pre> tag around text you want to preserve the formatting of. In Figure 4.7, you see the result of placing <pre> around a piece of text.

In the figure, you can also see the drawback to using <pre>—namely, if your sentence is too long for the browser, it will not be displayed on the viewable page; you'll have to use the bottom scroll bar to view it. The <pre> tag effectively turned off the browser's normal formatting on a HTML document, including putting text that strays outside the viewing window on the next line.

In spite of this snag, the <pre> tag is very useful for short sentences such as lines of a poem or where formatting is more important than keeping the lines within the browser window, such as computer code.

Relocating Pages

You may need to move your pages to a different directory or a different server. This can be a problem if other pages refer to them, because students will get a "file not found" error message if they try to access a page that has been moved. You should really change all the links in the pages that refer to the pages being moved, but this could be very time consuming. The way to conduct a move without spending time changing all referring links but enabling the students to find their way to a newly moved page is to leave a "forwarding address—a message saying the page has moved—and provide a link to where it has been moved.

Using the <meta> tag, you can have your page redirect visitors to the new page automatically. When a browser that supports the <meta> tag (the majority of browsers do) accesses the page, it will automatically go to the forwarding address. You should still provide a proper link like the one here in case the student hasn't got a browser that recognizes the <meta> tag.

```
<html>
<head>
<meta http-equiv="refresh" content="0;url=
http://server.name/path/newlocation.html ">
</head>
This page has moved to this location: <a href="http://serv-
er.name/path/newlocation.html">newlocation.html</a>
If your browser hasn't automatically loaded the new page then
click on the new location.
</html>
```

If you want to move your pages but don't want users getting "file not found" errors, you can also use a utility like HTML-Move (**www.Stars.com/Software/Perl/html_move.html**), which goes through a series of specified HTML pages and alters links that have been moved. Some Web creation packages such as Adobes Sitemill (**www.adobe.com**) automatically change links to a page if that page is moved.

Dealing with Links

Because many of your structures will depend on links to move from page to page, you need to know how to phrase links and avoid problems with them.

Links You create a link to a file or another page of html by typing the command

```
<a href="protocol://machine/location/file.ext"> Get this file
</a>
```

where:

protocol is the protocol the server is using to pass you the file, usually HTTP. (*Caution*: Make sure you do not put the protocol in capital letters, which could cause the browser not to recognize the protocol and so return a "Forbidden by rule" error.)

machine is the name of the computer the file is stored on (the server).

location is the path of the file from the server's Web root (the file is in the directory path "location").

file is the name of the file.

ext is the extension of the file. It is important that you give files their correct extensions; otherwise the browser may not know what to do with them. For example if you called an HTML file myfile.ork instead of myfile.html, its contents (all the information together with the HTML tags used to format it) would be displayed as opposed to interpreted. Suitable extensions for HTML files are .htm and .html; extensions for other file types (graphic, sound, etc.) were given earlier in the chapter.

Absolute and Relative Links You can create two forms of link: an absolute link and a relative link. An absolute link is one that gives the complete URL for the object that will be loaded when the link is clicked on. For example,

```
<a href="http://server.name/path/name.html">
```

will access the server called server.name and ask it for the document.

A relative link is one for which you do not give the server name, but the browser will assume that the document you want is stored in the same place as the document you are currently reading. For example,

```
<a href="file.html"> Load the menu</a>
```

means that when the user clicks on Load the menu, the browser will ask the server for the file file.html, which is located in the same directory as the file the user is currently reading, and load it into the browser. Relative links make it easier to move your pages around, because you don't have to worry about the server's name and paths. Using relative links also makes it easier to access your pages on

Table 4.12 Forms of a URL for Links

URL	*What It Does*
#name	Goes to a point on the page currently being displayed in the browser. This point will have been marked using a statement of the form: <a name="name">. The point</a>.file.html, Loads the file called file.html, which is contained in the same directory as the page containing the link, into the browser.
file.html#name	Loads the file file.html and goes to a point called name in it.
dirname/file.html	Loads a file file.html in directory called dirname located in the same directory as the page containing the link.
../dirname/	Goes to the directory dirname located in the directory above the one for the file currently displayed in the browser and loads the fileindex.html (the default when no filename is given).
/dirname/file.html	Loads a file file.html, which is located in the directory called dirname that is located in the server's root directory.
http://www.location. ext/	Loads the home page (index.html) at the site **www .location.ext**.
http://www.location.ext/	Loads the file file.htm' located at the site **www .location.ext.file.html**.
ftp://location.ext/file. ext	Loads the file file.ext via anonymous FTP from the site **location.ext**.
MAILTO:name@ address.ext	Starts the browser's mail program and attempts to send an e-mail message to username who has an account on the machine address.ext.
NEWS:group.name	Connects to the News server that has been set up as the browser's default and attempts to read the messages in the group called group.name.

a local disk or CD-ROM, because the relative paths relate to the path on the disk. You might need to use absolute links for some references, such as making links to pages that are not stored on your server.

Forms of URL A URL in a link can take many forms, and each form has a different meaning. Table 4.12 gives a list of URL forms and their meanings.

Link Problem Solving

Are your links not working? Make sure that the following are true:

- The file or machine to which the link is going is spelled correctly
- The link has the correct path

- The case of the file name is correct
- The permissions for the file enable it to be read
- The browser is set up to handle NEWS and MAILTO references if the link URL begins with NEWS or MAILTO
- The server to which you are making an FTP connection allows anonymous FTP connections if the link URL begins with FTP
- You have phrased your link correctly

Form of Links You can have a number of types of links. Each hyperlink is known as a trigger because it triggers the browser into loading another page. Either text or a picture can act as a trigger to any other file, whether that file is a page of text, a sound file, or a video. It is usual to tell the students that a picture is acting as a link, because some students may not notice the outline that appears around a picture when it is used as a link. A piece of text used to link to another file is known as a text trigger. For instance,

```
<a href="URL">Text Trigger</a>
```

means that when the student clicks on the words Text Trigger, the page URL will be loaded into the browser.

You can also use a picture as a trigger:

```
<a href="URL"> <IMG SRC="picture.gif"  ALT="[Go to next
page]"> </a>
```

When you use a picture as a trigger, the student clicks on the picture to follow the link. Note that if the student's browser cannot display graphics, you should supply a description of the action performed by clicking the picture in the ALT section of the tag (in our example, the action was to go to the next page).

You can also use a picture and a text trigger together:

```
<a href="URL"> <IMG SRC="icon.gif"  ALT="[Go to next page]">
Text Trigger </a>
```

Describing and Placing Links The easiest way for beginners to use links is to make it clear to them what to do. For example, your link could say "Place your

FIGURE 4.8 Navigation icons.

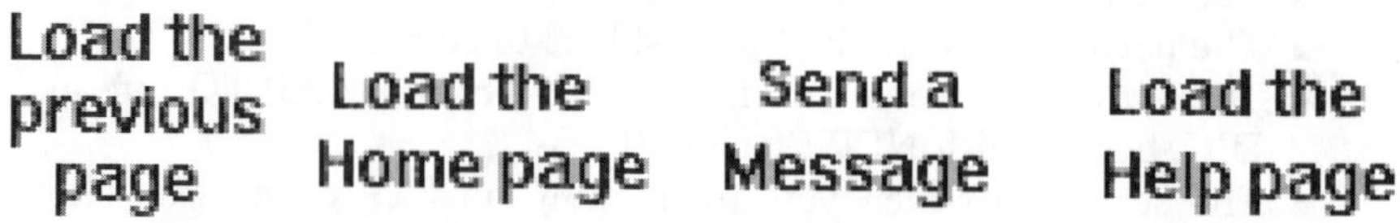

FIGURE 4.9 Text explanation for navigation icons.

mouse over this sentence and click on the left button to move to the next section." Try to make your links descriptive.

Using graphic buttons as links works as long as the students know what the graphic button represents. Such graphic buttons were introduced as navigation bars in Chapter 3. For example, you could use a right-pointing arrow to indicate that the student can click it to move to the next page and a left-pointing arrow to indicate that the student can click it to move to the previous page in the structure. A useful training method is to animate the graphic buttons on an introductory page so that the students know what they stand for. Figure 4.8 shows the graphic buttons for a navigation bar; these buttons are animated on the Web page so that at certain intervals a text image appears in their place, indicating what they do. These images are shown in Figure 4.9. The file containing this animated navigation bar is located on the CD-ROM in content/iconhelp/index.htm.

Ensure that your links are short; excessively long links can obscure text and distract the reader. *For example, if this whole sentence was a link to another document, it would look like this.* You can see that making a whole paragraph a link would result in text that is difficult to read and a link that is difficult to categorize.

Placing links too close to each other can make your page confusing:. *Go to next section. Go to previous section. Go to the index.* Which part of the sentence do I press to go where? You should try to space out and separate your links, like this: *[Go to next section] [Go to previous section] [Go to the index].*

Be careful of getting into a situation where every second word is a link to another page. This certainly takes advantage of hypertext as a means of exploring, but it can mean that the student is constantly clicking on links and thus loses the flow of the sentence that contains the links. Use links sparingly; they should add to the document, not distract from it.

Some browsers allow you to display a message on its bottom bar when a pointer is placed over a link. Such a message can give a further description of a link without cluttering up the text. For example, look at the link:

```
<a href="times.html"
onMouseOver="window.status='This link brings you to a list of
timetables';return true;"
```

Table 4.13 Utilities to Verify Page Links

Package	*Platform*	*Location*
MOMSpider	UNIX	www.ics.uci.edu/WebSoft/MOMspider/
BigBrother	Macintosh	hyperarchive.lcs.mit.edu/HyperArchive/ Archive/text/html/big-brother-11.hqx
jWalker	Java	www.webwrks.com.au/

```
onMouseOut="window.status=' ';return true;"
> Timetables</a>
```

Note that the quotes immediately after the second window.status are two single quotes and not one double quote. The message displayed when the user places the mouse pointer over the link marked Timetables is "This link brings you to a list of timetables." When the user moves the mouse pointer from the link, the message should disappear (that's what the onMouseOut command is there for), but on some browsers it remains until the mouse pointer goes over another link.

Avoiding "Missing Links" Nothing is more annoying than clicking on an interesting-sounding link to be told the browser cannot find it. Be sure you check your links to ensure that they point to a valid page. You can use utilities listed in Table 4.13 to verify that your links are pointing to a valid page.

You should also check that the links are pointing to the page that you intended them to point to. For example, a link labeled Current Assignment shouldn't lead to a list of tutors instead of the current assignment page.

Writing Equations

A problem that has always confronted educators is how to display equations on the Web. HTML does not yet have a standard way of representing equations, so they usually have to be placed in a picture file format such as GIF or JPEG. However, there are a number of ways of avoiding drawing each of your equations:

- Use a Java applet that will interpret the equation for you. Your students' browsers must be able to run a Java applet to see the equation. See **www.geom.umn.edu/~rminer/jmath/** for more details.
- Using a rendering service such as **www.lfw.org/math/**, you can write your HTML pages as you normally do and refer students to this site anytime they are accessed. The site handles the conversion of the math equations and shows the completed page to your students.
- By far the easiest way is to obtain software that will convert the equations into a graphical picture. Word processors like Microsoft Word allow you to create and edit an equation using their built-in equation editor and convert the file to HTML using an HTML converter component. During the conversion

process, the equation is converted into a picture. Latex2Html also translates equations into a graphic file. Another option in a similar vein is the tth package (**venus.pfc.mit.edu/tth/tth.html**), which will convert TeX files into a form of HTML using available symbols and tables to produce a close approximation to most equations.

- Use a browser that recognizes a form of math equation formatting. Version 3 of HTML is supposed to include tags for writing equations. Though the method is not very elegant or intuitive, it is a start. The problem at the moment is that very few browsers support this method. One browser that does is the Arena browser (**www.w3.org/hypertext/WWW/Arena/**), which is available for UNIX platforms only.
- Finally, you could construct your equations from files that contain pictures of common symbols. A repository of symbol pictures is available at **donald.phast.umass.edu/data/tutorials/kicons.html**.

Automatic Dating of Modifications

It is important to know the age of the page you're viewing. If a page contains time-related information such as announcements, students would like to know the last time an addition was made. Knowing the age of a page is also useful to help students figure out if any changes have been made to a page since they last looked at it. You can place the current date at the end of each page or you can use two automatic methods of reporting—Server Side Includes and JavaScript—when you modify it.

Using Server Side Includes If your server has a facility for using Server Side Includes, you can place the following command at the end of your document. (In this example, the name of the document is chap01.htm.)

```
<!--#flastmod file="chap01.htm"-->
```

Every time chap01.htm is loaded, the server looks at the file to see when it was last modified and prints the date in place of the above statement. The statement will appear on screen as "Friday, 19-August-97 14:46:05 GMT."

This method could be very useful for announcements. For example, you could place the following HTML in the main page of your course:

```
<a href="announce.html">Announcement page.</a>
Last announcement made: <!--#flastmod file="announce.html"-->
```

This displays the following: "*Announcement page.* Last announcement made: Friday, 19-August-97 14:46:05 GMT."

Using JavaScript If your students' browsers are equipped with JavaScript, you can place the following code at the end of your documents:

```
<script LANGUAGE="JavaScript">
document.writeln('This document was last modified: ');
document.writeln(document.lastModified);
</script>
```

This will display the following in your browser window: "Last modified: Tue Apr 29 18:11:02 1997."

RESOURCES

A list of links concerning topics covered in this chapter appear in this book's CD-ROM:

- HTML resources
- Hybrid systems
- VRML
- Animated GIFs
- Server-push mechanisms
- Systems for sound and video
- Client-side animation
- Specialized digital video cameras
- Web products for the hearing and visually impaired

5

Distributing Information

What do we mean by information distribution in a Web environment? It means you can use the Web as a repository students can access to retrieve any information that would be useful to them. Not only can you can use the Web to help you distribute information—you can also place the information in a form that goes beyond text and takes advantage of media that will help students understand better and to which they can relate more easily. As you know from reading the preceding chapters, you can make any form of media available for students to access: sound files containing speeches, video clips showing real demonstrations, animation illustrating abstract concepts, pictures, photographs, and straightforward text. You can combine these media and use specific structures of links to perform various functions. For instance, you can use the Web to give a lesson, display a slide show, or store materials. Information distribution can also become a two-way process, with students sharing information with the educator.

As you will see, each of these uses has its own method of preparation and will make various demands on your computers in terms of the amount of storage space they need and the power of the computer needed to display them, as well as making demands on the network and you in terms of preparation time. This chapter examines the components of information distribution in terms of what you can do and materials you need, examples of how others are using the Web to distribute information, and factors you need to consider in creating a distribution mechanism. The chapter also provides some troubleshooting tips.

INFORMATION DISTRIBUTION BASICS

As you saw in Chapter 1, apart from its usefulness as an electronic library, the Web has enormous advantages in terms of presenting and processing information.

The Web can come into its own if you have problems with the traditional methods of information distribution or you want to use something other than a text-based book, creating a "living" book that changes during the course in response to students' needs. Indeed, you can make an "electronic scrapbook" of your course, with students and educators contributing lessons, comments, and links to other resources. This makes for a much more active learning experience because students get a chance to help construct their own course. This approach can lead to a cooperative effort in education, which is facilitated by the ease with which information can be disseminated and altered using the Web. Your learning system could take the form of a contract between you and your students.

Using the Web for information distribution can help with the following tasks:

Material distribution. Placing material on the Web instead of photocopying and distributing it by hand saves time and resources and provides an archive for students who missed lectures or misplaced their notes.

Distance education. Distance students may need a great deal of time to obtain material by ordinary methods. With a Web-based information distribution system, they can access the material as soon as it has been placed on the server. They can even set up a system whereby they are notified if the material on the server changes so that they can investigate the additions.

Using a multimedia system that is independent of platform. Traditionally, multimedia displays are created and displayed using software packages like Authorware. This means that students' computers must contain a copy of a program that can display the Authorware presentation. Unfortunately, not all platforms are capable of using such a program, nor do they have the resources needed to make it work effectively. Using the Web and an appropriate format for the information enables the presentations to be independent of software packages or computer type. A specific type of computer is not needed to view the information as long as the computer has a Web browser that can display the multimedia files you prepare. You don't need to make a commitment to an expensive software package when material you produce with various low-cost packages can be stored in a Web browser-compatible format that can be used by all.

Dynamic publishing. Often, educators want to add parts to lessons or include supplementary materials. These can be added directly to the class Web site as soon as the educator has written them, which means there is no need to alter the class schedule.

Administrative information. Some classes maintain paper-based bulletin boards in specific buildings to help students keep up with changing course information. Using a Web-based information distribution system allows you to create an electronic bulletin board that is more accessible to students and easier for you to update.

Integration with other teaching methods. In a traditional environment, the course is run at a uniform pace, and it is assumed that the students are of a uniform type and standard. With a Web-based system, you can accommodate diversity of ability and attitudes of students by offering different explanations, remedial or advanced tutorials, and a chance for the students to proceed at their own pace.

Resource access. Resource material—files, explanations—can be placed online, where it is easily accessible.

Reference material. Reference material that was once available only in a library, where students may have had difficulty accessing it, can be placed online so all students have equal access to it.

Searchable information. You can use indexing programs and utilities to make it easy for students to search all the information you distribute on the Web, saving time and preventing frustration.

Supplementary material. In traditional education, material such as how-to instruction manuals and troubleshooting guides would not usually form part of the course due to lack of time. Using a Web-based information distribution system allows you to offer the students such help with all facets of the course.

Hyperlinked information. The ability to incorporate hyperlinks into text and create links for certain areas of pictures enables you to embed cross-links and reference links into text and pictures.

Applications. What can you use an information distribution system for? A number of things, each with its own possibilities: administration, personal material pertaining to both students and educators, resource repositories, and teaching.

Administrative Use You can use the system for distributing administrative information such as assignment results, announcements, tutor lists, contact details, timetables, grades, FAQs, study guides, and resources such as past exam papers, course syllabi, and college facilities.

For example, in the Web-based administrative system in Figure 5.1 there are entries for results, sample exam questions, contact information, and a course schedule. A rich resource like this encourages students to access the system at frequent intervals to check for new grades or new information. Allowing students to peruse such information at their leisure in a comfortable environment also makes it easier for students to notice relevant information.

Personal Space Information about the staff and students can be stored in a "personal space." Students can place details about themselves, such as their photographs and backgrounds or any other relevant information. Staff can include information about themselves such as their contact times and research interests. This system helps to build a sense of camaraderie in the class.

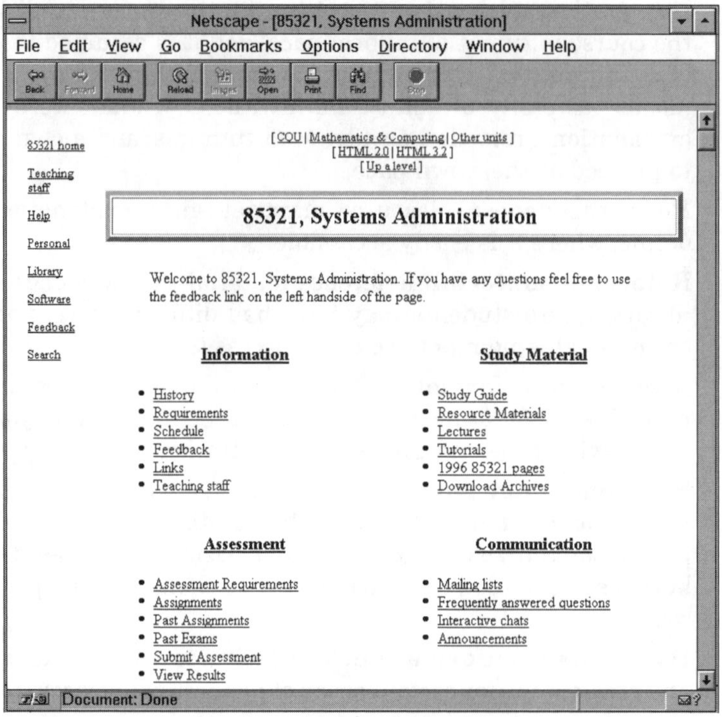

FIGURE 5.1 A sample class page.

Resource Center A resource center is intended to act as a repository for files that may be useful to students. For example, if you are giving a word processor course, you could place a collection of example documents in your resource center. You can have two types of resources: technical resources and student-related resources.

Student-Related Resources Material prepared by the lecturer in a form that is difficult or too time consuming to translate to a format viewable by a Web browser can be stored in a resource center site and downloaded by the student, whose computer must have a copy of the application to view the original file. For example, many lecturers prepare their lectures using Powerpoint so they can make their lecture notes available on a Web site for the students to download to view or print. By altering the Web server and the student's browser slightly, you can configure the browser to access a file on the Web site and automatically start the application associated with it, and even load the file into the application. (You were shown how to set up browsers and servers to automatically start applications in Chapter 4.) This means that if a student clicks on a link labeled lecture 2- Powerpoint slides, the Powerpoint file will be downloaded to the student's computer; Powerpoint will launch and load the slides from lecture 2.

This approach allows lecturers to make their material available with minimum effort and provides a valuable resource for the students.

Technical Resources Students may need access to utilities or programs that will allow them to display files or perform some other function. A technical resource facility can show them where to find useful programs or which programs contain a series of guides on how to install programs or cope with various technical problems they may encounter. A search facility could form part of a technical resource to help students search either the Web or the course server for information of interest.

Instructional Uses You can set up a number of information distribution systems that can on their own be used to educate or train. For example:

Tutorials. A tutorial could include a complete explanation of a topic or act as a supplement to a lecture. A number of types of tutorials are possible, as you shall see later.

Simulations. A computer program or Web page that will simulate some operation.

Reference manuals. A set of Web pages that the student can use to look up various topics, much like a glossary.

How-to guides. A step-by-step explanation of how to do something.

Troubleshooting guides. A series of question-and-answer links that students can use to guide them through a problem situation.

Considerations for an Information Distribution System

The question arises: "Why use an information distribution system?" An information distribution system does not have to address a specific problem to be useful. However, to ensure that you get the best result from any system you implement, you should examine your current educational system and see if any problems could be addressed using an information distribution system. The questions you need to ask are what problems are there at the moment? How can an information distribution system be used to help? Here are some common problems that can occur in an education system and how you can use an information distribution system to help:

Increased participation. As noted, the more students involved in a course, the more anonymous each student becomes and the less he or she feels part of the class. This situation can lead to a loss of motivation, a reduction in student participation, and a strain on resources. Using an information distribution system can ensure that students have equal access to resource material. You can create a personal space for the class to encourage cooperation and to make the students feel part of the class. Placing material, such as handouts, on an information distribution system reduces the need for the lecturer to spend time distributing and archiving material.

Increased variety. A class of students originating from many different backgrounds means you cannot assume students have a uniform set of knowledge or skills. Usually, time or resources cannot be obtained to help these students reach a uniform level. Using a tutorial system allows students who are not equipped with the prerequisites to be trained or given access to reference material. This gives the students the resources to catch up and enables educators to treat the students as though they were on a uniform level.

Need for increased flexibility. Flexibility in students' workload and study habits is a desirable feature in a course. Using a tutorial system can allow students to learn in their own time, at their own pace. Placing lectures on an information system can allow students who were unable to attend class to keep up. In your tutorial system, you can create material that is tailored to fit different types of student, thereby helping students learn using experiences they can relate to or by creating a tutorial that adapts to their needs.

Increased expectations. Students not only have increased expectations of the educator but also of themselves. Students who are exposed to an information distribution system are happy that they are getting an extra resource and use it to improve their performance.

The changing nature of knowledge. Information stored on an information distribution system can be updated as often as needed. Additions to courses can be made to train students on new topics that could not be incorporated into lectures.

Increased competition. Universities can offer an information distribution/tutorial system as added value. Private companies can create a tutorial system for which they can charge an access fee.

Distance education. Students are free to access course material whenever and wherever they are. Tutorials can be converted in order to use online access as little as possible if this is a problem for the students. Providing students with tutorials, access to educators, and commented lectures enables distance students to obtain as good an educational experience as they would have by attending a course in person.

Temporally distributed class. Records of lectures can be used as a focal point for training. Administrative information is available to allow students to keep track of their deadlines and results.

Poor results. Students can read the material and test themselves. Students can make their misapprehensions clearer to themselves through tutorials and question-and-answer sessions.

Including more material. Lecturers can add additional material as they see the need. They can include supplements to their lectures, offering different explanations, or make available advanced tutorials to sufficiently capable students.

Students memorize as opposed to understand. The usual key to helping students understand material is to provide multiple explanations of a topic. This increases the chance that a student will be able to grasp a concept because they might be able to relate better to a more specific explanation or example. In an ordinary education system, delivering multiple explanations could be very time consuming. An information distribution system not only allows you to offer extra explanations to the student, but to construct tutorials that will help student understanding. However, you need to educate students to be able to cope with this process. If students are too accustomed to memorizing and are faced with multiple explanations, they may attempt to memorize them all. This is one of the aspects of a problem known as "information overload."

Students have different goals. You can accommodate the goal of increasing student learning by matching the tutorials with a list of stated goals. In each of the goal-based tutorials, tailor a tutorial for the relevant groups of students by providing examples related to their field of experience or basing explanations in the context with which they are most familiar. For example, students taking a minor course might be interested in how it relates to their major. Material or the structure in which it is presented can even be molded to the individual student.

Shared course, different educators. Educators can place their material on an information distribution system to enable other educators to see what they have covered and their method of instruction. Educators may not even have to attend a course in person; instead, they could create lessons, lectures, and exercises and place them on the system.

Dropout rate. If prospective students are free to access a course information distribution system and see its content, nature, and level together with the assignments, they will have a better idea of what they are undertaking when they sign up for the course. Linking this information to a Web-based test system (see Chapter 7), you can create a system that will automatically perform initial grading of student abilities and inform them of their suitability for a course or what they will need to know before undertaking it. You can also use this pregrading system to identify specific tutorials that you need to construct for incoming students.

Advantages The development of an information distribution system, even a very basic one, has certain advantages:

Platform independence. Students will be able to access the information, no matter what type of computer they are using, as long as it supports a Web browser.

Industry support. You can create your course, safe in the knowledge that the system for distributing it and viewing it is tried and tested. Your material will also be usable if new and different types of computers are used.

Material format will not become obsolete. Material you place in a form that can be viewed using a browser can be easily converted into other forms, so you need not fear that your files will become unusable if you change computers or operating systems.

Increased flexibility. Students have more access to the resources, saving time, and staff can send messages and add and update material speedily and answer students' questions.

Phased development. You can develop the system a little at a time, allowing you to evaluate how the students react and enabling you to establish a plan for further development.

Problems

You may encounter the following problems that will affect the success of your system:

Speed. The network to which the students have access may not be fast enough to support the material you want to distribute. This usually happens if you want to distribute materials that take up a large amount of file space, such as video clips.

Equipment. Students' computers may not be powerful enough to handle material. Again this is a problem common to multimedia files such as video clips.

Cost. Setting up and maintaining an information distribution system requires the use of equipment and software packages and requires time to plan, write material, test, implement, and maintain.

Reliability of access. Even if students' equipment is suitable, how easy is it for them to gain access to it? Do they have to walk half a mile across campus? Do they have to wait until certain hours of the day?

Browser. Remember, browsers are capable of different things. So, if students are not using the browser on which you tested the system, they may have problems using the system.

Initial cost of production. Converting and creating material will require an investment of time and money.

Screen quality. Students may have difficulty reading the material if they are not using a good-quality display. This difficulty makes them reluctant to use the system extensively, because it may be physically uncomfortable for them to read the screen for prolonged periods of time.

Distraction. Ensure that the system acts as a resource to support the teaching of the student and not as a novelty item for the student (and sometimes the educator) to play with. Students might complain that they did not have enough time to complete their practical assignment because they were using their allotted practical time to access their information distribution system.

Overkill. You should ensure that you are setting up an information distribution system with a purpose and are not simply attempting to throw every possible resource you can lay your hands on at students in the hope that their performance will improve. You should also note that, to get the message across, your presentations need not use multimedia or the latest in Web presentation formats extensively.

Success Factors You may implement a system that is excellent in terms of content and technical implementation. However, other factors must be considered that can make a significant contribution to the system's success.

Training Make sure students know how the browser works and are familiar with the type of computer and operating system they will be using. (The CD-ROM contains an example of paper-based training material that provides an introduction to a system.) It's a good idea to make sure the training material is paper based, because trying to train students to use an electronic system *with* an electronic system is not usually the best approach. Handing out paper manuals also gives the student a usable reference they can easily consult when they are not using the computer.

Another good training component is the guided tour (discussed later in this chapter), which can introduce students to the information distribution system and guide them through it. They should also be familiar with not only the method of using the system (navigation bars, communication facilities, and so on), but also the function of the information distribution system. For example, the function of an administrative information distribution system is to allow easy dissemination of material; therefore, students should be told that they are required to access it frequently in order to keep up to date with course developments. This brings home to the student the philosophy behind the system and how they are expected to use it. (The CD-ROM includes an example of a document that you can distribute to students studying using a Web-based system. You can extend this document to cover the various systems that you implement.)

Ease of Use One of the most important factors contributing to the success of your system is ease of use. The students should find it easy to start the system and find their way around it. Things students find off-putting are having to log on to multiple systems in order to start a browser, being equipped with a browser that is very slow to start (some systems have a browser installed that is much too advanced for the system; consequently, it is very slow to load) or a browser that interferes with other applications they have running, and a poor download speed for information (because the server or network is too slow or overworked).

Resource Value The extent to which the students will use the system is often based on what they believe is its resource value. If they don't think the system contains useful material, they won't use it. If they find material that is difficult to understand or is inaccurate, this will also depreciate the value of the system from their point of view.

Design The system's design should make it easy to use. It should be easy to navigate around the system, and each of its parts should be clear and unambiguous. Poor system design, such as badly laid out pages and missing links, can prevent students from using the system, even if it has a high resource value.

Flexibility Students appreciate a system more if it is flexible. For example, can they print parts of the system? Can they use it to obtain tutorials to use on their own computers? Can they make requests for specific information? Are they free to peruse the material at will?

REQUIRED RESOURCES

You will need a variety of resources, depending on what you want your information distribution system to do. These resources can be categorized as follows: structure and page layout via a template, the actual information you will place on your system, viewing tools such as browsers, distribution tools, authoring tools, and utilities. (Viewing, distribution, and authoring tools were discussed in Chapter 4.)

Structure and Page Layout

You will need a structure for your Web site and a standard page layout for your system together with components such as navigation bars and icons. Keeping a consistent set of icons and a uniform page layout will make it easier for students to navigate around the system and become familiar with it. (See the development discussion in Chapter 3.)

Material

Begin with a list of material—announcements, resources, lessons—you plan to put into the information distribution system. Do you have objectives for each lesson, as well as enough material to adequately explain the topics it contains and to offer a variety of differently phrased explanations? Have you sufficient questions you can ask the student to test their knowledge of the material? Are your resources on paper or already in computer file form? Having plenty of material is important; you'll tend to alter the material you have to fit the new medium. Content development is usually the most time-consuming part of the whole process, so be prepared to invest considerable time creating new material and adapting old material.

Material can be used in four ways: straight distribution, conversion, value-added conversion, or purpose-built material.

Straight Distribution Many information distribution sites simply contain links to files in a common viewable format such as PostScript or files produced directly from an application such as Powerpoint or Word. Students use their Web browsers to download these files and view them or print them locally. If you already have your material in an existing electronic format doing a straight distribution will save you time because all you have to do is place the material on your Web site and prepare instructions on how to use it. Unfortunately, distributing material in a non-Web-based form means that students will usually have to make more effort to view that material—for instance, they must download viewers and set them up on their system. It also means that the material cannot be altered or used as easily; students may find it more difficult to cut and paste parts of the material. If these disadvantages do not deter you, you need to ensure that the format used for the material is as platform independent as possible—in other words, students with any type of computer (Macintosh, Windows, or UNIX based) should be able to view your files.

You might have resource material that cannot be easily translated for the Web and you have no option but to do a straight distribution. An example of a platform-independent format that is not easily translated is the PostScript format (files containing PostScript end in .ps). A viewer for PostScript called GhostScript (**www.cs.wisc.edu/~ghost/**) will allow you to make PostScript files available for students to download. PostScript allows you to have complete control over the way a document is formatted and appears to the reader. It runs on the Macintosh, Windows, and UNIX platforms. Thus, you can place a copy of GhostScript on students' machines or specify in a resources page where they can download a copy and use it to view the PostScript files.

Another popular format is Adobe's Portable Document Format (PDF). Files in the PDF format usually end in .pdf. PDF is popular because it allows you to include hyperlinks within documents and have complete control over the document's appearance. More details about PDF and details of how to obtain a free viewer, called Acrobat, can be obtained at **www.adobe.com/**. Note that you will need a special program to create files in PDF format, whereas most word processors have an option that enables them to output a file in PostScript form.

Conversion Conversion involves converting existing material into a form that can be more easily used on a Web page. There are two forms of conversion: from paper form and from a specific file format. If your material is on paper, you need to get it into the computer. This can be done using a scanner, which can convert the paper-based information into a picture file, or using optical character recognition (OCR) software, which can translate information supplied by a scanner into computer text. Once the material is translated from paper form into a computer file, you can convert the file into a Web form or leave it in picture or word processor file form.

If your material is stored in files in a specific format, such as Microsoft Word, you can convert it HTML pages using a utility that will perform the conversion for you. Fortunately, most word processors include conversion utilities that will allow word-processed documents to be translated directly into HTML. Many other applications, such as Powerpoint and Authorware, also have utilities that will allow their files to be translated. You'll have to make some trade-offs, however; for example, some word processor converters will not convert the pictures the documents contain, but in general the procedure works quite well and allows you to reuse existing material. (Chapter 4 contains some examples of conversion utilities.)

Value-Added Conversion Value-added conversion involves using material suitable for display in a Web browser and adding an extra component to it to take advantage of the Web media. For example, you could add narration to slides, links to related topics in your lecture text, or a structure for the course material with a navigation bar to guide the student through it.

Purpose-Built Material Purpose-built material is specifically designed for the Web. This usually involves developing a hypertext structure for the material, creating multimedia, and writing Java-based applications that are used for demonstration and simulation. This process usually requires the most effort of all the information distribution approaches, but it allows you to use the Web medium to its fullest.

Obtaining Material If you do not have enough material for use in an information distribution system, you can obtain material by a variety of methods The main source of educational links is the World Lecture Hall (**www.utexas.edu/world/lecture/index.html**). This site contains mainly college courses placed on the Web.

If you cannot find material of use to you there, you could consider looking at other Web sources for information. Sites such as the WWW virtual library (**www.w3.org/vl/**) keep a list of Web sites that contain information on particular subjects. The subjects are grouped under broad categories that you can browse.

You can also use a search engine to conduct a more detailed search of documents available on the Web. Certain Web sites, like Yahoo! and AltaVista, run programs that constantly look at the servers on the Web and compile lists of the files they contain, as well as their contents. Personal search engines like My Yahoo! produce even more relevant results. A meta search engine is one that will search a number of search engines for you. An example of a meta search engine can be found at **www.metacrawler.com/**.

Companies that have traditionally supplied educational material in print, like Encyclopedia Britannica (**www.eb.com**), now have Web sites you can access for a fee. Other sites such as the Electric Library (**www.elibrary.com**) provide a database of magazines and newspapers that you can use for research and reference or as sources for material.

Using Material You can use material you have located on the Web in two ways. You can insert a link to the material in your course or you can ask the author if you can make a copy of the material and use it.

If you want to use other people's material you should first evaluate it for suitability. Use the following checklist for evaluation:

Content. Does it cover the topic thoroughly? Can you distinguish between established fact and the author's opinion? Will the material be a distraction or will it augment the learning process? If the material is a supplement for students, you should indicate this; otherwise, students may assume it is essential knowledge and might fall victim to information overload.

Accuracy. Are you sure the information is accurate? Unlike a textbook, Web sites rarely benefit from editors checking through them to make sure that everything is correct.

Authenticity. Who developed the material? Is it provided as an altruistic gesture or will students be subjected to advertising—either direct advertising or, more dangerously, biased recommendations? Junk mail can be recognized as junk mail, but junk mail masquerading as a resource is a little more difficult to spot.

Author. Who is the author of the material? Remember that almost anyone can publish on the Web, so if you are unsure about the material, check the author's credentials.

Usability. Does the material contain elements the students will have technical difficulty with—videos, Shockwave presentations, or the like?

Speed of access. If you are recommending that your students access a site, you need to check if it takes a long time to access or whether the site is frequently unavailable. If students are depending on the site, access difficulties will cause problems. You should measure the speed of access at different times of the day because there may be "rush hour traffic" when your students are likely to use the material, making the access and downloading process very slow.

Copyright Questions It is important to ensure that you have permission from the copyright owners of the material you intend to use. Be especially careful of anything you copy from other people's Web pages, because they are still subject to copyright law. Usually, people will not mind you copying anything they have placed on the Web for your own local use (provided you do not use their work for commercial gain). However, it is best to get a written release for anything you are doubtful of. If people are reluctant to let you copy their material, you can provide a link to their site (although there is currently a heated discussion over whether this, too, breaches copyright).

Some publishers are starting to offer their paper-based texts in electronic format, so you can obtain parts of textbooks for your course. However, the publishers will charge you a fee, usually related to the size of your class, for any material you use.

Downloading Material and Mirroring Sites

If you obtain permission to use someone else's material, you can either copy the material page by page (load their pages one at a time and save each on your system) or you can use software that will go to the author's site and copy the Web pages and associated files (pictures, text, and so on) for you. This software will copy every file linked to the URL of the page you want to copy. So, if you supply your copying software with the main or home page URL, it will copy all the pages that the main page links to and place them on your site, using the same filenames and directory structure. This process is known as making a mirror of a site (see Chapter 1 for more details). You can also make these utilities available for students, who can then download a copy of your entire information distribution system to their own computers. Doing so will reduce telephone charges for students who need to access your Web site through a modem. Some of the mirroring software available is listed in Table 5.1.

Testing the Material Testing your material can mean two things. You can test the material's suitability for your students by having someone read through it,

Table 5.1 Mirroring Software for Downloading

Name	*Location*	*Platform*
WebWhacker	www.ffg.com/whacker/	Windows and Macintosh
Weblicator	www.lotus.com/	Windows
FlashSite	www.incontext.com/	Windows
Teleport Pro	www.tenmax.com/	Windows
NetAttache	www.tympani.com/	Windows
w3mir	www.ifi.uio.no/~janl/w3mir.html	For UNIX systems, written in Perl; requires a Perl interpreter on a UNIX system
wget	sunsite.auc.dk/ftp/pub/infosystems/wget/	For UNIX systems, written in C

checking to see it is understandable and correct. Another thing you need to do is check to see how the material will appear on-screen to the students. For example, a student may have access to a slow computer with very poor screen resolution and may not be able to see any of the pictures in your presentation. The student's system may also be configured to use as few colors as possible, which means that any colored text or pictures may not appear as you had envisaged. You should, therefore, try to test your Web material on a computer similar to the ones your students will have access to. This may not be always possible if you allow students to access using their own computers, but at least try to gain access to a computer that corresponds to the lowest-specification model that students will use. You can then inform the students that you tested with this particular platform and they should be capable of using the system if their platform is equivalent or better. If you are dealing with a more diverse student group, like distance students, you will need to involve them more in the testing process because you can never be sure of their computers' capabilities.

You should also use the type of connection the students will use. If students are using a modem to connect to your server or to an ISP, you should see how usable the system is, because a modem usually operates at a fraction of the speed of most local network connections.

Not only should you test whether the material is understandable and usable on students' computers, you should also check to see that students have all the components they need to use the material. Either check the computers students are using on campus or survey the students to see what their home machines can do. For instance, can their computers play sound files? (Some computers, such as Macintosh, have sound reproduction built in, but others need an extra component.) If they can play sounds, which format of sound file can they handle? Can they play video files, and if so, which ones? What is the display resolution of their current setup? How many colors can they display?

If students' computers are unlikely to be equipped with the necessary software, you can set up a training resource that students can use to find out how to install multimedia resources. (Don't forget to train them how to use the training resource.) You can also distribute a list of prerequisites, telling students that, for instance, their computers must be able to run Netscape 2.0 and have a facility for playing sound files. If you always prepare your course for the most primitive type of computer available, you may miss out on the rich information presentation capabilities that more modern equipment can support, so it's best to indicate the technical requirements to students up front. This does not mean that you should demand that your students have the latest equipment, just equipment of a reasonable standard.

One of the main things to check, if possible, is the screens students will use. Check to see how well graphics and text are displayed on the screens. The quality of text display is important because students can tire of looking at a screen for long periods of time. Check to see whether the screen is prone to flickering, which would indicate that it has been set to too high a resolution. Check the arrangements for viewing the screen—the seating posture students need to adopt, for instance. Seating posture in most laboratories is such that students will sit hunched over the screen and thus can become physically uncomfortable reading material. The quality of the display and the suitability of the students' physical environment can impact the success of your course; no matter how good the material and how dedicated the students, if they find it uncomfortable to use, they will not use it.

Using Utilities A number of utilities can make a Web-based education system more productive and manageable; these are discussed in detail in Chapter 10. You may need to consider which ones to incorporate in your system at this stage in your development plan. Utilities you may find useful include such programs as log analyzers (used to analyze what pages students are accessing, how often the system is being used, and so on), link checkers to check that all your links lead to valid locations, and search facilities to enable you or your students to search your information distribution system for relevant terms.

Limiting Access You can limit access to your system to authorized students by setting up accounts for students on your server system (see Chapter 10). You can limit student access to pages either by using the server's access protection system (again, see Chapter 10) or using methods of limiting access to the pages (see Chapter 7 and Appendix D on the CD-ROM).

Allowing Students to Alter Material If you want to set up a system whereby the students can alter the Web material, you need to give them permission to place material on the server. The easiest way of doing this is to set up an FTP server alongside your HTTP server. The FTP program is slightly different from an HTTP server in that FTP was designed to allow users with accounts to transfer files between machines. Most UNIX systems have FTP built in, but you need to give each student an account. For other platforms, there are programs that allow them to act as an FTP server. Students can access the system using FTP and upload files or using the upload feature on the Netscape Navigator browser. You can also allow students to upload material using an upload utility on the server.

CREATING AN INFORMATION DISTRIBUTION SYSTEM

You have seen what resources you need and how to create your structure. Now you need a plan of action. This series of steps shows what is involved in creating an information distribution system:

Define what you want to do and why. Decide what your needs are and what components would fulfill these needs— a tutorial system, a reference system, and so on. For example, you might want your students to be able to view a copy of your lectures before you give them together with a set of addenda and a link to outside references, both of which you will provide after each lecture is given.

Define what constitutes success for each component. Do you want to stimulate your students to think and to work independently? Do you want to see records that show students downloading the material that you have placed in the reference section? How many students should regularly use the system before it is classified a success? Will the system be a success if the number of dropouts falls? Do you want feedback from your students? Do you want your students to be more informed? Do you want to save time copying and distributing material? You can define success in these ways:

Usage. How many people are using the system? How many pages have they read? How often do they access the pages? Are students satisfied with the system?

Results. Are there fewer questions from students? Is there an improvement in students' performance? Has the system made things easier for you or addressed some of your problems? Does the system provide students with genuine benefits?

Consequences. How do others view your system? Do your institution's administration or your colleagues look favorably on your work and innovation? Do other educators ask for your help to set up their own systems? Are students more attracted to your courses because of your use of the Web?

Decide on a structure or work out how your components fit into an existing structure. Later in this chapter, you'll see an example structure for the components of an information distribution system and a set of templates for each. You can plan your own structure or use our structure.

Plan the content. Decide what you are going to put in the system (pictures, text, multimedia). What will your content look like on students' computers?

Check your server or method of information distribution. Before you start putting any work into the system, check that the server you plan to use can handle your system and that the owners of the server are willing to cooperate. If you have to set up your own server, do so before you create your material and construct your structure so you are guaranteed that your server will be operational and you have a home for your Web-based classroom.

Check that your students can and will use it. Will you be able to train your students to use the system? Will they be willing to use it? Will they have the necessary time and equipment available to use it? Check the available equipment to see that the browsers and all necessary components have been installed or can be installed.

Create or convert the content. Write the HTML pages from scratch or convert them from existing files. Create the multimedia files you intend to use or convert them into a particular format. Remember that all your content does not have to be converted, because you can do a straight distribution of material; however, conversion means material is in a form that is easier to use and adapt.

Pick a template and adapt it. Choose one of our templates and alter it for your content. This is the easiest way for you to construct your course.

Test the pages locally. Use your browser to see that all the graphics and text are clear and understandable. Check to see if the multimedia files are playable.

Install the pages on your server. Download the pages to your server. You can use an archive program to move your files or use one of the Web creation environments such as FrontPage. Ensure that all the components associated with a page (pictures, sounds files, and so on) are downloaded with your HTML files and that the filenames are not altered by the operating system.

View the information on the server and using other computers and browsers. Test to see that all the links are valid on the server and all the material is viewable on your browser. Perform the test with the same type of computers students will use, and see how their computers handle any multimedia components. Here is a series of tests for you to do on a student's computer:

- Turn off the image loading so that no pictures are loaded. This will show what will happen if the student's browser has trouble with images.
- Change the default font size to see if this impacts significantly on the way your pages appear. For example, students with poor-quality screens may have been told to increase their font size, which could mean a change in the way the information appears in their browsers.
- Reduce the number of colors that the system can display and see how this affects your Web images.
- Play any video or audio files to see if the system can handle them. Check to see that the videos are clear and that the audio files are understandable.
- Check the pictures to ensure they are not too dark.
- Ask a neutral party to view your pages and the material.

Distributing Administrative Information

This is one of the simplest information distribution systems to set up and one that a lot of educators find very useful. You do not need an elaborate structure or multimedia content to build an administrative information system. The structure commonly used is the hierarchical one. You saw from the discussion of administrative systems that you can distribute a wide amount of information.

Let's take a look at some of the things you may need to think about when distributing this information.

Assignments and Grades Most institutions have a policy about posting grades for general viewing. For example, your institution may require that grades be posted by student ID number to maintain some privacy for the student. Some institutions prefer that students see only their individual grades and not those of their peers. You must therefore ascertain what sort of format is acceptable to post grades online. If students' grades must remain private, you can implement a system whereby grades are placed in students' online personal space to which only individual students have access, or you can e-mail their grades to them.

You can post grades under a link to the relevant assignment. For example, the links Assignment 1 Marks and Assignment 2 Marks could lead to the list of grades for those two assignments. It is useful to include a short explanation after each list of grades regarding the marking criteria applied, on what scale the assignment was marked and what it is worth overall. A sample solution can also be provided.

Announcements It is usual to place announcements in their own section of an information system. The problem with this system is that students may not always go to the announcement link after the novelty of checking for announcements every day has worn off.

To address this problem, you can do two things. You can place very important announcements at the start of the home page of the system so that all students will see the announcement as soon as they log on. Make sure the announcement is brief and to the point and that you do not clutter up the main page with announcements. Don't overuse this method, either, or the students will soon learn to ignore a message like "Urgent announcement in announcement page" if no urgent announcement has appeared there for the past three weeks.

Another method of ensuring students will look at your announcement page is to include the last date that the announcement page was altered, along with the page link on the main page. This message will tell students when the last announcement was posted. You can either change the announcement date entry on your main page manually every time you make a new announcement or use one of the methods for reporting file modification times that you read about in Chapter 4.

If you are setting up an area in your Web page where you can post announcements, put the newest announcement first on the list so students do not have to wade through old announcements. To keep your announcements page tidy, delete announcements that are no longer current. Alternatively, older announcements can be kept because they could be useful for any students who are absent from the course for a long time and want to know what they missed. Leaving all the announcements there also gives the casual observer an idea of what has happened in the course over time.

Try to keep each announcement short and to the point. If the announcement is long by nature, provide a link to a separate page containing that announcement. Identify announcements by date of posting.

It is often the practice to combine an announcement page with a list of deadlines. The deadlines could appear at the top of the page and the announcements can follow. This makes it easier for students to get an instant overview of their priorities. An example of an announcement page is available on the CD-ROM in the file /infodist/example/announce.htm.

Frequently Asked Questions Students often ask the same questions as their fellow students or students from earlier courses—questions like, "How do I change my practical time?" "What grade do I need in order to pass?" Answers to these common questions can be placed in your information distribution system to save repetition and maintain consistency.

Study Guides and Other Resources Many students have problems coming to terms with the methods of study they are expected to use when they first start a course. You could have students on your course who have not studied for many years or students who previously were in a different education system. It helps them if you can offer some advice, not only on what to study, but *how* to study and what is expected of them. Students also appreciate advice on stress management, time management, and how to participate in student networks. Ask students to make suggestions themselves as to what they need help with. Many institutions have developed their own guides for students; if yours has one, see if you can obtain permission to place it on the Web.

You can make a list of tutors that the students will have available to them. Each tutor's name can have a link to a personal space where the tutors can place their contact details and background information. You could even place a link to a communications facility that would enable students to get in contact with tutors (see Chapter 6).

Many resources are available to students—the problem is for students to get hold of them. You can make life a little easier for your students if you provide them with some relevant resources— copies of past exam papers, a course syllabus, a list of college facilities (student counselors, mentors, etc.), class timetables, and a list of the expected attendees, for example—on your system.

A brief summary of what was covered in each lecture with links to useful resources or terms would also be helpful to students. You can even include a short survey the student can fill out, similar to the one shown in Figure 5.2. Try to include a link that will allow students to send you feedback. Feedback will enable you to build on your system in response to students' requirements or to address any problems students may have. (Implementing a feedback facility is discussed in more detail in Chapter 8.)

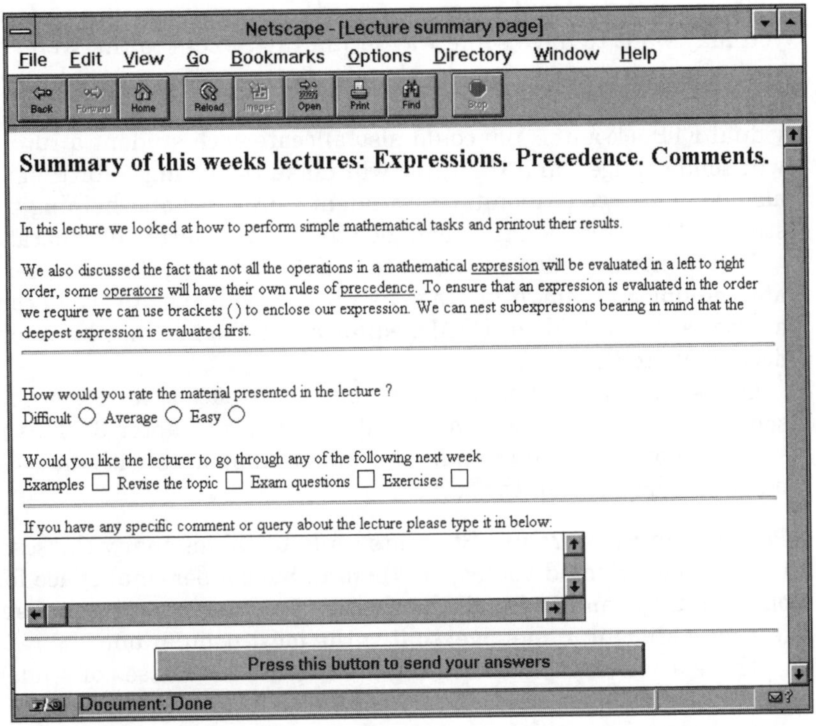

FIGURE 5.2 A lecture summary page with survey.

Creating a Personal Space

As discussed at the beginning of this chapter, a personal space is an area students and staff can use to describe themselves or store personal information. A personal space could involve giving each student and staff member the ability to create their own home page with information about themselves (hobbies, background, interests) and perhaps a photograph. This helps the students relate to each other and to the teaching staff. Students can also use the system to track their personal progress, which is handy if they want to ask a fellow student for help. Students can use their space to provide a list of useful links for the class. Staff members can place contact details and interests on their own home page.

If you are worried about following students' progress through the course, you can ask them to keep an online journal in their personal space detailing their learning activity. The journal may contain a list of tutorials they have completed, interesting links they have found, and comments about various topics. They can also use their personal space to build their own tutorials as part of an assignment.

To create a personal space, you need a server. To prevent "electronic graffiti," you may want to have some way of limiting access to the Web site so that only authorized students can make changes to their own personal space. Usually this is done by allowing the student to upload information to the server using individual FTP accounts. You could also allocate each student a tutor to whom they will send changes, and the tutor will make the changes for them. The tutor can also be in charge of monitoring students' progress and helping them with their studies. This process has a tendency to become overly bureaucratic, though.

If students are allowed to create their own pages, they will need a tool to create and upload them. A package like Netscape Navigator Gold contains not only a browser but a built-in HTML editor and a facility that helps students upload documents to the server.

One simple method of creating a personal space is to give each student a personal message board, such as WWWBoard (see Chapter 6). This message-board system allows students to add and update messages without having to directly upload information to the server.

Personal Space Structure Students could be taking many classes while they are taking yours. Should you expect them to have a personal space for each class or one that they can use for all the classes? One common personal space is the easiest for a student to manage, so it is the most popular one.

There are two ways of creating a structure for classes of students: divide per status or divide per class. Divide per status means that you divide the personal space based, for example, on the course and year of study of the students. (The easiest approach is to divide the students by expected year of graduation.) Divide per class means that each class will have a list of student personal spaces. One way to do it is to divide per status, then create a list of the students in each class and link the names in each class list to a common set of student pages.

The Scrapbook Approach Allowing students to add their own material to their personal spaces will encourage them to keep a scrapbook of their learning experience. That is, they can keep their own notes on their own progress. Annotations are important considerations for many online systems; they allow students to keep their notes online as well and note the links to the pages on which the notes were made. Students can be encouraged to prepare their own tutorials or to provide exercises or questions for other students to answer.

If students are asked to prepare their own tutorials, will they become resentful and think they are doing your work for you? It depends on what the student is used to. In some education systems, it is common for students to give seminars and to be actively involved in teaching each other. In other systems, the student never gets involved in the learning process.

What happens if a student posts inappropriate material or copyrighted information without permission? You can reduce your liability by having students sign an agreement (called an acceptable usage policy; see the CD-ROM for more information) that they will be liable for anything they place on the system.

Web-Based Instruction Structures

This section describes standard tutorial types and discusses a hyperlink structure for each. Each of the tutorials discussed in this section has a corresponding example on the CD-ROM. (Load the file /infodist/tutorial/index.htm into your browser for a menu of choices.). Be advised that these are not hard-and-fast methods of producing tutorials. You can make your tutorial use a combination of tutorial types; for example, one topic might be best expressed using a step-by-step tutorial, another by using a troubleshooting tutorial, and so on. An example introductory page for a tutorial system is shown in Figure 5.3.

As you can see, in the sample page in Figure 5.3, an indication is attached to each tutorial element as to its relevance for the student. This feature helps students avoid missing out on important information or attempting to assimilate

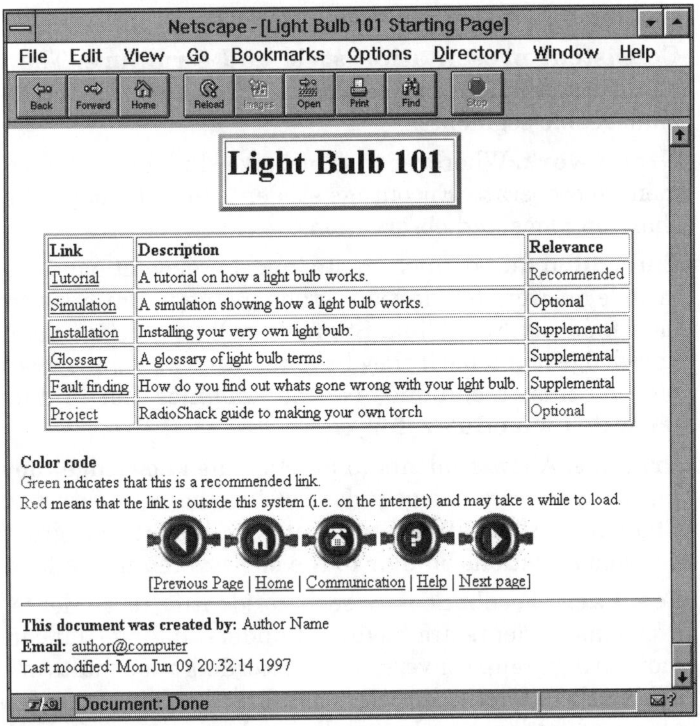

FIGURE 5.3 A tutorial introduction page.

the entire contents of the tutorial system verbatim. You can also use the same material for a variety of instruction structures and offer the students a choice.

Pedagogy In order to fully understand a lesson, students need to be able to form their own ideas about the material and understand the material in their own way. We can say that the student is constructing a *map* of the knowledge presented in the lesson. Instruction that encourages students to construct their own knowledge structure as opposed to learning a specific one is known as constructivist instruction. To set up your Web-based instruction system to facilitate constructivist learning, you should ensure it contains the following elements:

An attention grabber. A section that will gain students' attention. We could use an interesting example of a problem, a multimedia description of the problem—anything that draws students' attention to the problem or subject of the tutorial.

Recall of prior knowledge. A summary that places the lesson in the context of the information students have already learned and provides links to that information for revision.

Consistent presentation style and structure. The presentation should be clear and follow a style that is consistent with the material, divided into manageable segments.

Group work. Wherever possible, give students a chance and the encouragement to cooperate. Encourage students to go through the lessons together or share opinions and observations.

Embedded questions. Create links to relevant pages using statements that include answers to questions students may want answered. This approach is known as the "why" link. Students will be able to expand their background knowledge of a topic if they have relevant why links available. (A good example of this technique is the Engines for Education resource at **www.ils.nwu.edu/~e_for_e/**.)

Practice. Allow students to practice the knowledge they have learned. This can be most conveniently done using the self-testing method discussed in Chapter 7. Alternatively, students can be put into groups and told to solve problem situations similar to the one covered in the lesson.

Feedback. Feedback is needed to identify to students (and the educator) problems students are having in understanding. You can obtain feedback by monitoring group conversations, recording the results of student self-tests, or asking the students directly or indirectly through feedback forms. Students also need feedback on how well they have done (using self-tests, for example) and the relevance of the knowledge they have learned.

Review. Reviewing the lesson is important to consolidate students' knowledge and to outline a context for the subject.

Learning guidance. You can provide students with a general guide as to how to approach the material or the path they can take through the various instructional methods that you use. For example, for a course with lessons, problems, and a real-world example section, show students that they can do the following:

1. Read the lesson.	1. Read the summary.	1. Look at the examples.
2. Do the problems.	2. Look at the examples.	2. Try the problems.
3. If you didn't get full marks, go back to the lesson.	3. Do the problems.	3. Try the lesson pages for answers to wrong problems.
4. Read the summary.	4. If you didn't get full marks, read the lesson.	
5. View the examples.		

Post knowledge. Students often need to put the knowledge learned in the lesson in their own words before they can identify problems they are having in understanding the material or the concepts. Encourage students to write up what they learned in the lesson in their own words or to write their own tutorial.

Setting Up a Standard Start Page At the start of each tutorial, place a standard starting page that may contain:

- An introduction and a brief summary of the tutorial
- A list of tutorial objectives
- What is expected of students and how the tutorial is intended to be used
- The resources the student will need to complete the tutorial (plug-ins, helpers, and the like) and links to guides on how to obtain them and install them
- A guide to completing the tutorial and a rough schedule for doing so, which enables students to allocate enough time to complete the work
- A list of the prerequisites required (and links to those prerequisites)

Creating a Help Facility A help facility can be included as part of the navigation bar. Context-sensitive help can be related to the purpose of a page. For example, the student could need help to do a quiz, so the help link could send them to a quiz help page. It is easier to have every page contain a link to a general help facility that covers all the aspects of the course. Your help page can take the form of a reference tutorial, which we will discuss later.

Parts of a Tutorial A tutorial system can have three distinct parts:

- A lesson area, where the instruction can take place and examples are presented
- A practice area, where students can test their knowledge by answering quizzes or problems (discussed in more detail in Chapter 7)
- A laboratory area, where students can perform "experiments" and try simulations using what they have learned

Creating a Structured Tutorial A structured tutorial simply presents a lesson as a hierarchy of topics, one following the other, like a lecture or a textbook. An example of such a tutorial is shown in Figures 5.4 and 5.5. As you can see from the figures, students are presented with a list of possible topics, some of which have subtopics. The page also includes a navigation bar that students can use to move from one level of topic page to another, backward and forward. Each page in the tutorial has a navigation bar. You can also provide a navigation link that will bring the user from page to page, as in the presentation structure (discussed later in this section).

A structured tutorial need not take advantage of the capabilities of hypertext from a structural viewpoint; in other words, hyperlinks leading to related topics

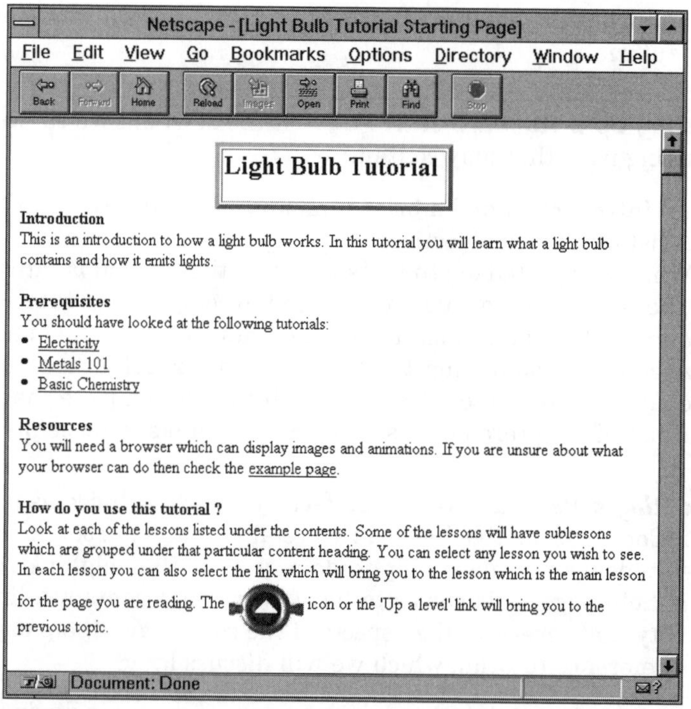

FIGURE 5.4 Page 1 of a structured tutorial.

needn't be embedded in the text, because all you want is a simple training course without providing too many links for the student to get tangled up in. Although not necessarily ideal as an instruction method, because it really only represents an electronic book, this is a straightforward tutorial to construct, and you can add elements, such as animation and sound clips, that improve the learning experience for students. For example, Figure 5.6 shows a page from a tutorial. It consists simply of some text and a picture. We could have included in the text or as part of the picture hyperlinks to other areas of interest, but the current arrangement is sufficient from an instructional point of view.

The student should be told that the material is provided in the form of links to topics and subtopics. They can be informed that they are free to follow any links that they come across and view the material in any order they want. You can also tell them to try the test at the end of the tutorial and revise if necessary.

You should consider some issues regarding structured tutorials. One is information overload. To prevent students being burdened by excessive information, try to keep the information relevant and to the point. Furthermore, shy away from very long pages full of separate topics that would be better off on their own separate page. To make the tutorial more flexible, you can use a system whereby

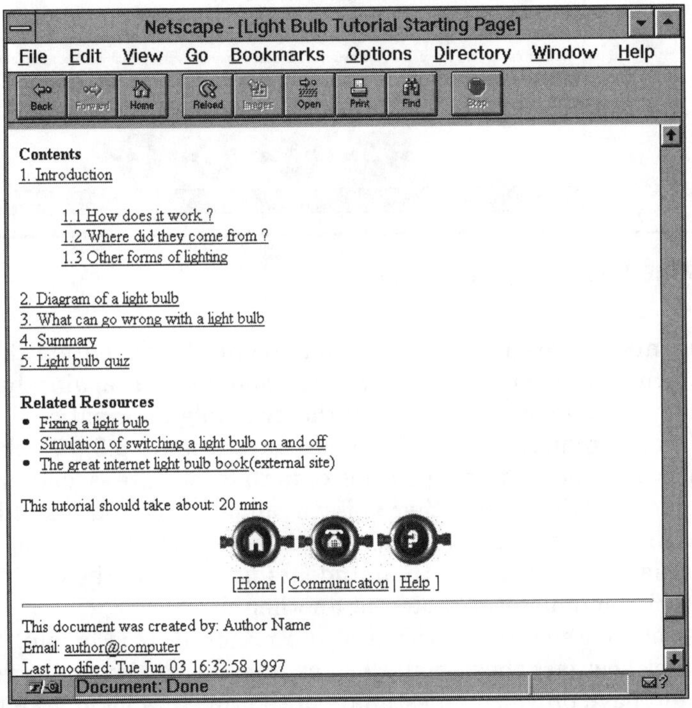

FIGURE 5.5 Page 2 of a structured tutorial.

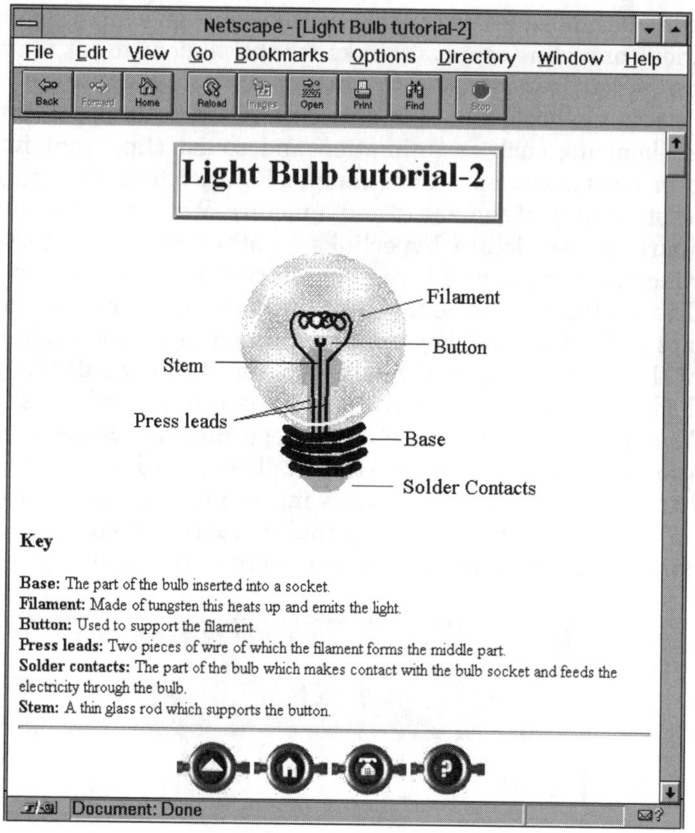

FIGURE 5.6 A simple tutorial page.

students are given a choice of the amount of information that they receive and its form (either in terms of layout or content), but again, there is a danger that students may try and absorb all the available information.

In our example tutorial, the main page (Figure 5.3), which contains the list of topics, is formatted using a color code that indicates whether the topic is recommended viewing or whether it is an outside link You may like to point out outside links for two reasons: one, they may take longer for the student to load; two, you may want to ensure that students understand the distinction between your material and material stored at another site.

Another issue is the pacing of the material. It is helpful to give students an idea of how fast they should be reading the material. On your start page, you should have provided an estimate of the time it should take to complete a tutorial. You can also create a small JavaScript program to time how long a student has spent reading a page. The code of that program is available on the CD-ROM in the directory /infodist/example/timed.htm.

When the student has exceeded a preset time (indicated by the JavaScript timelimit variable), a window will pop up that will ask if the student needs help (see Figure 5.7). If the student responds by clicking OK, a new browser window will open, loaded with the page to which the help variable is set (helpfile.htm in the example).

Other things you can do to help pacing are as follows:

- Have students keep journals of their learning progress in their personal space.
- Have students send you their journals or a message when they have completed a tutorial. You can also ask students to reflect on their journal notes of their progress and send you that as a summary.
- Keep an eye on the server logs to see if the students are accessing the material (see Chapter 10).
- Give students a schedule for the course with specific instructions such as, "You should have done the following tutorials before the end of the month" and "You need to do the following tutorials before you attempt any others."

The structure of the structured tutorial is shown in Figure 5.8. The navigation path that students will be most likely to follow is shown as a dotted line.

A structured tutorial has the following elements:

A standard starting page. The student accesses this page first.

A structure of elements into which the course content is divided. This structure can be hierarchical or linear in nature. In a hierarchical tutorial, a topic has a number of subtopics, and so on. Each topic page has a link to one or more subtopic pages.

A consistent set of links. Each page usually contains a link to the next topic in the tutorial (if there is one) and a link to the tutorial's main page. Each page can also provide a link to a relevant example and a help facility.

The recap page. At the end of the tutorial, students will have a chance to view a summary of what they have learned. The text used for the recap page can contain links to the relevant pages where the element mentioned was discussed in detail.

The test page. This page can test students' grasp of the tutorial material. The test is usually a self-test students can try as many times as they want. (For more information on testing, see Chapter 7.)

Creating an Unstructured Tutorial If you want to provide a tutorial that will allow students to follow links to relevant keywords or words that grab their attention, an unstructured tutorial is a good device. Think of the unstructured tutorial as an encyclopedia; look up a word in an encyclopedia and it will provide

FIGURE 5.7 Window presented to student after preset time elapse.

a list of cross-references you can then proceed to look up, and so on. When applied to an online tutorial, this system allows students to see how a knowledge space is structured. Such a tutorial structure is ideal for testing whether students understand the knowledge structure of a topic; you can give them a task that involves following the correct knowledge trail. As a very simple example, say you asked your students to gather information about Thomas Edison, developer of the light bulb (among other things). You could give them a tutorial on modern electrical appliances, and if they make the connection with Edison, they can follow links that lead them to the history of the light bulb and, finally, to Edison.

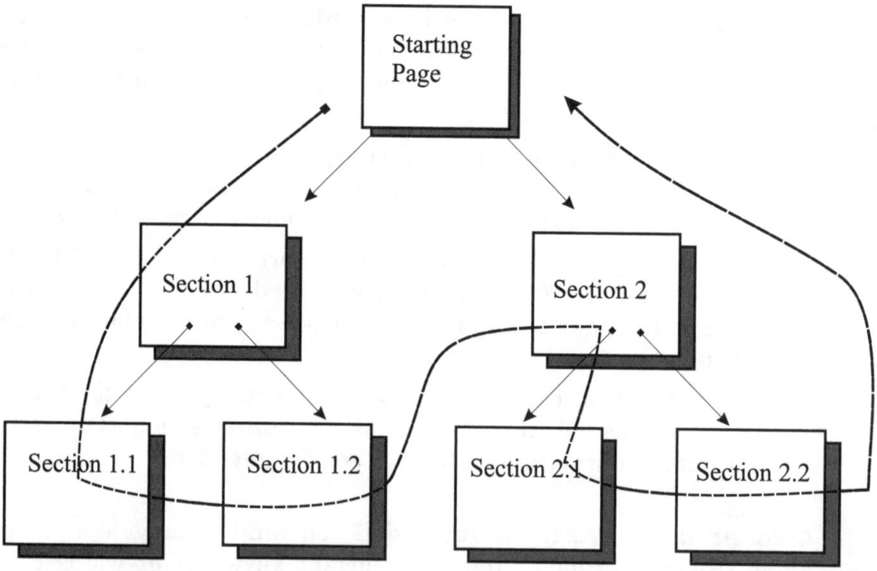

FIGURE 5.8 Diagram of a structured tutorial.

When employing an unstructured tutorial, tell your students that they should use the system to explore the knowledge space of the topic. They can then construct their own knowledge maps of the system, showing how the elements relate (or you can provide one as a reference). They could even be asked to build a structured tutorial from the information in the unstructured tutorial, thus teaching them to categorize and create a hierarchy of information.

The unstructured tutorial begins with a start page leading to a main page that introduces the topic or provides a summary of the topic. A diagram of the structure appears in Figure 5.9. In the topic's description, words act as links to other pages in the tutorial that explain the topic related to the word and provide yet

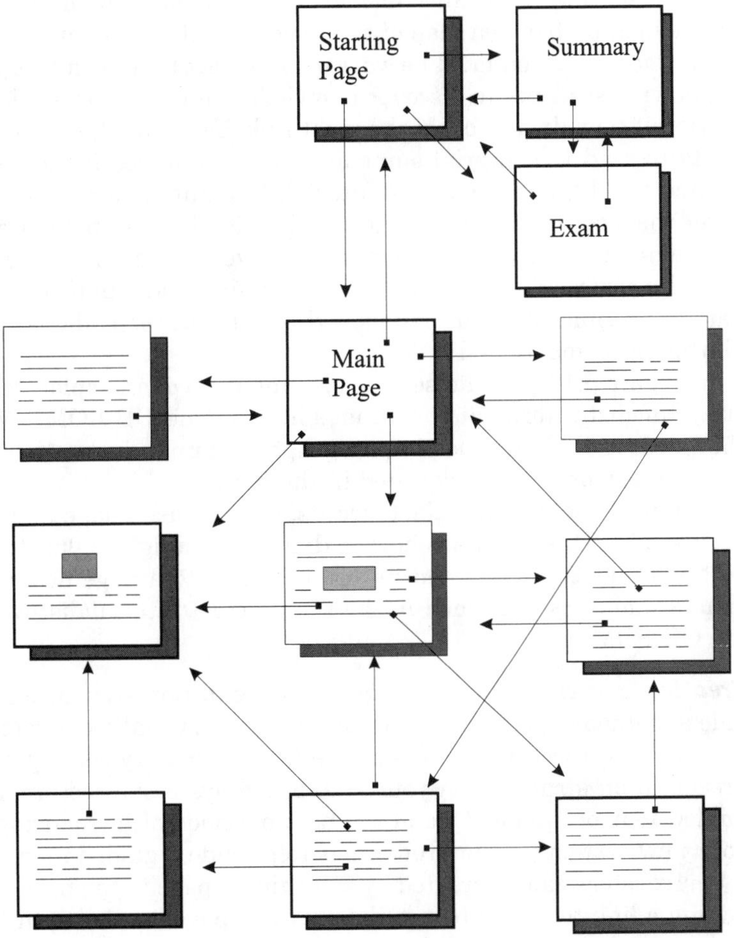

FIGURE 5.9 Structure of an unstructured tutorial.

more links. This sort of tutorial allows students to explore the available knowledge very easily and to see how the pieces of information relate to each other. Each page should have a navigation bar that will enable students to return to the main menu page if they get lost. You could set up the links so that they open a new browser window using the target tag (see the end of this chapter), but if there are many links that may open many new windows, the student's screen may become cluttered with browser windows.

As with a structured tutorial, there are issues to consider when setting up an unstructured tutorial. One we like to call "lost in hyperspace" addresses one of the big problems students can encounter: They can become disoriented. You can overcome this by providing a navigation bar that enables them to return to the start of the tutorial at any time. You can also help them by providing a link on the navigation bar to a map of the hyperlinked documents.

Another thing you must be wary of is the fact that, by its very nature, a method of allowing students to discover knowledge can result in students missing information if they do not follow the right link. You should, therefore, encourage students to read the tutorial summary carefully to see if they encountered pages related to all the topics in the tutorial. In addition, structure your tests so they cover the most material possible, and provide links to the material that students are having trouble with or seem to have overlooked. Providing a link to an index of topics covered in the tutorial also benefits students if they want to look up a particular topic. Students can view this index at the end to see if they remember all the topics mentioned in it.

In Figure 5.10, you can see the opening page of an exploratory light bulb tutorial (/infodist/tutorial/discover/index.htm on the CD-ROM). Note that many of the words in the introductory paragraph contain links to other pages in the tutorial. These words are underlined in the figure.

You need not confine links to words; you can use image maps, too, as shown in Figure 5.11. This example shows a diagram of a light bulb; students can click on sections they are interested in and be taken to a page describing that section. (This example is contained in the file /infodist/tutorial/discover/imgmap.htm on the CD-ROM.)

Creating a Presentation Structure A presentation structure is designed to provide a method of presenting information and is usually delivered in a linear fashion, such as a lectures. You can give a number of types of presentation using a presentation structure on your Web-based system: a lecture, a slide show, or a guided tour of a topic. One of the best methods of introducing the resources in your new system to your students is to provide a guided tour of them.

A slide show can be created by attaching a page to the next page by a link, and adding a link to the bottom of the previous page, as shown in Figure 5.12.

A slide show usually follows a linear structure. Students can proceed to the next slide or return to the previous one using a navigation bar. Most presentation systems come with a navigation bar at the bottom that makes it easier for

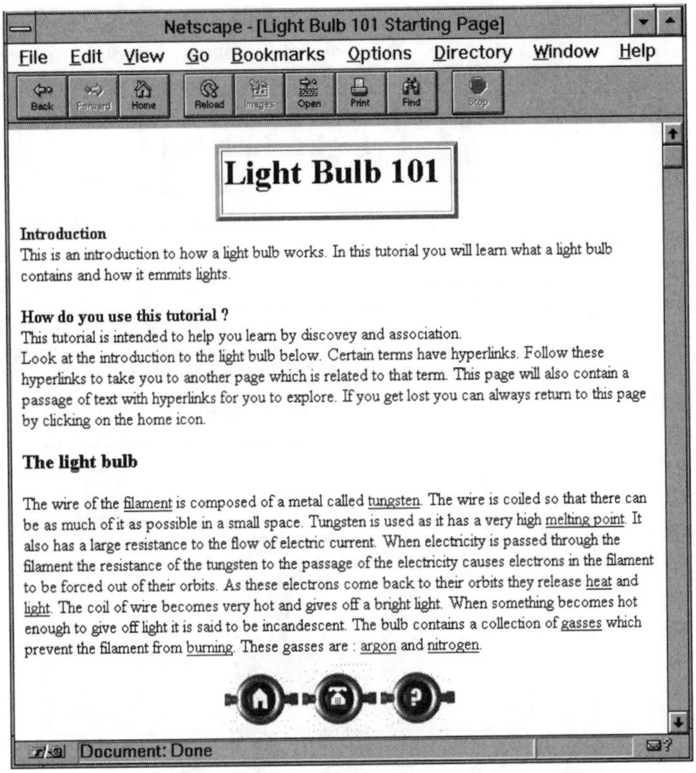

FIGURE 5.10 The text opening page of the light bulb unstructured tutorial.

students to become accustomed to the method of navigation. One of the links for the navigation bar should connect to a feedback facility so that students can send the educator a question about a slide they are having problems with. Links on the navigation bar can also be connected to a sound file that will provide a narration of the slide currently being observed.

Make it clear to the students that your linked pages are intended to be a presentation. Tell them that they are free to move from slide to slide, going backward and forward, taking their time to read and understand each slide. If the pages in the slide show window have links in them as well, clicking on the links will take the students out of your slide show (because they will have lost their navigation links), so you should encourage the students not to touch any of the links in the slide show pages unless told to do so.

You can limit the amount of time a student has to view each slide by placing a <meta> tag in the HEAD section of each HTML page in the slide show. The code shown here loads the page with the URL **machine/slide1.html** 60 seconds after the student's browser loads the page that contains this tag. Note that limiting

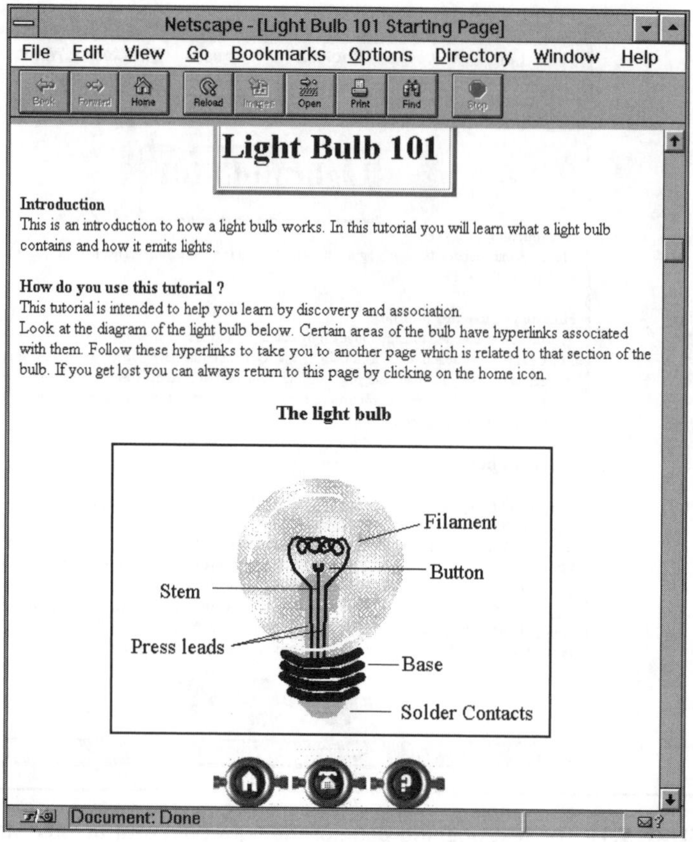

FIGURE 5.11 The image map opening page of the light bulb tutorial.

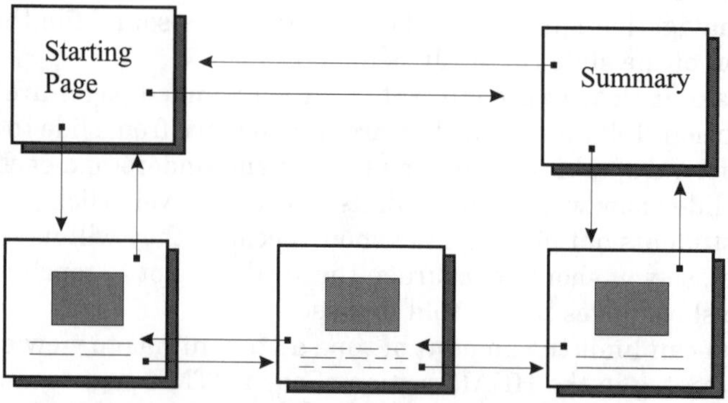

FIGURE 5.12 Using links to create a presentation.

students to a specific viewing time is not a particularly nice thing to do, and this facility is best used for automatic displays or flash-card presentations.

```
<HTML>
<HEAD>
<META HTTP-EQUIV="REFRESH" CONTENT="60;
URL=http://machine/slide1.html">
</HEAD>
.........
</HTML>
```

The previous code calls the file slide1.html after 60 seconds. This means that each page in the slide show should contain a <meta> tag that calls the next page in the slide-show sequence. So, for example, the file called slide1.html would contain the <meta> tag:

```
<META HTTP-EQUIV="REFRESH" CONTENT="60;
URL=http://machine/slide2.html">
```

which would call slide2.html (the next slide in the sequence) after 60 seconds. (An example of this type of presentation is contained on the CD-ROM in the file /infodist/tutorial/present/timed/index.htm.)

Figure 5.13 shows the result of using the JavaScript slide-show program and is on the accompanying CD-ROM (/infodist/tutorial/present/js-slide/index.htm). The slide show uses a frame to display the navigation bar and a frame to display the slide itself. Using this method, you do not have to alter the page forming the slide in any way—simply add its URL to the JavaScript program. It is best to use an absolute URL, one that starts from the root directory. You can add a sound clip or a narration page for each slide. Each time a slide page with an associated commentary is loaded, the student is asked if he or she wants to hear/see the commentary. Pressing the Commentary button will also play the sound clip or display the page associated with that slide; if there is no commentary associated with a slide, pressing Commentary will have no effect. Students can navigate the show by pressing the Next and Previous buttons. The code necessary to customize the slide show is available on the CD-ROM.

Three example slide shows constructed using these methods are included on the CD-ROM; load the file /infodist/tutorial/present/index.htm. An example that uses a navigation bar to show the same slides is given in /infodist/tutorial/present/linked/index.htm. Again, the disadvantage with this presentation approach is that you must alter pages that are being directly included in a slide show to include a suitable navigation bar.

Creating a Choice of Explanation Tutorial A choice of explanation tutorial uses a method in which the student is offered a choice of the explanation or topic they wish to see. They may be offered an outline, a detailed explanation, or an explanation written with their particular needs or experience in mind. In a choice-based

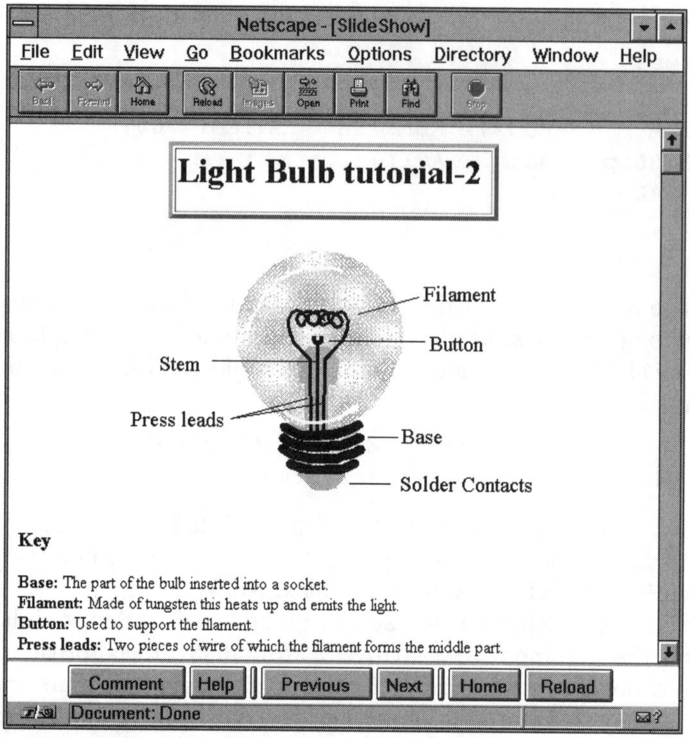

FIGURE 5.13 JavaScript slideshow program in operation.

tutorial, the choices are displayed to students and they pick one. In an adaptive tutorial (discussed later in this chapter), the server or the browser decides what information students should see based on information about each student stored in the server's or the browser's memory. In the case of choice of explanation, students can return and view an alternative explanation if the initial explanation they choose was not satisfactory.

The structure of a choice-driven tutorial can consist of an ordinary page with a link to a page that contains a list of choices of explanations (the choice page in Figure 5.14). The student views any of these explanations and carries on to the next topic or returns to the choice page and views another explanation.

Students should be told to choose an explanation they want to see. They are told that they can make any choice and that there are a number of explanations available to them in order to help them understand the topic better. As in the other tutorials, you can place an exam and a summary at the end of the tutorial.

Using our old friend the light bulb tutorial example, we provide a choice-driven tutorial (/infodist/tutorial/choice/index.htm) on the CD-ROM. The starting

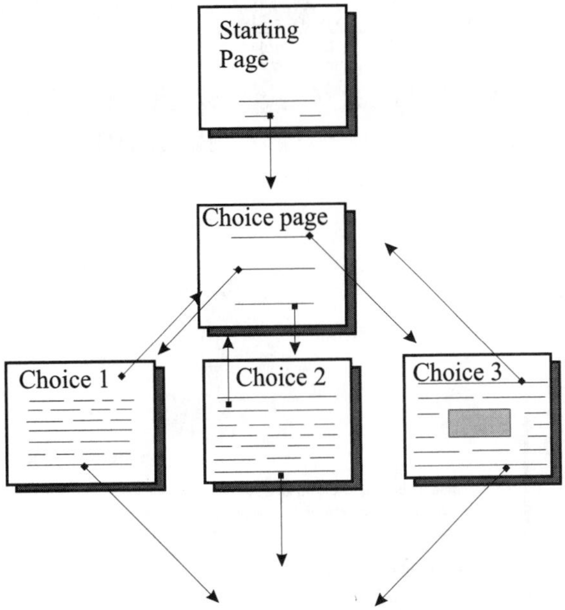

FIGURE 5.14 The choice of explanation tutorial structure.

page and the choice page for this tutorial are shown merged in Figure 5.15 so you can get an idea of their contents.

Creating Adaptive Tutorials An adaptive tutorial is one that picks the material to display based on information about the student or a profile. You can establish a profile of students at the beginning of the tutorial using the JavaScript program supplied on the CD-ROM and use JavaScript programs contained in other pages to automatically direct them to a relevant page. This is similar in nature to the choice of explanation tutorial except the student has no idea that there are other explanations available. There are a number of possibilities for collecting information about the type of tutorial the student will get. You could give the student a quiz and set the level of the tutorial accordingly or you could give the student a choice of tutorial.

Why not just create a different tutorial for each student group? If you were using an adaptive tutorial just to make an initial choice, this might make sense, but the real power of an adaptive tutorial is that you can cause the student's profile to be changed at any stage in the tutorial. So, for example, if the student is having difficulty with an explanation, you can assume he or she was too ambitious in an initial selection and use a JavaScript program to place the student at a lower level to receive simpler explanations.

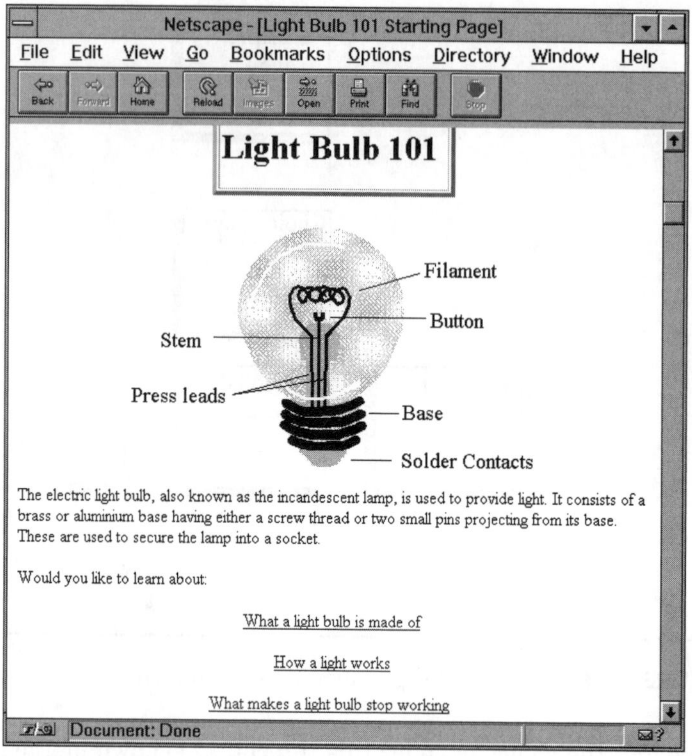

FIGURE 5.15 A sample choice-driven tutorial.

Explain to the students that the system will ascertain what to put in their tutorials. They should be told how either filling out the quiz or selecting a preference will mean that they may see a different presentation of the same course. Students should be encouraged not to select a level that is too high for them if they have a choice of the level at which the tutorial is aimed (beginner, average, expert).

The structure of an adaptive tutorial is shown in Figure 5.16. The first page collects information that will allow a JavaScript program to make choices about the student. This can be done by asking students to select the type of presentation that would appeal to them or to give them a test that places each of them in a category.

Once students have selected their areas of interest or completed a quiz, they move on to an action page that makes the choice for them automatically. This page then passes students on to an appropriate page without them selecting any links.

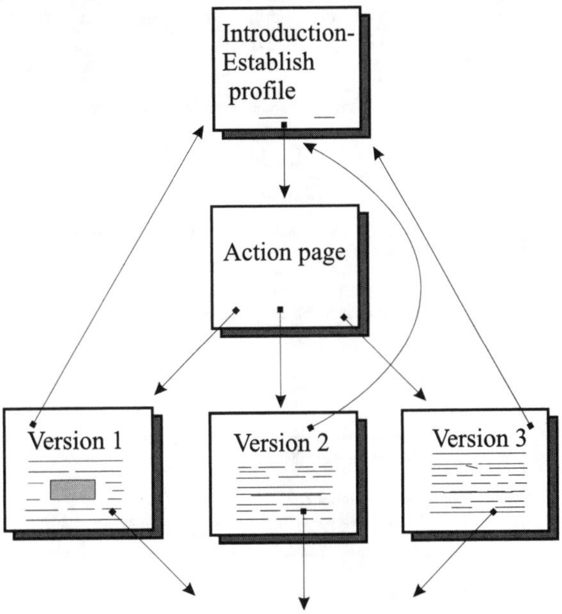

FIGURE 5.16 The adaptive tutorial structure.

The appropriate page could take a number of forms: You could set up your adaptive tutorial so that it asks students what form of page layout they would like (heavily graphical, perhaps) or whether they would like their pages in a different language. Or the action page could automatically direct students to different forms of an explanation.

In the structure diagram in Figure 5.16, you can see that you must set the links in the pages shown to the students to point back to the preceding page. This is necessary because if your links point back to the action page, the action page will reload the same page again. If the page before the action page is another set of pages, you must establish the correct links between versions of the tutorial—for instance, beginners' page 1-2 must have a link that will bring it to beginners' page 1-1.

An example of the page displayed at the start of this tutorial is shown in Figure 5.17.

Information about the student is stored in the form of a cookie, which is a piece of information stored by the browser and that can be retrieved from the browser by a CGI or JavaScript program. There are different methods of setting your browser's cookies. For example, the cookies could have been set as the result of an exam or students could have set the cookies themselves. Note that when using cookies, students must use their own copy of the browser to maintain the cookie

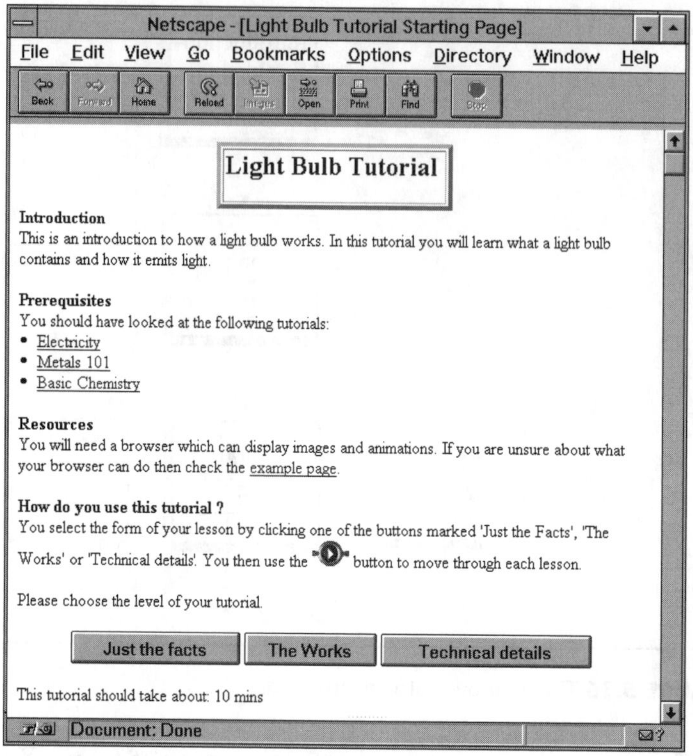

FIGURE 5.17 A level selection page.

information. When students exit their browsers, the information about them acquired using the establish profile page will not be present when they return.

Another point to watch about cookies is that it is possible to disable cookies in some browsers, so the programs given will not be able to work. If your students use this type of tutorial, you should inform them that they need to enable cookies on their browsers.

The piece of JavaScript below implements the action page. It will ascertain the level of the tutorial. (It knows what tutorial it is dealing with because the tutorial name is in the cookie TutorialName.) It will then open one of three pages depending on the value of the cookie for that tutorial. If the value is 1 (the student selected "beginner"), it loads the URL topic1-1.htm. If the value is 2 (the student selected "intermediate"), it loads the URL topic1-2.htm, and so on.

```
<html>
<script LANGUAGE="JavaScript">
```

```
// The name of the tutorial
var TutorialName="Tut1";
var Choices = new Array();

// The locations which match the corresponding choice
Choices[1] = "topic1-1.htm";
Choices[2] = "topic1-2.htm";
Choices[3] = "topic1-3.htm";

function GetCookie(name) {
   var arg = name + "=";
   var arglen = arg.length;
   var cookielen = document.cookie.length;
   var count = 0;
   var found=false;
   while (count <  cookielen)
      {
      var offset = count + arglen;
      if (document.cookie.substring(count, offset) == arg)
       found=true;
      count = document.cookie.indexOf(" ", count) + 1;
      if (count == 0) break;
      }
    if (found)
     {
     var endstr = document.cookie.indexOf (";", offset);
     if (endstr == -1)
      endstr = document.cookie.length;
      return unescape(document.cookie.substring(offset, end-
str));
     }

}

location=Choices[GetCookie(TutorialName)];
</script>
</html>
```

It is best to name the pages students will be shown based on their initial choices. For example, in the JavaScript example above we named the files topic1-1.htm for the beginner, topic1-2.htm for the intermediate student, and topic1-3.htm for the advanced student. You can place an Establish Profile page at different points in the tutorial to enable students to change their profiles.

Creating How-To Tutorials A how-to tutorial guides students though the process of performing some specific task (like installing a light bulb). Therefore, the structure is usually linear, but it isn't always, because there may be slight diversions to other tutorials (a troubleshooting tutorial, for instance) along the way.

In this type of tutorial, students are told to follow the system from one step to another. You can provide a feedback link so that students can indicate if there is a problem with an explanation in the tutorial.

If you are showing students how to use a program, you can capture parts of a screen to use as illustrations. You can then use the pictures as is or animate them using a GIF animation utility. An alternative is to use one of the following utilities:

- Lotus ScreenCam (**www.lotus.com/screencam/**) for Windows 95 allows you to record a series of actions on screen (as though you were videotaping what you were clicking on and typing) and enables students to view the "video" of your actions. You are required to buy the application to make these "videos," but the utility to view them is available as a browser plug-in (for Windows only). Alternatively, you can translate your ScreenCam video into an AVI format video file.
- Microsoft's Camcorder97 (**www.microsoft.com/office/office97/camcorder/**) also allows recording of "videos" of screen actions. However, you can save the videos only in an executable file for Windows 95/NT or as an AVI format video file.
- Pedagoguery Software produces a program called Gif.gIf.giF for the Macintosh and Windows platforms (**www.cafe.net/peda/ggg/**). The program allows you to create animated GIFs of sequences of actions on screen. You can designate an area of the screen for capture and save these captures as an animated GIF.

Figure 5.18 shows the linear structure of a how-to tutorial. You could combine it with a choice of explanation structure to take account of situations in which students are starting from different points You could also combine it with a reference structure to facilitate students who want to look up a term that they are unsure of. You can even incorporate a troubleshooting guide for students who run into problems.

There is a how-to tutorial on the CD-ROM showing installation of a light bulb (/infodist/tutorial/howto/index.htm). Figure 5.19 shows the first page from that tutorial.

Creating Supervised Tutorials A supervised tutorial is one students undertake with the help of a tutor with whom they are in communication. Various types of tutorial activity are possible. For example, a tutor can send the student to a certain Web page, and a tutor can monitor the student's actions there. Similarly, a student can monitor the actions of a tutor, thereby learning by example. A student can start a communication session with a tutor to discuss a page or other relevant topics. The tutor can assign a list of pages for the student to read.

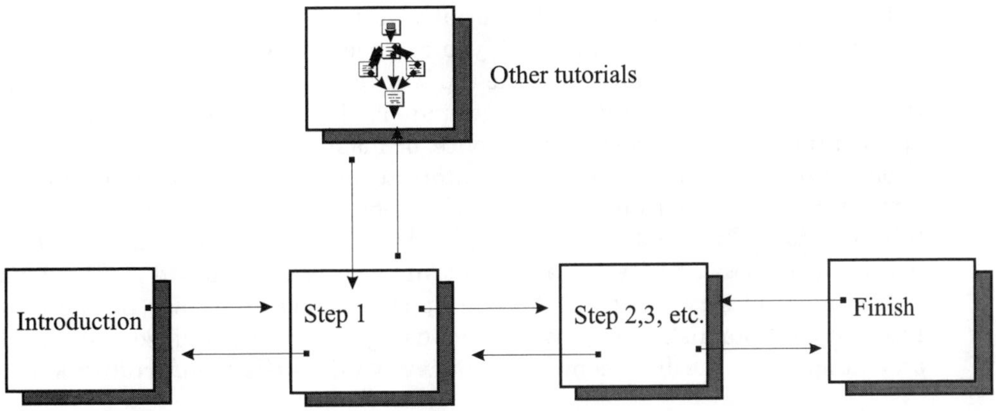

FIGURE 5.18 The structure of a how-to tutorial.

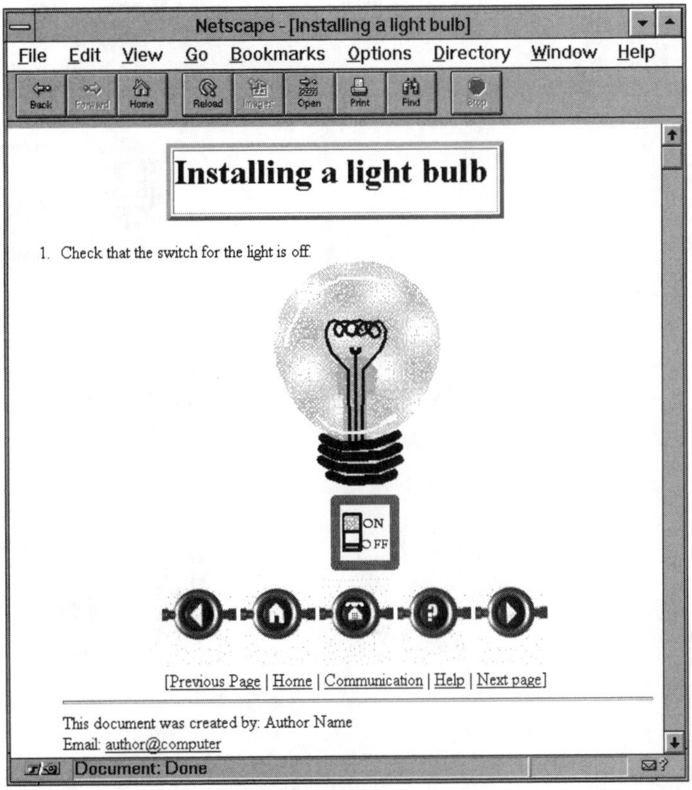

FIGURE 5.19 A sample page from a how-to tutorial.

The structure of a supervised tutorial will vary depending on the system of supervision you use. In Figure 5.20, you can see two possible structures. In the directed tutorial, the tutor sends the student to a page. In an observed tutorial, the tutor observes the student's page and can intervene to point out relevant parts of the page, give the student advice, or make suggestions.

Software is available that allows tutors to take remote control of students' computers to demonstrate a sequence of actions or allow students to observe the tutor's actions. Table 5.2 shows a list of such software. Communication software to establish a session between a student and a tutor is discussed in Chapter 6.

A number of services watch for the appearance of particular people on the Internet and establish contact with them using text, voice, or video systems. (For an example, see the ICQ home page at **www.mirabilis.com/products.html**.)

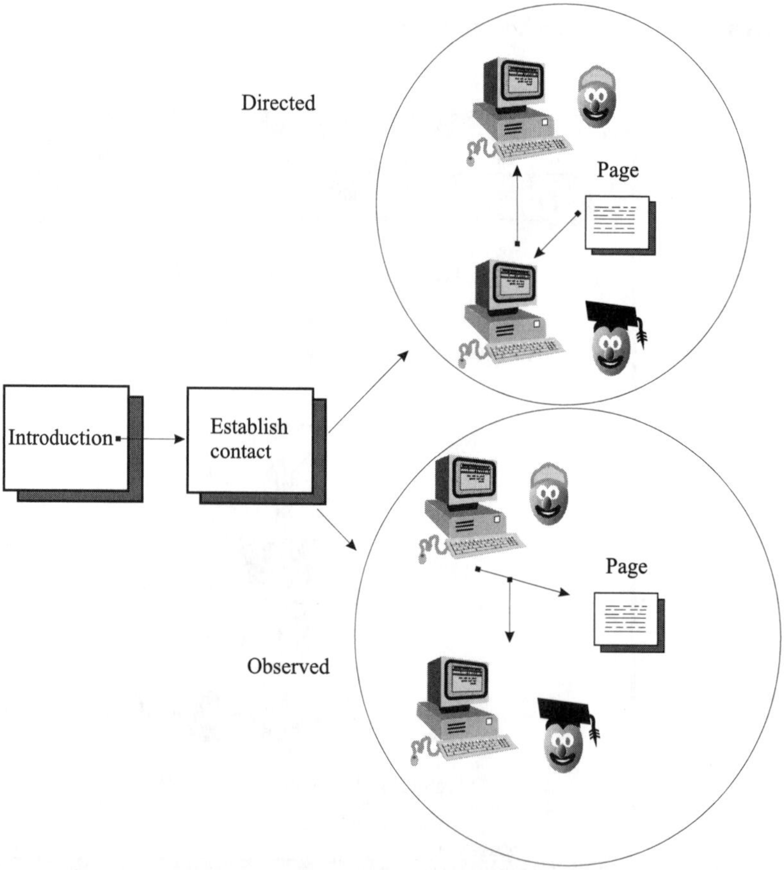

FIGURE 5.20 Supervision structures.

Table 5.2 Software for Remote Tutors

Name of Package	*Platform*	*Location*
Remotely Possible	NT and Windows	www.avalan.com/
Look@Me	Windows and Macintosh (Netscape plug-in)	www.farallon.com/www/look/ldownload.html
DoubleVision	X Windows-based UNIX systems	www.maxtech.com/

Such a service allows tutor to wait for their students to log on and establish a connection with them.

Creating Knowledge-Driven Tutorials A knowledge-driven tutorial is one that operates by asking students a question at the end of the presentation of a topic. Selecting the correct answer will bring students to the next page of the tutorial.

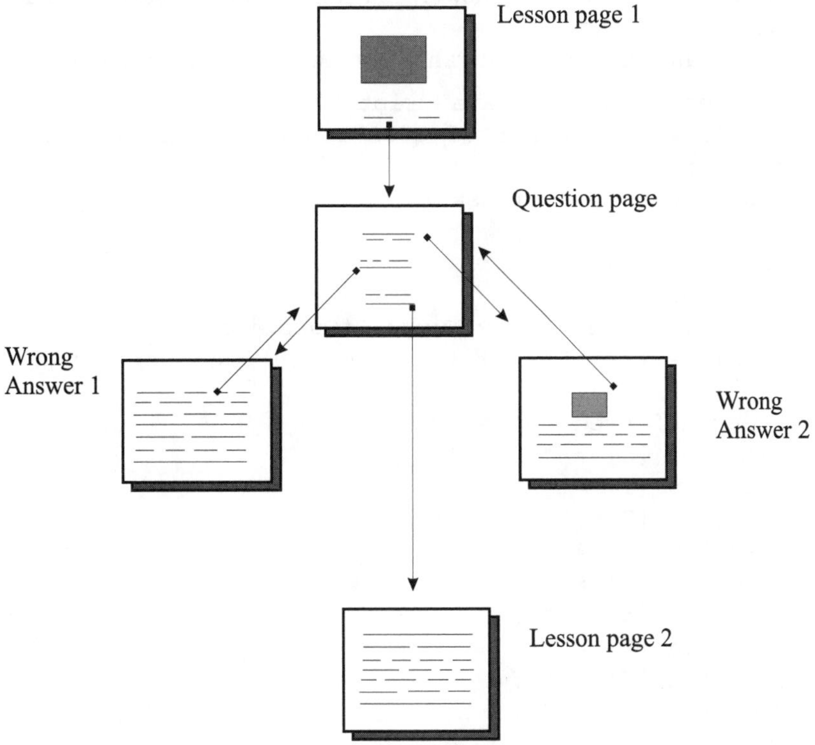

FIGURE 5.21 Progress-by-question structure.

In our example structure shown in Figure 5.21, the questions are asked on a separate question page that immediately follows the tutorial page. Students will select the link for the next page and be brought to the question page. The questions usually take the form of links to pages that contain responses to students' answers. For example, you could have three possible answers to a question leading to three different pages. Two answers could be links to pages that say that the answer was incorrect and give an explanation of why it was incorrect. Students who reach these pages are directed to try again and would follow a link back to the page with the questions. This is not a particularly reliable mechanism for preventing students from proceeding unless they know the right answer, but is useful to encourage students to read the lesson more carefully.

We use simple hypertext links as an answering mechanism; if you want to build in a more advanced set of questions, such as multiple choice or fill-in-the-blanks, see Chapter 7. (Chapter 7 also discusses an advanced system, known as a gateway, that prevents students from proceeding until they answer a series of questions correctly.)

In the knowledge-driven system, students can keep pressing the answer links until they get the right answer. You can discourage such behavior by using random question pages.

You can ask a questions randomly using the following piece of JavaScript:

```
<script LANGUAGE="JavaScript">
// Place the number of question pages the student can be
given here
var NumberOfQuestions=3;

var time=new Date();
var Random;
Question = new Array(NumberOfQuestions);
// Place the URLs of the question pages that the student can
be
// transferred to here
Question [0] = "1.htm";
Question [1] = "2.htm";
Question [2] = "3.htm";
Question [3] = "";
Question [4] = "";
Question [5] = "";
Question [6] = "";
Question [7] = "";
Question [8] = "";
Question [9] = "";
Random=(time.getSeconds())%10;
location=Question[Random%NumberOfQuestions];
```

```
</script>
```

To customize the script, change the variable NumberOfQuestions to the number of question pages you want to choose from. Place the URL for each question page in a corresponding Question variable. In our example, the script makes a random selection between three question pages, 1.htm, 2.htm, and 3.htm.

Use the JavaScript for selecting a random question page as follows: Get your topic page to point to a page that contains the script. This script then automatically passes students on to one of the question pages (1.htm, 2.htm, 3.htm). In each question page, place a link that enables students to get back to the lesson page; if they go back to the page that contains the JavaScript, they will be sent to a new random question page. Figure 5.22 gives a representation of how this system needs to work. You can also look at the example on the CD-ROM (/infodist/tutorial/knowled/random/index.htm).

The structure of a knowledge-based system is very much related to the questions asked. The student proceeds from a topic page to an answer page; usually a wrong answer page provides a link back to the topic page, but you can also provide a link back to the prerequisites given in the starting page so that students have a chance to do some basic revision before trying again.

An example of a plain knowledge-driven tutorial using image maps as well as hypertext links can be found on the CD-ROM in the directory /infodist/tutorial/knowled/index.htm. Figures 5.23 and 5.24 show two pages from one of the knowledge-driven tutorials in which students are asked to select the correct text answer and the right part of the light bulb before they can proceed.

Creating a Troubleshooting Guide A troubleshooting guide usually consists of a set of questions representing common problems and actions to perform in response to those questions. One example of a such a guide is the troubleshooting section of a car manual, which takes the form of a list of questions and procedures (if your car won't start, check that it contains sufficient fuel, that the battery isn't dead, and so on). A troubleshooting guide is ideal for a hypertext implementation because you can provide links to relevant pages to match the answers to the questions students ask.

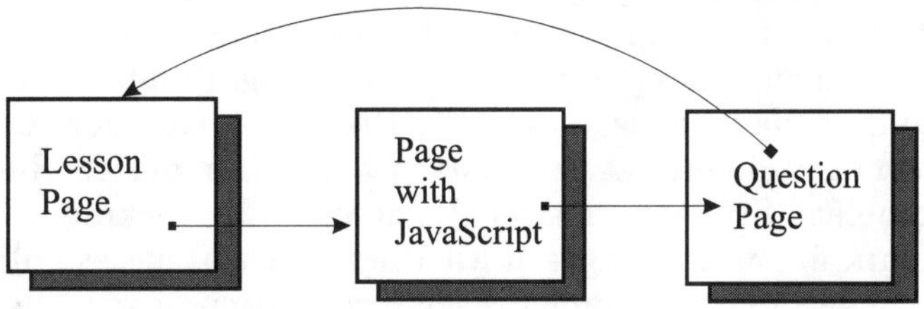

FIGURE 5.22 The structure of a random page selector.

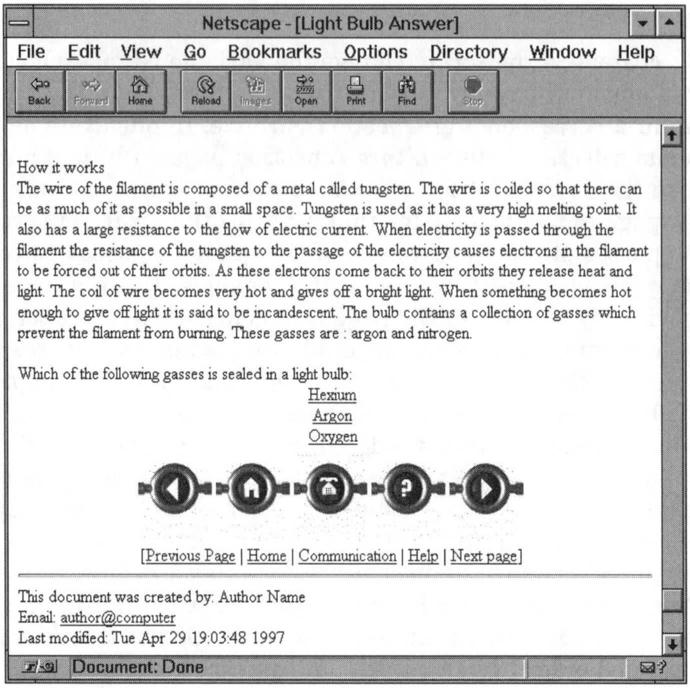

FIGURE 5.23 A text-based question page.

A troubleshooting guide may need to provide links to other sections of the system. For instance, if students find themselves in a situation where they need to follow a step-by-step guide, you can place TARGET="NEW" (see the code at the end of this chapter) inside a reference to a link to instruct the browser to open a new browser window and load the new link into it. This is done to prevent the student from getting lost after completing a step-by-step guide or another tutorial.

Figure 5.25 shows the typical structure of a troubleshooting guide. (You'll find a troubleshooting guide on the CD-ROM in the file /infodist/tutorial/trouble/index.htm.) The start page or introduction to the guide should consist of a series of conditions that apply, such as the requirement for a particular type of computer or, in our example, a specific type of light bulb. Once students have established that the guide is suitable for them, they can move on to the next page.

Each subsequent page consists of a question designed to narrow the area of the problem. Students answer the question by clicking on an appropriate link. Students follow the pages until they reach a successful solution or there is nothing else to try. Students reach a resolution page if they obtain a successful solution or a failure page if a resolution to the problem could not be found. The

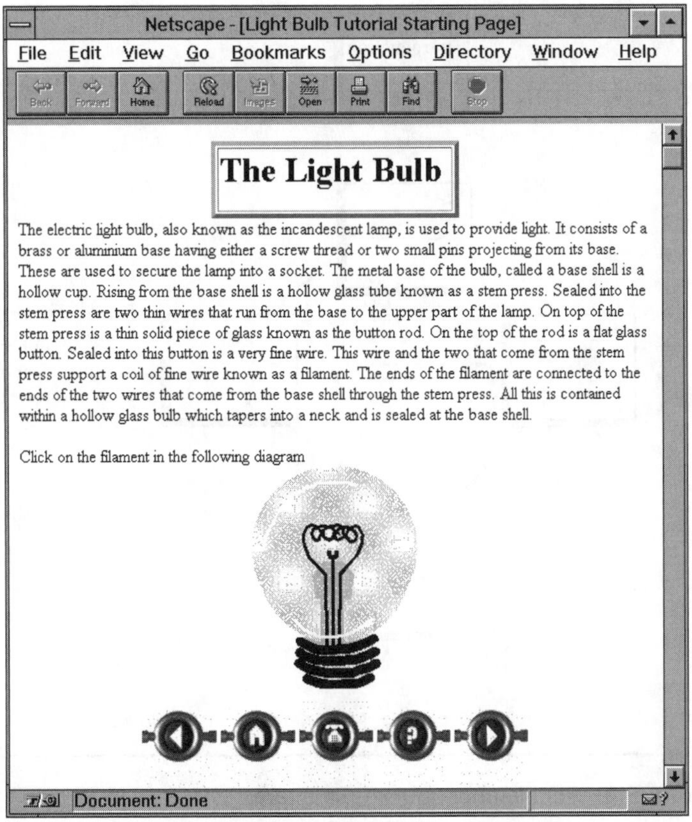

FIGURE 5.24 An image map-based question page.

failure page should contain contact information for someone who may be able to solve the problem. Make the contact information appropriate; for example, if students cannot configure their e-mail connections, do not provide an e-mail address as the method of contact. This contact information should be included on the failure page as opposed to the start page; otherwise, students tend to be reluctant to try and go through a problem-solving process at all.

Creating Simulations In a simulation or a laboratory tutorial, you can give the student a chance to interact with something. It could be a very simple interaction, such as selecting a link representing an action, which causes the link to load a picture or a video of an experiment after the corresponding action has been performed. Alternatively, you can write complicated simulations and laboratories using languages like Java.

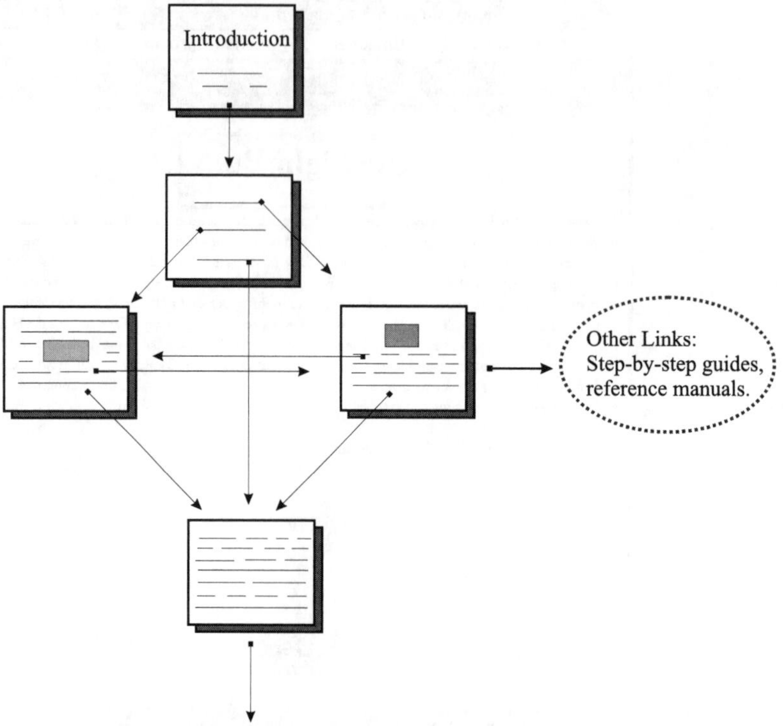

FIGURE 5.25 Troubleshooting guide structure.

A simulation should be relevant to the topic you are trying to teach the student. There is no point in providing an entertaining experience if the student does not learn anything.

Simulations can also be used to draw students into a discussion by getting them to record and discuss their predictions. This process turns students into active observers of the simulation's outcome; they make a commitment to a certain result. It also helps students build a mental model of the process as they question how their predictions differed from or agreed with the result of the simulation. The results can be discussed by a discussion group, allowing students to explore other students' perspectives.

One other thing you should do is to make clear the simulation's limitations and assumptions beforehand to prevent misconceptions.

The structure of a simulation could be similar to that of a choice of explanation tutorial because various options are presented for the student to try, and the simulation builds on each step. A troubleshooting type of structure is more appropriate for a "looser" type of simulation or an experiment in which students could return to previous pages based on certain conditions. For example, in a chemistry experiment, students could have a choice of the amount of a particular chemical to add to a solution. Their choices will have an impact on later choices they make.

In the light bulb simulation on the CD-ROM (/infodist/tutorial/simulate/on.htm), we show how two pictures can be used to simulate switching a light bulb on and off. The two pictures are image maps, with the section representing the switch linked to the corresponding HTML file. So, for example, if students click on the switch part of an image of an unlighted bulb, a page containing a lit bulb will be loaded and vice versa. Figure 5.26 shows how the page appears to the student.

Creating a Reference Guide A reference guide is usually a simple list of terms students may find useful. It can consist of a menu of terms that provides links to a more complete description of terms, either on the same page or a different page. It is customary to put the referenced elements all on the same page unless it makes the page too large, as might be true if it contains an image for each reference.

A reference guide usually consists of a single page with a main menu and a menu of terms. An illustration of a reference structure is shown in Figure 5.27.

The glossary HTML page creates two frames side by side and a frame on top that holds instructions. (A template for a glossary is supplied on the CD-ROM in the file /infodist/tutorial/refer/gloss.htm; an example is shown in Figure 5.28.) The left frame contains letters of the alphabet, which, if clicked on, will cause the main page to go to the section indicated by that letter. This is one of the few

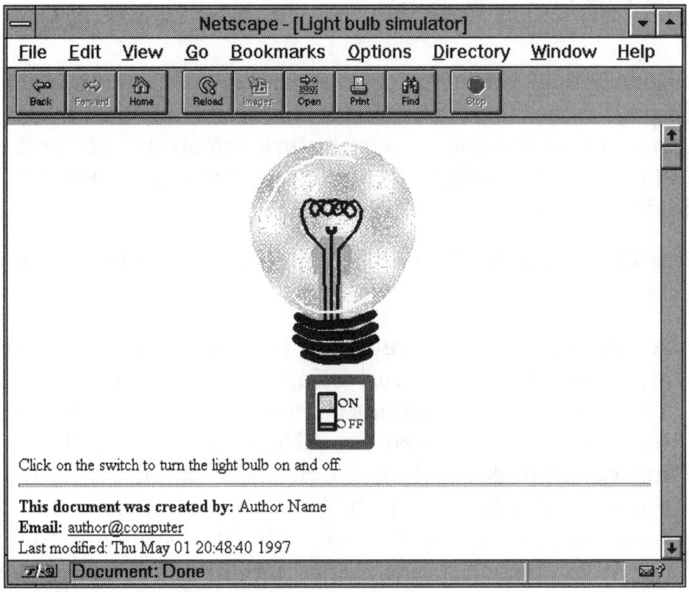

FIGURE 5.26 The light bulb simulation.

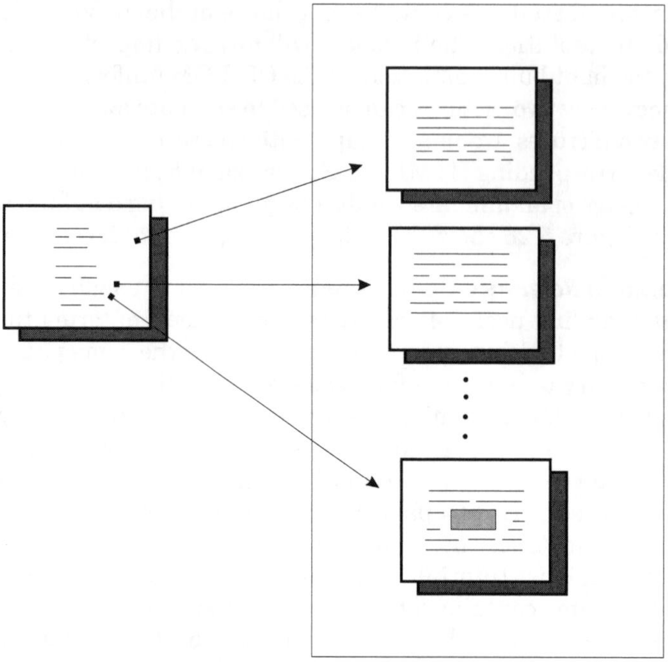

FIGURE 5.27 A reference structure.

appropriate uses of frames; because the alphabetical list does not move when the main page moves to the relevant section. You can also implement a glossary without frames (see the file /infodist/tutorial/refer/anchor.htm on the CD-ROM, and the file /infodist/tutorial/refer/index.htm for a description of the glossaries with and without frames.)

A Few More Details Here are a few more things to consider when setting up a tutorial:

> **Do students have to read the lesson all in one session?** Stopping in the middle of a lesson and restarting later is an important consideration if students have time restrictions on using the system. You can encourage students to use the bookmark feature of Netscape to mark their place in a tutorial so they can go back to it later on. Students can mark their position at any point in the tutorial by adding the current page to their list of bookmarks. If students are sharing a computer with other students, they should be asked to keep their personal bookmarks separate to avoid confusion. Students can save their own personal bookmarks on floppy disks after each session and reload them when they want to restart from where they left off. Alternatively,

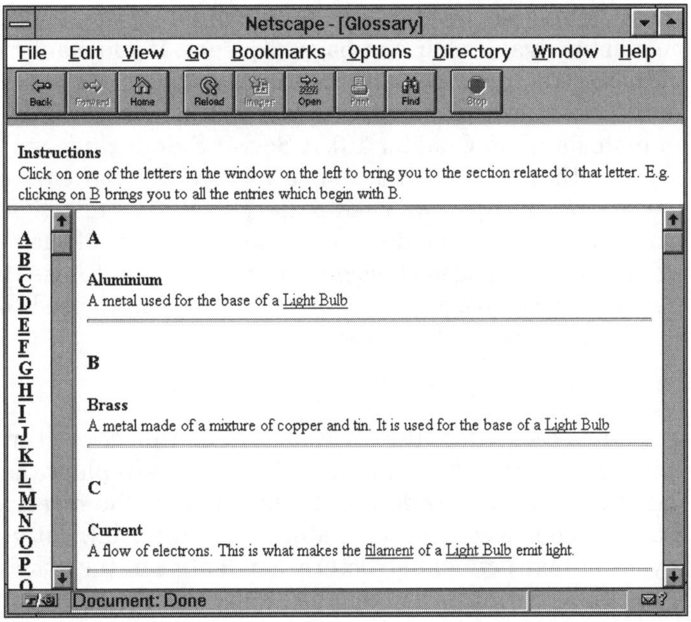

FIGURE 5.28 A glossary page.

they could be encouraged to place their bookmarks in their personal space. Bookmarks can also be kept for URLs students find of use, such as related sites and summaries.

Resource centers. Resource centers can either contain programs students will find useful, such as helper applications, or files that they can download for viewing. Be careful that files you make available for downloading are in a format usable by all the platforms your students have access to. For example, some files created with a Macintosh application may not be viewable by a PC. Be careful also when making Macintosh files available for downloading, because each Macintosh file really consists of two parts, a data fork and a resource fork. If you FTP a Macintosh file directly from one computer to another, you lose the resource fork, which identifies the application that created the file. Therefore, make sure that you use the binhex utility (available with most Macintosh archivers) on any Macintosh file before downloading it or put the Macintosh file in a format such as HTML or GIF that can be more easily transported.

Varying the instructional structure. In this chapter, we examined a number of structures that you can use to present material to your students. All of these structures have their own individual merits, and most have their own custom navigation bar and page sequence. If you want to use more than one of these structures for your material but do not want to have to cut and paste multiple copies of the material, you can use Server Side Includes (discussed in more detail in Chapter 10). A Server Side Include will allow you to create a file with your material and to include the contents of that file in other pages. For example, we used material relating to a light bulb in the structured tutorial and the discovery tutorial. Copies of the material were placed in the relevant pages of each of these tutorials. To use the same source files for different instructional structures, you simply need to prepare your page as usual and insert the directive:

```
<!--#include file="path/page.html"-->
```

where path is the path to the file called page.html. Every time the page with this directive is requested from a server, the server will place the contents of the file indicated (page.html) inside the document with the directive. This means you need only keep one copy of the material in page.html, but you can use it in several types of instructional structure. Students can take their pick of the type of structure they are interested in, and you need only update one file if you need to make changes.

RELATED TOPICS

Here we explore a few additional topics related to information distribution systems.

Are Students Using It?

The easiest way to check if students are using the information and their patterns of usage is to use the logs kept by the server to provide summaries of the requests made by students' browsers. Chapter 10 shows some utilities that can indicate the number of times a page has been accessed; Chapter 8 describes a utility called Follow that allows you to track the pattern of access of students, such as the order of pages visited. If each student has his or her own personal account on the server, these utilities can also be used to track pages each student has accessed.

What can you do if students are not using the system? First, you need to examine the reason. Are they having trouble accessing computers or the network? Do they understand how to use the equipment and the browser? Do they view the system as offering any resource value or advantage? What is their attitude to the system? Do they understand that the system is there to help them and how it is to be used? Is the system easy to use?

You can do a number of things to encourage students to use your system:

- Explain how the system should be used and what advantages the system will bring to students.
- Release material exclusively over the Web. Place handouts, solutions, and the like on the Web only so that students are "coerced" into using the system.
- Release material at regular intervals. Place new material on the system once or twice a week. This will encourage students to access the system to check for new material.
- Build a guided tour of the components and pages that you think students should see, and place this guided tour at the start of your system.
- Award marks based on use of the system. Using logs, you can estimate how extensively each student uses the system and award marks accordingly. This is not a particularly appetizing approach, because it amounts to bribing students to use the system, and the students in turn will start to see the system as just another hurdle or "mark earner" as opposed to a learning facility.
- Start a treasure hunt. As students hunt to find an answer to a problem located somewhere on the information distribution system.
- Actively solicit feedback. Ask students what they would like to see or what they think of the system. Students can give feedback anonymously (see Chapter 6) or by using formal evaluation techniques.
- Have students write their own tutorials or to rewrite a tutorial in their own words. This is a useful exercise because it is difficult to explain something unless you really understand it.
- Give students exercises based on their online tutorials.
- Give a "tip of the week" online.
- Liven up your system by adding a daily joke to the home page, a gentle inducement to students to log in each day. This requires minimum effort; large libraries of jokes are available on the Internet.

Sometimes it is tempting to try to continuously improve the presentation of the information, to use fancier graphics, interesting backgrounds, and Java gimmicks. This may engage students' attention temporarily, but remember that educational content should be the primary focus of your development effort, and constantly developing a new look for your presentation will have no educational impact on students. Design your system from the start to be clear enough for students to use *and* to be visually attractive, as discussed in Chapter 3.

Avoiding Information Overload

Sometimes when an educator makes the effort to provide a large amount of resources for students, students treat the resources with equal priority and attempt to read every referenced or online resource, even trying to learn them verbatim or printing them all. This tendency, known as information overload, can cause students trouble distinguishing between what is necessary and what is useful.

One way of dealing with this problem is to show the minimum amount of material on a page and provide links to expansions on other pages. This technique is known as providing a hub for basic information and a knowledge wheel for expansion. If you are providing a great deal of supplementary material, you can reassure students by providing them with a list of the material that is truly essential or mark the essential material in some way, such as with an asterisk or a different color. In our example information distribution system in Figure 5.3, we showed a presentation method that listed the importance of each link.

Avoiding the "Lost in Hyperspace" Syndrome

To prevent your students from getting lost among the series of hyperlinks that make up your Web system, you can do a number of things. The easiest is to put all your material into one document; therefore, no one can get lost. For reasons we've discussed, this is not really a desirable thing to do, so the next best option is to ensure that students can navigate the structure of your presentation easily. This can be facilitated by placing a navigation bar in each page that allows students to go to certain predefined places in the structure of the group of documents that they are reading. It is also helpful to give a clear title for each page and provide a map of the structure of the system for the reader.

One other thing you can do is add TARGET="name" in your link—for example:

```
<a href="doc.html" TARGET="window1"> More Information</a>
```

The TARGET="name" method will open a new browser window (called name) and load the information specified in that link (the file doc.html in the example) into that browser window. You can open a new browser for each link—all you need to do is change the name of the window you want to open. For example, if you place another link on the same page as the link above, you could give it the reference

```
<a href="doc.html" TARGET="window2"> Even More
Information</a>)
```

Your original window stays intact, leaving you with a reference point to manage navigation. Note that there is a maximum number of browser windows that can be open at any one time (the number depends on the memory available), so it is best to open new windows sparingly. If you want your new window to be usable by several links, keep the same window name. For instance, in our two examples, you would use TARGET="window1" for both, meaning that a new window would open the first time either link is selected, but the new window would be loaded with documents associated with each of the two links.

Building a Map of Your Web Site To show your students a map of the site and how documents lead to each other—a helpful tool—the easiest thing to do is to build a text map of that section when you were designing the system. For example:

```
                         |Section A.1
            |Section A ->           |Section A.2
Main menu -> |
            |Section B-> |Section B.1
```

A number of packages can build a map of your Web site for you. Table 5.3 shows a list of some of these packages.

Apple's HotSauce MCF (Meta Content Framework) allows the construction of a 3D representation of an information map or link space that visitors to your Web site can "fly" through. The map has two parts; you need a tool that will allow you to construct such a 3D space, and your students need a plug-in for their browsers so they can navigate the 3D space (available for Macintosh and Windows '95/NT only). More details are available at **hotsauce.apple.com/**.

Creating Expandable Menus Another good way of showing students the structure of your system is to use a utility that provides an expandable series of links. This usually looks like the graphical display for a file browser utility used to navigate through a file system where the user clicks on a folder, and that folder expands to show that user its contents.

An example of Evan Meir's expandable menu for a university Web site is shown in Figure 5.29. The structure of the site has been built into the menu on the left side of the main page. Clicking on a folder icon opens that folder; clicking on a document page loads that document into the frame to the right.

Table 5.3 Packages for Building a Map of Your Web Site

Name	*Platform*	*Location*
SiteTree	Windows '95	www.kobixx.com/
WebMapper	Windows '95	www.netcarta.com/
Treelink	UNIX	aorta.tat.physik. uni-tuebingen.de/ ~gaier/treelink/
Cmap	Perl	www.stars.com/Software/Perl/
ClearWeb	Windows	www.clearweb.com/

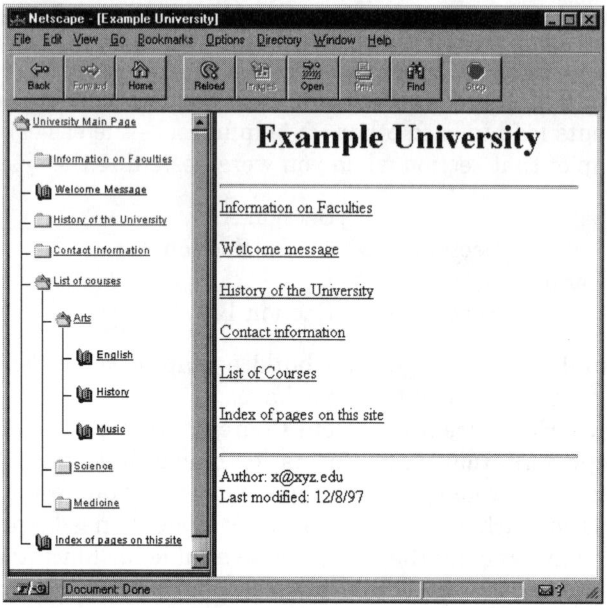

FIGURE 5.29 An expandable menu.

A copy of this menu is available on the CD-ROM in the directory /infodist/meirmenu.

RESOURCES

A list of general resource sites related to the field of Web-based information distribution can be found on the CD-ROM. Topics covered include the following:

- Purpose-built tools
- Information distribution systems
- Search engines
- Web copyright issues
- Online study guides
- Constructivism and other learning theories
- Slide shows
- Remote-control tutorials

6

Enabling Communication

Most people recognize the importance of human interaction to the learning process, but there are many situations and factors that can make it difficult to incorporate interaction into a learning experience. The use of computer-mediated communication (CMC) to address these factors and provide a medium for human interaction has a history going back more than two decades. This chapter aims to help you demonstrate some of the possibilities of CMC and to provide guidance as to how you can incorporate appropriate and effective interaction into your Web-based classroom.

The first part of the chapter examines the theoretical aspects of interaction and the use of CMC and examines a number of issues. It starts with the benefits and drawbacks of communication, regardless of the medium, before examining the advantages, disadvantages, and reasons you would want to use CMC as a communications medium. Included in this discussion is an examination of the factors that contribute to the success of CMC and examples of how people are currently using CMC in a Web-based classroom. A significant body of literature examines the advantages, disadvantages, and characteristics of CMC; this section includes references you'll find helpful.

The second part of the chapter examines the more practical issues of implementing interaction in a Web-based classroom using a four-step approach:

Educational purpose. Before using CMC in your Web-based classroom, be aware of why you are using it. What is the problem you are trying to address? What are you trying to achieve through the use of CMC?

Appropriate pedagogy. The use of CMC offers a wide array of possible approaches to achieving your educational purpose. Drawing on the characteristics of your Web-based classroom, as discovered from reading Chapter 2, you must decide on the most appropriate approach for you. In some cases, the most appropriate approach may not include the use of CMC but rather the use of more traditional methods.

Identification of a suitable tool. An increasing number of tools can support the use of CMC in a Web-based classroom. Each tool has different capabilities and requirements that make it appropriate for some purposes but not for others. Your use of CMC will be more successful if you are able to choose the most appropriate tool for your purposes.

Implementation. Effective interaction does not occur simply by selecting and installing a tool. Discussion must be motivated, participants urged to contribute appropriately, problems and misbehavior responded to, and discussions kept on track and eventually brought to a close.

WHY COMMUNICATE?

Communication among members of a class—whether student to student or student to educator—provides a number of benefits, including the following:

Decreasing the sense of isolation. Many students in a Web-based class can feel isolated and alone. Communication with the educator and other students can increase the sense of belonging and decrease the sense of isolation. Combating this sense of isolation can help decrease the attrition rate in a class.

Increasing flexibility. The ability to simply and quickly communicate with students improves students' ability to adapt to new conditions.

Increasing variety. An environment in which students interact with other students who have different views and experiences exposes them to a larger variety of opinions and experience.

Increasing communication experience. A class in which communication is an essential part of the learning experience provides students with invaluable practice.

Enabling variety of pedagogy. Interaction in learning allows the adoption of pedagogies that rely on interaction, such as collaborative and cooperative exercises. Many of these new approaches help improve learning outcomes.

Problems with Communication

Given that communication is such an important part of the learning process, why isn't it encouraged more? In most situations, the lack of interaction is a result of certain characteristics of interaction that make its use difficult or ineffective. These characteristics include time (considerably more than that required with more didactic teaching methods), skills, personality, synchronicity (the participants need to be at the same place at the same time), and ephemeral interaction (a discussion with a student in the hallway, for example, is by nature ephemeral; only individuals participating in the discussion benefit from the exchange of ideas, mainly due to the fact that there is no archive of the discussion).

The Advantages of CMC

Looking at the characteristics of CMC, it is important to recognize that CMC comes in a number of forms. Each form, because of its different characteristics, provides a number of advantages and suffers from problems. The three basic forms mentioned in this section are as follows:

Asynchronous CMC. This form includes such standard CMC tools as e-mail, Usenet news, and computer conferencing tools. With asynchronous CMC, individuals participate in communication without the need to come together at the same time. They participate when they want to.

Synchronous CMC. Includes all of the text-based synchronous systems such as Internet Relay Chat (IRC), MUDs/MOOs, and interactive chat systems. Unlike asynchronous CMC, synchronous CMC requires participants to communicate at the same time.

Almost face-to-face CMC. This type of CMC includes the more modern systems such as Internet Phone, CU-SeeMe, MBone, and other video- and audio-conferencing systems. Until recently, most CMC systems were limited to text-based communication; these systems provide an experience approaching that of face-to-face communication.

In general, CMC has a number of characteristics that enable it to address many of the problems associated with more traditional forms of communication. These characteristics include the following:

Geographic independence. Use of computer networks means that, regardless of their physical location, participants can communicate as long as they have access to a computer and a network. The requirement for participants to be in the same place disappears, which can help reduce the demand on buildings and classrooms.

Temporal independence. In asynchronous forms of CMC, it is not necessary for participants to come together at the same time. Temporal independence means that participants do not have to synchronize their schedules, and they are no longer restricted to the hour or two of scheduled class time. This is of particular benefit to people who require more time to consider and formulate their responses.

Absence of physical cues. Most CMC systems are text based; consequently, they do not rely on physical cues or appearance, which can help increase the participation of students with low self-esteem and, with appropriate support, can enable the participation of handicapped individuals who may not be able to take part in traditional interaction.

Silent participation. In face-to-face interaction, listening and not contributing can be embarrassing for some people. In online forums, the act of "lurking" (silent participation) is common, and lurkers generally do not suffer from the same feelings of inadequacy.

Computer mediation. In CMC, all communication passes through and can be stored by a computer, so it can be archived and quickly searched, which helps reduce the ephemeral nature of communication. Computer mediation also allows the manipulation of the communication into different structures or formats that may better suit the participants' requirements.

Interactivity. A number of studies have shown that use of CMC, coupled with appropriate pedagogy, actually increases the amount of student participation and interaction.

The Problems with CMC

The use of CMC brings its own set of problems and drawbacks of which you should be aware so that you can design approaches that address and minimize the impact of these problems. As with the advantages of CMC, the problems listed here apply only to certain types of CMC. The problems with CMC include these:

Absence of physical cues. Many CMC interactions suffer from problems caused by the lack of physical cues that in a face-to-face interaction supplement or even change the content of a conversation. Sarcastic comments and humor often lose much of their effectiveness and can be misinterpreted without the presence of physical cues.

Training. A prerequisite for any successful interaction is that the participants are comfortable and familiar with the environment in which the interaction takes place. Although familiarity with the Web and the Internet is increasing, the majority of people do not yet have sufficient experience with the medium. As a result, they are not familiar with its capabilities, unwritten rules, or operation. Some form of training and familiarization is necessary.

Imperfect technology. While becoming easier to use, Internet and Web technology is still occasionally unreliable, slow, and difficult to use, especially for the first time.

Reading online. Because most interaction in CMC takes place online, it is necessary for participants to become comfortable with reading text on a computer screen. That aspect of the technology and the previous experience of the participants (or lack thereof) can make communication difficult, especially if the amount of information to be read is significant.

Access. Even though the number of people with Internet access is increasing, the great majority of people do not have such access. This is especially true in less developed countries.

Asynchronous problems. Asynchronous communication has a number of advantages, but it also has drawbacks and is less suitable than synchronous communication for some tasks. With asynchronous communication, participants may not be certain whether other participants have received their contributions; it can also be difficult to track the progress of a conversation.

Increased interaction. Increased interaction, although bringing many positives, can also become a negative, especially if the interaction becomes exceedingly time consuming. An interactive use of CMC generally requires more teaching staff time in moderation duties than does lecturing, especially if there are problems with implementation. Students also can feel the burden of increased workload if they move from passive learners to active participants.

Moderation issues. As with any interaction, a number of moderation issues must be addressed: spurring participation, unwanted or incorrect discussion, interaction overload, and various forms of harassment.

Success Factors

Simply using the Web to enable interaction between students and educators will not guarantee increased interaction and better learning outcomes. In fact, achieving any form of success with CMC, at least in the first instance, can be a difficult and time-consuming task. The use and evaluation of interaction in a CMC environment, especially in learning, has led to the identification of a number of factors that contribute to the successful use of CMC. Three common characteristics of a successful CMC-based interaction are high levels of use, high subjective satisfaction, and participants' enjoyment and recognition of genuine benefits. For more on this topic, see Starr Roxanne Hiltz, *Evaluating the Virtual Classroom in Online Education: Perspectives on a New Environment*, Linda Harasim, ed. (New York: Praeger, 1990).

In a CMC system, use is measured by combining the number of people using the system and the amount of communication being performed with the system. Alejandra Rojo (**www.oise.on.ca/~arojo/tabcont.html**, 1995) identified the following conditions for high message contribution in a CMC forum:

Balance between new and old members. Long-standing members of a CMC forum provide examples of appropriate behavior and a link with the original aim of the discussion. New members bring innovation and fresh ideas that can help a discussion keep ticking. Achieving this balance in a classroom can be difficult, given that the nature of a classroom is to have one "old" member (the educator) and many new members (the students).

High number of regular contributors. A CMC forum will not be as successful as it could be if only a small percentage of the participants contribute.

Active owner or moderator. An active moderator who spends time, both in and outside of the CMC forum, urging contributions and responding to queries contributes a great deal to the success of a CMC forum.

A participant's subjective satisfaction with CMC is formed from a combination of factors:

Training. Feeling lost or incompetent while trying to communicate is not likely to increase a participant's feelings of satisfaction with the process. A participant in a CMC discussion should be provided with sufficient information about how to use the tools, the purpose of the communication, and how to communicate in a new environment.

Access. One of the benefits of CMC is the ability for communication to take place where and when it is convenient for the participants. If significant effort is required to participate in CMC, such as driving to a study center in order to use a computer with a modem, the freedom provided by the medium is reduced.

Charging. Face-to-face communication usually has a small, fixed cost (bus fare, fuel) that is not dependent on the amount of time spent communicating. Internet access, on the other hand, is, for many people, charged on the basis of time connected. For many participants, this can lead to worrying more about the cost of the communication than the purpose and content.

System characteristics. If the system or tool used for communication is unreliable, difficult to use, or expensive, it can reduce the satisfaction of participants.

User characteristics. A participant's personal preferences will influence that person's satisfaction with CMC.

Sense of community. A group of people who feel no common sense of purpose, interdependence, or common frame of reference will find it difficult to relate to each other and be motivated to communicate with others.

Genuine benefits. It's not enough that participants *can* receive genuine benefits from CMC. They must be aware of these benefits, and their experience needs to reinforce this awareness.

USING CMC

The introduction of interaction into the Web-based classroom opens a wide array of possible pedagogy that can be used. One online resource, by Martin Plausen (**www.hs.nki.no/~morten/cmcped.htm**), describes 20 techniques that can be used in CMC. This section briefly describes some of the approaches educators are using to implement CMC in the Web-based classroom.

One-to-One Approaches

One-to-one approaches using CMC usually cause some form of close relationship between the two individuals to develop. In the case of student/teacher communication, it is common for one-to-one communication to take on some sort of guiding role using such approaches as internships, apprenticeships and mentor relationships, and virtual office hours. One-to-one communication can also take place between students and result in peer assessment and e-mail "buddies."

One-to-Many Approaches

One-to-many approaches, related closely to the concept of information distribution, usually consist of one person giving a presentation to a group. These approaches might include lectures, student presentations, panel discussions, and scripted interaction.

Many-to-One Approaches

Many-to-one approaches are especially suited for a group of students to provide feedback on some particular aspect. These approaches can be used for peer assessment and class evaluation. Such approaches can differ in a number of ways, including:

Level of Anonymity. Anonymity can be total (identities are hidden though accessible if need arises, such as in the case of harassment or abuse) or full identification (where every piece of feedback identifies the sender).

Level of Comment Distribution. Possibilities range from immediate and total release of comments received to comments released only after moderation, to comments visible only to the original receiver.

The Introduction to Software Development course at Monash University in Australia (**www.sd.monash.edu.au/sft1101/**) uses a completely anonymous feedback mechanism via a simple Web-based form. In order to assure students that the process is anonymous, the source code for the script and the feedback file are publicly available.

Many-to-Many Approaches

Many-to-many or group-oriented approaches open a wide range of possibilities: online debates, simulations and role playing, discussion groups, transcript-based assignments, voting, group projects, and discussion forums.

A lecture at which all students are in attendance is a perfect opportunity for discussion and announcements of interest to the entire class. However, it is rare to have a lecture that all students attend, and—in some circumstances, such as distance education—it is impossible to attend. The use of CMC as a group communication system, whether via mailing lists or conferencing systems, offers a number of advantages over face-to-face approaches.

Another advantage of using CMC as a group discussion facilitator is that a record of the interaction is kept and can be reused for future offerings. This record provides a "class memory" that can be reused by both the students and the staff.

STEPS IN CMC

Having looked at the benefits, characteristics, problems, and possibilities of Web-based interaction and CMC in general, we now turn our attention to the nitty-gritty of actually implementing some form of interaction for your Web-based classroom. To do this, we have broken the process into four steps:

1. Identify the purpose.
2. Identify the pedagogy.
3. Select the tool.
4. Implement CMC.

The following sections describe the important concepts and tasks for each step. These are emphasized by case studies of the steps taken by other educators in developing their Web-based classrooms.

Identify the Purpose

As mentioned in Chapter 3, there is no point in using technology for the sake of using technology. Use of CMC in your Web-based classroom should be for a specific educational purpose. Therefore, the first step in using CMC is identifying the purpose. The discussion about the advantages of CMC in the first part of this chapter may help provide some ideas. In addition, Chapter 3 includes a step that may help you develop a purpose for your use of CMC.

Decide on a Pedagogy

Having identified your purpose, you need to decide on the best approach to achieving it. As always, the use of technology is just one of a number of approaches an educator can use. There may be other, non-Web-based approaches that you can use to achieve the desired purpose, with none of the Web's problems. Your choice of pedagogy should be influenced by the purpose to be achieved and by the characteristics of the educator, students, and class.

Choose the Tool

A seemingly endless number of tools are currently available to help incorporate some form of interaction into a Web-based classroom. There are so many, in fact, that it is impossible for this chapter to examine all of the available tools, describe their features, and make recommendations. This task is made more difficult by the fact that each Web-based classroom is different; consequently, the most appropriate tool for one classroom will not be appropriate for another.

Therefore, rather than make recommendations, this chapter aims to provide you with the information you need to make an informed judgment about the tool that is appropriate for you. To achieve this goal, you will be first given a tour of the categories of tools that are available and an introduction to the role they perform. This tour includes descriptions of a small selection of the tools from each category. After the tour, you are shown a collection of characteristics that you should use to identify the tool that best suits your situation.

E-Mail Tools Electronic mail, or e-mail, is a major form of personal communication on the Internet. An individual reads and composes e-mail using a program called a mail user agent (MUA). Early MUAs were text-based programs, such as Elm and Pine, which ran on UNIX machines and other central computers. Today, most people use MUAs with familiar graphical user interfaces and many more complex capabilities. A typical MUA today provides, among other features, the following capabilities:

Message threading. E-mail messages that are in some way associated—about the same topic or sent by the same author—are grouped together. This feature makes it easy to keep track of ongoing discussions.

E-mail filtering. The MUA automatically sorts, deletes, and resends e-mail based on certain user-defined characteristics. This ability is extremely useful for anyone making significant use of e-mail.

Address books. Usually combined with nicknames, address books provide a simple mechanism by which regularly used e-mail addresses can be associated with names.

Multimedia attachments. Older MUAs were restricted to text only. Today, most MUAs support the MIME standard for attaching and delivering files of any description. The more complex MUAs also support the management and display of attachments.

Enhanced text. A recent trend among MUAs is allow the use of HTML or other enriched text formats in e-mail messages. This can be a drawback if significant numbers of your correspondents use MUAs that do not support enhanced text.

Table 6.1 lists some of the common MUAs.

Table 6.1 Mail User Agents

Package	*Platform*	*Cost*	*Requirements*
Netscape Navigator 3.0	UNIX, Macintosh, Windows 3.1/'95/NT	Free for educational users	Win 3.1: 386, 8MB RAM, 3MB HDD Win95/NT: 386, 8MB RAM, 9MB HDD Macintosh: 68020, 9MB RAM, 6MB HDD Unix: 32MB, 15MB
URL	home.netscape.com/comprod/products/navigator/version_3.0/index.html		
Comments	Collection of Web, news, and e-mail client; e-mail client offers a number of advanced features.		
Netscape Communicator	Windows, Macintosh, and UNIX	Free during beta release	Win 3.1/95/NT: 486, 8MB RAM Macintosh System 7.1: 68020, 16MB RAM UNIX: 16MB
URL	home.netscape.com/comprod/products/communicator/index.html		
Comments	Next version of Netscape's product. Messenger, the e-mail client, adds a number of useful features, including filtering support, a spell checker, improved search, and others. Currently in beta release.		
Pegasus	Windows, DOS, Macintosh	Free	Runs on most standard computers
URL	www.pegasus.usa.com/		
Comments	A popular free client.		
Eudora	Macintosh and Windows	Various packages ranging from $89.00 to $45.00 per user, depending on number of users for Eudora Pro; Eudora Light is free	Platform CPU Mac System 7.0 Mac Plus or later Win 3.1/95/NT 386+
URL	www.eudora.com/		
Comments	Eudora comes in two versions: a free, "cut-down" version, Eudora Light, and the commercial product, Eudora Pro. Recent versions of both offer a number advanced features. Possibly the most popular e-mail-only client.		

E-Mail Servers MUAs fulfill the simple role of allowing users to read and compose e-mail messages. The actual delivery of e-mail is the responsibility of server programs, also referred to as mail transport agents (MTA). MTAs perform a number of tasks, including message routing and storage. Message routing consists of deciding how an e-mail message will travel from its sender to the recipient. Message storage involves storing any incoming e-mail in a "postbox" until the recipient next checks his or her mail.

The protocol used to route and deliver e-mail messages from one MTA to another is called the simple mail transfer protocol (SMTP). When an e-mail message is sent from a MUA, the MUA uses SMTP to communicate with a local MTA. Having received the e-mail message from the MUA, the MTA delivers the e-mail message to the MTA used by the recipient. The recipient's MTA in turn stores the e-mail message in the recipient's e-mailbox.

With older MUAs such as Pine and Elm, it was common for these programs to run on the same computer as the user's e-mailbox. In other words, older MUAs were able to read the contents of an e-mailbox directly from disk. By comparison, modern MUAs such as Netscape and Eudora commonly run on a completely different machine from the one on which the e-mailbox is stored. How then can the MUA access the contents of the user's e-mailbox? There are two common solutions to this task: Post Office Protocol (POP) and Internet Message Access Protocol (IMAP).

POP is the much more common and widely used solution; most MUAs support POP. POP is a protocol that allows a MUA to transfer the entire contents of an e-mailbox from a server onto a local machine. The only options POP provides are to either transfer all messages from the server to the local machine or leave all messages on the server. POP has been around a long time, is simple to implement, and is an effective solution if you are reading your e-mail on the same computer all the time. However, in some situations—for example, if a student is restricted to reading e-mail from any one of a large number of laboratory machines—POP poses a number of problems.

A more recent and much more complex protocol, IMAP, can do everything that POP can but with additional functionality that allows users to retrieve only certain parts of specified messages. IMAP also provides the ability to create and manipulate folders on the server. These abilities make IMAP particularly useful to people who use multiple machines to read their e-mail. IMAP is only now starting to be supported by MUAs; some offer relatively poor support.

Most UNIX computers come with the appropriate SMTP, POP, and IMAP servers. For other operating systems, you are generally required to purchase these protocols as separate software packages. Table 6.2 lists some of the common MTAs. The contents of this table demonstrate the newness of IMAP in that very few of the MTAs support it. Recent MTAs from Netscape and Microsoft do support IMAP.

Free E-Mail Clients A recent arrival are free Web-based e-mail clients such as Hotmail (**www.hotmail.com/**) and RocketMail (**www.rocketmail.com/**). These services provide users with free e-mail addresses and a Web-based MUA. If you

Table 6.2 Example Mail Servers

Package	*Platform*	*Cost*	*Requirements*
AIMS	Macintosh	Free	Macintosh Plus or higher, Systems 7.0 or later, MacTCP 1.1.1 or later
URL	cybertech.apple.com/AIMS.html		
Comments	Free POP3/SMTP server produced by Apple.		
LSMTP/POP	Windows NT (Intel and Alpha), OpenVMS	Not available	Not available
URL	www.lsoft.com/LSMTP.html		
Comments	Heavily used at L-Soft's own site.		
Mercur SMTP/POP3	Windows '95/NT	5-, 10-, 20-, and unlimited user licenses for $122, $250, $330, and $640, respectively	NT 3.5 or higher, 95, or TCP/IP networking
URL	www.atrium.de/mercur/mcr_eng.htm		
Sendmail	UNIX	Free	UNIX and TCP/IP
URL	www.sendmail.org/		
Comments	A legend, often regarded as a bit of a nightmare program. Reputedly hard to use; not for a simple installation. Offers more flexibility. Full of security holes, as is every one of these MTAs.		
Windmail	Window	From $70 to $130	Not available
URL	www.geocel.com/windmail/		
Comments	A drop-in replacement for sendmail under Windows. Very useful for Perl-based tools that require Perl.		

cannot access an e-mail server for your Web-based classroom, an alternative is to suggest to students that they obtain accounts with these services. Be aware that these services generate income by advertising to people with e-mail accounts.

Mailing-List Managers E-mail, MUAs, and MTAs are generally designed specifically to support the creation and delivery of e-mail between individuals. It is common for e-mail to be used as a communication mechanism among a group of people; it is possible to achieve such a purpose with MUAs and MTAs, but it is not suggested. Using e-mail for group communication introduces a number of additional tasks that must be fulfilled, including these:

Membership management. This task involves controlling who is included in the group of individuals who will receive messages and how people can be added or removed from the list.

Archive maintenance. A common desire in most group communication is to retain a copy of discussions for future reference.

Message delivery. Somehow, messages sent by the individuals in a group must be distributed to all the other members of a group.

It is possible to perform these tasks "by hand" using MUAs and MTAs. However, the job is time consuming and repetitive. Most of the tasks involved in managing group communication can and have been automated by computer programs, called mailing-list managers (MLMs).

MLMs are computer programs that understand a small command language that can be used to perform many of the tasks listed above. There are a number of MLMs, each one using a unique command language and providing a unique combination of capabilities. Table 6.3 provides a short list of some available MLMs.

Table 6.3 Mailing-List Managers

Package	*Platform*	*Cost*	*Requirements*
Majordomo	UNIX, perhaps portable to other platforms with Perl	Free	Majordomo, program to send e-mail
URL	www.greatcircle.com/majordomo/		
Comments	Free, small, and being actively developed. Very popular.		
ListProc, free version	UNIX	Free	Not available
URL	ftp://cs-ftp.bu.edu/pub/listserv/		
Comments	Free version of Listproc for nonprofit uses. No longer being developed. May not be a "good" Internet resident.		
CREN ListProc	UNIX, NT port rumored	Non-CREN members $2,000 or $2,500 per copy	Not available
URL	www.cren.net/www/listproc/listproc.html		
Comments	A number of extra features, including graphical management clients for X and Microsoft Windows.		
LISTSERV Classic	UNIX, VMS, VM/CMS, Windows '95/NT	Not available	Not available
URL	www.lsoft.com/listserv.stm		
Comments	Most features, well supported. Win95 version is shareware.		

Continued

Mailing-List/Web Command Interfaces Issuing commands to a mailing list manager to join a list, leave a list, obtain a list of the people on a list, and various other administrative functions usually involves sending an e-mail message containing a particular command to a particular address. Although not overly complex, this process can be an annoying task, especially if you are a member of a large number of lists managed by a number of different MLMs, each of which uses its own command syntax.

To combat this problem, a number of individuals have created Web-based interfaces to mailing-list managers. These interfaces allow you to perform most of the same commands as the original e-mail interface but with the benefits of the Web's improved interface. Table 6.4 lists some of the available mailing-list/Web interfaces.

E-Mail/Web Gateways One of the advantages of CMC over face-to-face communication is the ability to archive communication records for future use and to

Table 6.3 Continued

Package	*Platform*	*Cost*	*Requirements*
Listserv Lite	Windows NT (Intel and Alpha), Windows '95, Unix	Not available	$500 to $2,000
URL	www.lsoft.com/listserv-lite.html		
Comments	Limited to a maximum of 10 mailing lists with up to 500 subscribers each. Only free if not used for commercial purposes (hosting a list for a subject is classed as a commercial activity). Does not provide all the features of Listserv classic.		
EASE	Not applicable	Prices vary according to level of service and number of subscribers; start at $500 per year	
URL	www.lsoft.com/EASE-head.html		
Comments	Expert Administration and Supervision of E-mail (EASE). Basically, L-Soft will host your mailing lists on their machine.		
Macjordomo	Macintosh	Free	32-bit clean system; problems for machine before IIci; POP3/SMTP server, one e-mailbox per list.
URL	leuca.med.cornell.edu/Macjordomo		
Comments	Appears easy to set up, uses a Mac interface, and is free.		

Table 6.4 Mailing-List/Web Interfaces

Package	*Platform*	*Cost*	*Requirements*
LWGate	UNIX, but may be portable	Free	Perl, a Web server, and sendmail
URL	www.netspace.org/users/dwb/lwgate.html		
Comments	Supports mailing lists managed by Listserv, ListProc 6, Majordomo, and SmartList. Also provides Web-based archives of a list.		
Mailserv	UNIX, possibly portable	Free	Perl
URL	iquest.com/~fitz/www/mailserv/		
Comments	Supports Listproc, Listserv, Mail-list, Maiser, Majordomo, MLP, Manual, PMDF Mailserv, and Smartlist (not necessarily all commands).		
Pandora	UNIX	Free	Perl
URL	www.ed.umuc.edu/products/pandora.html		
Comments	Supports only Majordomo.		

manipulate that communication into different formats. E-mail-to-Web gateways are programs that translate collections of e-mail messages into Web pages. Using this technique, archives of e-mail discussions can be placed, in some cases automatically, onto the Web for future reference.

The major differences between e-mail/Web gateways is differing support of message structure and mail formats. Archives of e-mail messages can be structured by threads, by author, by date sent, and a number of other possibilities. Some of the e-mail/Web gateways support a limited number of these possibilities.

Traditional e-mail contained text only, but today e-mail comes with attachments in a number of formats, including uudecode, binhex, and MIME. Some of the e-mail/Web gateways support these other formats and automatically translate attachments into appropriate Web formats. This means that pictures, sound files, and audio sent as attachments to e-mail messages can be viewed and played from the Web page generated from the e-mail.

Table 6.5 lists some of the common e-mail/Web gateways.

Web/E-Mail Gateways Web-to-e-mail gateways provide a mechanism by which the information entered into Web-based forms can be sent via e-mail to a specific person. An example of Web-to-e-mail gateway use is a simple feedback mechanism. A Web-based form can be set up as part of your Web-based classroom, allowing students to enter comments without associating their names with those comments. When submitted, the information entered into the form can be delivered directly to the person in charge of the class. Table 6.6 lists some available Web-to-e-mail gateways.

Table 6.5 E-Mail/Web Gateways

Package	*Platform*	*Cost*	*Requirements*
Hypermail	UNIX	Free	C compiler
URL	www.eit.com/software/hypermail/hypermail.html		
Comments	No longer being developed; provides useful structuring options.		
MHonArc	UNIX, MS-DOS/ Windows, WinNT, Win95, OS/2, and possibly Macintosh	Free	Perl
URL	www.oac.uci.edu/indiv/ehood/mhonarc.doc.html		
Comments	Includes support for MIME, which means pictures, sound, and other attachments are displayed on the Web. Can also be used on Usenet news.		

Usenet News Usenet news is collection of asynchronous, text-based discussion forums that are now one of the major group communication tools on the Internet. (Originally, they had nothing to do with the Internet.) Today, thousands of newsgroups are discussing topics ranging from computer science to religion and everything in between. Usenet newsgroups are quite widely used as group communication tools for education.

News Readers Users employ client programs, often called news readers, to read and post news articles on the Web. A similarity with e-mail is the trend toward

Table 6.6 Web/E-Mail Gateways

Package	*Platform*	*Cost*	*Requirements*
FormMail	Windows NT/95, UNIX, Macintosh	Free	Perl
URL	worldwidemart.com/scripts/formmail.shtml		
Comments	Widely used script.		
Form Mailer	Any	Free	Perl
URL	www.netexpress.net/~mkruse/www/scripts/mailer/mailer.txt		
Comments	Simple and effective script.		
AutoMail	UNIX, possibly other	Free	Perl and Sendmail
URL	www.stepweb.com/		
Comments	Allows an e-mail message to be sent to many people but to appear as though it is a personal e-mail message.		

news readers that use graphical user interfaces and provide a number of advanced features. Table 6.7 lists some common news readers.

News Servers Unlike e-mail, Usenet articles are not posted to individual mailboxes for each user; instead, each article is posted to a newsgroup. News servers are programs that store and forward news articles. Each news server accepts a subset of newsgroups and "expires,'" or deletes, articles after a specified time. Very few news servers accept all newsgroups; most specify a subset of newsgroups and accept articles only from those groups. It is common for a news server to contain a number of local newsgroups that no other server stores. Table 6.8 lists a few news servers.

Using Usenet news as group communication mechanism can cause a number of problems:

Newsgroup creation. Creating a new, global newsgroup can be a complicated business. In most educational situations, you create a newsgroup on a local news server.

Newsgroup access. If the newsgroup is local, participants can access it only via the local news server. This causes problems due to the trend for people to gain Internet access through local ISPs. It can sometimes be difficult for these people to gain access to remote news servers.

Article expiration. If articles are set to expire, it is possible to lose past communication via the newsgroup. This leads to a problem common to large newsgroups of new members always asking the same question.

Recent development in Usenet technology—for example, Netscape's release of Collobara—provides some steps in addressing these issues as well as a number of additional features.

Table 6.7 News Readers

Package	*Platform*	*Cost*	*Requirements*
Netscape 3.0	Provides e-mail, news, and Communicatorand Web clients. See entries in Table 6.1.		
InterNews	Macintosh	Shareware, $20	Not available
URL	www.dartmouth.edu/~moonrise/		
Comments	Fewer resources required than Netscape and other "fat" clients. Some nice features.		
Agent	Windows 3.1/95/NT	Free version and an enhanced commercial version for $29	Not available
URL	www.forteinc.com/agent/agent.htm		
Comments	Also a mail reader.		

Table 6.8 Usenet News Servers

Package	*Platform*	*Cost*	*Requirements*
DNEWS News Server	Windows NT/95, UNIX, Macintosh, Novell, VMS	Unlimited user license on one machine, $485	Not available
URL	netwinsite.com/dnews.htm		
Comments	Various advanced features and GUI management methods.		
INN	UNIX	Free	Not available
URL	www.isc.org/isc/inn.html		
Comments	The traditional news server for UNIX.		

Free News Free Web-based Usenet news services similar to e-mail services are available. Two examples are FeedMe (**www.feedme.org**) and BillyBoard (**www.billyboard.com/**). Both provide visitors with a personal news client they can use to read and post to newsgroups. Some free systems also provide the ability for users to create their own newsgroups.

As with the free e-mail services, these services are useful if you do not have access to appropriate software or computers.

News/Web Gateways News-to-Web gateways are programs that convert Usenet news articles into a Web format. Table 6.9 provides a pointer to gateways that are currently available.

Conferencing Computer conferencing is a term used to describe some of the earliest CMC tools that were based around mainframe computers and text-based interfaces. The use of these tools in education started in the mid- to late 1970s and extended into the early 1990s, when the Internet's popularity boomed.

Table 6.9 News/Web Gateways

Package	*Platform*	*Cost*	*Requirements*
MHonArc	UNIX, DOS/Windows, Win NT/95, OS/2, and possibly the Macintosh	Free	Perl
URL	www.oac.uci.edu/indiv/ehood/mhonarc.doc.html		
Comments	Also provides e-mail-to-Web gateway.		
Forum News gateway	UNIX	Free	Perl and News Server
URL	forum.swarthmore.edu/forum.news.gateway.html		
Comments	Beta version from 1995; appears not to be under development.		

The years of experience using these tools led to asynchronous group communication systems that provide a number of useful facilities such as shared documents, tracking of messages that have been read, and voting systems. The usefulness of these features led to the development of a number of new products designed specifically for the Web, such as CoW and HyperNews. Table 6.10 lists a number of Web conferencing tools.

Table 6.10 Conferencing Systems

Package	*Platform*	*Cost*	*Requirements*
CoW	UNIX	Free	Perl
URL	thecity.sfsu.edu/COW2/		
Comments	Full-featured, free Web-based conferencing system.		
WWWBoard	UNIX and possibly others	Free	Web server and Perl
URL	worldwidemart.com/scripts/wwwboard.shtml		
Comments	Simple Web-based bulletin-board system that provides some support for multimedia.		
Hypernews	UNIX	Free	Perl and Web server
URL	union.ncsa.uiuc.edu:80/HyperNews/get/hypernews.html		
Interaction/IP	Macintosh	$200; beta versions can be used for free	Not available
URL	www.ifi.uio.no/~terjen/interaction/		
Comments	Provides a number of features, including conferencing and chats.		
Motet	UNIX	Ranges from $500 for educational institutions to $5,000 for commercial Internet use	Not available
URL	www.sonic.net/~foggy/motet/index.html		
Comments	Commercial conferencing system written in C.		
WebBoard	Windows 95/NT 3.51+	$59.95; extended version $299	486 (or higher), CD-ROM drive, 5MB disk space for software alone, 32MB RAM
URL	webboard.ora.com/		
Comments	Cheaper version comes with a book and is limited in the number of conferences it can support.		

Continued

Table 6.10 Continued

Package	Platform	Cost	Requirements
Caucus	UNIX, NT version soon	Prices start at $2,995, with special prices for educational institutions	Not available
URL	screenporch.com/welcome.htm		
Comments	Commercial Web-based conferencing system built using many years of experience in traditional conferencing.		
FirstClass	Servers for NT and Macintosh; clients for Macintosh, Win 3.1/95/NT, and DOS	Clients are free	Servers: NT 3.51+, 16MB RAM, 10MB HDD Macintosh: 1.5MB RAM, 3MB HDD
URL	www.softarc.com/		
Comments	Uses proprietary clients that can interact with normal Internet e-mail.		

MOO, MUD, and MUSH These three acronyms—MUDs (multiuser dungeons, discussions, and domains), MOOs (MUD object oriented), and MUSH (multiuser shared hallucination)—describe computer programs that provide a virtual environment, usually text based, that users can explore via a computerized "personality" that has the ability to interact with and manipulate other characters and objects within the virtual world. From a user's perspective, there is no great difference between a MOO, a MUD, or a MUSH; the main difference is that a different program, with slightly different features, hosts the virtual world. There are a large number of MUDs, each with its own use, including social, educational, and role-playing adventure games.

MUDs attempt to simulate a full virtual world, so learning to use a MUD can have a significantly greater learning curve than the more straightforward tools discussed in this chapter. Creating a new MUD is especially difficult and not something most educators have the time or ability to do.

The complexity of MUDs does, however, come in handy in situations requiring the features of a virtual world. Educationally, MUDs are particularly useful in simulating complex situations.

The virtual world created by a MUD, MOO, or MUSH is hosted by a program called the server. A variety of MUD servers are available for most platforms. Servers understand different programming languages used to create the virtual worlds and the objects that inhabit them. Programming and maintaining a useful MUD server is not for the technically timid or time strapped. One popular MUD program, CircleMud (**www.circlemud.org/**), operates on the UNIX, Windows

95 and NT, OS/2, and Macintosh platforms. It is based on stable code and widely available.

Participation in a MUD occurs via a MUD client. The simplest MUD client is the standard Telnet application. The more complex clients are full-blown graphical user interface clients that provide advanced features.

Chat Systems Chat systems allow two or more people to participate in synchronous, usually text-based communication, but many of the new tools use multimedia. Chat tools generally don't attempt to recreate a virtual world as MUDs do; as a result, they can be simpler to use. Most chat tools support multiple discussion areas, often called channels or rooms, and the use of an anonymous "handle" or nickname. More complex chat tools offer other features, including logging of conversations, support for multimedia, shared whiteboards, and group Web browsing.

Chat systems are invariably client/server based. Participants in a chat use a program called a chat client to connect to another program called the chat server. The client presents a friendly interface by which the participants chat. The server is responsible for distributing the contents of the chat to all the participants.

Types of chat systems include the following:

Web forms-based chat. These programs use Web forms as the primary form of communication, so any forms-capable Web browsers can be used as interfaces. The server is some sort of CGI script that uses the form input to modify a Web page that must be reloaded by all the participants.

IRC. Clients range from simple text-based programs through full-featured graphical user interface clients written in Java and other high-level languages. IRC has the most participants of any chat system.

Java-based chat. Usually clients and sometimes the servers of these chats are written in Java. That means any Java-capable Web browser can be used as a client, providing a more interactive chat than forms-based chats.

Proprietary systems. Chat systems that are available from one company usually can't interact with other systems. These systems are usually tied to a particular computer platform such as Windows.

Avatar chats. In a normal chat, each participant is represented by nothing much more than a name on a screen. In an avatar chat, participants are graphically represented as virtual characters standing around in a virtual room. Most chats provide some measure of freedom as to what image can be chosen as a participant's avatar. The participant can control the character, moving the avatar around the room and, on some systems, having the avatar display emotion by changing the graphical representation.

Table 6.11 lists some of the available chat systems.

Table 6.11 Chat Systems

Package	*Platform*	*Cost*	*Requirements*
Chat	UNIX	Free	Perl (may run on other platforms)
URL	www.cabinessence.com/cgi/chatpro.shtml		
Comments	A free, forms-based chat system with a very nice interface and support for multiple rooms, both public and private.		
mIRC	Windows 3.1/NT/95	Shareware	Windows and Winsock
URL	www.mirc.co.uk/get.html		
Comments	Popular Windows IRC client		
Conference Room	Windows NT/95	$99 to $249	486+, 16MB RAM, 2MB HDD
URL	www.webmaster.com/products/conferenceroom/index.html		
Comments	IRC/chat server for Windows; has Java clients and advanced features.		
The Chat Server	UNIX, Windows 95/NT (Intel)	About $1,550	100MHz Pentium for 15 chat rooms with 40 simultaneous users, 300K RAM for each chat room, 1MB HDD for product, additional storage for discussion logs
URL	chat.magmacom.com/		
Comments	Forms-based chat system.		
Ewgie	Any Java-capable platform	Free	JDK 1.02
URL	www.eit.com/ewgie/		
Comments	Both client and server are written in Java. Full-featured, easy-to-use chat system that includes features such as a shared whiteboard and Web tours.		
The Palace	Clients: Windows 3.1/95/NT, Macintosh Servers: Windows, Macintosh, UNIX	Clients: Full , version $39.95 retail **Servers:** 100 concurrent users $995, 1,000 users $8,495**Personal server**: 40 users, $50	Not available
URL	www.thepalace.com/		
Comments	A very popular Avatar chat.		

Groupware The distinction between the other tools discussed in this chapter and groupware can at times be a touch fuzzy. In fact, one quite valid definition of groupware is any software that supports and augments group work, which could be taken to mean all of the tools mentioned in this chapter. For our purposes, the distinction between groupware and the other tools mentioned here is based on the functionality the tool provides. The tools labeled as groupware in this section provide significantly greater support for group collaboration, including not only fairly standard asynchronous and synchronous communication functions, but also the concept of shared documents, applications, and workplaces. Table 6.12 lists two free groupware products.

Audio Communication Tools Recent developments, including the increasing availability of bandwidth and improved compression technologies, have led to use of the Internet to distribute reasonable-quality audio. Some applications that this technology makes possible include one-to-one voice discussion, audio-based lectures, and audioconferencing. Table 6.13 lists some audio products.

Synchronous uses of the medium, such as one-to-one discussion and audioconferencing, do not provide some of the benefits of text-based, asynchronous communication. For example, there is no temporal independence, which means that participants must be together at the same time, introducing the problem of synchronization and also removing the time to reflect and frame their contributions available in asynchronous forums.

In addition, audio communication requires further infrastructure in order to work effectively. Students' computers must have sound cards, microphones, appropriate software, and reasonably fast connections to the Internet. These requirements add an extra burden for many students.

On the other hand, these approaches provide a number of advantages:

Familiarity. One-to-one verbal communication and audio based lectures are much closer to the traditional teaching and learning methods used in classrooms. This similarity helps increase the comfort level of the participants and eases the transition into the Web-based classroom.

Personal touch. A solely text-based medium can be particularly impersonal, especially for people new to the medium. Audio communication that allows you to actually hear the other person's voice can help increase the sense of a personal relationship.

Less work. Preparation of an audio-based lecture that explains a topic can be less work than preparing a study guide (Web or print based), especially when existing material can be reused.

Video Communication Tools Videoconferencing using satellites and microwave technology has been used at some educational institutions. However, the high costs involved in such systems have limited their appeal. Fortunately,

Table 6.12 Groupware Products

Package	*Platform*	*Cost*
BSCW	Servers: UNIX Clients: Any Web browser	Free
URL	bscw.gmd.de/	
Comments	An environment for sharing documents, including event notification (e.g. reading, modification).	
TeamWave Workplace	Macintosh, UNIX, Windows 95/NT	Free for educational institutions
URL	www.teamwave.com/	

the same trends that make possible audio communication over the Internet are making video over the Internet possible using relatively cheap cameras and existing computers and network connections.

Videoconferencing over the Internet provides many of the same advantages and suffers many of the same problems as audioconferencing, only more so. It

Table 6.13 Audio Communication Products

Package	*Platform*	*Cost*	*Requirements*
NetMeeting	Windows 95	Free	Suitable microphone and sound card
URL	www.microsoft.com/netmeeting/		
Comments	Version 2.0 is in beta and supports NT.		
Netscape CoolTalk	Windows, Macintosh, UNIX	Free for educational users	Suitable microphone and sound card
URL	www.netscape.com.au/comprod/products/navigator/version_3.0/communication/cooltalk/index.html		
Comments	Functionality to similar NetMeeting's but available on more platforms.		
RealAudio	Clients: Windows, Macintosh, UNIX	Some versions of both client and server available free	Win 3.1/95/NT or PowerPC, 16MB RAM for Video, 4MB for audio, t least 14.4kbps a Internet connection, for Windows greater than 256 colors and 16 bit sound card
URL	www.realaudio.com/		
Comments	Most widely used streaming audio on the Web. Can purchase a client with more features.		

provides a personal touch in that you can place not only a voice, but a face to another participant. However, it places more emphasis on physical appearance, unlike text-based CMC. You can answer an e-mail query from a student after just stepping out of the shower; this is not something you can do with videoconferencing. Table 6.14 provides information on CU-SeeMe, the most popular video communication tool.

The technical requirements for videoconferencing over the Internet are also higher than any of the previous technologies. To use videoconferencing, you will need the following:

Client software. Possibly the most popular Internet-based videoconferencing software is CU-SeeMe, which is available in both free and commercial versions. This software not only provides the ability to send and receive video; it also provides shared whiteboards, text-based chats, and a number of other features.

Video camera. Not all the participants in a videoconference need a camera. In a lecture situation, students can receive the video of the lecture and ask questions using a text-based chat facility. Suitable black-and-white video cameras and connections can be obtained for a couple of hundred dollars.

Distribution mechanism. In a group videoconference, just as in other CMC-based group discussions, there must be a way for distributing the communication to all participants. In most forms of CMC, this task is taken care of by a server that is responsible for accepting the communication and passing it on to the other participants. In CU-SeeMe terminology, this server is called a reflector. Some other videoconferencing tools bypass this requirement by using multicast protocols that allow a host to send information to a group of machines.

Network connection. Although videoconferencing is possible over modem connections, the quality of both the video and audio may be patchy. For most purposes, a LAN connection is the most appropriate means of conducting a videoconference.

Comparing Tools In the end, you are the one who must decide which tool is most suitable for the application you have in mind. This section describes some of the factors you should consider when choosing a communication tool.

Buying or Renting Most CMC tools require the installation and maintenance of a server program that manages and distributes the communication. The traditional approach in most Web-based classrooms is to obtain and install the necessary server program. For most of the tools discussed in this chapter, the installation and maintenance of these tools is quite a technical and time-demanding responsibility, especially if the tool has a high level of usage. As a result, the cost of maintaining the tool can outweigh the benefit gained from using it.

Table 6.14 Video Communication Products

Package	*Platform*	*Cost*	*Requirements*
Enhanced CU-SeeMe,CU-SeeMe	Clients: Macintosh, Windows 3.1/95/NT Servers/reflectors: Windows 95.NT, Unix	Clients: From $69	To be seen by others, you need an appropriate video camera, receiving only requires Windows clients: 486 DX/66+, 256-color video with 640 × 480+ resolution, 8-bit sound card, 16MB RAM+, bandwidth of 28.8KB or better Mac clients: 25MHz 68040+, MacOS System 7+, 10MB HDD, 8MB RAM, QuickTime v2.0+, Sound Manager v3.0+ audio out, MacTCP v2.0.6+, or Open Transport v1.1+; bandwidth of 28.8KB or better Servers/reflectors: 16MB RAM, 8MB HDD, 100MHz+ CPU
URL	Commercial version: www.cu-seeme.com/ Free version: cu-seeme.cornell.edu/		
Comments	Possibly the most popular videoconferencing software on the Web. The free version of CU-SeeMe is released by Cornell University. White Pine Software sells Enhanced CU-SeeMe.		

An alternative that is becoming widespread is to use someone else's server. The advantage is that someone else is responsible for maintaining the server, and you can concentrate on moderating discussions and the educational goals of the interaction. At many universities, this hosting service is provided by a central information technology division. However, it is increasingly common for commercial companies or other organizations to provide chat servers, MLMs, or MUDs that anyone can use.

In addition, a number of educational MUD servers may provide your class with space and access. In the end, the decision to buy or rent should be based on the relative costs and benefits associated with each choice.

Suitability Above all, your communication tool should be suitable for your educational aims. Even though the way in which the tool's use is designed plays a large part in achieving any aim, certain tools are more suitable for particular tasks than others. For example:

- The lack of immediate interaction when using asynchronous tools means they are not as good for achieving consensus or making decisions as similar synchronous tools.
- The use of synchronous tools in distance education removes one of the primary freedoms of distance education: students' ability to study when they want.
- Groupware tools that provide a number of features designed specifically to help manage the management and synchronization of groups are more likely to create a feeling of group identity than unrelated sequences of e-mail messages.
- The tendency for Usenet newsgroups to expire articles older than a few weeks makes it difficult to reuse discussions from one course offering to the next.

Capabilities Your chosen tool should provide all the capabilities you require now and for future versions of your Web-based classroom. Aim for a balance between selecting a tool that provides the minimum required capabilities and the widest range of capabilities.

A tool that provides just the capabilities you require for your current Web-based classroom may cause problems in the future, when your class requirements grow. In some situations, moving from one tool to another can be quite time consuming or even impossible.

On the other hand, choosing a tool that provides everything, including the kitchen sink, can cause you to pay for features you never use and a program that is so bloated as to be slow and inefficient.

Price Software on the Internet comes in three basic price ranges: free, shareware, and commercial. There is usually no correlation between the price charged for a tool and its quality and usefulness. Many of the free CMC-related tools have a number of advantages over their much more expensive commercial rivals.

It is important to recognize that for most CMC tools, the price tag does not form a significant component of the overall cost of using a tool. Training in the use and management of a tool, combined with the cost of maintaining it, usually contributes a far greater proportion of the cost of a piece of computer software. When evaluating the cost of a tool, try to keep in mind issues such as the support provided by the tool's vendor, how much support costs, how often you'll have to use support, how much of that support you'll require locally, the level of technical skill required for local support, likely costs for upgrades, and how often upgrades will be released.

Leading-Edge versus Complete Tools Once your Web-based classroom gets under way, you'll want to waste a minimum of time due to computer or software malfunctions. All good computer software should have been through testing procedures, but as the saying goes, "Testing proves the presence of bugs (mistakes), not their absence." Another old computer industry saying suggests that you should never use the first version of a piece of software, because it almost always contains a number of errors.

The recent Internet-based software trend is for companies to release unfinished (referred to as alpha or beta) versions of products. This practice has come about in part due to the fast development of Internet products, the cheap and fast distribution methods provided by the Internet, and a large group of people who want to be using the latest and greatest tools and who consequently provide software companies with a cheap and large army of testers.

To minimize disruptions caused by computer errors, we suggest you use tried-and-tested versions of software rather than the "latest, greatest," not yet complete version.

Requirements Most communication tools discussed in this chapter have certain requirements, including these:

> **Server requirements.** The server is the machine on which the server program that manages and distributes the communication resides. Such requirements are usually expressed, for both server and client computers, in terms of operating system, type of CPU, and size of memory and hard drives.
>
> **Client requirements.** These refer to computers that the participants in your Web-based classroom use to access the online forum.
>
> **Network requirements.** The mechanism by which information is passed between the client and the server. The bandwidth, the speed by which information can flow, required by the tool should not exceed the bandwidth of the network used to connect the participants. It does not make sense to run a videoconference over a 2,400bps modem.

Most tools specify a minimum and recommended level of requirements needed in order to use the tool. In most cases, you should always aim to fulfill the recommended level of requirements. Most tools running on the minimum level of requirements operate less than effectively.

Cost versus Benefit An online forum's benefits for participants must be greater than the costs and effort involved in participating. As mentioned earlier, if participants feel that the costs outweigh the benefits, the on-line forum will suffer. The approach should be to maximize the benefits while minimizing the costs.

The cost in time and effort to the participants includes at least two components: the effort to become comfortable and familiar with the tool and the effort required to use the tool from day to day.

The more complex tools such as groupware systems, computer conferencing, and MUDs have a significantly greater learning curve and are unlikely to be familiar to most participants. Tools such as e-mail and simple chat systems may be familiar to participants or considerably easier to learn.

A common approach with tools such as Netscape Navigator and Microsoft Internet Explorer is to provide one tool that does it all. These sorts of tools offer Web, e-mail, news, and Chat clients, all in one program. One advantage of this approach is that new users require just one tool, with one interface, and need not learn how to use multiple tools.

An added advantage of a tool such as Netscape Navigator is that it is available on multiple platforms. This means students with Windows, Macintosh, or UNIX machines can use the same program with basically the same interface. This significantly reduces the overhead required to identify tools for various platforms and train students in the different tools normally required to support multiple platforms.

Openness One of the advantages provided by systems such as the Web and Java is that they remove the old problem of platform dependence. When using multimedia CD-ROMs or computer-based training systems, it was once necessary to specify exactly what type of computer the student must have in order to be able to use the resource. The alternative was to produce many different versions of the system to accommodate the various types of computers students might have.

With the advent of platform-independent tools, these problems almost disappear. At least they do when you are careful in your choice of tools. Where possible, choose tools that accommodate the widest range of computer platforms to give students the freedom to use the platform they are most comfortable with.

Ease of Use The move from text-based clients to graphical user interface clients has been, in the most part, driven by the desire to make it easier for people to use the tools. If students find a tool difficult to use or understand, they will be less likely to continue using the tool. This is of particular importance with the more complex tools such as MUDs and groupware systems.

Implement CMC

This section examines the process of actually starting and maintaining a CMC-based forum in your Web-based classroom. It starts by defining the characteristics that make a good moderator of an online forum. It then discusses the tasks that a moderator will be expected to perform during all phases of the forum's life. Finally, it offers some general hints and tips that may be helpful in running your online forum. Given the widespread use of CMC in an educational setting for more than 20 years, considerable resources are available that can help in running a CMC-based classroom. A list of these references appears on the CD-ROM.

What Makes a Good Moderator? Moderating a CMC forum can require skills and abilities that differ from those necessary for leading a traditional face-to-face class. In many cases, the success of the CMC forum will depend on the moderator's characteristics and performance to harness the abilities of the tools and participants.

The following, far from exhaustive list provides some idea of the characteristics that contribute to a successful moderator:

Experienced. Communication in an online forum is, for most people, a totally new experience, unlike any previous form of communication. Online discussions have their own feel and flow. A prospective moderator will find it useful to have had some experience with this environment as a participant before taking on the moderator role.

Flexible. The combination of technology and people who are often new to the technology often leads to problems that disrupt the best-laid plans. A moderator must be flexible and inventive enough to cope with unplanned events and help continue the discussion toward its aim.

Tolerant. Nothing reduces the effectiveness and sense of community in an online forum more quickly than anger and disagreement among the participants, especially if the forum's moderator is the source of that anger. A moderator's tolerance might be stretched to the breaking point, but a good moderator will deal with all situations and individuals with an absence of even the appearance of anger and frustration.

Supportive. One of the factors that governs the success of a CMC forum is a high level of participation. A prime responsibility of the moderator is urging participants to contribute and offering support when required.

Knowledgeable. A good moderator, while careful not to dominate a discussion, should be capable of correcting misunderstandings and have the ability to make useful and proactive statements about a topic that points the discussion in interesting directions.

A good listener. Given the lack of physical cues and the increased possibility of misunderstanding, it is important that an online forum moderator be good at discerning not only what participants have said, but what they meant to say.

A good communicator. The moderator of a forum must demonstrate all the characteristics of good online communication, including clarity and conciseness. Remember, communication in an online environment is considerably different from traditional communication.

Not authoritarian. A good online forum is one in which all participants feel free to contribute without fear of ridicule or embarrassment. The presence of authoritarian figures in an online forum may well cause or increase this fear.

Organized. The moderator of an online, educational forum is responsible for bringing together a collection of students from a variety of backgrounds, often with little or no online experience, introducing them to each other and a new environment and helping them achieve some predefined goal. To perform such a task effectively, it is essential that significant planning and organization be carried out.

Responsive. A fear of many new participants in online forums is that their messages are not being received, especially if participation is being assessed by the educator. The moderator should respond to messages and questions within an acceptable time frame.

Has the time. Moderation of an online forum takes time and is not restricted to any particular day or time. Time investments of more than an hour a day, seven days a week, are not unusual.

Understands technology. A moderator must have a sufficient understanding of the technology, or appropriate technical support, in order to respond to difficulties that will occur during the running of the forum. Additionally, one of the unofficial roles of a moderator is that of help desk operator. The moderator will usually become the first stop for participants when they are unable to participate in the forum for technical reasons.

Enthusiastic. For participants, especially newcomers to the online world, not many things will affect their feelings about the new environment more than a reluctant, unenthusiastic moderator.

Choosing a Moderator The role of moderator of your online forum is an important one that will directly affect the effectiveness of your Web-based classroom. In most cases, the moderator role will be taken on by the educators directly involved in the class. Another option to consider is to employ an independent moderator. In an ideal world, such a hired moderator would be experienced and skilled in maintaining and building online forums and be able to comment knowledgeably on the topic being discussed. This is an especially attractive option if you are likely to have a large number of online forums or participants. One possible source for independent moderators may be the pool of students who have previously passed through your Web-based classroom.

Some of the benefits of providing an independent moderator include freeing your time to concentrate on other tasks; providing a skilled model for staff who don't have moderator experience or skills; filling a role that is independent of the educator, thus giving students another person with whom they can discuss problems and another perspective on the material, and providing a balance between old and new participants. However, using an independent moderator has a number of possible disadvantages: expense beyond your budget, dissent from your opinions on how the forum should be run, lack of availability, and difficulty in evaluating performance. Furthermore, the absence of the educator from the moderator role may provide some students with the perception that the online forum is less than important.

The Moderator's Tasks In moderating an online forum, a wide array of tasks must be completed. This list increases if the purpose of the online forum is educational. It is common for these tasks to be broken up into the following categories:

> **Organizational tasks.** The participants in a CMC-based forum should be made aware at all times of the "how, why, and what" of the forum. They should not be worried about these issues and should instead be free to concentrate on taking part in the interaction. If the participants have to worry about these issues, it can take away from their enjoyment as well as ability and desire to participate. It is up to the educator to ensure that participants have all the required information and resources required to participate in the discussion.
>
> **Educational tasks.** In order to achieve the educational aim of the forum, the moderator is required to perform tasks that point the participants in the right direction.
>
> **Social tasks.** Learning, especially in CMC forums, is a social process. The moderator must ensure that the social climate of the forum promotes participation and exchange. Problems to be combated include "flames," temper tantrums, inappropriate posts, and fear of ridicule and embarrassment.

Before Starting As with all aspects of the Web-based classroom, thorough planning and preparation are essential to an effective online forum. The extra effort invested before starting the forum will be paid back in less time wasted dealing with problems, as well as increased positive feelings about and participation in the forum. Before the interaction commences, someone must decide on the following:

> **Format.** The format of CMC includes many of the issues mentioned previously in this chapter, including the tool to be used, the goal, the approach, what is required from the students, a rough idea of the time table, and any other information that defines the shape the interaction will take.
>
> **Scene setting.** From the start, participants should be aware of as much information as possible about the purpose, expectations, and details of the online forum.
>
> **Requirement fulfillment.** In order for an online forum to proceed smoothly, all of the technical and nontechnical requirements must be in place. These requirements include software, hardware, and support procedures.

Training. In identifying the purpose of the forum, you should have outlined the difference between what the students are expected to do and their current skill levels. It is important that you supply any additional training required to bring participants up to speed.

Alternatives. At some stage, the technology will fail. It is good practice to always have an alternative or a backup plan that does not rely on technology, just in case. For example, if student cannot obtain their e-mail for two weeks, they should have a list of tasks they could be performing or an alternative method for participating. You might tell students up front that if they receive no communication within a set time period, they should contact the moderator via alternative means such as the telephone or in person.

Access. It is important that all participants have access, especially if participation in the online forum is compulsory. At the start, make sure all participants have access and that everyone has joined the online forum.

Etiquette. Training does not end in telling people which buttons to press. Online forums are a new world with their own rules, regulations, and expected standards of behavior. Participants should be aware up front what behavior is expected of them while they participate.

Testing. Software being used for educational purposes should, where possible, be tested under the conditions in which the majority of the participants will use the tool. If all your students are using a conferencing system over 14,400bps modems, it is not useful to test the conferencing system over a LAN.

Starting. A very useful method for providing the necessary training, ensuring everyone is aware of what is required, and providing a method for breaking the ice is to hold a face-to-face meeting before the online forum commences. Of course, circumstances may make this impossible.

Introductions. An additional approach is to use an exercise to introduce the group members to each other. Both this and the previous step are aimed at providing the sort of interdependence and comfort among group members that is necessary to ensure a successful online forum. One approach is compiling an online class photo album, placing a photo and some personal details about each student on the Web. This approach helps increase participants' recognition that the other forum members are human beings, not just e-mail addresses.

Once Under Way Like any complex life form, an online forum requires certain maintenance tasks to be performed during its lifetime to ensure that it continues operation. First, the climate of the online forum must be set from the start and maintained during its lifetime. If it starts to become somewhat heated, the moderator needs to step in to cool things down.

At the start of the online forum, each group or member of the group should be assigned a simple first task that draws on previous knowledge rather than new knowledge. The aim of the task is to allow participants to concentrate on how to perform the task in the new environment rather than on the content. Once familiar with the environment, participants can then move onto more complex tasks.

Use pseudonyms, ex-students, or other lecturers to act as other class participants. These class participants are meant to help demonstrate good or bad practice and possibly present opposing views that push others to participate.

Where possible, send all new members of the online forum a personal e-mail message welcoming them to the group. This helps reinforce that they have actually joined and can help provide positive feelings about the forum.

Where possible, either in the forum itself or via private communication means the moderator should be asking for opinions and prompting other participants for their thoughts. However, inappropriate or disruptive behaviors must be stopped as soon as possible. If allowed to continue, these behaviors can adversely affect the climate and outcomes of the online forum. A response to bad behaviors is best handled via private communication, possibly requiring the offender to apologize to the group or excluding the offender from future participation.

Having specified what is expected of the participants, the moderator should at all times model and reward this expected behavior. Never respond immediately to any form of computer-based communication that creates anger or frustration. Always take at least a day before responding. If an immediate response is required, keep it short and possibly say an answer will be available tomorrow. Posts made while angry are invariably detrimental to an online forum.

The lack of physical cues in most forms of CMC means that recipients of your messages will not be aware of the situation in which you found yourself when answering. They will not know that when you sent that simple "No" in your last e-mail that you were rushing out the door to keep an appointment, for example. The lack of physical cues and uncertainties about the new environment may lead to such short answers, reducing students' comfort with the environment. If you are short of time, either don't respond or mention that you are out of time and will provide a fuller answer later on.

From time to time while moderating a forum, summarize a conversation, weave together the comments made by participants, and move the discussion in the required direction. This serves two purposes: It keeps the discussion on track, and it provides positive reinforcement to the contributors.

Ask participants to justify their responses and occasionally play devil's advocate. Don't overload the participants, though. An online forum takes more time due to increased interaction and the unfamiliarity of the medium for most participants. Do not set too many goals; aim instead for quality.

Do not let any one individual or group dominate a forum. Enforce this either through personal discussion or by limiting their ability to contribute.

The feeling of satisfaction participants feel is directly related to the speed and quality of the responses they receive. Where possible, answer queries quickly.

In an educational setting it is not unusual for the educator to have more regular access to the forum than other participants. Consequently, the moderator is often able to respond to all queries before others in a group forum. This should be avoided; it allows one individual (the moderator) to dominate participation, limits participants to one approach, and prevents others from gaining experience in answering questions.

Finally, it is important for most online forums in an educational setting to come to a satisfactory and appropriate close.

CONCLUSIONS

Setting up and moderating any form of online forum can be a time-consuming task that requires a number of new skills, a great deal of planning, and a good serving of perseverance. However, the use of communication in a Web-based classroom can be the most exciting and rewarding use of the Web in education. It enables a tremendous freedom that addresses many of the problems with face-to-face communication and provides a number of new educational possibilities. As we've seen in this chapter, the importance of communication can be seen in the wide variety of tools of many types that can be used to enable communication in the Web-based classroom.

RESOURCES

A list of sites related to the following topics covered in this chapter can be found on the CD-ROM:

- CMC
- E-mail gateways
- Usenet resources
- Conferencing resources
- MUDs
- Chat services
- Groupware
- Audio and video communication

7

Online Student Assessment

Methods of assessment are an important aspect of every course. How else can you tell how well your students are doing or demonstrate to the students themselves how much progress they are making? How also do you know that your method of instruction is succeeding?

There are a number of methods for assessing students, each useful its own way:

The quiz. The quiz is usually a short exercise that consists of questions students can answer simply—by choosing an option or filling in a word. A quiz can be automatically marked by a computer.

The essay. A longer exercise involves the use of knowledge in the production of an explanation, an essay, or a piece of work such as a segment of computer code. Essays cannot usually be marked by computer.

The evaluation. An evaluation usually involves an assessment of a student's behavior or progress through observation, conversation, or feedback.

In general, we can say that any mechanism involving information gathering that can be used to improve instruction and learning constitutes an assessment. An ideal assessment is said to be one for which the goal is to make the student successful.

Traditionally, handling assessments manually incurred major overhead in the marking and processing of those assessments. So, in most courses, assessments or quizzes are usually kept to the minimum necessary to accurately assess progress or competence. With a Web-based classroom, it is easy to construct systems that automatically correct and handle quizzes for you and that reduce the time taken to carry out other forms of assessment.

In this chapter, we look at methods of assessing students. We examine the individual attributes of these methods and discuss what they are appropriate for measuring. We look at how you can design assessments in order to ensure that they do a competent job of assessing students' knowledge of and ability to apply a subject. A number of factors are involved in determining what is considered a competent job; these factors relate to an assessment's ability to establish what a student has learned and the effectiveness of an assessment as a teaching tool so students can learn by their mistakes. We also look at the mechanisms for handling assessments in an online environment and some tools that can help. It is important to note that the methods of assessment and the contents of the assessments are highly dependent on the local educational circumstances. Therefore, all the information in this chapter should be read as general information as opposed to specific advice.

The chapter is divided into the following sections: a general look at assessments and the advantages of an online assessment, the various types of assessment, online implementation of assessments, and custom quiz creation.

We rely on JavaScript for a number of quizzes in this chapter. Although we have tested the JavaScript programs we discuss on a number of browsers and platforms, you should be aware that some browsers may have problems with them. As always, the rule is to try them out on the equipment that your students will use to see if they will work properly. In general, Netscape browsers are the most JavaScript-compatible browsers available (after all, Netscape developed JavaScript).

WHY USE ASSESSMENT TECHNIQUES?

Assessments have two main purposes: to evaluate students' progress and to help students learn. Some of the other uses for assessments are testing teaching effectiveness, encouraging educators to reflect on their teaching and material, provoking student thought and action, encouraging students to ask questions, and motivating students to learn. Let's examine these and other uses of assessment in more detail.

You can use assessments to indicate whether components of the course have been clearly understood by the students. You can record the results of assessments and check the results of student assessments to see how well they are performing. Students' wrong answers can also be recorded and analyzed to determine the nature of the misunderstandings. Based on the results of assessments, you can implement remedial lessons or expansion and clarification of material.

Once a lesson has been developed, constructing an assessment based on it helps the educator to review the material and determine whether it is sufficient to answer a series of questions. This enables the writer of the material to reflect on it and work out the best way of helping students master it. It may also show up shortcomings in the material on which the assessment is based. The construction of an assessment can be done as the basis of a comprehensive revision exercise—that is, you can include questions that test students' knowledge of all aspects of the lesson.

Assessments can often be used to provoke students to consider the material they have just seen in a lesson. If the lesson material is not sufficient to answer a question in full, the student may be encouraged to read further about the topic. If the outcome of an assessment is unexpected, it may challenge the student to think more thoroughly about the material on which the assessment is based.

Assessments need not consist only of questions that have "right and wrong" answers; they can contain questions that act as leaders to other questions or that encourage students to start a discussion with fellow students or an educator.

Students are often motivated by success or failure in an exam. You can use an assessment to encourage students to work harder by making assessments more difficult to do well on. A difficult assessment may encourage students to put more effort into the course. Unfortunately, this approach usually increases motivation by increasing students' stress levels, which can eventually result in a negative impact on student performance (not to mention the effect on the student personally). If students are successful in an assessment, they receive satisfaction and reassurance that they are reaching the required standard. This success can improve students' motivation and reduce stress.

Many topics are open to various interpretations. Providing an assessment that suitably probes understanding of a topic can make students think further about that topic.

You can use recorded results from an assessment to chart the progress of individual students through the course. Recording and analyzing students' answers enables you to see if you can discern trends in misunderstandings. The average abilities of students and areas of weakness in their abilities can also be pinpointed.

Students can use computer-marked assessment to ascertain whether they have sufficiently understood the material in the course or have retained mastery of a subject. A test bank of assessments can be assembled from each lesson and used as a revision aid by the students.

Students can use an assessment to assess their standard of knowledge before beginning a lesson. You can place the assessment at the start of a course or a lesson in order for the students to find out if they have the relevant prerequisite knowledge. You can also post the average results of an assessment to let students know how they compare with their peers.

An assessment can be used to determine students' levels for an adaptive tutorial (see Chapter 5) or to allow them to access areas of the course that have been restricted. This way, you can ensure that students reach a required standard before proceeding to more advanced material.

Questions in the assessment can be phrased in such a way as to consolidate the knowledge learned or to apply it to a particular set of circumstances. This acts as an additional form of instruction for students.

Students may think they understand a topic completely, but until faced with an assessment, they may be overconfident. An assessment forces them to confront shortcomings in understanding and may expose areas or aspects of the course students were unaware existed or for which their knowledge is inadequate.

Examinations are a major cause of stress for students. Studying for examinations can help reduce anxiety because students can become accustomed to the types of questions that the exam will ask. If students subject themselves to continuous self-assessment, they become more familiar with the process of studying for exams, pacing themselves, and answering questions.

Students can be encouraged to construct their own assessments for particular sections or be required to do so as an exercise. This strategy encourages students to reflect more closely on the material that they have just learned, because they must formulate questions about it. Questions developed by students can then be made available to all the students to try out.

In a conventional face-to-face course, it is usually easy to pace delivery. If students are expected to learn autonomously, we must find another way of ensuring that students keep up. You can use assessments as an instructional mechanism. A course following this system does the following: Material as well as a set of assignments for the course are made available to students; students read the material in an order of their choosing, then use the assignments to ascertain their mastery of the subject and to point them to other relevant material. You can set a series of suggested targets for the students—for instance, they must complete an assessment every two weeks—or use the assessment as a gateway mechanism for the next part of the course.

WHY USE ONLINE ASSESSMENT METHODS?

Paper-based assessment has been around for many years. Using an online system for assessment can improve the assessment process in the following ways:

Saving time. Assessments can be created using software tools and adapted and reused as needed. They can be distributed and collected using a Web-based system. This saves development and distribution time.

Reducing turnaround time. Using a system whereby assignments are corrected by computer or the computer is used to reduce the correction time means the results (and appropriate feedback) can be returned to students as quickly as possible. This will enable students to use the knowledge obtained from their corrected assessments to address their deficiencies as soon as possible.

Reducing resources needed. Human resources can be reduced because simple assessments can be electronically corrected and software can reduce the processing and correction time for essay-type assignments. Assignments can also be created, collected, corrected, commented on, and returned entirely electronically, saving paper and printing time and resources.

Keeping records. Computerized correction and collection facilitation utilities can automatically keep records of results for individual students. These records can be stored centrally and accessed by interested parties, such as staff and students.

Increasing convenience. Collection and (to a certain degree) correction of assessments can be automated, meaning that students can obtain instant feedback for some assessments. Students find assignments for which they can receive an instant correction more useful when assessing whether they have mastery over a particular topic and more convenient because they can do the assessment at any time and any number of times.

Increasing ease with which data can be used. Because the data from assignment corrections is stored in electronic form, it is easier to analyze and use the data in spreadsheets and other statistical packages.

Electronic assessment is not a completely foolproof method, however. Many of the difficulties that accompany conventional assessment, such as cheating, lost assignments, and privacy, are also present in electronic assessment methods.

SUCCESS FACTORS

Before we take a look at the various types of assessment, we should look at the factors that influence the success of an assessment. We can define success in a number of ways. An assessment can be successful if it ascertains the extent of students' knowledge or if it teaches students something. We can also define an assessment as successful if students choose to do it or if it teaches the educator something about the students, the material, or the educator's teaching methods.

Some of the factors that can positively affect an assessment are as follows:

It is clearly signposted. Students should be able to find an online assessment, or they should encounter an assessment if they are following a linear path. For example, in Chapter 5 we recommended placing an assessment at the end of each tutorial, which would be encountered by students as they work their way through the material.

It provides meaningful feedback. To result in students using an assessment to improve their performance, you should try to provide meaningful feedback with the results, including meaningful and useful hints or a link to a location where the students can find supplementary knowledge.

Training is adequate. To ensure that students will be able to make the most of the assessment, they should be trained to use the assessment submission mechanisms, how to interpret questions correctly and to understand the output or feedback they receive from an assessment. Students should also be able to appreciate the philosophy behind assessment—that it is designed not just to categorize them but to help them learn and help their teachers to teach them.

It is usable. Usability refers to both students' and educators' ability to use the assessment method with the minimum of effort. You should consider such factors as ease of preparation, ease of use, ease of administration, ease of scoring, and interpretability of results.

The question content is of good form and is understandable. The form of your questions influences how well students can answer them and how eager they are to involve themselves in an assessment. For example, in your questions, if you use unusual vocabulary, terms, or complex expressions that are unrelated to the material being examined, students will become confused. You should also ensure that all the material included as part of the assessment questions is accessible and clear. For example, if you are using illustrations, make sure the pictures are discernible; if you are using a video clip, ensure that students can view it. Another point to watch out for when framing questions is the danger that your questions will depend on nonreferenced prerequisite knowledge of a particular student group, such as phrasing questions for the engineering students in your class as opposed to a students from a liberal arts background. Students should be made aware of the focus of the assessment and any prerequisites they need and where they can get them. This is particularly important if students are learning modules of the course according to their own schedules, because they may not have encountered a unit prior to doing an assessment that depends on it.

The purpose should be clear. Assessment is not usually a game to see if the student can outwit the educator or the system. The students should be made aware of the purpose of the assessment in order to enter into the spirit of it.

FORMS OF ASSESSMENT

This section looks at three main methods of assessment, what they can involve, and their associated considerations. In the implementation section later in the chapter, we see how each of the assessment methods can be used in practice. The methods we examine here are the quiz (a short-answer assessment), the assignment (a long-answer question), and the student evaluation.

The Quiz

When we talk about an online quiz, we are talking about a form, displayed in a browser window, with questions and spaces where students place their answers. Students then press a button that results in correction of their answers. The results are then displayed to the student.

An example quiz is shown in Figure 7.1; one student's corrected answers are shown in Figure 7.2. The idea of such a self-test is that it is done without any need for a person to mark it. Marking is done by either a program on the server or a JavaScript-based marking mechanism contained in the HTML page on which the quiz is displayed.

Why Use a Quiz? It is important to have some simple mechanism, such as a quiz, for evaluating students. This is useful not only for the educator but also for students, who can obtain an idea of their abilities and their progress in the course.

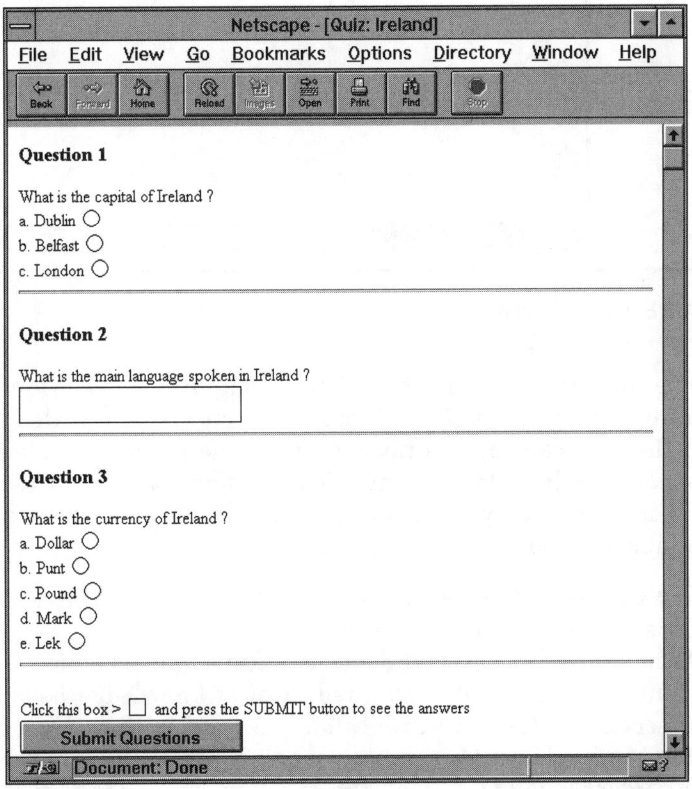

FIGURE 7.1 An example of a quiz page.

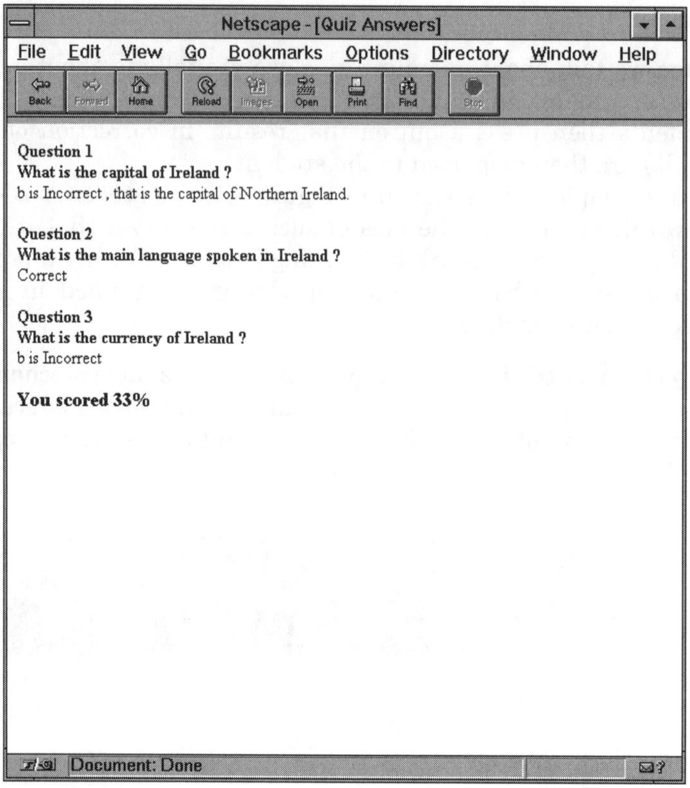

FIGURE 7.2 A marked quiz.

The advantages of using a simple computer marked quiz are that it offers instant feedback to a student; students can make repeated attempts to pass it; and the quiz can contain hints that will help students identify problem areas. Furthermore, links to relevant resources make it easier to revise the quiz, so that labor is needed only to create the quiz, which can be done easily using freely available software or code templates.

Other Uses of a Quiz A quiz can be also used as a gatekeeper, as a pointer to knowledge, or as a coaching mechanism.

As mentioned in Chapter 5, you can use a quiz as a mechanism to ensure that students have reached a required level of knowledge before proceeding to the next section of the course. We call a quiz used in this way a gatekeeper.

You can implement a gatekeeper quiz by defining a "reward" that is displayed to a student who answers all the questions in a quiz correctly. This reward can be a password to new section of the course, if the course is password protected (see the discussion on the CD-ROM in Appendix D), or the location of a new section of the course. The danger with this approach is that the quiz may assume the status of a game for the student, where the only purpose is to obtain the password and not to indicate the areas the student is weak in. Another problem that can arise is that students may share "rewards" with each other. You can address these problems by a variety of solutions (see the implementation section in this chapter for more details) or by making clear to students the philosophy of the gatekeeper quiz—that it is there to help students, not to act as an obstacle or a challenge to be sidestepped in some way. If students appreciate this explanation, this system can act as an excellent filtering method to let them know that they need to do a little more work to proceed.

You can publicize to the rest of the class the number of "gates" that the average student has passed through or the level of achievement of individual students. This method helps bring home to lagging students the fact that they are falling behind and that they may need some help.

Students who give wrong answers to quizzes can be directed to relevant resources though the use of hints. For example, associated with three out of four possible answers, you could have hints that direct students to particular pages. The questions themselves can be constructed using links for keywords; these links would bring the student to the relevant page in the course. A good idea is to write a link so that it opens up a new browser window and puts the new page in it. This approach, discussed in Chapter 4, makes navigation easier for students. Basically, you write the link to resources like this:

```
<a href="http://machine/ref.html" target="new">word</a>
```

Problems with Using Computer-Marked Quizzes As with every form of assessment, computer-marked quizzes have their place in the scheme of an education process. A number of problems of which you should be aware can arise; most of these problems can be solved by careful design, but others may not be possible to address:

Overreliance. If you intend to rely on computer-marked quizzes solely as opposed to supplementing them with traditional assessment methods such as assignments, you may encourage students to become accustomed to the point-and-click method of evaluation, with the result that, when students encounter final examinations that require much greater depth in answers, they may have a problem because of inexperience.

Impersonal. Students may feel anonymous and isolated if they are evaluated continuously by computer. To counter this, on each quiz, you could include the name of a person to contact in case of difficulty. Students could also be told that the philosophy of online testing is to help them assess themselves as opposed to imposing a computerized examiner on them. You could supplement the online quizzes with assessments for which human feedback is given or get the students involved in discussion groups to integrate them more with the class and the educator.

Overtesting. Be wary of subjecting students to too much testing. A constant barrage of testing may cause students to avoid using the self-testing system, because they will feel that the resource value of the test is too low.

Fostering a false sense of confidence. If the standard of the tests is set at a reasonably low level to encourage students, then students who do well may become overconfident. Students can also look back over the material covered in the test and attempt the test many times before arriving at the right answers, sometimes by chance. Once students see that they have obtained the right answers, they may assume they know all they need to know about the subject. You should caution the students about this "I know it all" syndrome when discussing the philosophy of the assessment system.

Encouraging rote learning. If the quiz questions place too much emphasis on regurgitation of knowledge, students may get the impression that simple memorization is all that is required in learning. Simple recall is fine to demonstrate whether students have read all the material properly, but you should include questions that test students' deeper understanding of the topic or their ability to make logical deductions from their knowledge.

Encouraging cue seeking. A popular pastime among students is trying to guess the contents of the final exam as opposed to acquiring the knowledge and understanding that will help them do well on it. Students may use the quizzes in an attempt to deduce the contents of the final exam or may assume that the quiz questions will closely resemble those in the exam. You could, therefore, end up with a situation in which students who perform satisfactorily on the quizzes will do poorly when it comes to a final exam. Perhaps you can make sample examination papers available and caution the students about assuming too much from the contents of their assessments.

The nature of the answers may be restrictive. With the quiz system software discussed in this chapter, the majority of software permits answers only in the form of words that can be matched to a correct answer or multiple-choice questions. This system restricts the educator to writing questions that can be answered in this way. More advanced quizzes are possible (see "Advanced Quizzes" in this section), but for the present we are left with single-word answers or the selection of a multiple-choice option.

Examples of Quizzes You can present quiz questions in a number of ways: one at a time, all in one page, or in image maps.

If you use the one-at-a-time question method, questions appear in an area of the screen, and students type in their answers and press a button to have the computer mark the answers. The computer's response to their answers will then appear in another text box. This code is created in JavaScript and is contained on the CD-ROM in the file /assess/examples/jsone.htm. An example of the quiz page is shown in Figure 7.3; the marked quiz is shown in Figure 7.4.

You can also incorporate a revision list, which means that students will be required to answer the questions until they get them all correct. Any questions they miss will be added to a revision list that will be used to ask students the same question again and again until they get them right. An example of this type of quiz is also contained on the CD-ROM in the file/assess/examples/repeat.htm.

In the all-on-one-page method, as you might guess, you place all the questions on one Web page. An example appears in Figure 7.5 and on the CD-ROM in the file /assess/examples/jsall.htm. Students can answer multiple-choice and true-or-false questions by typing in answers. The marked quiz is shown in Figure 7.6. This method is possible with JavaScript or using a server-based program to mark the question.

Alternatively, you can create an image map using one of the programs discussed in Chapter 4. You can then use this image map to build a JavaScript quiz. In our example in Figure 7.7, we have taken the light bulb image map from Chapter 4, used the coordinates created by the image map creation program, and added a JavaScript program to create the questions and the answers. Students answer the questions by clicking on part of the image map. You can view this technique on the CD-ROM in the file /assess/examples/imapq.htm.

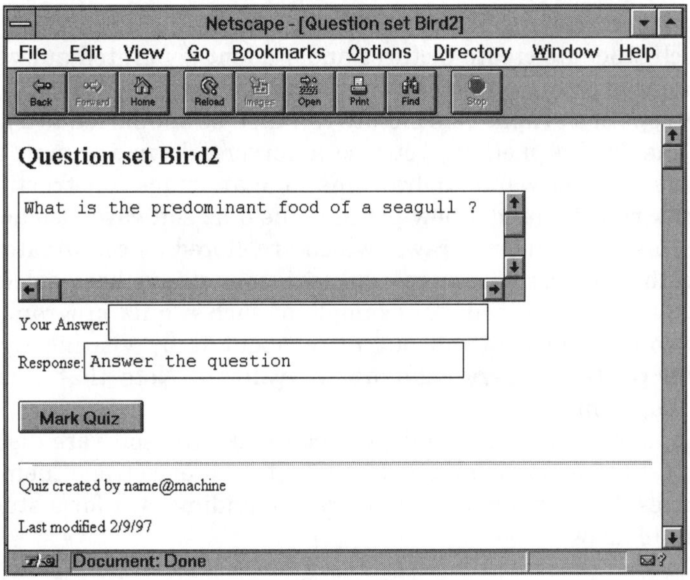

FIGURE 7.3 A JavaScript quiz page.

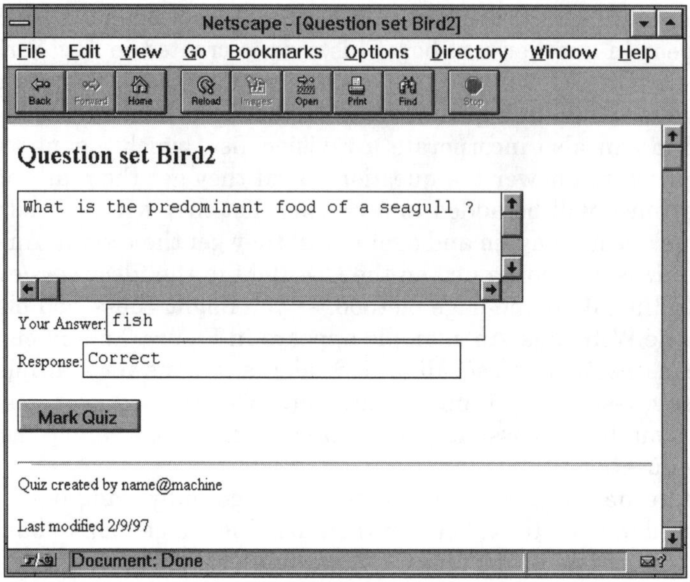

FIGURE 7.4 A marked JavaScript quiz.

We'll see how to implement these quiz types later in the chapter.

Advanced Quizzes There are several more advanced types of quiz: quizzes in which students create pictures and student-generated quizzes.

You can create a Web page in which students can draw a picture—for example, the slope of a graph. This picture can then be submitted to a server for correction. To enable this method, you use a server-side image map to locate the points where the user wants to draw lines and an image construction program that the server runs to build a new picture. The quiz software also needs to keep track of the lines the student draws (which are stored as coordinates) in order to ascertain that the correct range of picture points have been selected. This range will have been predefined. An example of such a quiz program, WebDraw, is being developed; you can find out more about it by visiting **cyber.ccsr.uiuc.edu/cyberprof-docs/general/draw/draw.html**. Note that this method is still in development.

In another advanced quiz, you can make the software discussed in the implementation section available to students and encourage them to create their own quizzes. It is usually a much more demanding task for a student to build a quiz than to answer one.

Providing Feedback with Answers There are a number of methods of feedback you can have the computer supply when students request that their quizzes be marked.

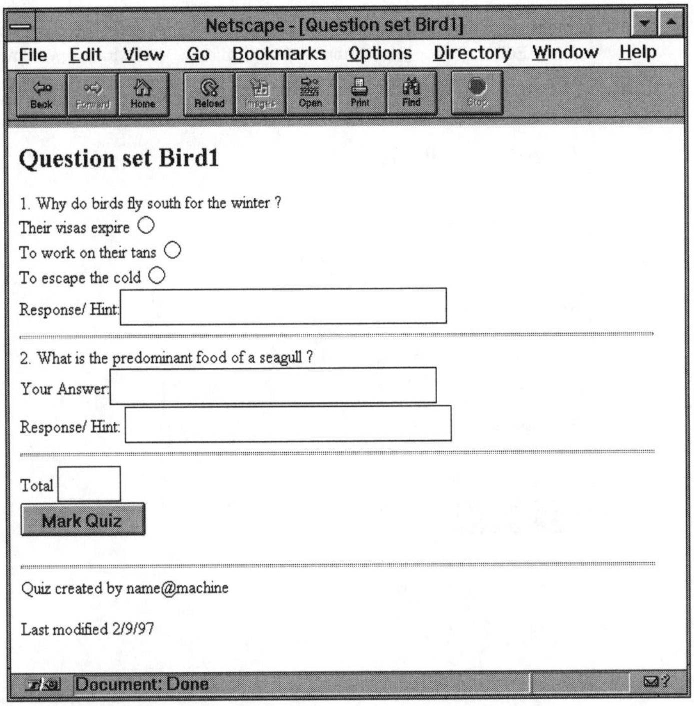

FIGURE 7.5 An example of an all-on-one-page quiz.

The marking software can indicate whether the answers students supplied were correct or incorrect. It can supply a hint if a student's answer is incorrect. If the answer given by the student is typed in, a standard hint is printed, no matter what the answer the user gives. If the answer is in multiple-choice form, you can define a different hint for each option. The hint can even contain the correct answer.

You can also give students blind feedback, in which the software gives students a mark for their answers—for instance, "You got 25%"—but does not tell them which questions they answered incorrectly. This makes it difficult for students to answer the quiz using a process of elimination or guessing. No hints are returned with this method.

In another alternative, when students submit their answers, the system will print the correct answer if students give an incorrect answer. This can save students from frustration if they encounter a particularly difficult question. A number of the software tools discussed in this chapter have made this facility an option for students, who can ask for the correct answer to be displayed.

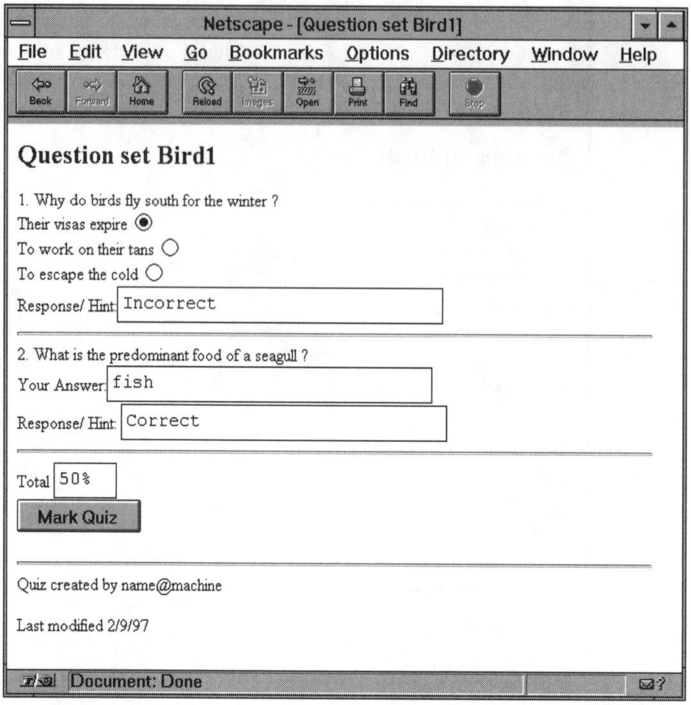

FIGURE 7.6 A marked all-on-one-page quiz.

Success Factors To help your students get the most out of quizzes, provide them with a facility they can use extensively and that aids the learning process. In doing so, you should consider a number of factors.

To make our interactive exercises effective, you should do the following:

Set the quizzes at the right level. You can create quizzes for different levels and use the adaptive or choice tutorial methods discussed in Chapter 5 to select the appropriate quiz for students or allow them to select their own level.

Insert a link to a source of resources for each question. Links can be inserted either as part of the question or as part of the hint for a wrong answer. Students will thus have easy access to resources related to the question to make revision more straightforward.

Provide a link or a contact point for a tutor to whom students can address questions. It is important for students to know that there is someone they can talk to if they are having problems with a quiz. You can provide such information at the bottom of a quiz page.

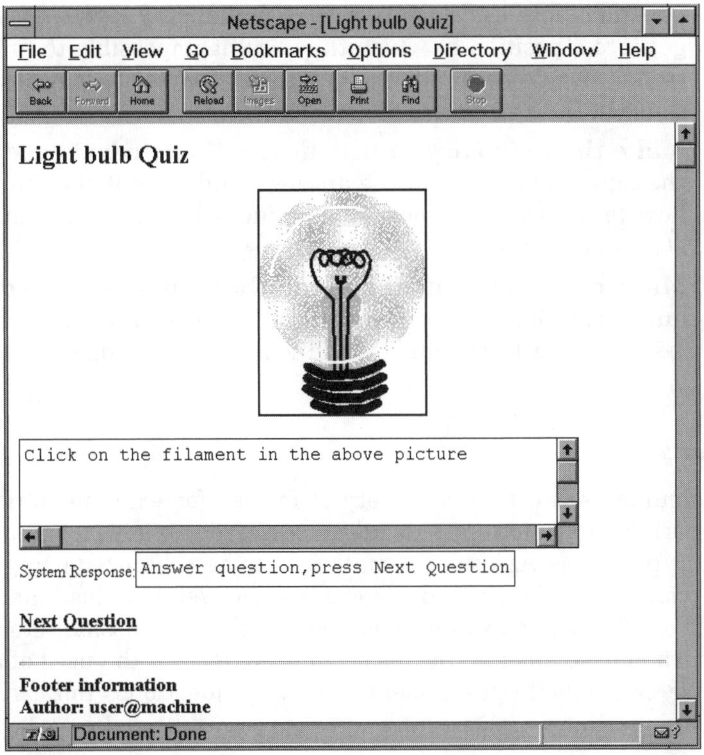

FIGURE 7.7 An image map-based quiz.

Link the questions to objectives or points in the teaching program. Each lesson has a particular objective, and groups of lessons should combine in order to fulfill a common goal. You can construct question sets to match these objectives and goals.

Be interesting, simulating, and motivating. Most educators do not want to encourage students to adopt a rote learning practice. They also do not want students to view quizzes as boring, pointless exercises. Construct quizzes to be as interesting and simulating as possible. This approach motivates students to attempt the quizzes and to use the answers to improve their understanding of a topic.

Help the student. Your quizzes should make the level of their knowledge clear to students. Students will do most quizzes on their own, and the results will not be seen by educators.

Build confidence without encouraging overconfidence. You need to strike a balance in the difficulty of your quizzes. One suggestion is to split the questions into easy, medium, and challenging levels. Try not to let students get into a position in which they find it impossible to finish the quiz; at the same time, do not make the quizzes so easy as to leave students with a false sense of their abilities.

Make the quiz easy to use. Ensure that students understand how to use the quiz—how to fill in the answers and submit the quiz for marking—and how to interpret the output. Provide a link to a relevant help page at the start of the quiz.

Make quizzes frequent enough that students won't fall behind. Place quizzes at all relevant points in the system—after each lesson or before each lesson—to test prerequisite and learned knowledge.

Assignments

Assignments can take a variety of forms. For example, students could submit materials in the form of a word-processed document, a spreadsheet file, or computer programs. Assessment material can be submitted using Internet tools such as e-mail and FTP, or students can use the Web to upload material onto the class server. Chapter 8 examines managing the submission, storage, marking, and return of assignments. In this section, we look at the uses of assignments.

We can refer to assignments as essay questions. You can have two types of essay questions:

Extended response questions. For instance, "Explain the circumstances under which a company should not computerize. Indicate what the circumstances depend on."

Restricted response questions. For example, "Give 10 reasons a company should not computerize."

The extended response question can be used as a very general specification, allowing students to form their own opinions on what the question is about and how to go about answering it. A restricted response question is useful when you know the specific domain of knowledge that you want to assess and want to ensure that students keep relevant any information they provide. A restricted response question, therefore, involves giving a more detailed specification for the answer, which reduces students' ability to be creative but also reduces their ability to misinterpret the question, bluff, or provide an incomplete answer.

Why Use an Assignment? The problem with the quiz as an assessment mechanism is that quizzes are generally useful only for determining a limited set of learning accomplishments, such as the mastery of a set of facts. Quizzes cannot tell you if a student's incorrect choice was the result of a guess or a mistake in reasoning. You might need to use the assignment form of assessment to allow students to demonstrate that they have acquired a more thorough competence in the topic and its application.

Table 7.1 compares quizzes and assignments, highlighting their relative merits and showing the conditions under which each may be appropriate.

Problems with Using Assignments

The problems that can arise using assignments include the fact that it is a labor-intensive process and only a limited sample of the course can be tested. Due to the nature of assignments, it is necessary to constrain their scope to a limited

Table 7.1 A Comparison of Assignments and Quizzes

	Quiz	*Essay/ Assignment*
Learning outcomes measured	Acquisition of facts, understanding, thinking skills	Writing abilities, problem-solving skills, originality, ability to select and organize ideas
Preparation of questions	A number of questions that reflect the knowledge domain to be tested need to be prepared; can be time consuming	Few questions needed
Sample of course covered	Can cover entire course using a large number of questions	Limited coverage of course material
Control of student response	Response is limited, reducing bluffing and the need for skill of expression but allowing guessing	Students can choose the form of response unless the question is restricted; guessing is eliminated, but students can use their writing skills and bluffing to hide lack of knowledge
Ease of scoring	Scoring is straightforward and consistent and can be automated	Scoring can be labor intensive; need to prepare and revise scoring criteria; scoring can be inconsistent
Influence on learning	Encourages the student to acquire a factual knowledge of a subject and to analyze questions carefully	Encourages development of good writing habits, expression, and organization and use of ideas
Consistency of marking	High consistency possible	Consistency for restricted and unrestricted essays is usually low

part of the course. This means that students who may demonstrate ability on the assignment may be weak in other areas of the course.

Forms of Assignments Assignments can consist of questions that require students to perform one or more of the following tasks: making summary notes, making lists, matching items from lists, assigning items to particular categories, and drawing and interpreting diagrams.

You can use communication mechanisms and students' personal spaces (see Chapter 5) to set up a group assignment, which encourages students to learn to cooperate. The usual problem with cooperation is conflict over each member's contribution to the project. Various resolution schemes are available if students disagree about workload, such as voting on the distribution of marks or having a tutor decide on the distribution based on conversations with the students. A number of resources for setting up group cooperation systems are provided in Chapter 6.

As we saw in Chapter 5, students can be encouraged to keep journals of their learning activities and results. As an assignment, students could write and submit reflective accounts of their journals in report form. The entire journal can be examined or submitted at stages in the course to verify students' reports.

Evaluations

An evaluation is another method of assessing student progress. Unlike the quiz or the assignment, an evaluation involves an observation or reporting of students' activities or abilities.

Why Use an Evaluation? The quiz and assignment methods may not be sufficient to produce a complete picture of the development of students' problem solving abilities, work habits, or social attitudes, which you may need to create an environment in which the learning process as a whole, not just the learning outcome, is monitored and fostered. For instance, neither assignments or quizzes can effectively establish whether a student has become an independent learner, has acquired creative ability, is interested in the topic, or has acquired an ability to work effectively as part of a group.

An evaluation can have a number of outcomes. For instance, you could use it for grading purposes or to categorize students into types (reluctant or eager to learn, for example) that can be dealt with appropriately. An evaluation can help you change your instruction methods or understand students' learning mechanisms. You can even encourage students to use the evaluation process to suggest methods of evaluation and grade students accordingly, helping students appreciate educators' difficulty in assessing them and giving them an opportunity to improve and feel part of their education.

Evaluation provides another tool for ascertaining if students are having learning difficulties. With an evaluation, you can investigate the nature of student difficulties more closely. Unfortunately, all this means that evaluation is a much more labor-intensive undertaking than the other methods of assessment and one that can be only facilitated using electronic methods rather than using electronic methods to reduce the workload involved.

Evaluation Methods You can use a number of methods for evaluation:

Peer review. Students can be asked to evaluate their peers or their peers' work.

Self-review. Students can be asked to evaluate themselves, perhaps using their journals.

Observed behavior. Students can be observed. during a discussion group and their behavior or ability noted.

One-to-one evaluation. You can communicate with students using online communications facilities in order to conduct the equivalent of a face-to-face examination.

Staged submission. You can have students complete an assignment in set time periods, such as an hour-long lab session each week, and obtain the result after each session. This result, a partial solution to a task, gives an insight into the path students are following to solve the problem.

Access records. You can analyze the number and nature of accesses to the course material stored on the server using activity logs stored on the server (see Chapter 10 regarding utilities for accessing and interpreting these logs), and you can make deductions about students from these. For example, if a student rarely accesses the system and performs poorly in assignments, you can deduce that the student is not trying or may have a problem.

Level of participation in discussions. Students' contributions to debates and discussions can be used as a basis on which to award marks.

Level of help given to fellow students. Certain students tend to become mentors to other students. You can either encourage this behavior and attempt to get mentor students to make themselves available to act as tutors for weaker students or you can investigate whether students are having a negative effect on their peers by doing too much for them.

Tests

You can use any of these assessment methods as a basis for awarding marks to students. They can also be used to implement a test, which is defined as an assessment (quiz, assignment, or evaluation) that students must perform in a specified time period in order to receive a grade.

The function of a test could be to establish students' relative standings in a group, to indicate whether students are competent in a clearly defined knowledge domain, or to measure students' achievement of a specific instructional objective.

You could have a number of other reasons for conducting a test. For instance, the use of tests tends to encourage students to keep up with the course. As most educators have found, marks are usually the most effective way to motivate the students to do something, so it is not always safe to assume that students will try the available quizzes diligently if there is no associated reward. However, this approach is usually viewed as bad teaching practice in that it rewards students for following an imposed set of steps toward learning as opposed to taking responsibility for their own learning. Unfortunately, though, the technique often works.

You could also want to use a test to obtain feedback on how students understood a lesson. The most effective way of getting the maximum number of students participating in the feedback process is to make it a compulsory undertaking or to offer marks for its completion.

Online Testing Issues The main issues involved in online testing are impersonation and security. It is worth noting that any conventional assessment situation in which students are not strictly monitored is open to abuse; online tests are no exception. Students can impersonate other students or tap into a network and record the answers sent by other students because answers are sent in unencrypted form (although with the volume of traffic on most networks, this is pretty unlikely). There are ways of addressing these issues, but they are so cumbersome as to be suitable only for extreme circumstances, such as when an online test receives a high proportion of student marks. There is no need to be impeded by this limitation, however, because paper-based methods of cheating are also well established (impersonation, copying, interception), so online exams should be regarded as being as secure as conventional exams.

You can consider two methods of addressing the problem of cheating. First, you could offer a level of marks that would mean cheaters would not gain that much. Second, you can introduce some sort of system that will ensure that the correct students are doing the test and they are not using any material they should not use. This method involves proctoring, or supervising, to some degree. Arrangements can be made for students at remote locations to take the test at a test center or to be in the company of someone of standing in the community who will certify that they performed the exam without cheating. Alternatively, you can implement a system of keeping an eye on the student, like the real-time video systems discussed in Chapter 6, where you can install a video camera at the test site and monitor students during a test. As an extra fail-safe method, you can introduce an oral test that will enable you to examine students in real time to ensure that they produce the results themselves.

Online Testing Methods The easiest method of implementing an online test is to use your server-based quiz as a testing mechanism. For example, you could use the TestCreator program (shown in the tools section of this chapter) to record the results from each quiz. You can allow students to try the quiz many times, or the "one-shot" option can be selected, indicating that students have only one go at the test. The one-shot test can be set up with a blind response system so students get their marks straight away but do not get enough information to help their peers cheat. The test can be made available as a quiz with answer viewing enabled when test submission time has passed to enable students to find out where they went wrong. The advantage of using quizzes as a form of test is that there is very little labor involved—just that necessary to set up the test, notify students, and collate the results. The system corrects and collects the results automatically, allowing an educator to conduct more tests on a class than were previously possible and enabling them to gain a truer picture of trends in the class and individual student abilities.

You can set up a time limit for a test to minimize the possibility that students can share results. The easiest way of doing this is to make the quiz accessible on the server for only a certain period of time, such as an hour. This time limit must take into account whether sufficient machines are available to allow all students an opportunity to complete the test and whether the students themselves are available within that particular time frame. Some quiz creation systems have automatic time limits built into each test, which mean that students have only a certain amount of time in which to submit answers once they have started the test.

The other assessment methods, such as assignments and evaluations, are equally useful, and indeed preferable in some cases, as testing methods. Testing that awards a significant portion of marks based on the result of an online test is hardly ever used due to the logistical and verification problems that accompany it. Most of the logistical problems can be put down to the requirement that testing take place simultaneously for all students. This requirement means that you must guarantee that students will be able to perform the test free from technical impediments. For example, what would your policy be for a student whose network connection broke down as he was sending a test to the server? How do you ensure that equipment used by students does not contain material that could help the student cheat? Many online distance education systems have used written tests and proctors who will ensure that students do not cheat; these can be adapted for online use only to a certain extent, because you cannot be sure that proctors will have the technical ability necessary to administrate an online test. One possible method of online testing advocates abandoning the notion of a specific time period used at the end of a course to ascertain students' achievements but bases students' overall results on a combination of assessments methods carried out over the duration of the course. This technique, however, requires administrative change in the majority of education establishments.

When to Give Tests You can set a number of points in your course at which to deliver tests: after a lesson, at specific times (end of the week or end of term). You can also use tests as a mechanism for encouraging students to use the system. For example, you can create a test if, in analyzing the system logs, you notice that students aren't accessing a particular lesson.

The frequency of testing depends on what you hope to accomplish with a test and the worth of a test to students. Administering tests too frequently can cause students to assume learning is simply a matter of absorbing enough information to pass a test; administering tests too rarely can result in students who are falling behind in the course being denied a safety mechanism to inform them that they are below an acceptable standard.

Another factor to consider is that there are two main student types: students who need to be encouraged to learn and need their learning planned out for them and students who will learn at their own pace and using their own paths. Making tests compulsory may disturb students who are following their own learning paths because they will be forced to learn specific material at specific times. On the other hand, making tests optional allows students who are weak learners to avoid having to face the fact that they are falling behind and delays bringing their inadequacies to the attention of the teaching staff. Therefore, it is best to adjust your testing policy to fit the types of learners you have in your class and the way in which you want to encourage your students to learn.

Test Design We have discussed how to build each assessment. Follow the guidelines for the relevant assessment method when you are building a test using that particular method (quiz or assignment). One other criterion you need to examine when designing a test is what you want to establish from a test:

- Teaching effectiveness
- Areas of difficulty for students
- Whether students can use the knowledge they have learned or are simply regurgitating it
- The average standard for the class

If you give tests frequently, it may be worthwhile to assemble the results and make them available to students, either individually or by posting the results in the administration area of your information distribution system. Posting the results for the entire class will give students a chance to assess their overall standing in the class.

How will the students respond to the tests? Will constant testing burden them or encourage them to keep up with the course? You should consider providing remedial action for students who are falling behind and not just simply let them slide out of the course. Another possibility to consider is that students will accept testing as simply another hurdle and ignore the results or any recommendation that accompanies them.

With the quiz-based testing system, students get their marks instantly, but if your system is set up to record students' identities along with their test results, you should consider notifying students of their marks by e-mail in some personal message. You can examine students' progress through the course using your logs and incorporate this information in your comments. An example e-mail message: "You scored 25% on the final section test even though you have covered all the relevant lessons. Perhaps you should have attempted more of the quizzes after each lesson. If you are having problems, feel free to contact me." Be careful that you do not sound too "big brotherish" or "big sisterish," but let students know that you are interested in their learning and that you are watching their progress.

IMPLEMENTATION OF ASSESSMENT METHODS

In this section, we look at how to design the various forms of assessment and the tools that are available to implement them.

General Design Considerations

Follow these steps in constructing and using an assessment:

Determine the purpose of the assessment. What is the learning aim of the material? How can students' achievement of this aim be measured? In other words, what is the most appropriate form of assessment? Is your intention to evaluate students or help them?

Develop the test specifications. This step involves producing a list of the material students should cover for the assessment, determining the types of questions that can be asked, and deciding what you want to find out from your questions (factual knowledge, deductive logic, etc.).

Select appropriate test items. Construct the test items using the guidelines discussed in the rest of this section.

Assemble the assessment. The assessment is assembled, students are informed about it, and, if necessary, signposts to the assessment are created. Nominate an educator to be responsible for processing students' queries about the assessment.

Administer the assessment. Some methods of assessment, such as the quiz, do not require administration, whereas a test may require you to set a time period for carrying out the test and to collect the results after the expiration of the allotted time.

Analyze the results. Most assessments produce some form of result you can use to gauge students' abilities or problems with sections of the course. Collate and analyze the results in order to draw conclusions from them.

Use the results. Make additions to your course or alter or create assessments based on the results of the test. Alterations could take the form of providing remedial tests for students, providing extra material, or sending personal messages to relevant groups of students about their performance.

To provide an effective assessment, you need to know what you are assessing. For each course's assessments, you should have prepared a set of instructional objectives in terms of learning outcomes. Usually, you want to evaluate whether students reached the learning objectives for a course or a segment of a course.

For example, in the tutorial about a light bulb we first examined in Chapter 5, the objective may have been to show the student how a light bulb works. The expected learning outcomes were that the students should be able to do the following:

- Identify the parts of a light bulb.
- Explain the principle of operation.
- Understand how a light bulb is replaced.

An assessment for this course can be broken down into a knowledge component (the student knows which part of the bulb is which), a skill component (the student should be able to replace a bulb), and an ability component (the student should be able to write a report on light bulbs and how they work).

These objectives make it easier to not only focus instruction, but to ascertain what should be assessed and what methods of assessment should be used.

Implementing a Quiz

This section looks at two methods of automatically marking a quiz. One involves using a program on the server, known as a CGI program; another method involves writing a quiz in JavaScript. (There is yet another method that involves creating a quiz that students can e-mail to a corrector. This method is discussed in the "Custom Quiz Creation" section of the chapter.)

Implementing CGI-Based Quizzes Within your HTML quiz page are form components (boxes for text and buttons for selecting multiple-choice options) that students use to fill in the answers. Each form has a button that, when pressed, will cause the information students have filled in to be sent to the server. The common gateway interface (CGI) method of information handling is a standard way of sending information contained in a form to a program on a server.

Each HTML quiz page contains (within a tag) the name of the program on the server that will mark the quiz; it passes this name to the server along with the information the student has supplied. The named program on the server will then be started by the HTTP program, will process the information from the quiz, and will print the results in the form of an HTML page the student will see.

The CGI program can also add the results of the quiz to a database of results for students. If students need an account to access the server (see Chapter 10 for a discussion of setting up an account), the database system will store students' user names along with their results. Because the program is stored on the server, the server must be able to execute the program, and students must have access to the server any time they want to do a quiz. One problem with relying on a server this way is that the programs to create and mark quizzes shown in this chapter can be used only on certain types of servers. Another problem is that quizzes created on one operating system cannot easily be moved to a different operating system because of the differences between file formats for various platforms.

Implementing JavaScript-Based Quizzes JavaScript is a language you can include in an HTML page to cause the browser to perform various tasks, such as correcting a quiz. If you want to use a JavaScript-based quiz system, you must ensure that students are using a JavaScript-compatible browser.

The big advantages of this method of quiz construction are that students do not need to access a server to correct their quizzes and your quizzes can be constructed to be server independent, so you can provide students with a method of doing quizzes on their own computers using a course distributed on a CD-ROM. However, it is not usually possible to keep a record of the results of a JavaScript-based quiz; the only record that can be kept of their use is if they are stored on the server, which can be used to track the identities of students who access the quiz page on the server (if you're using an account-based system) or the number of accesses made to the quiz page. If you want a reliable method of recording quiz results, you should use the CGI-based method.

Another problem with using a JavaScript-based quiz is that the answers are included with the JavaScript program necessary to implement the quiz and can therefore be viewed by students if they know how to display the source of an HTML page. You can address this problem by encrypting or encoding the answers (see Appendix D on the CD-ROM for information).

Implementation Guidelines Before using a quiz for any assessment method, you should establish its purpose—is it a gateway, a reinforcement for the lesson, a test of prerequisite knowledge, an eye opener (where students are introduced to an extension of knowledge presented in a lesson), or a "frightener" (used to scare students into changing behavior)? Be careful; as mentioned before, scare tactics may lose their effect if overused.

To make using quizzes as smooth as possible, you can:

- Test the quiz to ensure correct answers are reported as such.
- Try out the quiz on a sample student population or on other educators to ensure that questions are readable and understandable.
- Make sure the quiz is signposted and/or added to a list of quizzes placed at the start of the online system, where students can easily find it.
- If the quiz has been set up to record results, test that the results are being recorded correctly.
- Request feedback from the students about the quiz by providing a link to a feedback facility in the footer of the quiz page.

Design Guidelines Your quiz questions may be presented as any of the following or a combination:

- An inline image
- A link to an image
- A link to a simulation
- A link to a sound file
- A link to a video file or animated GIF
- A piece of text, either formatted or unformatted (formatted maintains the tabs and spaces associated with the text)

In most of the tools, you are limited to 10 questions. This should be a sufficient number to test students without overwhelming them. If you need more than 10 questions, you can place a few links to quizzes together on a page; for instance, "Do quiz a," "Do quiz b," and so on.

The most common use of a quiz is for revision purposes. If you are designing a quiz to help students consolidate their knowledge, the quiz should reflect the lesson's activities and content without focusing on only the small details, but also on a deep understanding of the larger issues.

Quizzes become meaningless if students cannot understand the questions. Try to put questions in as simple a form as possible. If you must phrase a question in a way likely to cause confusion, link terms of the question or even the question itself to a page that explains more fully, such as a glossary. Using numbers or color, you can give questions difficulty ratings that could ease students' minds if they are having trouble with a question.

Many students may want to print the quiz for later reference. The ability to print a quiz is important because the quizzes form part of the notes for the course, so you should construct it in a form that makes questions and/or results easy to print. Alternatively, you could provide solutions to the quiz at a later stage in the course, and students can print those.

You can create a number of quizzes and use the random page selector introduced in Chapter 5 to select a quiz at random for students. This will take some of the repetitiveness out of doing a quiz for students who go through material repeatedly.

Quiz Chains You can assemble quizzes together to form quiz chains. For example, in Figure 7.8, students starts with a main quiz, Quiz 1. Depending on the result, they can be taken to further material or another quiz (Quiz 2), which checks to see if they need remedial material and what form of material it should be. Once students have completed the remedial material, they have a chance to attempt the first quiz again. As we shall see later in this chapter, you can implement such a quiz chain using cookies or reward/punishment messages.

Question Groups You can write a number of quiz questions based on one main question. For example, in the first question in a quiz, you could include an image or a video clip and have a number of subsequent questions refer to it. This is known as a question group. The use of a question group enables students to concentrate on different aspects of a theme or topic.

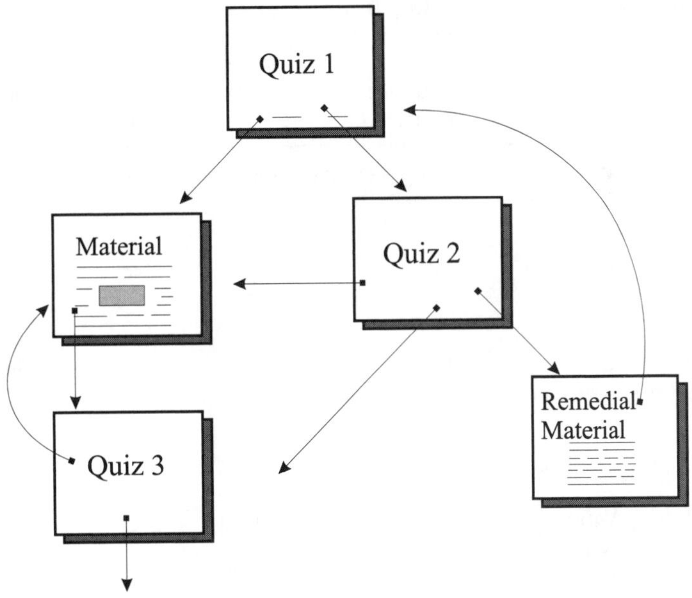

FIGURE 7.8 An example quiz chain structure.

Tools This section presents a number of tools for creating online quizzes. (We also provide JavaScript code for the quizzes in this chapter that you can use to create your own customized quizzes on the CD-ROM.) All the software discussed in this section is available on the accompanying CD-ROM in directory /assess/utils.

A summary of each tool and its facilities is shown in Table 7.2.

Test2000 The Test2000 package (located on the CD-ROM as file /assess/utils/win3-1/test2000) is a Windows program for constructing JavaScript-based quizzes with multiple-choice answers. The construction window is shown in Figure 7.9. As the figure shows, you can insert questions and possible answers as well as indicating the correct answer. Material relating to the question, such as related links, can also be inserted; this material appears in a frame to the side of the main question page.

Figure 7.10 shows what the quiz looks like in a browser. When you are finished creating the quiz, you can make a Web page of it and upload this page to your server. (Each test will actually consist of three HTML pages; one page is used to start the quiz, and the others provide the contents of the frames used in the quiz.)

Students take the quizzes by pressing the Grade Test button. The numbers of the questions for which students gave incorrect answers are shown at the bottom of the browser window. Students can click on the numbered question in the bottom section of the quiz (shown under the heading "Correct Answers") to see the

Table 7.2 Tools for Creating Online Quizzes

Tool	*Platform*	*Type of Questions Supported*	*Automatic Marking?*	*Result, Records Kept?*	*Hints Displayed?*	*Students' Requirements*
Test 2000	Windows 3.1/95NT	Multiple choice	Yes	No	No	JavaScript-capable browser
Jquiz	Windows 95/NT	Text	Yes	No	Yes	JavaScript-capable browser
Test Creator	UNIX, written in C	Multiple choice, text	Yes	Yes	Yes	JavaScript-capable browser or network connection
Web Work-sheet	Various, written in Perl	Multiple choice, test, essay	Yes	Yes	Yes	Network connection

reference material, and the correct answer is displayed in the frame on the right (the "Answer Window"). You can use Test2000 to save the quiz and reload it later for alteration.

TestCreator TestCreator is a program written in C for creating and editing various types of tests.

TestCreator is placed in the cgi-bin directory of a Web server (see Chapter 10) and is called using a URL (such as **machine/cgi-bin/testcreator**). You then use a form as an interface to the server-based program. (A number of versions of TestCreator appear on the CD-ROM, so you may not have to construct the program from scratch. These versions and instructions for creating and installing the TestCreator program are given in directory assess/tools/unix/tc on the CD-ROM. If there is no version of the TestCreator program for your particular platform, follow the instructions contained in the README file to compile your own version.)

TestCreator can be used to produce CGI server-based quizzes and JavaScript quizzes. If you use it to produce a CGI server-based quiz, you will need another program called TestMarker to mark the quiz. (You'll find TestMarker located in the same directory as TestCreator on the CD-ROM.)

When you start the TestCreator program, you are asked to name a quiz and to indicate the directory in which the quiz will be placed, as shown in Figure 7.11. If you give the name of a quiz you have created previously, it will be loaded again; otherwise, a new quiz will be created in this directory. The TestCreator program places a number of files in that directory, including the HTML file that will contain the quiz. You may move the HTML file that the quiz program creates in this

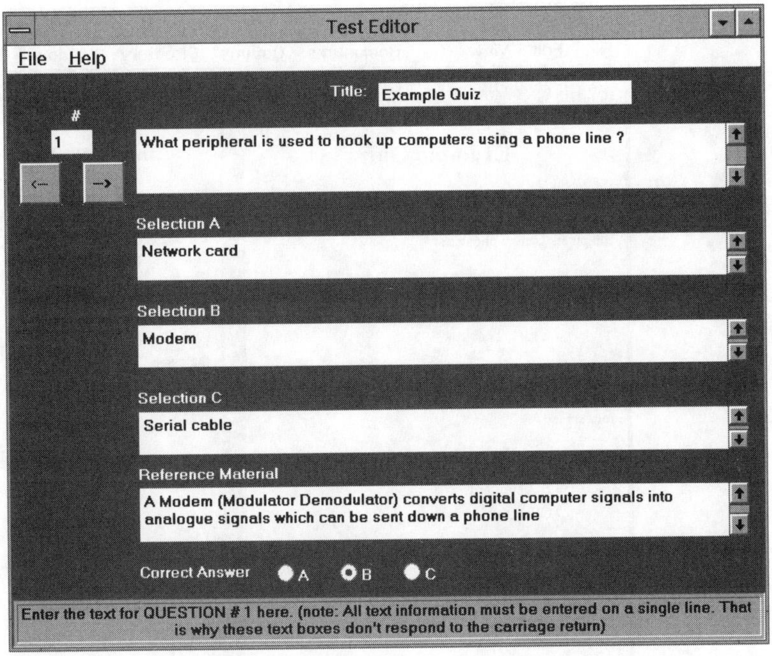

FIGURE 7.9 The Test2000 quiz creation page.

directory to any other directory, but you should not move the other files that TestCreator creates—namely, the record of the contents of the quiz (which has the extension .ans) and the results obtained by students who use the quiz (stored in a file with the extension .res).

Make sure that if you are creating a quiz, you have permission to write to the directory name you supply; otherwise, the program cannot create the quiz. If you do not have permission to write to a directory, TestCreator will produce an error message but will still allow you to create a JavaScript quiz, which you must then save on your local disk. For easier maintenance, create a new directory for each quiz before using TestCreator. The directory you create should not be accessible using a browser—in other words, it should not be within the root directory. If it is accessible using a browser and the directory is unprotected, students can read the answer file (but are unlikely to be able to interpret it) and read the record of marks for the quiz.

Once you have named your quiz and given a location for it, you are presented with a page into which you can input the questions, as shown in Figure 7.12. You can supply a maximum of 10 questions for each quiz. Answers can be supplied in the form of multiple-choice options or text.

Place the text for the question in the question box. By default, questions re displayed in formatted fashion but can be left in the format you type them in by

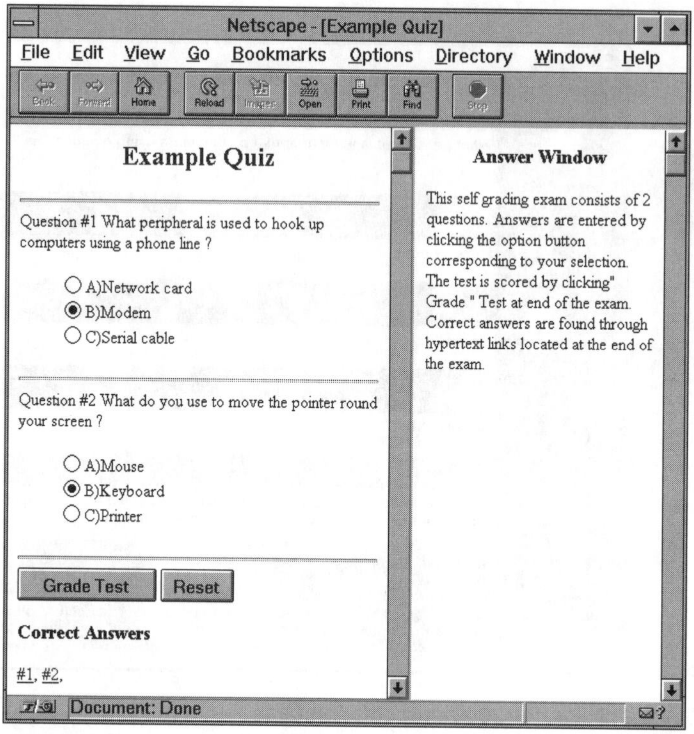

FIGURE 7.10 A Test2000 example quiz.

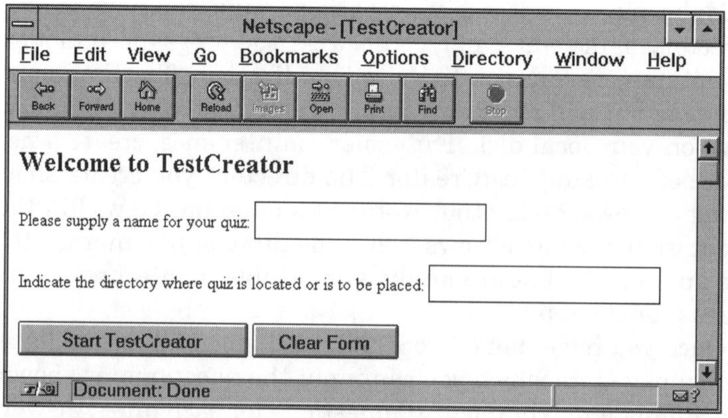

FIGURE 7.11 The TestCreator initial page.

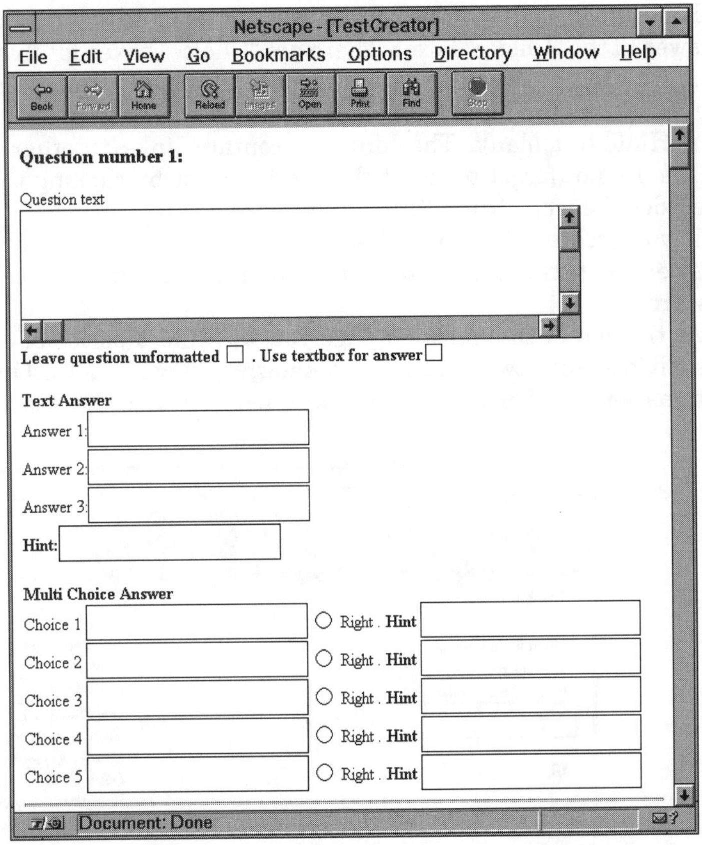

FIGURE 7.12 A TestCreator question creation page.

clicking on the "Leave question unformatted" box. The text of a question can contain HTML tags that allow links to be placed in questions or inline images to be loaded as part of the question. Students can type in or paste in a large answer to a question by selecting the "Use textbox for answer" option, which must be used in conjunction with the "Record results" option; any text students put into a text box on a quiz page will be written to a file that records the test results. You can enable this option if you want to obtain more comprehensive answers from students or use the system as an assignment submission mechanism.

The correct answers for text questions are placed in the "Text answer" box. Hints for the text answer are placed in the hint box following the answer boxes. There is a choice of three types of text answer box, so you can supply up to three acceptable answers to each question.

For multiple-choice answers, place the text to be displayed as a possible answer in the "Choice" boxes. There are "Choice" boxes for five answers. Place the hint for each answer in the box beside it labeled "Hint." This hint will be displayed if the student selects that answer. If the answer is the correct one, leave the "Hint" box blank. The hint can contain links to other pages or an inline image. Do not forget to select the right answer by clicking the radio button that precedes the word "Right" after the choice.

If you create a question that has both a text answer and a multiple-choice answer, the text answer will be used and the multiple-choice answers and hints discarded.

At the end of the question page you will find a series of options. The options are divided into two columns, as shown in Figure 7.13. One column contains options for JavaScript quizzes; the other contains options for the CGI server-

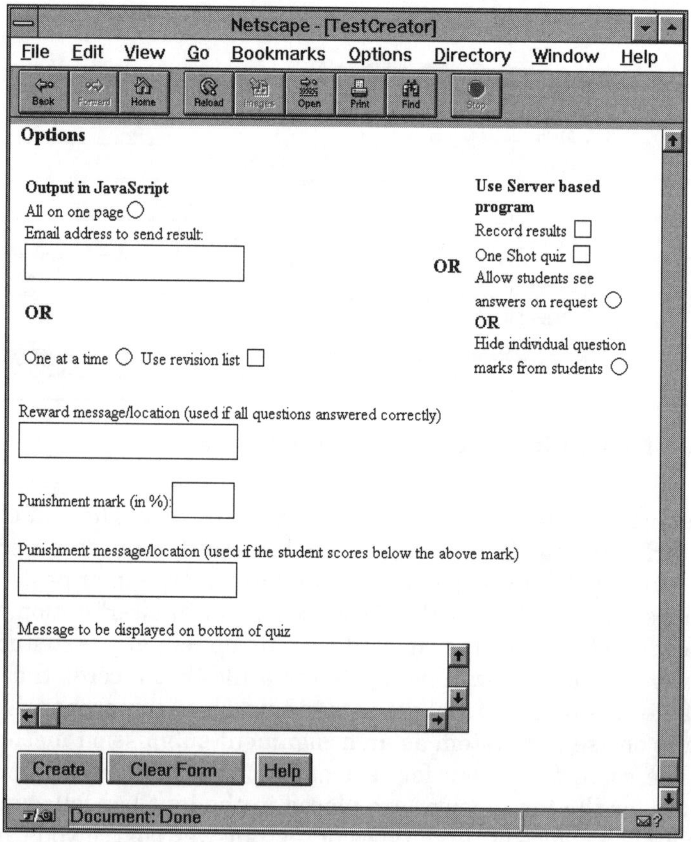

FIGURE 7.13 The TestCreator option selection page.

based quiz. If you do not select any of the options, the TestCreator program will create a CGI-based quiz.

The CGI-based quiz options are as follows:

Record results. The program that corrects the quiz will also make a record of student IDs, their marks, and the answers they supplied. If the system cannot read the students' IDs, just the marks and answers will be recorded.

One shot quiz. Students will get only one go at the quiz. For this option to work, your quiz must be access protected (see Chapter 10). If students attempt the quiz a second time, the system will refuse to record their results or mark their attempt.

Allow students to see answers on request OR hide individual question marks from students. These are the two possibilities of output form to students. If you choose neither of these options, students will simply be informed whether they got questions right or wrong.

If you select the "Allow students to see answers on request" option, students will have a box displayed in their question form that, if checked, will show students the correct answer to a question if they answered the question incorrectly. With the "Hide individual question marks from students" option, students will get only a final mark when they submit their quizzes for marking; they will not be told what questions they answered correctly or incorrectly.

You can create three types of JavaScript test: one in which all the questions are answered on one page (referred to as an all-in-one quiz), one that asks the questions one at a time (referred to as a one-per-page quiz), or a version of the one-per-page quiz that asks questions until the user gets all the questions right (referred to as a repeat-until-done quiz because it presents questions one at a time until they are all correctly answered). Let's look more closely at these quiz options:

All-in-one quiz. This type of quiz allows students to fill out an answer form (refer back to Figures 7.5 and 7.6). The answers are then corrected by a JavaScript program. Responses to answers ("correct," "incorrect," "hint") are placed in text windows following the question. This means that the hints cannot contain direct links; links must be supplied in URL form and students must be told to copy the link and visit that URL themselves. When a student gets all the questions right or obtains a mark below the punishment mark, an alert window appears. If the reward that has been supplied as an option contains a URL, the student is transferred to that URL after pressing OK on the alert box. If there is no URL, the text of the reward/punishment message is displayed. If you create an all-in-one JavaScript quiz, you can supply an e-mail address to which the results of the quiz will be sent. This address should be placed in the text box following "Email address to send result, as shown in

Figure 7.13. When you supply an e-mail address students completing a JavaScript quiz clicks on the button to mark the quiz, and the browser not only marks their quiz but sends their answers and their results to the e-mail address you supplied. This feature will be discussed in more detail later in this chapter.

One-per-page quiz. Questions are printed in a text window, answers must be typed into an answer window (multiple-choice answers are not permitted for this quiz), and a button is pressed to mark each question in the quiz, as shown in Figures 7.3 and 7.4. Once the question is marked, the student must press the button to get the next question. This process continues until the student completes all the questions in the quiz. This method is only suitable for typed-in answers, such as for spelling tests.

Repeat-until-done quiz. Similar to a one-per-page quiz except that the student does not receive a mark for the quiz but continues on with it until all questions have been answered correctly. Questions that are answered incorrectly are stored in a revision list that is used to present the incorrectly answered questions to the student again until all the questions have been answered correctly.

Other options shown on the TestCreator option selection page include these:

Reward message/location. A message appears when all the questions are answered correctly. This message may contain a link to another section, a password for another part of the course, or simply a congratulatory message.

Punishment message/location. A message appears if the student scores below a preset percentage, which you should input into the box marked "Punishment mark (in %)." The punishment message can contain a link to a remedial lesson or a message stating that the student should contact a tutor. Note that if a URL is supplied for the punishment and reward results, the URL will be automatically loaded into the browser only if the quiz is of a CGI or an all-in-one JavaScript type. If students use a one-per-page or repeat-until-done quiz, the URL will be displayed in the question box; students will be required to copy the URL from the text box and open it themselves.

Web Worksheet Web Worksheet is a CGI-based system written in Perl. It presents one question at a time as part of an HTML page. Web Worksheet is included on the CD-ROM in the directory /assess/tools/unix/webwork. Features of Web Worksheet include interactive exercises, feedback and scoring mechanisms, and scoring that can vary from question to question and for various degrees of "right" answers (allowing for partial credit).

Three types of questions can be used with Web Worksheet: multiple choice, fill in the blank, and essay/short answer (not marked by the correction program).

The exercise types Web Worksheet can accommodate are quizzes (answers are marked but the results are not stored), tests (results are recorded on the server), and one-shot questions or tests that allow a number of attempts. Students can get transcripts (via e-mail or Web page) of how they did for each exercise.

Web Worksheet's report features include summary reports that allow instructors to see how many students performed a test and their results and individual student reports that allow instructors to see how students did on each question as well as access to the essay answers.

JQuiz JQuiz is a Windows '95 program written by Martin Holmes. Its purpose is to allow you to easily design, store, and revise quizzes. It enables you to create Web pages that contain a JavaScript program that implements your quiz and a file that can store the questions and answers and be used at a later stage to alter the quiz. The answers can be supplied in text form only. JQuiz contains such features as these:

> **Choice of three possible answers.** You can supply three different possibilities for your answer.
>
> **A "safety" option for Microsoft Explorer.** This option makes the quizzes safe for use on an Explorer browser (sometimes Explorer has problems with JavaScript programs).
>
> **Individual answering.** Questions are answered in a separate frame. When an answer for a question has been filled in, students click on a link, and the answer is displayed in a frame located above the question.

Figure 7.14 shows the JQuiz application used for editing a quiz; Figure 7.15 shows the Web page this application generates.

Other Methods As mentioned, not all the answering possibilities that you might like to use— image map and gateway quizzes, for example—can be facilitated with available tools. In that case, you may need to modify the code that makes up the quiz. Let's examine what needs to be done, then take a more detailed look at the code involved in the "Custom Quiz Creation" section later in this chapter.

A JavaScript Image Map Quiz We looked at two ways of using an image in a quiz: You can include it as an inline image and ask students to identify relevant parts using multiple-choice or fill-in-the-blank questions, or you can combine a JavaScript program and the results from a client-side image map creation process to create a JavaScript quiz in which students answer questions by clicking on the relevant part of a picture.

Figure 7.16 illustrates the first method. You can include the image as part of the question (either as a link or in inline form) and ask students questions related to it. For example, "What part of a light bulb is represented by section A of the image?" This is the easiest way to include images in quizzes.

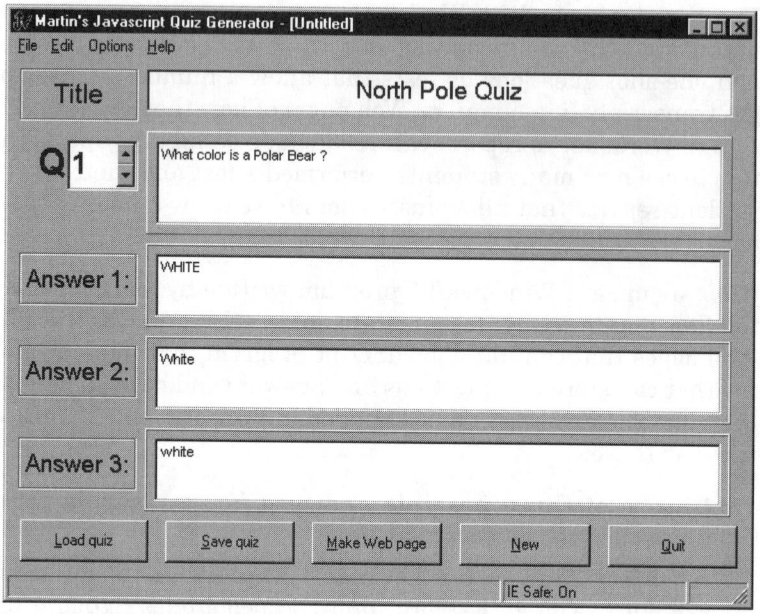

FIGURE 7.14 The JQuiz quiz creation page.

You can achieve the second way to involve an image in a test using the JavaScript code discussed in the "Custom Quiz Creation" section, the results of which are illustrated in Figure 7.7. (This code is available on the CD-ROM in directory /assess/examples/imapq.htm.) In this quiz, you can ask students to click on parts of the image; these clicks will be interpreted by the JavaScript program as answers. Using the JavaScript code means you must obtain the coordinates from a client-side image map creation program. (We saw how to create client-side image maps in Chapter 4.) Add these coordinates and the corresponding questions, answers, and hints to your JavaScript program. The JavaScript program is based on the one-per-page program described earlier, which asks the question in a text window and places the response to the question in another text window.

Setting Cookies in a JavaScript Quiz Chapter 4 gave some JavaScript code for reading a cookie that could contain a value indicating that the user belonged to one of three levels and transferring the user to the page associated with that cookie. You can use a quiz to set the level of the cookie. See the "Custom Quiz Creation" section for further discussion.

Quizzes as Gateways If you do not want to use a system in which students are transferred to a URL if they get full marks (discussed in the "TestCreator" section earlier in the chapter), you can give students passwords to other parts of the

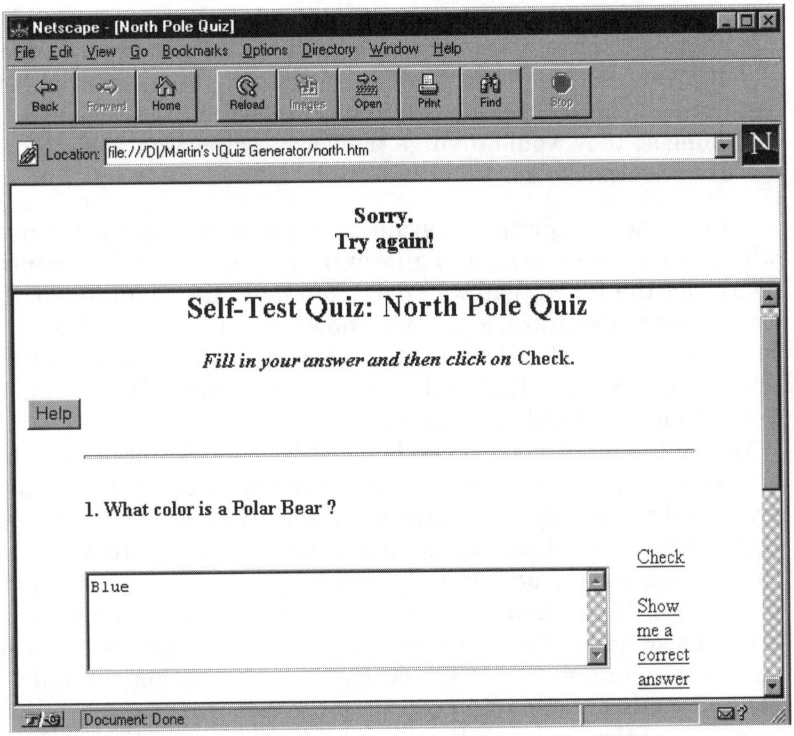

FIGURE 7.15 JQuiz example quiz.

course as "rewards" for a perfect score in a quiz. You can implement a password protected system in three ways.

Use a JavaScript program as a "door" the password will unlock. This method is open to compromise because students could find a way of breaking the password.

Use the access protection system of the HTTP server to create areas of the course that can be accessed only with a particular password. For example, you could create different users, Lesson1, Lesson2, and so on, and set up the system so that only these users have access to specific parts of the course. You can then provide students with the account name needed to get to the next part of the course (Lesson1) and its associated password. (We look at how to set up accounts on the server in Chapter 10.)

Add students to an access list based on their quiz results. Access lists control users' ability to access a single directory or a group of directories on the server (see Chapter 10 for more details). A file containing a list of account names can be created so that each directory has a group of identities that are allowed to have access to it. When students perform satisfactorily in a quiz or an assessment, their IDs can be added to the permitted list. Students will not be able to share passwords to protected areas of the course because in doing so they would divulge their own passwords, something most students are reluctant to do.

To use the JavaScript program as a gateway, you must convert the URL to which students are sent into a form users cannot read by simply looking at the source for the HTML gateway page. You must translate the location into a form users cannot recognize, a process known as encryption. This encrypted location must then be translated back into its correct form so users can tell their browsers what page to load. This is known as decryption. Details on encryption and decryption are provided on the CD-ROM.

One of the problems you can have with a JavaScript quiz is that it is easy for students to examine its source and read the answers from that. Students can even read the encrypted reward used to go through a gateway page. To hamper this method of cheating, you can use a system of encryption for your answers. You can use pieces of JavaScript code to create encrypted answers and add a function to your quiz that, when called, will decrypt the answer and compare it to one the user has supplied. You can also encrypt your reward value so students cannot obtain the location they will receive upon competing the quiz. Note that this method offers only limited protection because it is possible for students to copy your decryption code and use it to break the code for the answers. (The JavaScript code for this scheme is given on the CD-ROM.) A more reliable way of ensuring that the student cannot see the answers is to use the server-side, CGI-based method of quiz answering discussed earlier.

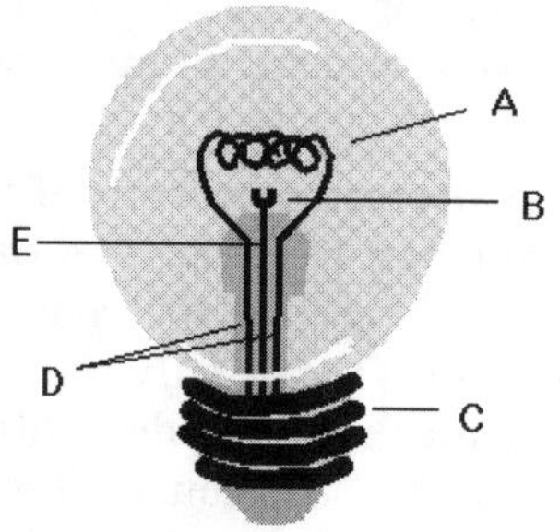

FIGURE 7.16 An image-based quiz.

The Assignment

Designing an Assignment To design an assignment, you need to do the following:

- Formulate it to support the desired learning objectives.
- Phrase each question so that the task is clear.
- Give a time estimate for the completion of the assignment.
- Identify and note irrelevant factors that will be ignored in the marking scheme; items such as bad spelling, poor formatting, or expression may be omitted because they are usually not major contributors to evaluating students' abilities.
- Decide whether the assignment is restricted or unrestricted.
- Prepare a marking scheme for the assignment.

Marking the Assignment There are two common marking schemes:

- The point method, in which markers look for common points in assignments and mark accordingly
- The rating system, in which you assign a number of grades and markers and place the assignment in the appropriate category

Form of Submission Assignments can be submitted in the form of word-processed documents, standard print file output (such as PostScript), HTML pages, links to HTML pages in students' personal space, computer code, drawings, simple text, or executable programs.

Be careful that students' submissions have been screened adequately for viruses. Executable programs are the main culprits, but Word and other word processor files can also contain viruses.

Submission Mechanisms Assignments can be submitted in a number of ways:

> **As e-mail.** Files can be sent as attachments to e-mail messages. This method has the disadvantage that the files must be extracted from e-mail upon receipt by the corrector. A way of overcoming this hurdle is to use the MHonArc utility (discussed in Chapter 6) to convert mail received into HTML form. This utility also extracts attachments and either includes them on the same page as the message (if the attachment is a type that is viewable in a browser window, such as a GIF image or a HTML file) or provides a link to the attachment file. If you want to prevent students from intercepting other students' assignments, you can set up a system that allows them to encrypt their e-mail messages. E-mail can be encrypted using a number of mechanisms, such as the PGP method (**web.mit.edu/network/pgp.html**).

Uploaded to a server. You can use the methods discussed in Chapters 4 and 1 to allow students to upload their assignments to a server using either FTP or an upload system. Once the assignments have been uploaded, the correctors can access them. Students can be prevented from uploading files after a particular deadline has passed by removing an upload script or changing the permissions on a directory so that nothing can be written to it.

As part of a quiz utility. The text box of a quiz form can allow students to paste in an assignment. This method is usually suitable for text-only assignments.

As a location. In this method, students prepare their assignments and place them in a particular location, for which they send you the URL. This location can be in students' personal space, where they may have written the assignment in HTML form, or in a file containing the assignment.

Acknowledging Submissions It is important to acknowledge receipt of students' assignments as soon as you receive them. Otherwise, students tend to resubmit assignment, which will cause confusion. A method for acknowledging receipt of e-mailed assignments is to use an autoreply program, which sends a message to users who have sent a message to your particular account, telling them that their message has been received. An example of such a program is Vacation (**www.amherst.edu/~atstarr/computers/vacation.html**). Be very careful about using such programs on general e-mail accounts, though, because they invariably reply to every message they receive. This leads to big trouble if you also receive mailing-list messages at that account. The best thing to do is to set up a special e-mail account for assignments, called, for example, grader.

Online Correction Tools Correcting assignments is usually more labor intensive than correcting quizzes or tests. Some tools can help you streamline the process of assignment correction. Let's look at a few.

Ceilidh The Ceilidh system, developed at the University of Nottingham, England, was created to allow users to submit computer code that could be automatically corrected by a server that produces a result and a series of comments to be returned to the user. This system overcomes a big problem with introductory programming courses: It can give rapid feedback to students with respect to the quality of their code. A Web interface has been developed but is not yet generally available (**www.cs.nott.ac.uk/~ceilidh/**). Ceilidh is being further developed to allow automatic marking of other forms of submitted information.

Markin Markin, written by Martin Holmes, is a Windows-based application designed to simplify the task of assignment correction. Markin enables the corrector to place a text assignment into a window and highlight various portions, such as spelling mistakes, that require a corrector's comments. The corrector can select the comment to be made from a panel that contains a number of appropriate marking criteria. The comment the corrector has defined as being associated with a criterion is then added to the assignment result. The program has the option of outputting the corrected assignment in the form of a text file, which can be e-mailed to the student, or a Web page. If the corrected assignment is output as a text file, the list of comments is added at the end in the form of footnotes associated with each occurrence of the mistake. If the marked assignment is output as a Web page, each portion of the text that was corrected acts as a link to a relevant comment, so students can click on a highlighted part of their text to discover what was wrong with it. This system enables correctors to construct a complete explanation of a problem and reuse this explanation for each student as opposed to repeating themselves for each new occurrence of a mistake. Students' grades are placed in text boxes in the marking program.

Figure 7.17 shows the layout of the Markin program. The assignment (which can be cut from an e-mail message or a Web page and pasted into this form) appears in the main text box. To the left of this box are a series of buttons, each of which contains a three-letter code for a common mistake or comment defined by the educator. If the comment that you want to add to the assignment is not defined beforehand, you can add extra comments or feedback information. Martin Holmes has also developed a toolbar for Microsoft Word and WordPerfect that works on the same basis as Markin. Details of these items and a paper describing computerized marking can be found at (**www.aitech.ac.jp/~iteslj/Articles/Holmes-ComputerMarking/index.html**).

CleverX Like the Markin program, CleverX is a package intended to allow a more streamlined correction procedure. It enables an educator to construct a list of assignment criteria. Correctors can then use this list to select elements that relate to what they find in students' assignments. Each selected element has a standard set of comments and advice associated with it that are assembled into one file and sent to the student. Each element also has an associated mark that is automatically added (or subtracted) to a total that is stored once the assignment is corrected. When the assignment is corrected and submitted to the database, students are sent their grades for the assignment and the material relevant to the selected comments. For example, the corrector could select a one-line comment, and the system could then add a page related to that comment or even a customized lesson to the material sent to the student as part of a corrected assignment.

The advantages of the CleverX system are that it enables students to make direct comparisons with peers, encourages educators to completely define assessment criteria, reduces time spent by correctors writing comments, increases the clarity of the comments as each failing can have an associated comprehensive comment written by the educator, and increases the amount of feedback obtained by the student. Furthermore, results are easier to analyze because they can be

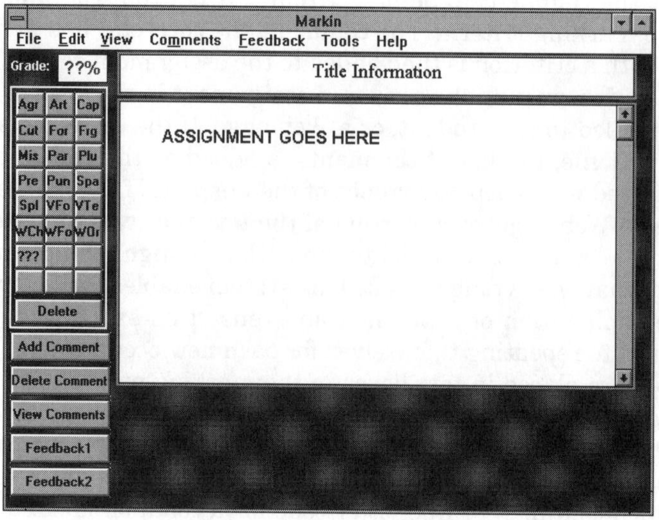

FIGURE 7.17 The Markin program.

broken down into areas, and turnaround times for returning assignments are decreased.

The CleverX program is currently in development, and evaluation versions will be made available for Windows 95 at (**www.cleverx.com/**).

Returning the Assignment After correcting an assignment, you should attempt to return it as quickly as possible and to provide students with a solution, a marking scheme, and a list of common mistakes. These can be posted in the administration area of your information distribution system. Individual assignments can be e-mailed to students or placed on a Web page students can access.

The Evaluation

Designing Your Evaluation You can design an evaluation for the following purposes:

Procedure evaluation. To test students' grasp of procedure.

Product evaluation. To assess the process by which students create something.

Social skills. To evaluate how students behave as individuals and in groups; the character traits of the students.

When designing an evaluation, you should be aware that because of their subjective nature, evaluations are more prone to error than assignments. For example, your evaluation could be influenced by what you think of the student in general, the criteria being evaluated may change during the course of the evaluation, or the marks awarded may fluctuate based on items not strictly related to the criteria of the evaluation but that tend to influence the evaluator.

Determining Evaluation Criteria Determine the goal of the evaluation and develop criteria for it as well as suitable methods of assessing students' conformance. Apply the criteria equally to all students.

Peer and Self-Evaluation The processes of peer evaluation, in which students assess each other, and self-evaluation, in which students assess themselves, are popular ways to introduce students to the mechanisms behind evaluation. In order to overcome students' natural tendency to overrate themselves or their peers, you can tie self- or peer evaluation with tutor evaluation—in other words, students receive marks based on how close they get to the standard set by the tutor. One problem with this method of evaluation is that it may teach students to learn the "tricks of the trade" as opposed to concentrating on the subject matter.

Tools You can use the following tools to help in evaluation:

Feedback forms. Feedback forms, shown in Chapter 5, enable students to submit self- or peer evaluations. The results can be added to a database and be examined by tutors or educators. These forms can be created using one of the quiz creation programs we looked at earlier in this chapter.

Logs. You can examine server logs using software discussed in Chapter 10. These logs can help you determine students' use of the system.

Communications facilities. The communications facilities discussed in Chapter 6 can allow one-to-one evaluation.

Discussion group archives. You can examine the archives of discussion groups to ascertain the nature and frequency of student contributions.

Journals. Student journals, created in their personal space, can also be used for evaluation purposes.

CUSTOM QUIZ CREATION

This section presents a more advanced discussion of the possibilities of a JavaScript-based quiz. It gives some code for various forms of the JavaScript quiz discussed in previous sections and shows how you can adapt these forms to facilities such as answer encryption, gateways, image map quizzes, and e-mailable quizzes.

Hiding Answers

One of the simplest methods of presenting self-tests is to hide the answer and tell students how to reveal the answer when they want to see it. For example, in Figure 7.18, you can see a question and, in parentheses, the instructions on how to reveal its answer. Figure 7.19 shows the same page with the answer revealed.

Each question in this type of quiz has a hyperlink to the answer. To create this link, you declare an anchor for your answer just before the answer, and the link for the answer points to that anchor. Therefore, anytime students click on the answer link, they stay in the same place on the page, but the color of the link will change, thereby revealing it.

In our example in Figures 7.18 and 7.19, this is done by defining the answer as the following link:

```
<a name="ans1"></a><a href="#ans1" >Polar bears can't fly
anywhere,they hibernate for the winter.</a>
```

Hiding the links is done by changing the background color of the links to be the same as the background color of the page, thus making the link "invisible." In our example, this is done by placing the declaration

```
<body bgcolor="#FFFFFF" link="#FFFFFF" vlink="#000000">
```

at the start of the page. As you can see, the color for each hyperlink is the same as the background color (bgcolor); in our example, the color is white. When students click on the link, they are said to have "visited" the link, and so the link changes color to indicate this visit. In our example, a visited link (vlink) changes to black. The HTML for this example is on the CD-ROM in directory assess/examples/hidden.htm.

A problem with this method is that the color declaration makes all unvisited links on the page "invisible"; therefore, you need to include a picture-based navigation bar on the page to allow students to follow a link to another page.

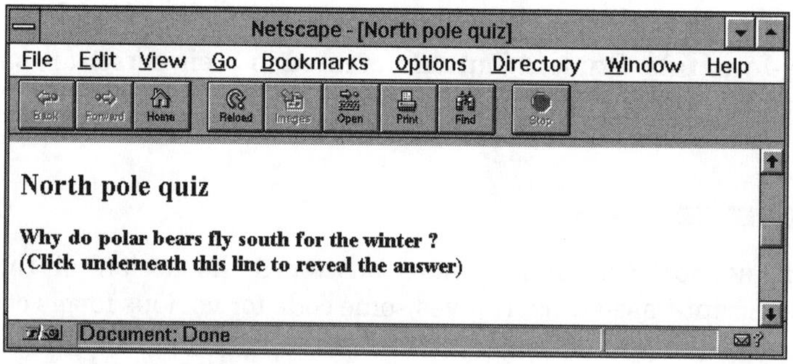

FIGURE 7.18 A hidden answer.

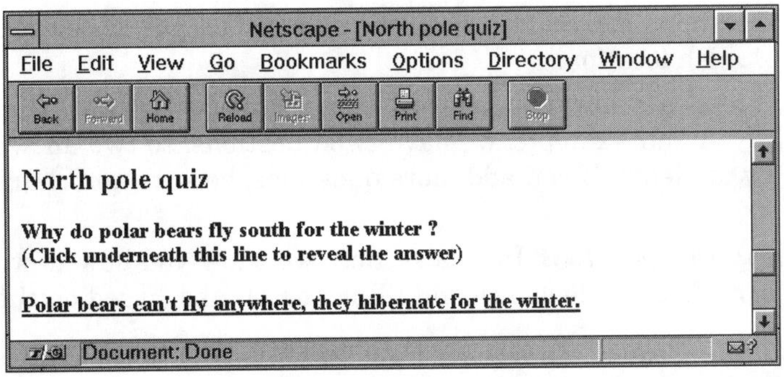

FIGURE 7.19 The answer revealed.

If students' browsers are able to handle JavaScript, you could use the pop-up windows discussed on the CD-ROM. This method allows you to put the question in the form of a hyperlink; when students' mouse pointers go over the link, the answer will appear in a window. When they move the mouse pointers away, the window will disappear.

All-on-One-Page Quiz

The following is a description of the JavaScript code for the all-on-one-page quiz shown in Figure 7.4. Each answer has its own separate section of the JavaScript program, known as a function, which is called from the main code. There are two different types of function: one to mark multiple-choice answers and one to mark text (fill-in-the-blank) answers. If you want to customize the code, you should alter the following:

In the main function (called check) you need to change the following:

Reward. Set the reward to the message you want to be displayed when students get all the questions right. Alternatively, you can include a location to which students are transferred upon receiving full marks. In our example here, we have set reward to display "Well done."

Punish. This is the location to which students are taken or the message received if their marks are less than that set in PunishMks. In our example, we have set the Punish variable to go to the location http://machine/ when the student gets less than or equal to the marks contained in PunishMks.

PunishMks. The percentage below which the Punish message is displayed or students are taken to the Punish location. In our example, we have set the percentage to 20, so if students get less than or equal to 20 percent of the questions correct, they will be shown the punish message or taken to the Punish location.

NumAnswers. This indicates the number of answers that students will supply. In our example, we have two questions, so two answers will be supplied by students. If you add more questions, be sure and change NumAnswers.

Setting Up Questions In this section, we show you how to write your own questions, both multiple choice and fill in the blanks, based on the following code.

Multiple-Choice Questions Function Answer1 in the code is a piece of the program that marks the answer to a multiple-choice question. Each function and its variables are named according to the number of the question they mark—for example, function Answer1 marks question number 1 (Why do birds fly south for the winter?). Each function needs some of the values changed so that you can insert your correct answer and hints. We denote the number of the question by attaching an X to the variables below. So, for example, in our function Answer1, we need to change the values associated with RightAnswer1, NumAnswers1, and Hints1.

To create more multiple-choice answers, simply alter the following for the relevant function:

RightAnswerX. This indicates the correct answer, so if you have four choices and the fourth choice is the correct one, you should replace the 2 in the example shown code with 4.

NumAnswersX. This is the number of choices; in our example, we have three possible answers.

HintsX[?]. Each incorrect answer has one hint. To supply a hint for an answer, simply subtract 1 from the answer number and place your hint between the quotes. For instance, hint for answer number 2 would appear like this:

```
Hint[1]="Hint for answer 2";
```

Text Questions Function Answer2 in the JavaScript code marks a text question. To add your own text question, you need to change the line in the function

```
if(form.answerX.value== "answer")
```

by replacing the word answer with your correct answer.

You can provide multiple correct answers with the following code:

```
if((form.answerX.value=="answer1")||(form.answerX.value=="ans
wer2")||(form.answerX.value=="answer3"))
```

where answer1,answer2, and answer3 are all acceptable correct answers. In our example, we have defined two acceptable answers: fish and Fish:

```
if((form.answer2.value=="fish")||(form.answer2.value=="Fish")
)
```

Question Text and Options You will also need to add your own question text to the form at the end of the code. Remember to add different choices for answers if the question is a multiple-choice one.

For instance, if you want to ask the question, "What day is today?" you add the question text and the number of the question this way:

```
<form>
1. What day is today?
```

If the question is a text question, you need to add an answer box in which students can write the answer and a hint box in which the hint will be placed. This is done by writing a line like the following :

```
Your Answer:<INPUT TYPE="TEXT" NAME="answer1" VALUE=""
SIZE=30><br>
Response/ Hint: <INPUT TYPE="TEXT" NAME="response1" VALUE=""
SIZE=30 ><br>
```

The number following answer and response must correspond to the number of the question. In the case above, the number is 1 because the question is the first question.

If you are adding a multiple-choice answer, you need to create each answer and provide a hint box:

```
Monday <INPUT TYPE="RADIO" NAME="answer1" value="ans1"
onClick=0><br>
Tuesday <INPUT TYPE="RADIO" NAME="answer1" value="ans1"
onClick=0><br>
```

and so on for the other possible answers, finishing with:

```
Response/ Hint:<INPUT TYPE="TEXT" NAME="response1" VALUE=""
SIZE=30 ><br>
```

Finish your form with the code that displays the button students press to correct the form:

```
<input type="button" value="Mark Quiz" onClick="check(form)">
</form>
```

Do not forget to add author and contact information at the end of your quiz.

This source code for this quiz is available on the CD-ROM in the directory /assess/examples/jsall.htm.

One-per-Page Quiz

To customize the one-per-page quiz, alter the code by changing the following options:

NumAnswers. This is the number of answers that students will supply. In our example code, there are two questions; therefore, there will be two answers.

Reward. The message displayed when students answer all questions correctly.

Punish. The message displayed if students below a certain grade (PunishMk).

PunishMk. The grade at or below which a punishment message will be displayed.

Setting Up Questions For each question, you need to put the text of that question into a variable. Put the question text into a variable called Question[X], where X is the number of the question minus 1. So in our code we put the question text for the second question, "What is the predominant food of a seagull?" into Question[1]:

```
Question[1]="What is the predominant food of a seagull?";
```

Put the answer to each question into the Answer variable. Again, remember that X is the number of the question minus 1. So, for our answer 1, we write the following code:

```
Answer[1]="fish";
```

Finally, put the hint for the question in the Hint variable:

```
Hint[1]="They swim in the sea";
```

The source code for the one-per-page quiz is available on the CD-ROM in the directory /assess/examples/jsone.htm.

Repeat-Until-Done Quiz

To customize the repeat-until-done quiz, you can alter the code by changing the following by changing the following options:

NumAnswers. The number of answers that students will supply. In our example code, there are two questions, so there will be two answers.

Reward. The reward message displayed when students answer all questions correctly.

Other than these two options, the repeat-until-done quiz is almost identical to the one-per-page quiz.

Setting Up Questions For each question, you need to put the text of that question into a variable. Put the question text into a variable called Question[X], where X is the number of the question minus 1. So, for example, in our code, we put the question text for the second question, "What is the predominant food of a seagull?" into Question[1].

Put the answer for the question into the Answer variable. Again, remember that X is the number of the question minus 1. Finally, put the hint for the question in the Hint variable.

Do not forget to change the quiz creator and include contact information at the end of the quiz.

The source code for the repeat-until-done quiz is available on the CD-ROM in the directory /assess/examples/repeat.htm.

JavaScript Image Map Test

To create an image map quiz using JavaScript, you need to take a number of preparatory steps:

1. Create an image map and select the sections that will form answers to your questions. In an image map creation program, each area of a picture selected is associated with a filename or URL that will be loaded when that section of the picture is clicked on. Create the image map using your answers for these URLs, the idea being that a click on the image will send the name of the file associated with that section of the picture to the JavaScript program, which will interpret the answer.
2. Insert the points obtained by the image file into the JavaScript program given at the end of this section. In this step, you place into your JavaScript quiz the coordinates produced by the image map program that represent the boundaries of the areas of the picture and that form the answers to your questions .
3. Alter the JavaScript program so that the answers it contains correspond to the names of the files associated with each of the points in the image map. Insert the questions and the hints into the JavaScript code.

For example, Figure 7.7 showed a quiz dealing with a light bulb. To create that quiz, we first mapped out the sections of the light bulb that we needed using an image map program. We want to ask students to identify the areas of the bulb that correspond to the filament, the stem, and the base. The image map program we used (see Chapter 4 for a list of available image map creation programs) produced an HTML file as it prepared a client-side image map. The code of this file is:

```
<html>
<img src="bulb.gif" usemap="#bulb">
<map name="bulb">
<area shape="rect" coords="76,119,190,161" href="fil">
<area shape="rect" coords="62,358,207,454" href="base">
<area shape="rect" coords="114,161,152,333" href="stem">
<area shape="default" nohref>
</map>
</html>
```

We called the files that outline the sections of the picture fil, base, and stem (note that these are not particularly good names because they give the game away when the student puts the mouse over the picture sections in the browser). We then inserted these coordinates into the JavaScript program below and changed the hrefs to point to JavaScript:check('name'), where name was fil, base, or stem. These names were then inserted into the part of the JavaScript program that marks the questions as the correct answers.

The quiz starts when the user presses the Next Question button, which displays the question in the question box. The student clicks on the part of the picture that represents the answer, and the response appears in the response box. The response indicates whether the answer is wrong or right; if it is wrong and a hint is associated with that answer, the hint also appears. If the answer is wrong, it is added to a revision list and the student will be asked the question again.

Do not forget to add the text for the reward students get when they answer all questions correctly. In our example, we have set Reward to "Well done," so the program prints out the message "Well done" when the student gets full marks. The rest of the changes are similar to those discussed in the section dealing with repeat-until-done quizzes:

```
<
```

This source code for the reward is available on the CD-ROM in the directory /assess/examples/imapq.htm.

Setting a Cookie

To have your quiz set a cookie based on the mark a student receives and then use this cookie as a basis for selecting the next page the student sees (see Chapter 5), you need to use a few extra JavaScript statements. The code you need to modify is a subsection of the all-on-one-page JavaScript quiz and should not be used on its own. Simply modify the function called check, which is the part of the JavaScript quiz that marks the questions, so remember to include all of the other functions that mark the question and the form for inputting the answers (seen in above sections). You can see the code in a complete form on the CD-ROM (/assess/examples/cookie/jscook.htm).

You can set a cookie using a JavaScript quiz by defining the levels of marks for each cookie. First, you remove the reward/punishment section from the JavaScript quiz code and replace it with code that checks the level of marks achieved and sets the relevant cookie.

For example, in the piece of JavaScript code here, we have taken out the reward/punishment section and set the level of marks for cookies 1, 2, and 3 (which correspond to beginner, intermediate, and advanced levels, as discussed in Chapter 5). That is, the cookie associated with this quiz is set to the following levels:

```
Beginner=1
Intermediate=2
Advanced=3
```

With this code, if the user obtains a beginners' mark (less than or equal to 20 in our example), the cookie is assigned the value 1, which will be used by the adaptable quiz action page to route the student to the page relevant to his status.

You need to set the following options in the JavaScript program for your adaptive quiz:

Beginner. The percentage of marks for which the beginner cookie will be set. For instance, the beginner cookie will be set if a student gets a total percentage less than or equal to the beginner value (20 in our example).

Intermediate. The percentage of marks up to which the intermediate cookie will be set. For example, the intermediate cookie will be set if the student gets less than or equal to the intermediate value but more than the beginners' value.

Advanced. The advanced level will be set if the percentage of the marks obtained by a student exceeds the percentage set for the intermediate marks.

CookieName. The name of the cookie that will be used in the page that acts on the cookie value (the action page). In our example, the name is set as Quiz1.

Jumpto. The location to which the student is transferred after completing the quiz. This is most likely an action page (see Chapter 5), which will read the cookie value and decide which page to bring the student to.

Look at the action page for the example quiz on the CD-ROM to see how it works: /assess/examples/cookie/action.

```
function check(form)
{
```

```
Beginner=20;
Intermediate=60;
CookieName="Quiz1";
Jumpto="http://machine/page";
var cookie;

NumAnswers=2;
var correct=0;
if(Answer1(form))
 correct++;
if(Answer2(form))
 correct++;
form.total.value=Math.round((correct/NumAnswers)*100)+"%";
Result=((correct/NumAnswers)*100);
if(Result<=Beginner)
  {cookie=1;
  Level="beginner";}
else
  if (Result<=Intermediate)
        {cookie=2;
     Level="intermediate";}
   else
        {cookie=3;
     Level="advanced";}
 document.cookie=CookieName+'='+cookie;
 alert("Quiz Completed.\nThe level you achieved was "+Level);
 location=Jumpto;

}
```

Sending JavaScript Quiz Results via E-Mail

JavaScript quiz results are usually shown only to the student who took the quiz, but you can alter the JavaScript quiz slightly so that not only does it provide students with instant feedback, but it also e-mails them the answers and their total marks. This is possible only with the all-on-one-page type of quiz.

All that needs to be done is to change the <form> tag in the JavaScript quiz to read

```
<form name="form" action="mailto:user@machine?subject=test-
name" ENCTYPE = "text/plain" onSubmit="return check(form)">
```

You need to change user@machine to the e-mail address to which you want the quiz results sent and testname to the name of the relevant test. You also need to change the line

```
<input type="button" value="Mark Quiz" onClick="check(form)">
```

so that it reads

```
<input type="submit" value="Mark Quiz" >
```

The new JavaScript quiz will appear exactly like any other quiz but will e-mail the results once the student has clicked on the Mark Quiz button. For example, if we altered the JavaScript quiz about birds, the e-mail message sent will look like the one below:

```
Date: Sun, 04 May 1997 19:03:07 -0700
From: student20 <student20@courserver>
To: quizmaster@courserver
Subject: Bird2

answer1=ans1
response1=Correct
answer2=Carrots
response2=They swim in the sea
total=50%
```

This message indicates that the user's first answer (answer1) was correct; the second answer (Carrots) was incorrect (response2 provides the hint for that question as opposed to the message "Incorrect"). The user therefore obtained only 50 percent.

For this method to work, students' browsers must be set up to send e-mail. For an example, see the quiz on the CD-ROM in the directory/assess/examples/jse-mail.htm.

Submitting Quizzes via E-Mail

Perhaps none of the above JavaScript or CGI-based quiz methods is suitable for your local setup. In that case, there is one other option to enable you to use a browser to administer a quiz. You can get students' browsers to e-mail the quiz answers to you. This involves preparing an answer form page as in the case of the other quizzes. However, when students submit or "mark" the quiz, the form's contents will be sent to you in an e-mail message. There is no JavaScript on the quiz page, so students will not see the result of the quiz.

The basic requirement for this technique is that students' browsers must be set up so that they can send e-mail. The easiest way to get the students to check this is to require them to send you an e-mail message at the start of the year using their browsers' built-in e-mail program. Do this using a link known as a mailto link. For example, when students click on the link "Send a message," the HTML code

```
<a href="mailto:user@machine">Send a message</a>
```

causes students' browsers to start their mail programs.

On most browsers, the e-mailable quiz will not call up a mail program to send the e-mail message containing the contents of the quiz. The big advantage of an e-mail quiz is that it is simple to set up and alter. The disadvantages are that students do not get immediate feedback and marking the answers will require labor.

Figure 7.20 shows a quiz like the one discussed here; the corresponding HTML code is located on the CD-ROM. As you can see, four types of answers are possible: a selection of one of three different options, a selection of any number of four options, a text answer, and a passage of text.

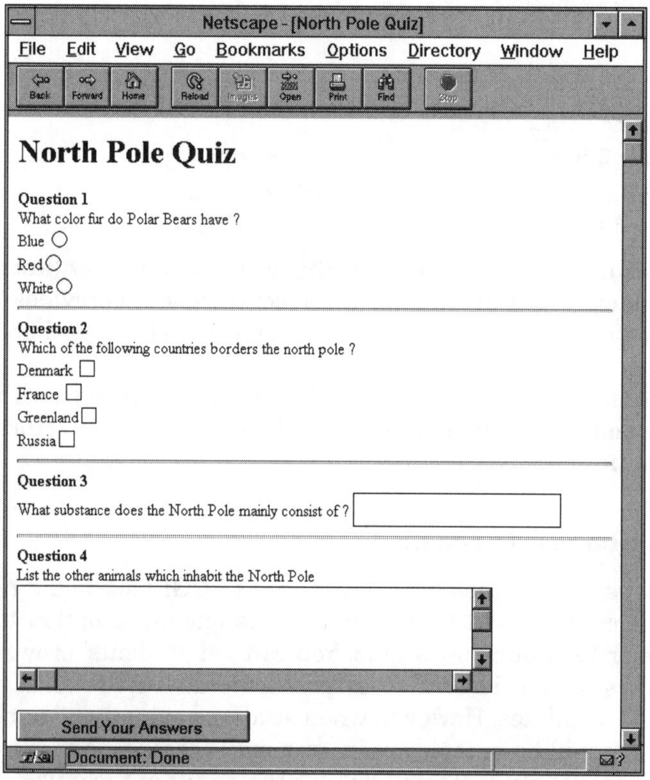

FIGURE 7.20 A question form.

To change the quiz to suit your purposes, just pick the type of question that you want to ask and change the following:

Name="..." This needs to contain a description of the question that will be sent with the e-mail message.

Value="..." This needs to contain an answer for multiple-choice questions.

For example, when we write the line

```
Blue <input type="radio" Name="Polar Bears fur" Value="Blue">
```

we are saying that the answer shown to students as a possible choice is "Blue," which is also the answer that is sent to you when the student submits the quiz.

The code for this quiz is available on the CD-ROM in the directory /assess/examples/emailq.htm.

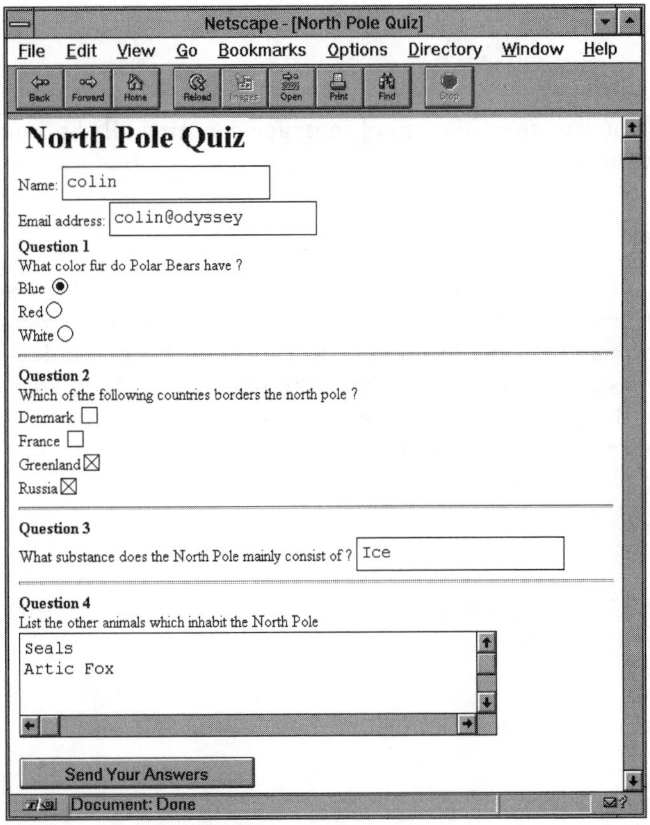

FIGURE 7.21 A filled-in question form.

Figure 7.21 contains the form filled in with some answers.

If students press the button marked "Send Your Answers," for the quiz in Figure 7.21, the following e-mail message will be sent to the e-mail address teacher@server:

```
Date: Wed, 23 Apr 1997 21:07:07 -0700
From: Any Student <astudent@student.edu>
To: teacher@server
Subject: North Pole Quiz

Students name=colin
Email=colin@odyssey
Polar Bears fur=Blue
Borders North Pole=Greenland
Borders North Pole=Russia
North Pole consists of=Ice
Other animal inhabitants=Seals
Artic Fox
```

As you can see, this e-mail message contains all the information necessary to mark the quiz.

CONCLUSION

In this chapter, we looked at a number of methods of assessment. Each one has its relevant merits and weaknesses and is suitable for ascertaining levels of achievement among students. We saw that various online methods of applying these assessments can improve the ease with which they can be administered and reduce the resources needed to operate them. Assessment is a valuable tool for learning, and it should be used in an appropriate fashion as part of your Web-based classroom.

RESOURCES

A list of sites related to the following topics covered in this chapter can be found on the CD-ROM:

- Quiz systems
- Mail-based forms

8

Class Management

Class management tasks are the clerical and administrative tasks necessary to ensure that a classroom operates efficiently. Duties include enrollments, course registration, assessment management, student tracking, and many others. These are tasks that educators must perform, but most would prefer to avoid. The combination of the characteristics of the Web, the information-processing power of the computer, and appropriate administrative practices can make existing class management practices more efficient. This combination can also lead to the development of completely new administrative procedures that may help you achieve either the same or completely different goals.

This chapter answers these questions:

- What is class management?
- Why would you use the Web to perform class management tasks?
- What are other educators doing with Web-based class management?
- How can you do it?

WHAT IS CLASS MANAGEMENT?

Class management is all those things that need to be in place to ensure that a class runs smoothly, with minimal fuss and maximum satisfaction for all participants. Many of these tasks are less than interesting and involve simple but time-consuming clerical and administrative processes. Class management tasks are often difficult to maintain an interest in, but are essential for the operation of a class. Many of the tasks are performed at a departmental or institutional level and often involve a number of support personnel, including secretarial, postal, clerical, finance, publicity, and counseling professionals.

The following section describes some of the tasks included in class management. It examines the steps required before a class starts, while it is running, and after it has finished.

Before the Class Starts

The quantity and quality of preparation for a class has a direct influence on its success. A Web-based class in particular requires more preparation than a traditional face-to-face class. This preparation is necessary for a number of reasons including the reliance on technology, the participants' unfamiliarity with the technology and the lack of administrative support that Web-based teaching methods generally receive compared to traditional teaching methods.

Some of the pre-class tasks include the following:

Class promotion. Two reasons to promote a class are to ensure a suitable number of students enroll and to ensure that those students who do enroll are fully aware of the class's purpose and requirements. Promotion can include traditional tasks such as writing the description of the class for an institution's handbook and talking to students, as well as nontraditional tasks such as using Web page meta data to cater to the requirements of Web search engines.

Time-tabling and scheduling. Timetabling and scheduling ensure that all participants know when, where, and what they are expected to do in order to complete the class. It also ensures that the necessary rooms, cameras, laboratory equipment, and other resources are available to the participants.

Enrollments. Due to the size and complexity of the enrollments task, it is usually the responsibility of a centralized administrative department that uses a large commercial database to store student information.

Course advice. Course advice incorporates a range of tasks: recognizing prior learning, checking prerequisites and qualifications, and providing advice on career paths.

Preparation of the delivery system. Any mode of teaching involves the use of a delivery system that must be tested and ready to go prior to the start of the class. In a traditional class, the delivery system may involve a lecture theater, whiteboard, overhead projectors, or possibly a computer-based presentation. In a Web-based classroom, the delivery system includes the network, Web servers, software, and other resources. The issues involved in preparing and maintaining a Web-based delivery system are discussed in more detail in Chapter 10.

During the Class

Classroom management tasks that occur while the class is running include the following:

Getting to know one another. Learning is a social process requiring interaction with other participants in the class. This process can run more smoothly if the participants are familiar with each other.

Information management. A major component of many class management tasks is the retrieval, update, and management of information such as contact information, past academic performance, and current progress. Assessment management forms a major portion of this task and includes chores such as submitting, distributing, grading, and moderating assessment.

Group management. The use of group work and collaboration in learning is becoming increasingly widespread. The introduction of group work brings with it a number of group management tasks that must be completed by either the educators or the students themselves.

Adapting to change. It is a rare class that proceeds as planned. Sickness, Mother Nature, or just plain human error can make it necessary for a class to adapt to a new situation. In doing so, the class's characteristics such as the syllabus or assessment may need to change, and students must receive notification of the change.

Student counseling. Students can have problems that affect their performance. Student counseling provides the necessary support, advice, and assistance that helps students complete their studies.

Evaluation. Formative evaluation may be used to discover information about certain factors.

Delivery system maintenance. Whether you use lectures, print-based distance material, television, or the Web, the course delivery will require maintenance. In the case of traditional delivery systems, an existing maintenance and support system is usually in place. With a Web-based classroom, the educator may be responsible for maintaining the hardware, software, and possibly the network used by the Web-based classroom. Chapter 10 discusses this large task in more detail.

After the Class

Some of the tasks required after completion of a class include these:

Collection, moderation, and distribution of grades. At the end of the class, collecting results from graders will enable students' final grades to be calculated. In some instances, students' performance will need to be moderated and compared with their performance in other classes to ensure the absence of discrepancies. Finally, the grades must be distributed to students.

Archiving course records and materials. It is often necessary to archive class-related information and records for future reference due to a desire to reuse class material or administrative policy reasons.

WHY USE THE WEB?

Most class management tasks deal with the entry, storage, manipulation, retrieval, and distribution of information. Because computers are very good at storing, manipulating, and retrieving information, they have been widely used in class management tasks. For example, student records are stored on large-scale, commercial databases, and individual educators keep class records in spreadsheets or personal databases. Most of these tasks are already performed using computers; however, several problems with these methods can be addressed by the use of a Web interface. Some of the problems with existing approaches include the following:

Inflexibility. Centralized student records never seem to provide the information or services required and often do not have mechanisms to request specific information.

Too much freedom. Although the student records systems at most institutions are centralized, most individual educators will keep separate records of student progress while a class is running. The method used to store this information may be paper based, a computerized spreadsheet, or some other computer-based approach. Whatever the format, when various people are free to use different methods to store information, it is difficult to share information and analyze information to identify trends. For example, could your institution identify all students who have yet to submit their first piece of assessment by the end of week five of your class?

Duplication of data entry. The use of various storage methods usually results in duplication of data entry, which slows down the flow of information, increases the likelihood of human error, and makes it difficult to maintain consistency between multiple copies of the data.

Distribution problems. The reliance on paper as the means of information distribution brings with it the standard problems of slow distribution and the possibility of lost information.

You can use a Web interface to existing class management tasks to do the following:

Solve problems with existing approaches. Most of the problems associated with current approaches to class management tasks have to do with the difficulty involved in distributing information. The Web's information distribution capabilities promise to address many of these problems.

Support the new environment. A Web-based classroom is a new teaching environment and needs the support of a number of new class management tasks.

Enable new practice. As a new environment the Web-based classroom makes it possible to perform old tasks in new ways. To take advantage of this environment, the methods used to implement some class management tasks will need to change.

WHAT CAN YOU DO?

This section will introduce you to some of the ways in which people are currently using the Web to perform class management tasks. The following sections include descriptions of class information distribution, student counseling, managing assessment, a class photo album, attendance tracking, accessing databases, timetabling and scheduling, and student progress tracking.

Class Information

Distributing class information via the Web includes such information as prerequisite knowledge, necessary resources, and contact details for teaching staff. Distributing class information on the Web not only informs current students, but can also be a method for attracting new students—a form of class promotion.

Some examples of distributing class information via the Web include these:

Simple conversion of existing information. The Department of Mathematics and Computing at Central Queensland University decided that in 1997 all its classes would have a Web presence. A few academics have built Web-based classrooms for their classes, but many have not. For these non-Web-based classes, the existing course information sheet was converted into HTML and placed onto the Web by secretarial staff using Webfuse and Microsoft Word.

Additional information. The Systems Administration class at the same institution extends the idea of distributing class information on the Web by distributing additional information that is not usually available. This information includes archives of feedback from previous students, a class history, and a collection of student photographs.

Student Counseling

Student counseling helps students by providing them with necessary information and someone to talk to. A large number of university student counseling services now use the Web to distribute information to use the medium's advantages, including geographic independence and anonymity. A smaller number of services are also using computer-mediated communication to offer students a forum in which they can ask questions, talk about their problems, and receive advice.

Assessment Management

The prompt return of appropriate feedback on student work can help improve student performance. However, the time-consuming nature of the submission, grading, and return of student assessments can often make it difficult to achieve a prompt return. The combination of the Web's information distribution advantages, the computer's information management capabilities, and automation can significantly reduce the effort that assessment management requires.

The use of e-mail for submitting and returning assessments is a simple approach that provides some benefits. As a result, it is widely used in a number of locations. Web-based submission of assessment requires a little more up-front investment in organization and technical ability, but can provide a number of long-term advantages.

> **Example**
>
> A description of an automated e-mail submission process that automatically records the submission of an assignment, forwards the assignment onto the grader, archives the assignment and any grader comments, and produces a Web page can be found at the site **science.cqu.edu.au/mc/Academic_Programs/Units/ 85321_Systems_Administration/Study_Material/1996_85321_pages/ 85321/assessment/submit/**. The Web page, shown in Figure 8.1, provides a summary of submission and return rate for assignments as well as listing both individual student and class performance.

Class Photo Album

A class photo album helps students and educators put names to faces and get to know each other on a more personal level. By providing a Web page that lists the names of all class members together with their individual photos, both the educators and the staff discover and remember the names of the members of the class. Useful for face-to-face classes, this feature can also be particularly successful for distance education classes in which students rarely meet face to face.

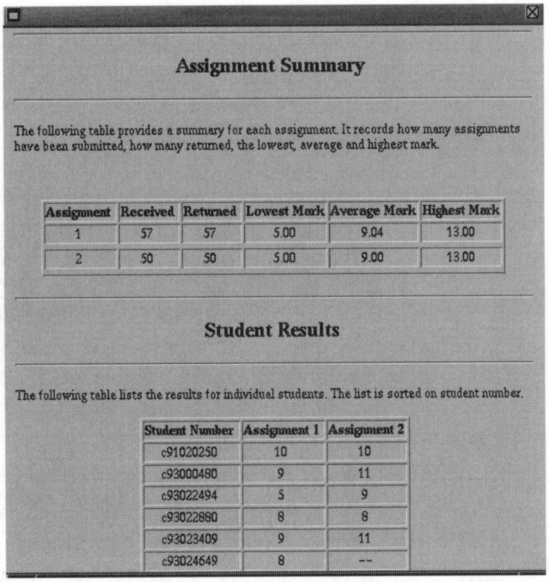

Assignment Summary

The following table provides a summary for each assignment. It records how many assignments have been submitted, how many returned, the lowest, average and highest mark.

Assignment	Received	Returned	Lowest Mark	Average Mark	Highest Mark
1	57	57	5.00	9.04	13.00
2	50	50	5.00	9.00	13.00

Student Results

The following table lists the results for individual students. The list is sorted on student number.

Student Number	Assignment 1	Assignment 2
c91020250	10	10
c93000480	9	11
c93022494	5	9
c93022880	8	8
c93023409	9	11
c93024649	8	--

Figure 8.1 A results summary.

A personal sketch page, which provides a small amount of personal background about each class member, can help other participants in the class feel that they know each other at least a little.

The Web-based photo album used by the computer science department at Rochester Institute of Technology is an excellent example of such a site. It provides three page types, including:

Lecture section pages. These pages allow users to quickly find the personal sketch page for a particular person in the lecture. The pages also provide a list of names, both students and staff, and links to their personal sketch pages.

Laboratory section pages. These pages (Figure 8.2) give a list of names and photos of the people in a particular laboratory group, also linked to each individual's personal sketch. The laboratory page can be used by staff prior to a laboratory to remind themselves of each student's name.

Personal sketch pages. These pages (Figure 8.3) provide a small photograph and limited background information about each class participant, possibly including a description of family, home town, and tastes in music and literature. This small amount of personal information can increase the sense of community in a class and help serve as conversation starters.

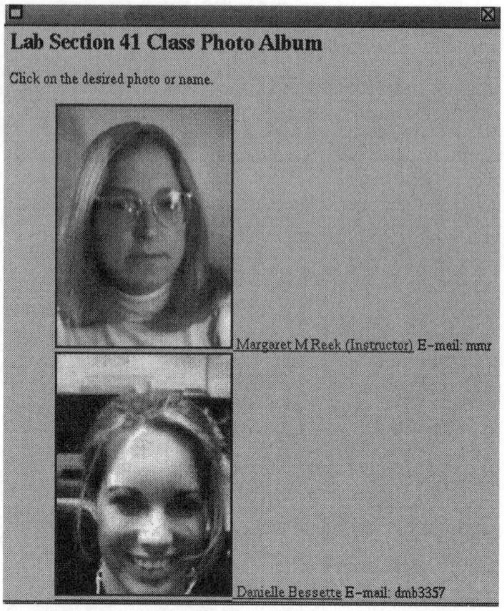

Figure 8.2 The laboratory section of the RIT photo album.

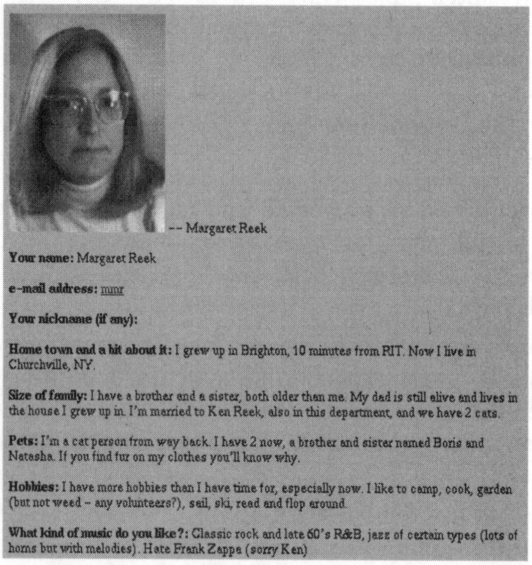

Figure 8.3 A personal sketch from the RIT photo album.

(For more detail on this approach, refer to Margaret Reek and Kenneth Reek, *An Electronic Class Photo Album,* SIGCSE Bulletin, 28(4), December 1996, pp. 15–19.)

Attendance

In classes in which attendance is compulsory, it is necessary to record and track student attendance. The traditional method, paper-based rolls, suffers from a number of problems:

Lost roll. It is not unusual for a paper-based roll to be misplaced or left in the office. This usually means some ad hoc method can introduce many of the problems of inconsistent data mentioned earlier in the chapter.

Lack of student access to records. Unless the a public version of the roll is updated after each session, there is no method for students to check their attendance to see if they have satisfied requirements or be sure that their attendance has been recorded correctly.

Difficulty with distribution. A paper-based roll does not scale well if there are multiple instructors, especially if they are geographically distributed.

A Web-based roll provides a number of advantages:

Global access. A Web-based roll can be accessed anywhere there is a connection to the Web.

Central storage location. Even though access is global, it always uses data that is stored in one central location. This means that everyone is using the same data.

Computer mediation. Because attendance information is stored on one central computer, it is possible to harness the capabilities of the computer to convert, analyze, and distribute the data. This makes it possible to track student attendance across all classes and to allow students to access only their attendance information.

Figures 8.4 and 8.5 show an example of a Web-based roll that was used for a class in 1996. Figure 8.4 is the page used by staff to modify the roll. This particular page is password protected so that only staff can access it. At any time, students could check their attendance records by viewing the page in Figure 8.5.

Database Access

Most institutions have some form of centralized student records system or other data stored in a database. The standard interface available to staff to access this information is often an antiquated, difficult-to-use, text-based system. To address

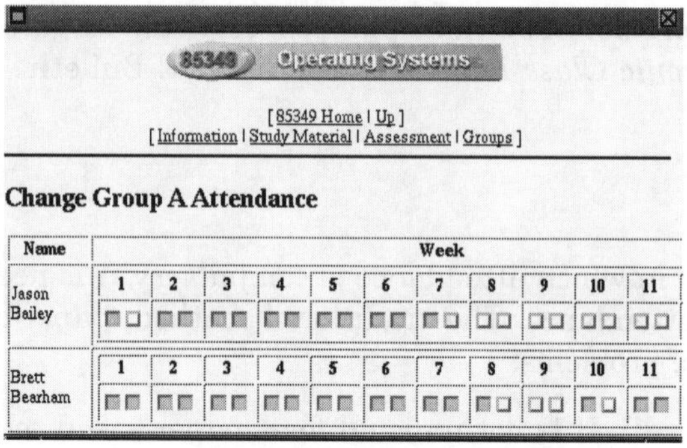

Figure 8.4 A Web-based roll, input form.

the problems associated with this primitive interface, a number of institutions are adopting Web-based interfaces to their existing databases. One such example is shown in Figure 8.6. These Web-based interfaces provide basically the same functionality as the text interface, but also provide the Web's advantages, including a simple, well-known interface, platform independence, and geographic independence.

Timetabling and Scheduling

The primary concerns of timetabling and scheduling are ensuring that class participants know when and where their class is, what they must do to complete it, and the resources necessary to achieve their aims.

At most institutions, centralized timetabling is increasingly accomplished using software. However, most of that software does not provide a Web interface. If it does, it is likely only in the form of an HTML file that displays the final timetable. Most software will not support the use of the Web for data entry. This will change as the influence of the Web increases.

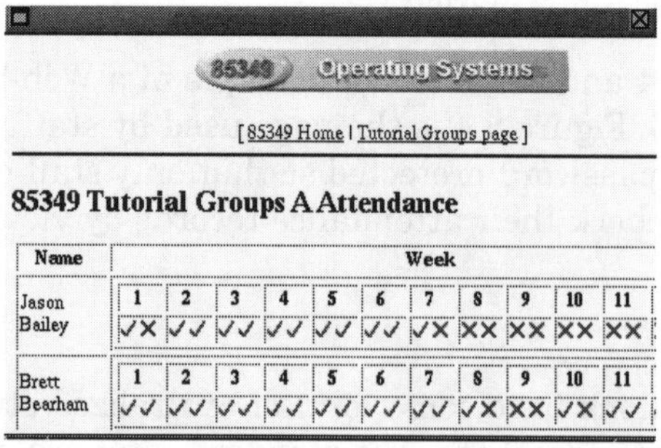

Figure 8.5 A Web-based roll with data in place.

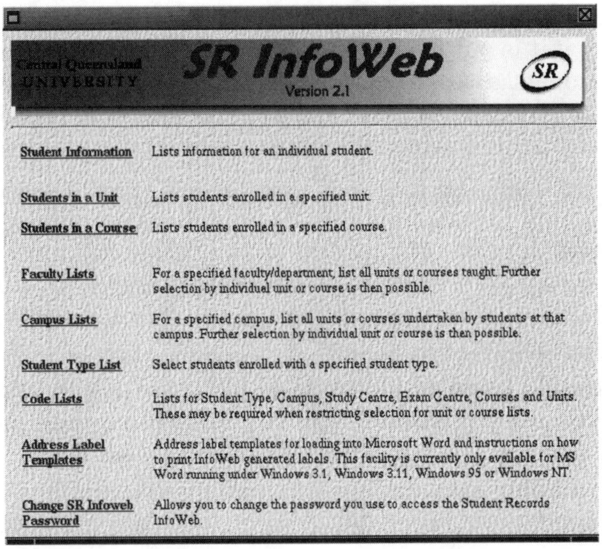

Figure 8.6 Accessing student record database.

Student Tracking

Tracking student progress and performance allows the educator to make decisions on how successful past methods have been, to see how many particular resources are being used, and to see some indicator of what the student should see in the future. Student tracking can be done on an individual basis or it can be done to track trends in an entire class or student group. In the past, student tracking was usually done manually in the form of keeping attendance rolls or analyzing student performance on assignments and class tests. In a Web-based classroom, where all student actions are computer mediated, it is possible to significantly expand the amount of data that is recorded and the methods by which it is analyzed.

To be beneficial, student tracking requires three steps:

Collection. Information about student participation, including assignment submission, results, level of participation in class discussion, and completion of class quizzes, needs to be recorded. Most of the programs used in a Web-based classroom keep logs of use that can be used to track student participation.

Analysis. Raw information is of little use. It must be analyzed in order to identify trends and generate useful information. Manually examining a large amount of raw information is a laborious and time-consuming job that may not provide many benefits. However, this is exactly the type of task computers perform very efficiently.

Response. The collection and analysis of student information makes sense only if it is put to some use. The resulting information could be used as part of student assessment, as a justification for increased resources, to discover if the student has fulfilled a prerequisite, or to identify concepts with which students are having difficulties.

Some examples of how student tracking can be used include the following:

Identification of problem areas. If students are constantly reviewing a Web page that describes a particular topic or all students are answering a particular quiz question incorrectly, this may point to some problems in understanding or delivery.

Identification of methods of use. Logs of how students interact with the Web-based classroom can provide ideas about their mental model of the Web-based classroom and whether or not it is suitable.

A basis for assessment. Students may be expected to perform certain tasks in order to obtain grades. For example, they might have to contribute a certain number of messages to a conference or discussion.

Currently, most Web-based systems have automated the first two of these steps; they are by far the easiest to implement via a computer. Consequently, although it is quite simple to collect and analyze the information, it is difficult and time consuming to actually do anything with it. Future generations of these tools will automate the last step, making student tracking via computer significantly more useful.

When storing information about students, it is necessary to keep in mind issues such as these:

Privacy. A common feature at most Web sites is a page that provides a record of how the site has been used, including how many people have visited, the most popular pages, and so on. Care must be taken when posting information that includes details about individuals to a public forum such as a Web page. Not only is it invading the privacy of visitors to your site, but also, in some countries, this is actually illegal.

Security. Once information is stored on computers, especially computers connected to a network, the question of security and unauthorized access must be examined. This is especially true given recent security problems with Web servers and other software on the Windows platform.

Freedom of information. Do students have access to information you store about them? In Europe, students are entitled by law to see any information kept about them on computer, and in some cases, educators' response has been to store information on paper.

Example

The provision of student tracking in a Web-based classroom requires specialized software support. An example of this support is the student tracking component of the WebCT system (WebCT is described in more detail in Chapter 9). Student tracking in WebCT records the first and last time students accessed the class (see Figure 8.7). This data is useful for identifying students who have not yet started work or have not done work recently.

Other services WebCT provides include identification of the distribution of use (see Figure 8.8). WebCT can provide a summary of the distribution of student visits to the various sections of the Web-based classroom. This can be useful for identifying resources that students are not using and that could be discontinued in future offerings (after discovering why the students aren't using it).

WebCT's page-tracking feature provides information on how particular pages within the class are used. How often do students visit? How long do they stay? This information can be useful to identify pages to which students are continually returning or are spending a large amount of time reading. Such behavior might be indicative of pages that contain concepts with which students are having difficulty.

Most of these services are available to both students and the educator. Students are able to access information about their own use of the system; the educator is able to track the participation of all and any students. For a more detailed description of WebCT's abilities in this area refer to the Web site **homebrew.cs.ubc.ca/webct/papers/ naweb/ index.html**. Chapter 9 also provides a description of the creation of a Web-based classroom using WebCT and compares it with two other available tools.

IMPLEMENTATION

The following section introduces you to some of the methods you can use to integrate class management tasks into your Web-based classroom. Implementing class management tasks can be achieved through the application of many of the information distribution and computer-mediated communication systems mentioned in Chapters 5 and 6. This section concentrates on more approaches and describes methods to promote your Web-based classroom, track student progress, provide a Web-based interface to an existing database, and allow assignment submission via e-mail or the Web.

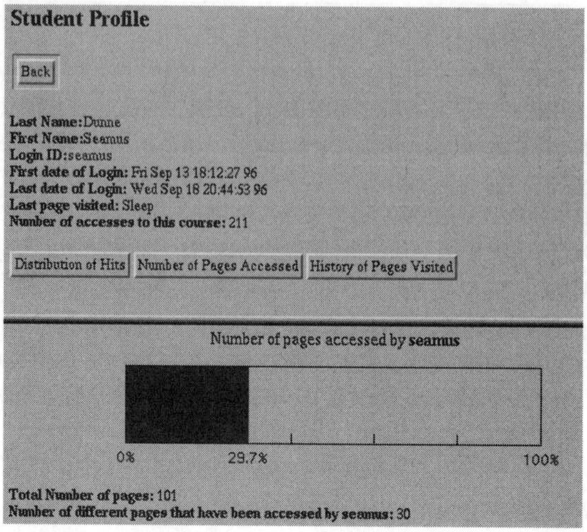

Figure 8.7 WebCT's student tracking facility.

Class Promotion

The global nature of the Web means that just by placing your class on the Web, you immediately make it available to a whole new group of students. With correct implementation and the appropriate administrative support, a Web-based classroom can provide a useful source of capable and interested students. However, before this can occur, potential students must know about your Web-based classroom and have access to the information they need in order to make the decision to enroll. This section looks at strategies that help make that task easier for your potential students and hopefully increase interest in your Web-based classroom.

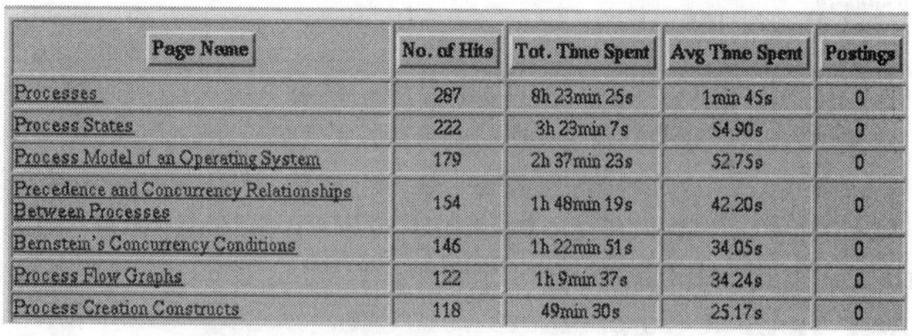

Page Name	No. of Hits	Tot. Time Spent	Avg Time Spent	Postings
Processes	287	8h 23min 25s	1min 45s	0
Process States	222	3h 23min 7s	54.90s	0
Process Model of an Operating System	179	2h 37min 23s	52.75s	0
Precedence and Concurrency Relationships Between Processes	154	1h 48min 19s	42.20s	0
Bernstein's Concurrency Conditions	146	1h 22min 51s	34.05s	0
Process Flow Graphs	122	1h 9min 37s	34.24s	0
Process Creation Constructs	118	49min 30s	25.17s	0

Figure 8.8 WebCT's distribution of use feature.

One possible process for promoting your class includes the following four steps:

Identify your students. Decide what type of students you want to attract and their characteristics. Where do they look for information on potential classes? What type of information will attract them to your class? What terminology will they use to describe your class and its field?

Design the site. Various types of students will have different expectations of the design of a Web site. A Web site that is not designed to suit the tastes of potential students will reflect badly on the class and discourage prospective students.

Determine the best method for promoting your class. There are a wide array of methods and forums that you can use to promote your class, some of which are mentioned in this section. You need to identify those most suitable to your class.

Respond to queries. If you attract student interest, you will need to have procedures in place for them to enroll. These procedures may include such tasks as handling online payment, distributing print-based enrollment packs, responding to queries, and providing information on accreditation and course credit.

Where to Promote

A maxim that applies in real life as well as on the Internet is that different people hang out in different places. In promoting your Web-based classroom, you should choose locations that are likely to attract the attention of your potential students. If you want to attract potential UNIX systems administrators, for instance, you need to promote your course in locations where people who want to become UNIX systems administrators hang out. Some of the online methods you can use to promote your course include banner exchanges, directory sites, search engines, submission services, and postings to online forums.

Banner Exchanges Banners are the small (and sometimes not so small) advertisements that you see regularly on the Web, particularly on commercial sites. Placing a banner on popular sites such as Yahoo! costs a significant fee that may be beyond most educators. An alternative approach can be found in banner exchanges.

Most banner exchanges work on a cooperative basis. When you join, you agree to display the banners of other people on your Web pages. In return, every time people visit your page, your banner will be displayed on someone else's Web page. For a list of the available banner exchanges, check out Yahoo!'s listing **www.yahoo.com/Computers_and_Internet/Internet/World_Wide_Web/Announcement_Services/Banner_Exchanges/**.

The use of banner exchanges is a personal preference and may be considered too brash for some educational purposes. Some people are so opposed to banners that they have written programs that automatically remove them from Web pages they visit.

Directory Sites Directory sites gather and organize references to Web pages and organize them into some form of hierarchy that is generally structured by subject. Such sites usually provide tools by which people can search the site for a particular phrase and submit their own sites. At one end of the directory site spectrum, you find large, general-purpose sites like Yahoo! (**www.yahoo.com**). At the other end, you find directories sites that concentrate on a particular topic. One well-known, education-related directory site is the World Lecture Hall (**www.utexas.edu/world/lecture/index.html**), which contains pointers to classes from accounting through zoology.

Search Engines Rather then search through a hierarchy, search engines allow users to enter a word or phrase, and the engine returns a list of links to pages that contain that word or phrase. The size of the Web means that some search engines can return tens and hundreds of thousands of links. Search engines use automated programs, called crawlers, to generate summaries of a large proportion of the pages on the Web. This means that if your course has been placed on the Web, it may be automatically indexed by one of these search engines. Popular search engines include InfoSeek (**www.infoseek.com/**) and Alta Vista (**www.altavista.digital.com**).

Submission Services Submission services allow you to register pages with multiple search engines and directory sites from one location. Although they can save time, submission services do not always allow you to customize your listing. An example submission service is Submit-it, located at **www.submit-it.com/default.shtml**.

Postings to Online Forums For most fields and areas of interest, there are particular newsgroups, mailing lists, or other online forums in which people interested in the field gather to talk and ask questions. If done correctly, a short announcement placed on these online forums can attract potential students.

What is a correct post? It is one that follows the rules of the particular forum to which you are posting. Most online forums that have been around for a while have established guidelines that define acceptable behavior for the particular forum. Before posting to an online forum, it is advisable to observe the conversation for some time so that you can become familiar with its "feel." General advice is that the post should be concise, relevant, and accurate.

Tips to Improve Web Ranking Many large Web search engines and directory services use programs, often called robots or spiders, to automatically traverse the Web to read, collect, index, and rank Web pages. Each of these robots uses a particular algorithm that controls how it performs its task. Being aware of how these algorithms work makes it possible to improve the ranking of your pages by following a number of simple guidelines. The ranking of a page determines where it will appear when the search site is asked for terms that relate to that page. For example, if your page contains a description of grape juice, a search by a search engine might produce a list of 100 pages about grape juice. Your page could be near the top of the list, making it more likely that the person who started the search will look at it, or your page could be toward the bottom, making it less likely the user will visit it.

Some of the guidelines for improving the ranking of your Web pages include these:

Place keywords in the title. Every Web page should have a title, the text that occurs between the <TITLE></TITLE> tags. By placing important keywords in the title, you can take advantage of the added importance that some robots place on the title's content.

Relevant keywords. Make sure you are using keywords your potential students will associate with a class. In particular, be sure that your keywords have the same meaning in other countries.

Meta data. Meta data is data about data. On a Web page, meta data takes the form of special tags that appear in the header of the page and provide information about the page, including the author's name, relevant keywords, date last modified, and a description of the content. Some robots use meta data to rank pages in their index. An illustration of the difference using meta data can make is given in the Example. (For more information on meta data refer to **www.nlc-bnc.ca/ifla/II/metadata.htm**.)

Punctuation. Some robots use only keywords that appear in sentences with full punctuation.

Write like a newspaper journalist. Most newspaper stores start with a summary of all the major points and then proceed to cover the details. Some Web robots access only a certain number of lines from the top of a Web page. If important keywords do not appear early in the page, they will not be used in the ranking. This can cause problems with pages that contain large JavaScript functions or frames, because the early parts of these pages do not contain content that can be indexed.

Promotion Activities to Avoid Marketing, promotion, and the Internet have for some time been uncomfortable bedfellows. This less-than-comfortable partnership has not been helped by a number of individuals and organizations that use what is considered by many to be inappropriate promotional activities. By repeating these unacceptable practices, you open yourself to ridicule and, in some cases, revenge attacks, not to mention the loss of potential students.

Example

One of the authors teaches a class in systems administration using a Web-based classroom. While writing this section of the book, the author performed a search on InfoSeek using the terms "systems administration." The search returned a list of more than 11 *million* documents. After looking through the first 100 entries and finding no mention of his class, the author, like most potential students performing this same search, gave up. To be promoted on the Web, it's important that a class appear high on the output list of a search engine.

To improve this ranking, the author added the following line to the class home page code:

```
<META NAME="Keywords" CONTENT="Systems Administration">
```

The class home page was resubmitted to Infoseek using its online submission system. Three days after the first search, another search using the exact same terms returned another list of more than 11 million documents. However, this time the author's class on systems administration was the first entry.

Promotional methods you should not use include these:

Using massive amounts of hidden keywords. Some algorithms used to rank pages will increase the ranking if particular keywords appear numerous times. To exploit this weakness in the system, some people have added lines like the following to their pages:

```
<! systems administration, systems administration, systems
administration, systems administration>
```

Some search sites are so upset by this practice that they have modified their robots to recognize this ploy and actually decrease the ranking given to such a page.

Names changing. Most lists are sorted using some sort of criterion, such as alphabetically. One approach to getting a Web site promoted more often is changing the title of a page to fit the ranking criteria—for example, altering "Zora the Fortune Teller" to "AAAA1111: Zora the Fortune Teller."

Regularly changing the title. For some Web robots, if the data it examines has changed, it will add the page to its collection again, even if it's already there. By regularly changing the particular data the robot looks for, such as the page title, it is possible to increase the number of times your page appears in its database.

Inappropriate posts to online forums. A post to an online forum can be considered inappropriate if it is too long, has nothing to do with the purpose of the forum, or contravenes one of the forum's rules. Before making any posting to an online forum, you should become fully aware of the conventions followed by that particular forum.

Spamming. With software, it is easy to send an e-mail message to millions of people without them wanting it. This practice, known as spam or junk mail, is usually directed to either a large collection of online forums, like newsgroups, or individual e-mail addresses. Spamming is probably the worst sin you can commit when promoting your class. Avoid it.

For more information on responsible promotion on the Internet, refer to **spam.abuse.net/spam/**.

Student Tracking

As discussed earlier in the chapter, student tracking involves a number of steps, primarily information collection, analysis, and action. How you can collect and analyze information in a Web-based classroom depends on the software you are using. Different types of software log (or store) different information in different ways and locations. The following section describes fairly common approaches to collecting information about student participation: the Web server log. The section finishes by examining some of the issues involved with computer-based student tracking.

Web Server Logs Most Web servers maintain log files that store information about the requests they receive for Web pages. A log stores information such as who made the request, what page was requested, how information was transferred, whether users requesting the page had user names, which page pointed them to the current page, and which browser they were using. The format in which this information is kept is usually an agreed standard format, known as the common log format. Most analysis tools require the log to be in common log format.

Useful analysis of Web logs is aided by two factors:

All student interaction with the Web pages is via the server. Student interaction with a Web-based classroom's Web pages is done only if students access those pages via the Web server. If students have installed a version of the pages on their hard drive and are viewing them locally, this interaction will not be logged.

All students can be uniquely identified. By default, a Web server can identify only the computers students use to access the Web; it cannot identify the particular students using the computers. In order for each person to be uniquely identified, the Web-based classroom must be password protected and each participant in the class given a unique user name and/or password. (Password protection is discussed in Chapter 10.) The advantage of being able to identify each student's operations must be weighed against the overhead in creating and managing student accounts.

Analysis of Web Server Logs Analysis of Web server logs is a widespread practice, and most analysis tools provide information about how many people visited a site and how many times they visited each page. These tools are quite common, are relatively simple to use, and provide some interesting information. (For more information on these tools, refer to Chapter 10 and to the Web site **www.yahoo.com/Computers_and_Internet/Software/Internet/World_Wide_Web/Servers/Log_Analysis_Tools/**.)

Session Analysis This section concentrates on performing session analysis of the log files of a Web server. A Web session is the time a visitor spends on a Web site from the first page he accesses to the last page he visits before leaving the site. By analyzing the sessions of individual students, an educator can examine the sequence of pages students visit during their use of the Web-based classroom and how long they spent viewing each page.

The following section explains how to perform a session analysis of a Web-based classroom using a Perl script called Follow. Follow, written by Mark Nottingham, takes a raw Web log file and produces output like that shown in Figure 8.9. You can see the sequence of pages this particular student followed during one session, including how long he spent viewing each page.

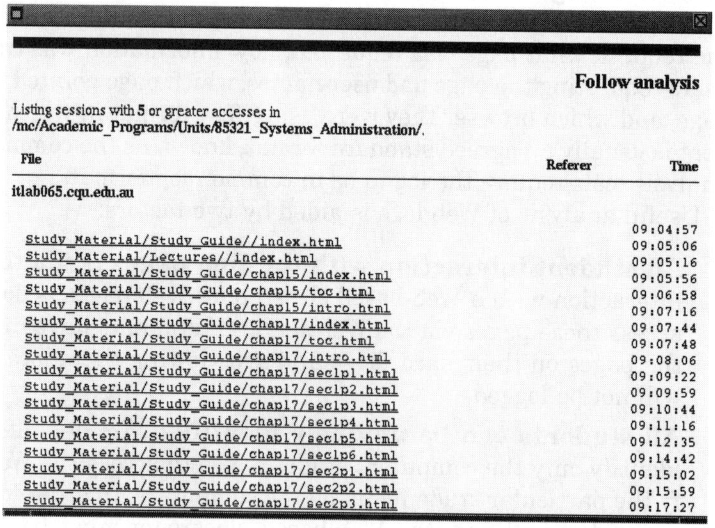

Figure 8.9 An example session analysis using Follow.

To use Follow, you will need the following:

A copy of Follow. Follow is available from the accompanying CD-ROM, and from Follow's own Web site (**mnot.cyber.com.au/follow/**).

A copy of Perl. Follow is written in Perl, an interpreted scripting language that is widely used for writing CGI scripts. In order to use Follow, you must have a copy of Perl. Versions of Perl are available for most common computer platforms. (For more information, refer to **www.perl.org/** and **www.perl.com/**.) Follow is known to run on UNIX and Windows 95/NT and should run on any platform that supports Perl.

Access to the log file of your Web server. Unless you have open access to your Web server, you may need to approach the Webmaster or systems administrator of your Web server before you can use Follow. Normally, access to the log file for a Web server is restricted for a number of reasons, including privacy and site maintenance, and you may have to make a special request to gain access. If the person responsible is reluctant to supply you with the entire log file, ask if he or she can extract just those entries relevant to your Web-based classroom or run Follow for you.

Follow can be used from the command line or via the Web by using a CGI script. If you plan to use the CGI script, which can be easier to use, it is likely you will have to ask for permission from your Web server administrator due to the fact that placing CGI scripts onto a Web server is usually restricted for security reasons. Figure 8.10 shows the Web interface produced by Follow's CGI script. (A version of the Web interface with which you can experiment is available on the book's Website.)

The installation and operation of Follow is explained in a README file distributed with Follow. It explains the small number of simple steps necessary to install Follow, so we don't repeat them here. The following discussion concentrates instead on examples of how to actually use Follow.

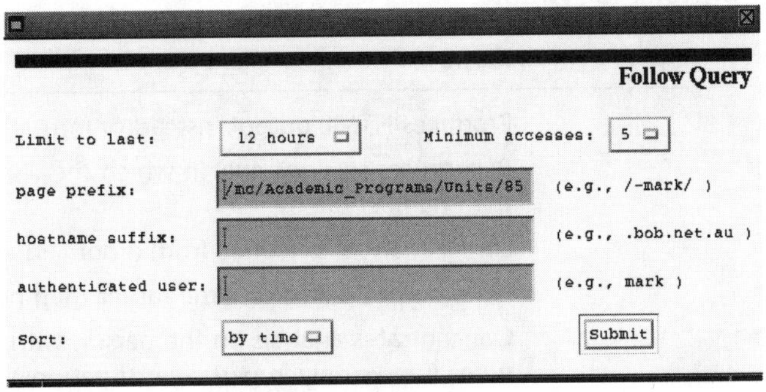

Figure 8.10 Follow's Web interface.

Assuming Follow is properly installed, the simplest way to run it is from the command line of your standard UNIX shell or from the MS-DOS prompt if you are using Windows 95/NT. An example follow command looks like this:

```
follow /usr/local/apache/logs/access_log
```

In this command, Follow receives the full path name of the log file that it should analyze. The absence of any other command-line options means that, by default, Follow will perform an analysis of all the Web pages stored in the log file. Follow supports a number of command-line options with which it is possible to customize the analysis in a variety of ways. Table 8.1 describes the command-line switches that allow you to customize the analysis Follow performs.

Some examples of using Follow's command-line options include

```
follow -n 1:30 access_log
```

which analyzes sessions that occurred in the last hour and a half. This command:

```
follow -d /subjects/85321/ -n 2:00 access_log
```

restricts analysis to accesses to pages in the directory /subjects/85321 that occurred in the last two hours. Finally,

```
follow -d /subjects/85321/ -u david -m 10 access_log
```

analyzes how the user, David, accessed the pages in the directory /subjects/85321, but lists only sessions in which he accessed more than 10 pages.

Creating a Web Interface to a Database

Databases, sometimes referred to as database management systems (DBMS), are the most efficient method currently available for storing and manipulating computer-based data. Any individual or company that deals with large collections of

Table 8.1 Options for Follow

Option	*Purpose*
-h	Produces HTML output instead of formatted text
-m *number*	Recognizes sessions only in which the visitor accessed more than *number* pages
-n *suffix*	Limits analysis to visitors from a domain ending in *suffix*
-s	Sorts output based on time rather than host name
-u *username*	Concentrates analysis on the person with the given *user name* (works only in particular situations)
-n *hh:mm*	Limits analysis to access that occurred *hh:mm* ago, where *hh* is the number of hours and *mm* the number of minutes

data uses some form of DBMS. Providing a Web interface to the information stored in a database combines the storage and retrieval power of a database with the familiar interface and geographic independence of the Web. Because most class management tasks rely in some form on the storage, retrieval, and manipulation of data, a Web interface to a database can be a useful tool that can provide services such as management of student results, online enrollment and registration, and online management of student information.

When using the Web with a database, consideration must be given to a number of issues, including these:

Data entry. At some stage, you will find errors in data entry. You must consider what checks are in place to pick up these mistakes and what avenues people can follow to check and change data. One simple approach is allowing students access to their own data, but that in turn opens up questions of security. You need to provide students with the ability to view data, but you may not want them to directly modify the data.

Security, privacy, and freedom of information. These considerations, mentioned in the section on information tracking, apply equally to the use of databases.

To provide some idea of how to set up and use a Web interface to a database, this section uses an example that takes you through five steps:

1. Choose the database engine.
2. Install the database engine.
3. Install the Web/database interface.
4. Produce the database.
5. Produce the Web pages that interface with the database.

Each step contains the necessary background information and provides a walk-through of the step using a particular set of tools.

The example implements a simple database for an example class, 85321 Systems Administration (referred to as 85321 in the remainder of this chapter). The class database will be used to store each student's name, student number, street address, e-mail address, and results for two assignments and the exam. The two tasks the Web/database interface will fulfill are these:

Distribute results to the students. A Web page will display student results, using just the student number, to allow students to check on their progress.

Allow the modification of results. The course has a number of graders who are geographically distributed. The Web interface will allow the graders to update results as they grade assignments.

Our example uses the mSQL database engine and associated tools to implement the database and its Web-based interface. mSQL is distributed on the Internet. (The main site for mSQL is **hughes.com.au/**, the home page for Hughes Technologies, the developers of mSQL, and there are a number of mirror sites. The FTP site **ftp://ftp.bond.edu.au/pub/Minerva/msql/** also contains a collection of mSQL-related software and the mSQL FAQ, **ftp://ftp.bond.edu.au/pub/Minerva/msql/faq.html**. You will also find copies of mSQL software on the book's Website, which provides working versions of the Web interface to this database. The reliance of this system on a database and Web server means that it is not possible to distribute our example on the book's CD-ROM.)

Given the scope and variety in database management systems and their associated tools, it is not possible to provide a discussion or comparison of each system in this chapter. Instead, we concentrate on describing the concepts most database management systems have in common. A demonstration of how each concept is implemented by mSQL is provided. It is hoped you will be able to apply this discussion of the basic concepts to the particular database management system you choose to use.

Choosing the Database Engine The database engine or DBMS is the collection of algorithms and data structures used to store, retrieve, and manipulate the information contained in the database. There is a large number of free, shareware, and commercial databases. all of which provide varying levels of performance, reliability, and features.

The first step in implementing a Web database interface is choosing the database you will use. Points to consider when choosing a database engine include price, performance, features, reliability, support, and available interfaces. Given the large number of databases, it is not possible here to give a detailed comparison of all systems. Instead, the following discussion focuses on the major features you must consider and describes how each feature influenced the choice of mSQL for our example.

Price Database engines range in price from completely free to thousands of dollars. A high price does not always mean a better system. mSQL is shareware for commercial organizations but is free for noncommercial educational institutions, research organizations, registered charities, not-for-profit organizations, and full-time students. For a university department, this makes mSQL very attractive.

Platform Obviously, you must be able to run the database engine on an available computer. Because most modern database engines, including mSQL, provide some sort of network support, it is not necessary for the database to sit on the same computer as the application that requires the services of the database. mSQL was originally a UNIX application, but there have been ports to both OS/2 and Windows 95 (see **blnet.com/msqlpc/peter/**). The main Web server for our example is a computer running Linux, a version of UNIX, on which mSQL is known to work.

Performance An important criterion for any database is how quickly it can respond to queries. Database engines use different algorithms that can drastically affect the performance of the system under certain conditions. For example, version 1 of mSQL was designed to ensure high speed for small amounts of data; consequently, its performance can be less than brilliant on large data sets, especially with complex queries. Version 2 of mSQL remedies this shortcoming.

The database to be constructed in our example is relatively small because the class has an average enrollment of around 120 students. For this data size, mSQL (both versions 1 and 2) provides performance that is considerably better than that of many commercial products.

Features Databases can supply a wide range of features, including a sub/superset of SQL commands, locking, indexing, the number of keys, rollback and commit, and a number of others. (For one comparison of a number of databases, refer to **www.postgresql.org/comp-comparison.shtml**.) mSQL, also known as MiniSQL, does not provide a lot of the complex features required in some situations. However, the relatively simple needs of the example system do not require additional functionality.

Reliability Reliability is an important feature for a system that will store all of the information for your class. The database system you use should not have a tendency to crash and lose the data with which you have entrusted it. mSQL is currently available in two versions: 1.0.16 and 2.0-B4. 1.0.16 is the stable version; 2.0-B4 is a beta version of mSQL 2. As a beta version, it still has a number of small bugs, and for this reason our installation example uses 1.0.16.

Interfaces For a database to be useful, it must support a number of interfaces that allow both people and programs to access its services. If the majority of your application programs are written in Pascal, you would probably not choose a database engine that does not have a Pascal programming interface.

Support Database engines are complex pieces of software, and, at some stage, it is likely you will need some support to solve problems or to figure out how to use a particular feature. Most commercial software products are supported by traditional documentation and hotlines. Increasingly, products like mSQL use the Internet to support users. mSQL support is provided by a collection of online documents and a mailing list. Use of the mailing list for problem solving is free and quite efficient.

Installing the Database Interface To use a database, you must be able to give the database commands to store, retrieve, and manipulate data. In most cases, you use some form of computer application as your interface to the database. The following sections introduce some of the concepts related to database interfaces and also describe some of the types of database interface. Once the basics are explained, the section describes how to choose between the types of database interface.

Database API Most databases include a predefined application programming interface (API) that specifies the services the database can provide to application programs. Each database system has a different API; in the past, that meant that an application for an Ingres database, for example, could not be used with a Sybase database. Recently, the advent of mSQL and, in particular, open database connectivity (ODBC, discussed in more detail later in this section) has made it possible for software developers to produce a single database application that can be used with a number of database engines. SQL and ODBC are described in more detail later in this section. A description of the API for a database is usually distributed with the database.

Programming Language API/Library Before you can write an application that uses the services of a database, you must have a database API for the programming language you are using. The programming language library provides a mechanism through which programs written in the specific language access the database API. Most modern database engines provide support for a large number of programming languages. For example, mSQL supports C/C++, Perl, Python, TCL, and Java, among others. All these are described in more detail in the mSQL FAQ.

SQL Structured query language (SQL) is a standard command language used to issue commands to a database. The official SQL standard, described on the Web page **www.jcc.com/sql_stnd.html**, is defined by a standards body. However, each database manufacturer implements its own subset or superset of the SQL standard. (The subset of SQL that mSQL supports is described in the mSQL documentation and on the Web at **Hughes.com.au/library/msql1/**.)

SQL queries look like this:

```
select name,address from students where name="David Jones"
insert into students ( name, student_number, address ) values
( "Fred Nobody", "X11123123", "8 Nowhere Lane" )
```

Databases usually support SQL by providing an application that accepts SQL queries and converts them into calls to the database API. The mSQL version is a command, msql, that allows you to enter simple SQL commands from a command line. For example

```
bash$ msql studentsmSQL > select name,address from students
where name="Fred Nobody"Query OK. 1 row matched. +-----------
--------+------------------------------------+
| name                | address
|
+-------------------+------------------------------------+
| Fred Nobody         | 8 Nowhere Lane
|
+-------------------+------------------------------------+
```

ODBC A long-held dream for database users is the ability to write programs that can store and retrieve data from any database system. The technology that provides this ability is ODBC, open database connectivity, a standard initiated by Microsoft. ODBC works by placing another program, called an ODBC driver, between the user's application and the database. The ODBC driver is responsible for converting ODBC queries generated by the application into function calls to the database's API. It is rare to find any modern database for which there are not ODBC drivers. Java database connectivity (JDBC) is an API that serves the same purpose as ODBC except it is specifically for the Java programming language. A Java interface to mSQL is illustrated in Figure 8.11.

mSQL is supported by a number of ODBC and JDBC drivers that allow database applications on a number of platforms to access and manipulate data in a mSQL database.

Database Applications A database application is a program that has been written to store and retrieve data from a database. An example of a database application is the simple SQL command interface used in the SQL example above. This command interface is a simple C program that accepts text-based input in the form of SQL commands and translates those commands into calls to the mSQL API. A number of people have also produced database applications for mSQL that perform the same duties as the msql command, but with a Windows or Java interface rather than a command-line interface. Database applications can access the information stored in a database using either the language specific database API or ODBC function calls.

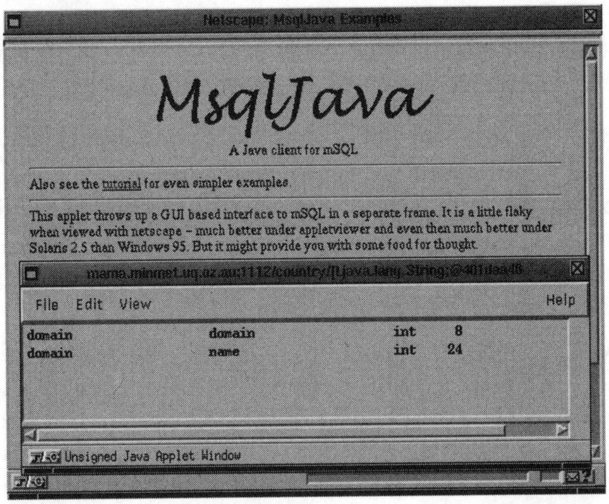

Figure 8.11 Java interface to mSQL.

Database Application Builders Creating database applications typically requires some programming experience in a language such as C, C++, Pascal, or Perl. This requirement makes it very difficult for nonprogrammers to use the services of databases. Application builders are computer programs designed to make it easier to create applications. Visual Basic is one popular example of an application builder. A database application builder is an application builder specifically designed to interact with databases. Database application builders are now widely available for most databases, and many standard application builders, like Visual Basic, also support ODBC, which means they can also be used to build database applications.

There are a number of database application builders for mSQL. This section, which describes the process for building a database, uses Jate (**aiace.lnf.infn.it/~ht/JATET/jate_home.html**), a database application builder for mSQL that uses a Web interface.

Web/Database Interfaces The programs that allow you to access database information from the Web are simply database applications designed specifically to use the HTML forms and Web pages as their primary interface. Like other database applications, Web/database interfaces must access the services of the database using either an ODBC driver or a language-specific API/library. A number of types of Web/database interfaces exist. The main difference between them is how they provide an interface with the Web. Later in this chapter we'll look in detail at the methods for providing a Web-based interface to a database.

Producing the Database The full process for designing the structure of a database is complicated, and many detailed books have been written about it. It is beyond the scope of this book to give anything more than a cursory introduction to this art. If you are required to construct large, complicated databases, you should take time to examine some of the resources listed on the CD-ROM.

Some of the terms you need to know and understand include these:

Field. The smallest piece of information accessible by a database. For example, a student's number, name, and address are some of the fields used in our example. Each field has a name and data type as well as the actual data. The name is a unique label used within a table to identify the field or column. A field's data type specifies the type of data it can contain, such as character strings, integers, or real numbers.

BLOBs. Short for binary large objects, BLOBs are elements such as graphic files, application programs, and sound files. Some databases, including mSQL, do not support BLOBs. However, that support can be emulated by storing the filename of a BLOB, rather than the BLOB itself. That filename points to the BLOB on disk from which it can be retrieved.

Row. Information about a particular person or object in a database is stored as a collection of fields called a row.

Key. A key is a special field that is used to access and structure information in a table.

Table. A table is a collection of fields that are related in some way. For example, a table called "student" might contain fields for student number, name, address, phone number, and e-mail address.

Database. A database in this context is a collection of tables. A database engine is likely to manage a number of databases. For example, the mSQL database engine for one academic department may manage one database for each of the department's classes.

Creating the Database The first step in storing data with a database engine is to create the database that will hold the tables. All database engines come with commands that allow you to create databases. To create a database with mSQL you use the msqladmin command:

```
bash:~# msqladmin create 85321
Database "85321" created.
```

This example command creates a new database called 85321. This database will be used to store the tables related to our example.

A database engine is likely to contain a number of databases. To find out what other databases an mSQL database engine has, you can use the relshow command:

```
bash:~# relshow

  +-----------------+
  |    Databases    |
  +-----------------+
  | test            |
  | 85349           |
  | 85321           |
  +-----------------+
```

In this example, mSQL is hosting three databases: 85321, the database that was just created; 85349, a database for another class; and a test database.

To delete a database from mSQL, you use the msqladmin command:

```
bash:~# msqladmin drop test

Dropping the database is potentially a very bad thing to do.
Any data stored in the database will be destroyed.
```

```
Do you really want to drop the "test" database?  [Y/N] y
Database "test" dropped
```

As the msqladmin command mentions, dropping a database destroys any data in the database. This command should be used with care.

The Tables The design of the table structure of a database and the determination of which fields go into which tables are the most complex parts of the database design process. The decisions made during this step control the efficiency and maintainability of the database. As a result, professionals are paid high salaries to perform this task in the commercial arena. It is beyond the scope of this book to provide a detailed introduction to this process, and instead we provide a simple process you can follow. If you are going to design any complex databases, you should refer to other resources, including **www.microsoft.com/access/productInfo/experttools/ureldes/ureldes.htm,** which is a more detailed description of designing a relational database available in both HTML and Word formats.

A simple process to design the table structure of a database includes the following steps:

Identify the fields. Identify all the information you want to store in the database, and identify the names and data types of the fields you will need. The database for our example includes the following data: student number, name, address, e-mail address, assignment 1 result, assignment 2 results, and exam result. The names and data types for this information are shown in Table 8.2.

Identify the tables. Organize the fields of the database into related tables based on what you want to do with the data. There are two main collections of data in our example database: student information, including number, name, and address, and student results. One way of dividing the example database is into two tables consisting of the following fields:

```
details: number, name, address, email
results: number, assign1, assign2, exam
```

Another reason it is important to get the design of a database correct the first time is that once you create a table, it is difficult, if not impossible, to change it.

Creating Tables Once you've identified the tables and their fields, you can create the database tables. The following section shows two methods of creating tables for an mSQL database:

The msql command. The msql is mSQL's simple text-based SQL interface. It allows you to issue SQL commands to mSQL.

Jate. Jate (**aiace.lnf.infn.it/~ht/JATET/jate_home.html**) is a CGI application that provides a Web interface to many of the tasks involved in setting up a database, including creating tables.

The code for creating the tables using the msql command looks like this:

```
bash:~# msql 85321

Welcome to the miniSQL monitor.  Type \h for help.


mSQL > create table details ( number char(10) primary key,
                              name char(100), address
char(200),
                              email char(50) )
    -> \g

Query OK.


mSQL > create table results ( number char(10) primary key,
                              assign1 real, assign2 real,
                              exam real )
    -> \g

Query OK.
```

The positive response of mSQL indicates that the tables have been created. To confirm that the tables are correct, you can use the relshow command:

```
beldin:~# relshow 85321 details

Database = 85321

Table    = details

 +-----------------+----------+--------+----------+-----+
 |      Field      |   Type   | Length | Not Null | Key |
 +-----------------+----------+--------+----------+-----+
 | number          | char     | 10     | Y        | Y   |
 | name            | char     | 100    | N        | N   |
 | address         | char     | 200    | N        | N   |
 | email           | char     | 50     | N        | N   |
 +-----------------+----------+--------+----------+-----+
```

Table 8.2 Fields for Example Database

Information	*Field Name*	*Data Type*
Student number	number	10-character string
Student name	name	100-character string
Postal address	address	200-character string
E-mail address	email	50-character string
Assignment 1 result	assign1	Real number
Assignment 2 result	assign2	Real number
Exam result exam		Real number

Using Jate or a similar tool, you can perform many of these tasks without being aware of the details of SQL. Jate provides a Web interface that allows you to perform many of these tasks. Creating a table using Jate involves the following steps:

Connect to the appropriate database.

Specify the number of fields in the new table. In Figure 8.12, you will see a space in which you must enter the number of fields in the new table.

Specify the name and fields of the table. Figure 8.13 shows the next screen, in which you specify the details of each field and the name of the table. Once this information is provided, click on the Create button to create the table.

Test that the table was created. Jate provides a method of viewing the details of a table to check that it has been created properly.

Populating the Database With the infrastructure in place, you can populate the database with data. You can use a number of methods to insert data into the database. This section discusses SQL commands, GUI interfaces, and importing data from other sources as methods of populating the database.

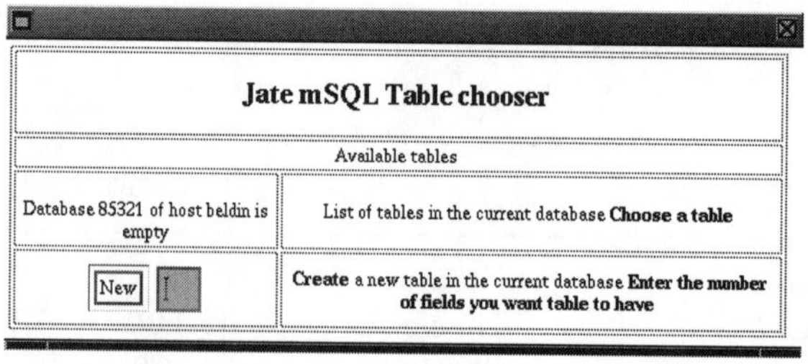

Figure 8.12 Creating a table with Jate, step 1.

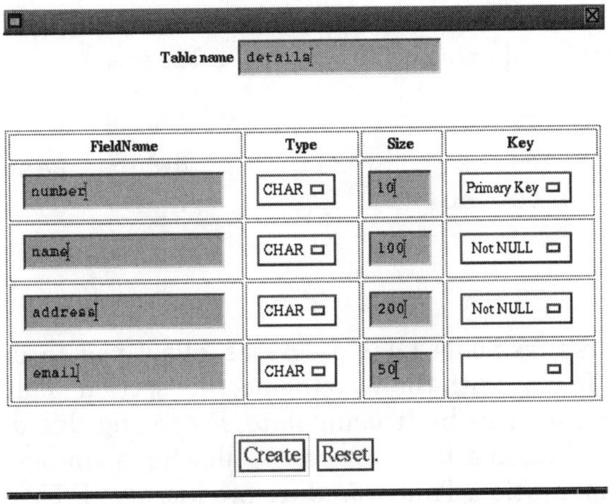

Figure 8.13 Creating a table with Jate, step 2.

SQL Commands To use SQL commands to insert data into an mSQL database, you should use the same msql command we used to create the table. For example:

```
bash:~# msql 85321

Welcome to the miniSQL monitor.  Type \h for help.


mSQL > insert into details ( number, name, address, email )
                      values  ( 'Q12345678', 'David Jones',
                             '8 Nowhere Lane',
'd.jones@cqu.edu.au' )
    -> \g

Query OK.
```

To test if the data was successfully placed into the database, you can also use the msql command:

```
mSQL > select * from details
    -> \g

Query OK.

3 rows matched.
```

```
+----------+------------+---------------+---------------+
| number   | name        | address        | email
|
+----------+------------+---------------+---------------+
| Q12345678| David Jones | 8 Nowhere Lane |
djones@cqu.edu.au|
+----------+---------------+------------+---------------+
```

GUI Interfaces Some GUI programs allow you to enter data into an mSQL database. To stay with the Web theme, this section demonstrates the use of a Web data-entry interface built using Jate. Preparing this data-entry interface was a matter of filling in a few forms and following a simple procedure outlined in the Jate documentation. This procedure produces an HTML file that, when placed on a Web server, provides a simple data-entry form. Figure 8.14 is an example of this form, edited to make it more presentable. Data entry entails entering the appropriate data and pressing the Input button.

Importing It is likely that the data you plan to store in a database is already being stored on a computer. Rather than duplicate data entry, it is usually possible to automate the procedure of importing data from one computer system to another. The fundamental problem with automating this procedure is working out how to convert the original format of the data into the format required by the destination computer. There are two common methods for accomplishing this goal:

Direct conversion. Some programs will convert one computer format directly to another. For example, Access is a common database used on the Windows platform. Some Access services take an Access 7 database and produce the appropriate SQL commands to insert data into mSQL. More information about these programs can be found on the mSQL FAQ, in particular **ftp://ftp.bond.edu.au/pub/Minerva/msql/faq.html#ms-access7**.

Delimited text files. A delimited text file is a normal ASCII text file that contains a number of lines, each line broken into fields by a special delimiting character. Most databases, mSQL included, provide a mechanism by which the contents of a table can be converted into a delimited text file. Most also provide a complementary function that allows a delimited text file to be inserted directly into the database. An example of this procedure is shown in the Example.

The distribution of mSQL version 1 did not include import and export functions for delimited text files. However, third parties produced these utilities, and version 2 of mSQL will be distributed with them as standard.

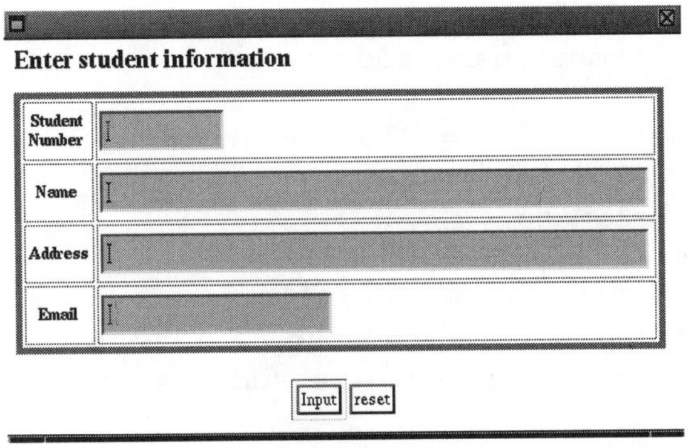

Figure 8.14 A data-entry page produced using Jate.

The data to be imported for our example course database is from the institution's existing student records system. The format of the data from this source is

```
"number","surname","given","middle","title","addr1","addr2","
addr3","pcode"
```

The data described in our example is not yet in a format that can be imported into the example database. The quote marks must first be removed, then the data must be manipulated to fit the requirements of the two tables in the example database. The forms for the two tables are as follows:

Details. The details table has four fields used to store students' numbers, names, addresses, and e-mail addresses. The student number is available as one of the fields from the output of the institution's student record systems. However, the name and address must be obtained by combining a number of the fields from the student record system's output. In addition, the student records database does not provide the student e-mail address, which means this field must be left blank.

Results. The results table of the database also has four fields storing students' numbers and their results on assignments 1 and 2 and the exam. Only the student number is currently available from the student records database; the rest of the information will be added as the semester progresses.

Before importing this information into our example database, we need to convert this file into a format that matches the requirements of the example. This task can be accomplished using a number of approaches: a word processor, a spreadsheet, or UNIX commands. Once the data is manipulated into the appropriate format, it is imported into an mSQL database using the msql-import command as follows:

```
bash:~$ msql-import -d 85321 -t details -c , -r \\n -i out-
put  -f "number,name,address"

 hostname            =  localhost
 column delimiter =  ,
 record delimiter =  \n
 database            =  85321
 table               =  details
 input_file         =  output
 fields      =  number,name,address

 Field: number   Type: char
 Field: name   Type: char
 Field: address   Type: char

116 rows successfully imported.  No row was rejected.
```

The command line for the msql-import command breaks down into the following components:

-d 8532 This switch defines the name of the database into which the data is imported. In this case, the database name is the example database, 85321.

-t details The -t switch defines the name of the table, in this case details, into which the imported data is placed.

-c , A switch that defines the character used to separate the fields of the imported data. In this example, the fields are separated by a comma.

-r \\n The imported data is a list of records, each of which specifies the information for each student. This switch is used to specify the character that separates one record from another. In this case, it is the new line character, which is represented by \\n.

-I output The data being imported must be read from a particular file. This switch specifies which file.

-f "number,name,address" Finally, the import command must be told into which fields of the database the imported data should be placed. In this example, the three fields of data will be placed into the number, name, and address fields of the database.

Producing the Web Pages With the database created and the initial information entered into it, it is now time to produce the Web pages that will allow users to view and manipulate the data stored in the database. There are at least five methods that you can use to produce a Web/database interface: static pages, embedded languages, CGI scripts, Java applets, and Web-based application builders. The following sections describe the various characteristics of each approach and provide examples of producing a Web/database interface using embedded languages, CGI scripts, and a database application builder.

Static Pages The production of a static page involves the use of a database application to extract the raw data from the database, then converting that data into an HTML format. Once the HTML format is available, it can be placed on the Web server. This approach is relatively straightforward, but it has a drawback in that the information on the Web is static. If the database is updated, the Web page will not reflect this change unless the static page is created once more. With static pages, it is also not possible to enter or manipulate the data in the database.

Embedded Languages The embedded language in mSQL is called w3-mSQL. Embedded languages work by inserting extra tags into an HTML file. Before a visitor sees the Web page, it is passed through a database application that recognizes these extra tags and replaces them with information taken from the database. In the case of w3-mSQL, the tags use SQL-like queries to retrieve data from the database; a couple of additional tags provide simple programming constructs and the ability to display output.

The following is an excerpt from a Web page that implements the results page for our example. The results page displays a list of student results information in a table. Figure 8.15 shows the Web page this w3-mSQL page produces.

```
<H2>
  Current Results
</H2>

<! msql connect >

<! msql database sysAdmin >


<! msql query "select * from results" q >

<DIV ALIGN=CENTER>
<TABLE BORDER=5 CELLPADDING=4>
  <TR>
    <TH> Number   </TH>  <TH> Assign 1 </TH>
    <TH> Assign 2 </TH>  <TH> Exam     </TH>
  </TR>
  <TR>
  <! msql print_rows q "<TD ALIGN=CENTER> @q.0 </TD>
                         <TD ALIGN=CENTER> @q.1 </TD>
                         <TD ALIGN=CENTER> @q.2 </TD>
```

```
                        <TD ALIGN=CENTER> @q.3 </TD>
                        </TR> " >
</TABLE>
<! msql close>
```

If you read carefully through the example w3-mSQL file, you will see that the name of the database in the example has changed. The command

```
<! msql database sysAdmin>
```

is the w3-mSQL command that specifies the database on which the following commands should work. Instead of 85321, the name of the database used in previous examples, it says sysAdmin. Why? It appears that w3-mSQL, at least the version used for this example, does not like a numeric database name.

The solution to this problem was to recreate the database with the name sysAdmin instead of 85321. This process involved the following steps:

Dumping the contents of the 85321 database. mSQL comes with a command msqdump, which produces SQL commands that, when executed, recreate all the data stored in a database. The command

```
msqldump 85321 > 85321.sql
```

produces a file called 85321.sql that contains all the commands to recreate the database.

Creating the sysAdmin database. A simple step using the msqladmin command msqladmin create sysAdmin.

Populating the sysAdmin database. Using the msql command and the file 85321.sql, insert all the data from the 85321 database into the sysAdmin database. The command

```
msql < 85321.sql
```

forces the msql command to execute the SQL commands in the file 85321.sql.

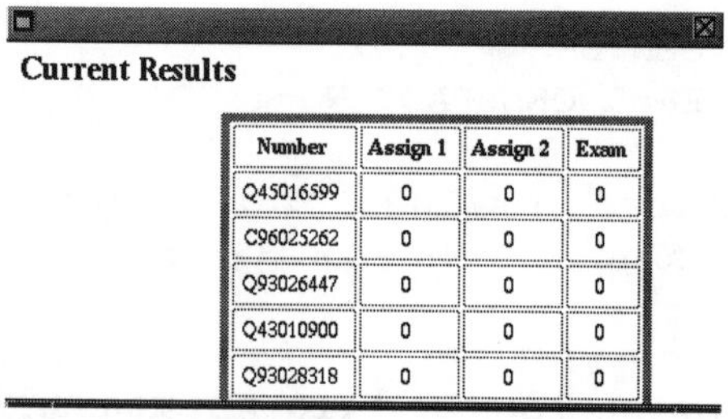
Current Results

Number	Assign 1	Assign 2	Exam
Q45016599	0	0	0
C96025262	0	0	0
Q93026447	0	0	0
Q43010900	0	0	0
Q93028318	0	0	0

Figure 8.15 An example w3-mSQL page.

CGI Scripts CGI scripts are programs written in any one of a number of languages that are run when someone connects to a particular URL. These scripts perform a certain task, then produce a Web page as output that is displayed in your Web browser. Some of the tasks CGI scripts can perform include storing, retrieving, and manipulating data from a database. CGI scripts that interface with a database use a programming language API to access the services of the database.

The following example uses the language Perl to implement a simple system that student assessment graders can use to enter and modify grades stored in the database. The implementation done here is available for testing on the book's Web page and involves creating two Web pages:

A list of students page. This list of students is similar to that produced in Figure 8.15, with one major difference. The students' numbers are linked to another CGI program. Following that link causes a CGI script to be run and the next page to be displayed.

Modification page for the student. Following a link from a student number gives the grader access to a page on which they can modify the grades for that student (see Figure 8.16). Pressing the Modify button on this page passes the information the grader changed back to the CGI script, which then updates the database.

The implementation of this system involves one CGI script written in Perl using the MsqlPerl package as the interface between Perl and the mSQL database. The script performs three separate operations, depending on what the grader is doing. The following sections describe each of these steps. Each step describes a section of code taken from the final script. (The full script can be found on the book's CD-ROM.) The example code below has had some code removed for brevity.

Displaying the List of Students The first task of the script is to display the list of students and their current results on a Web page. The following code performs this task:

```
# connect to Msql and select the appropriate database
# an MsqlPerl functions to access mSQL services
$dbH = Connect Msql;
SelectDB $dbH "sysAdmin";

# retrieve from the dBase the information we need
# an MsqlPerl function to access mSQL services
$queryHandle = Query $dbH "SELECT
number,assign1,assign2,exam
                                FROM results" ;
```

```
# displays the start of the Web page, and the table
# these are functions written by me
print &PrintHeader;
print &startTable;

# the following displays the rows of the table
# an MsqlPerl function to access mSQL services
@result = FetchRow $queryHandle;

$count = @result;
while ( $count )
{
  # a function to display each student's
  # information in a table
  &showRow( @result );

  # get the next student's information
  @result = FetchRow $queryHandle;
  $count = @result;
}
```

Allowing Data to Be Modified The next step involves obtaining one student's information from the database and displaying that information in an HTML form. The grader can then modify the data and press a Modify button. Figure 8.16 shows what this form looks like.

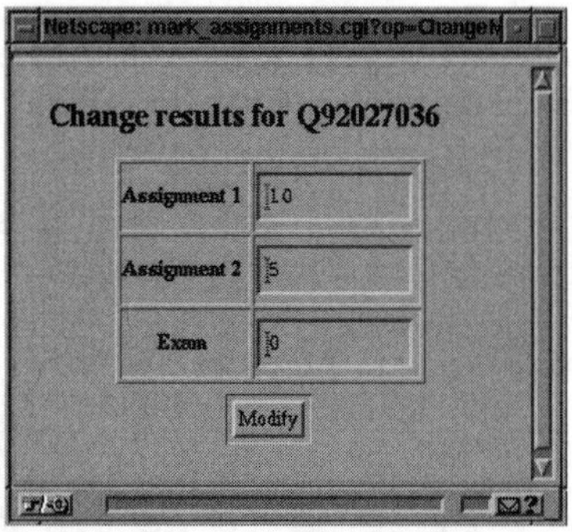

Figure 8.16 Modifying student grades.

```
# print the start of the page
  print &PrintHeader;

  # get information for the particular student, the number
was
  # passed in as a parameter to this script
  $queryHandle = Query $dbH "SELECT * FROM results where
                   number='$student'" ;
  @result = FetchRow $queryHandle;

  # display the HTML for the form
  print <<"EOF";
 <H2>
    Change results for $result[0]
 </H2>

  <FORM METHOD="POST" ACTION="/cgi-bin/mark_assignments.cgi">
  <INPUT TYPE="hidden" NAME="op" VALUE="setResults">
  <INPUT TYPE="hidden" NAME="number" VALUE="$result[0]">

  <DIV ALIGN=CENTER>
  <TABLE BORDER>
    <TR>
      <TH> Assignment 1 </TH>
      <TD>
        <INPUT TYPE="text" NAME="a1" VALUE="$result[1]"
SIZE=10
            MAXLENGTH=10>
      </TD>
    </TR>
    <TR>
      <TH> Assignment 2 </TH>
      <TD>
        <INPUT TYPE="text" NAME="a2" VALUE="$result[2]"
SIZE=10
               MAXLENGTH=10>
      </TD>
    </TR>
    <TR>
      <TH> Exam </TH>
      <TD>
```

```
        <INPUT TYPE="text" NAME="exam" VALUE="$result[3]"
SIZE=10
                 MAXLENGTH=10>
      </TD>
    </TR>
  </TABLE>
  <INPUT TYPE="submit" NAME="modify" VALUE="Modify">
  </DIV>
EOF
```

Modifying the Data The last step in the process is to place into the database the new data entered by the person grading the assessment. Once the data is inserted into the database, this script displays the list of students so that the process can start over.

```
  # retrieve the data from the form, this method is particu-
lar
  # to the tool we are using
  $number = $input{ 'number' };
  $a1 = $input{ 'a1' };
  $a2 = $input{ 'a2 ' };
  $exam = $input{ 'exam' };

  # use MsqlPerl to update the information in the database
  $queryHandle = Query $dbH
            "UPDATE results set assign1='$a1',
assign2='$a2',
               exam='$exam' where number='$number' ";
```

Java Applets A restriction of most CGI scripts, particularly for data entry, is the primitive nature of the interface provided by Web-based forms. JavaScript provides some additional flexibility in the interface, but it is still somewhat restrictive, and there are problems with compatibility of JavaScript between browsers. Java applets provide a fully programmable interface with the advantages of both HTML forms and JavaScript. The advent of JDBC further simplifies the process of creating Java-based interfaces to databases.

Database Application Builders Both embedded languages and CGI scripts require some knowledge of programming. Another method for performing these tasks without programming skills is to use a database application builder. An example of what can be accomplished with Jate was shown in Figures 8.12, 8.13, and 8.14. Database application builders like Jate allow you to produce a Web interface to a database by filling in a few forms.

Assessment Submission and Management

The submission and management of assessment can be achieved using a number of means, each with its own problems and advantages. This section does the following:

- Lists the desirable characteristics of an assessment management system
- Describes the standard problems that appear when performing online submission and management of assessment
- Provides some possible approaches to implement assessment submission and management using e-mail
- Examines the automated assessment management system that comes with Webfuse

Desirable Characteristics The following is a list of desirable characteristics for assessment management systems:

No delivery delays. No time should be wasted in delivering an assessment from the student to the grader and back again. This is especially important in distance education, where assessment may spend a number of weeks in transit.

Automatic acknowledgment of receipt. The first concern of most students after submitting a piece of assessment is whether or not the assignment was submitted safely. The assignment submission system should provide immediate feedback to the student, indicating whether the assignment was successfully received.

Automatic distribution and notification. Some classes have multiple graders, each responsible for grading particular assignments. Once an assignment is submitted, the grader should receive automatic notification and be able to immediately access and grade the assignment. Manual distribution opens up the possibility of delays and human error.

Centralized storage with distributed access. A number of tasks related to assessment management can be implemented only if all the information about a class assessment is centralized. Some examples include identifying how many assignments have been submitted and how many have been returned, comparing the work of one grader against others, and retrieving graded assignments to answer student queries. However, to gain full benefit, centralized storage must be partnered with distributed access that allows students and graders to view and modify information as necessary.

Common Problems and Solutions Computer-based assessment submission and management is not without its problems, which include:

- Lack of support for non-computer-based assessment
- Marker access to the technology
- Marking online versus printing
- Incompatible file formats
- Viruses
- Lack of administrative support

Let's examine these problems that are common to all forms of computer-based assessment management and some remedies.

Non-Computer-Based Assessment The most difficult problem to solve in computer-based assessment management is that some forms of assessment cannot be put onto a computer. Others can be put on a computer, but at great expense, and hence are not cost-effective. Examples include biological or geographical samples and musical or dramatic performances.

Grader Access to Technology Online submission generally means that the grader retrieves assessment from an online storage location and proceeds to examine and grade student assessment via a computer. This procedure requires the grader to have access to a computer and the network in order to grade. Online assessment management means that grading cannot be done under a tree or during a commute, though portable computers may make either possible in some instances.

Marking Online versus Printing With all assessment submitted electronically, the question of how the grader reads the assessment arises. There are two basic choices: online reading, an approach that does not suit all individuals and raises particular problems with long essay assessment, and reading a printout, which requires the grader to have access to a quality printer. The time taken to print and collate assessment may be such that any time saved by electronic assessment is lost.

There are no simple solutions to these problems; what works will depend on the class, the type of assessment, and the graders. However, a number of approaches, both technical and procedural, can help address some of these issues.

Incompatible File Formats To grade an assignment, the grader must be able to read it. In order to read a computer-based assignment, the grader must have access to a program that can read students' files. This access is not always possible. Common problems include "weird" applications that are not widely available and produce files that can't be read easily by other, more standard applications; software version changes; and platform dependency. A solution is to specify up front the file formats that are acceptable for assignment submission. Platform-independent formats such as RTF, HTML, and text are good choices.

Viruses The use of e-mail attachments to distribute binary and application files raises the possibility of infection by computer viruses. Traditionally, this was only a problem if the attachments were executable programs; however, the trend for Microsoft applications to support a macro language means that it is possible for data files produced by most Microsoft applications to carry viruses. If you have 100 students submitting essays via e-mail, chances are that at least a few will contain viruses, regardless of what you tell students.

One solution to this problem is to run every attachment you receive through a virus scanner before opening it. Automated virus scanners are available, but their use does add an extra level of difficulty and time to the task. In addition, scanning works only if the virus scanner you use is capable of dealing with the latest viruses. Trusting students to check for viruses before submission will never be a fool-proof solution; some students will forget, use an out-of-date virus checker, not understand how to do the check, or not have time to do it before submitting the assignment.

Another solution is to accept assignments only in file formats that cannot be used to distribute viruses; RTF, HTML, text, and PostScript are examples. Using these file formats does add another task to be completed by students, and some file formats may not support all the features of the original file.

A more recent problem with this approach is a Word virus that only pretends to save a Word document in RTF format. A version of Word infected with this virus will happily report that it has saved your file in RTF when in reality the file is actually a Word file infected with this particular virus. Recent virus checkers do identify and deal with this particular virus.

Lack of Administrative Support Having a couple of hundred students submitting assessment, either electronically or by traditional methods, is a major exercise requiring significant administrative support. The next section describes the implementation of assessment submission via e-mail, discusses the problem in more detail, and offers some solutions. Other solutions to this problem are provided by complete assessment management systems like the Webfuse system described later in the chapter.

E-Mail-Based Assessment Management The most obvious method for the submission of assignments is for students to send their assignments, via e-mail, to the educator. Although this approach removes the delay in delivery, it does not provide any of the other desirable characteristics of an assessment management system:

Automatic acknowledgment of assignment receipt. Some e-mail systems provide automatic acknowledgments, but to receive an acknowledgment, the student must wait for the educator to read his e-mail and respond.

Automatic distribution to graders. Again, the educator must play the part of a forwarding office and distribute assignments to graders.

Centralized storage. By default, assignments, solutions, and comments on assignments end up being distributed among the computers of the various graders and the educator in charge. It is possible to have one centralized storage location, but this can involve passing all information through a central individual.

In addition, the use of e-mail for assignment submission introduces a number of other difficulties:

Freedom or lack thereof. When submitting assignments via e-mail, students have complete control (or lack of it) over the format and information included in a submission. This situation makes it possible for students to forget information, include it in the wrong order or format, and even send it to the wrong e-mail address.

Incompatible attachments. Internet e-mail is a text-only system, and before any binary data can be sent via e-mail, it must first be translated into text. Translation methods include uudecode/uuencode, binhex, and base 64 (MIME). Not all e-mail programs can handle all encoding formats, and if you use e-mail submission of assessment, chances are that one of your students will use a format that your e-mail program does not understand.

Incompatible formats. Many recent mail programs, in an attempt to capture market share, have introduced a number of incompatible extensions to e-mail that not all e-mail programs understand.

Message limits. Some mail systems place a limit on the size of files that can be distributed via e-mail. This is an increasingly rare occurrence, but happens from time to time.

Mail overload. Assignments submitted via e-mail must end up in someone's incoming e-mail. Most e-mail users are already complaining about receiving too much mail. The overnight addition of 150 e-mail messages containing large assignments can add to this problem. This overload of e-mail can contribute to the loss of e-mail assignments.

These problems and shortcomings of e-mail as an assessment management system can be solved by a combination of practices and tools that help provide the necessary administrative support, as described in the following sections.

FormMail FormMail, available from the site **worldwidemart.com/scripts/formmail. shtml**, is a CGI script that provides a simple gateway between HTML forms and e-mail. With FormMail, you can create an HTML form containing input areas for the information you want students to submit. Students must cut and paste the information from their existing applications into the HTML form. When a form is submitted, FormMail generates an e-mail message containing the assignment and delivers it to any e-mail address.

There are a number of issues involved when using FormMail for assessment management:

Lack of freedom. FormMail reduces the choices and tasks a student must complete in order to submit an assignment. Hopefully, this limitation reduces the number of problems introduced by student mistakes.

Restriction to text. This approach can be used only to submit text information. This restriction removes the problems of viruses and incompatible file formats, but limits the type and presentation of the information.

Quasi-acknowledgment. Once submitted, FormMail displays a Web page claiming successful submission. However, the successful operation was the submission of the data and sending it via e-mail. The e-mail may still be lost while traveling from the Web server to the grader.

Mailing Lists Rather than have students send their e-mail assignments to the e-mail address of an individual, you can instruct them to use the address of a mailing list. The configuration of a mailing list could accept mail from anyone and distribute mail only to the graders. It can also maintain an archive of all assignments submitted on the mailing list server.

To return graded assignments, graders copy the graded assignments to the mailing list and the student. The mailing list archive then acts as the centralized store of grading information and allows moderation and retrieval of old assignments.

The characteristics of this approach include the following:

Automatic distribution of assignments to the graders.

Lack of automatic acknowledgment.

All-or-nothing distribution. All graders will receive copies of all assignments, not just those for which they are responsible.

A centralized store of all assignments. A centralized store of assignments makes it possible to implement student tracking, the production of assessment summaries, and moderation of grading.

Distributed access for graders. Graders would be able to access the central archive using standard mailing list commands from any machine at which they can access e-mail.

Possible security problems. In setting up the mailing list, in particular the archive, care must be taken to ensure that only authorized individuals can access the information.

E-Mail/Web Gateways Most of the problems with mailing lists are related to the way in which assignments are distributed to graders. A solution to these problems is to use an e-mail/Web gateway as the primary form of distribution. This process works as follows:

1. Students submit assignments to a particular e-mail address.
2. Mail to this address is run through an e-mail/Web gateway that produces Web pages.
3. Graders retrieve assignments from these password-protected Web pages.
4. Marked assignments are sent to another e-mail address, also connected to an e-mail/Web gateway.

This approach provides a centralized storage area for assignments with access anywhere there is Web access. Use of a e-mail/Web gateway, like MHonArc, that supports MIME can also address the problem of file attachments. (Chapter 6 discusses e-mail/Web gateways and MHonArc in more detail.)

E-Mail Filters The increasing use of e-mail—in particular, the increase in junk mail—has led to the development of e-mail filters. E-mail filters are programs that automatically scan incoming e-mail and perform a number of operations with that e-mail, including deleting it, forwarding it to someone else, acknowledging receipt of it, or copying it to a mail folder.

E-mail filters can be divided into two categories:

Client-side filters. Client-side filters are those implemented by mail readers such as the latest versions of Netscape Communicator and Eudora. Client-side filters are generally simple to use; however, they are applied only once e-mail has been downloaded to the mail reader, which may be quite some time after the message was actually sent.

Server-side filters. Server-side filters reside on the computer to which your e-mail is delivered and are applied as soon as e-mail arrives. Most server-side filters provide a simple yet powerful programming language to control their operation.

In practice, client-side filters are a useful aid in the management of e-mail assignment submission but do not provide the automatic acknowledgment of receipt. The desirable immediate acknowledgment of assignment submission can be provided only by server side filters.

Vacation programs are another possibility for providing immediate acknowledgments of assignment submission. The original purpose of vacation programs was to send a short e-mail response to any incoming e-mail, informing the sender that you are on vacation and won't be able to respond to e-mail for a while.

The WebFuse Assignment Submission System The Webfuse system, available from the Web site **webfuse.cqu.edu.au/**, is an integrated system for online learning. It is discussed in more detail in Chapter 9, but because it includes an integrated assessment management system that uses the Web as the primary interface, we begin to explore it here. The features of this system include:

- Submission of assignments via Web-based file upload
- Automatic acknowledgment of receipt
- Centralized storage with access via the Web
- Simple Web-based grading of assignments
- Automatic production of assessment summaries

Some problems with the Webfuse system include the following:

Lack of browser support for file upload. File upload is a draft Internet standard that defines a mechanism that allows Web browsers to upload a file onto a Web server. Currently, the only browsers that support file upload are Netscape browsers from version 2.0 and later. In June 1997, Microsoft announced support for file upload on Internet Explorer 3.1.

Lack of individual student accounts. Only graders can have accounts on the system, which they use to access assignment submissions. Students do not have accounts. Submitting an assignment involves entering a unique student identifier, choosing the assignment, then uploading the assignment. Once the assignment is submitted, the student, or anyone pretending to be the student, cannot submit the assignment again without the intervention of a grader. This prevents someone submitting a dummy assignment and replacing it with a real assignment later. However, in some circumstances—for example, if a student made a mistake and left something out or your assessment approach allows students to resubmit—this can be a problem. In particular, it requires the intervention of a staff member to reset the database.

Requirements The requirements for the Webfuse assessment management system include the following:

A version of Webfuse. Webfuse is distributed free of charge and is available from the book's CD-ROM. Versions of Webfuse are currently available for Windows 95/NT and most versions of UNIX.

Webfuse accounts for yourself and any graders.

Student details. For each student, the assessment management system requires a unique identifier, student name, and e-mail address.

Information about the assignments. For each assignment, you will need to provide the assignment number, names of the files the students will submit, and a short description to be displayed when a student submits the assignment.

Submitting an Assignment To submit an assignment using Webfuse, a student follows these four steps:

Visit the assessment submission page. On this page (see Figure 8.17), students enter their student numbers, select the assignment they want to submit, then press a Submit button. If that assignment has already been submitted or a student number does not appear in the student database, an error message is generated. If everything is correct, students proceed to the next step.

Visit the assignment page. The next page is specific to the assignment being submitted. It contains a general description of how to use the page, specific instructions for the assignment (supplied by the educator), and a sequence of file upload components. The number of file upload components depends on the number of files required for this assignment. Figure 8.18 shows the assignment-specific instructions and file upload components of this page. Students locate the files to upload and then press the Submit Assignment button. If they have not specified all the files, an error message will be displayed. Otherwise, the files will be copied onto the Web server running Webfuse.

Visit the acknowledgment page. By this stage, students' assignment files should have made it onto the Web server. To provide an acknowledgment of safe arrival, the system displays the names of the files and the size of the server copy of each file (see Figure 8.19). Students can compare the size of the server-based files against the size of the files on their computer. If the sizes match, they know that the assignment has been submitted safely.

Visit the results page. At any time, students can check on the progress of their assignments and the performance of their classmates by visiting the results page. This page provides the same information and uses the same format as that shown in Figure 8.1.

Grading an Assignment To mark an assignment using Webfuse, the grader performs the following four steps:

Go to the class assessment submission page. This is the same first page (Figure 8.17) used by students when submitting their assignment. However, the grader follows the assignment management link. This link is password protected; to access the subsequent pages, a valid user name and password are required.

Visit the assignment management page. This page (see Figure 8.20) provides a summary of current grading, including the number of assignments submitted and returned, and a list of links that split the student population into groups of 20 students. Following one of these links takes the grader to the next page.

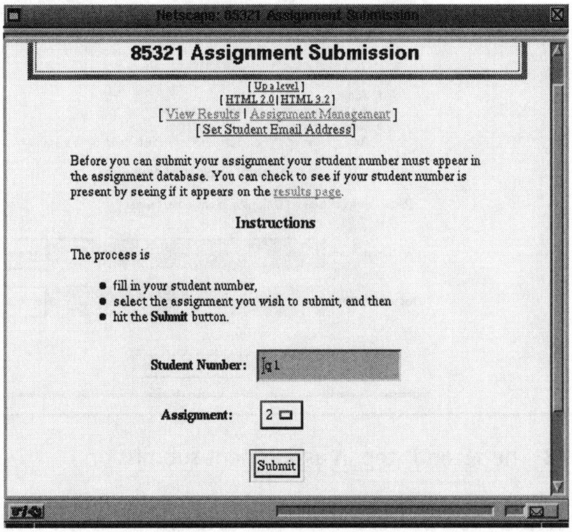

Figure 8.17 The first step in Webfuse assignment submission.

Go to the group grading page. As shown in Figure 8.21, this page provides a list of 20 students and links that allow the grader to e-mail the students, access their assignments, and grade the assignments.

Visit the individual grading page. This page (see Figure 8.22) allows the grader to enter comments about students' assignments and change grades. Comments about the assignments can be entered via the Web or loaded from disk.

Other Submission Methods E-mail submission and the use of the Webfuse system are only two of the online methods possible for assessment submission. Others include:

Anonymous FTP. An anonymous FTP area to which students can upload files but from which they cannot retrieve files is used by students to submit their assignments. This technique can be difficult to implement and use, and it allows students too much freedom of choice. With this technique, students are expected to do manually most of the tasks, including packing and uploading assignments. Even with specific instructions, this can result in multiple methods of achieving the same goal, which can increase the management workload.

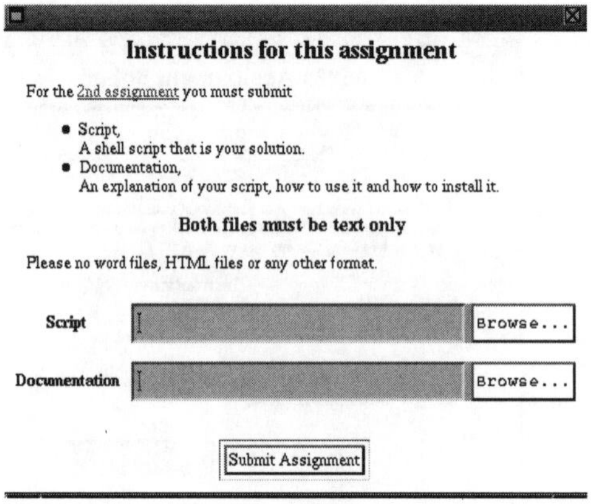

Figure 8.18 The second step in assignment submission.

The file system. This method originates from the pre-Internet days, when students had user accounts on a multiuser system. It exploits = the fact that on a multiuser system, all files are accessible if you have the appropriate permission. Typically, students either place assignment files into a particular location to which they can write but not read or the educator will gain permission to enter students' account areas.

Student Web sections. A modification of the file system approach is for all students to have their own section of the Web into which they can place files and to which they can restrict access to prevent other students obtaining their assignments. The WebCT system uses such an approach.

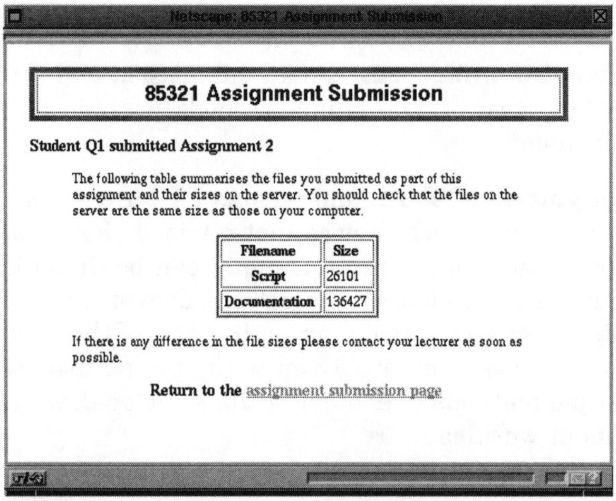

Figure 8.19 The third step in assignment submission.

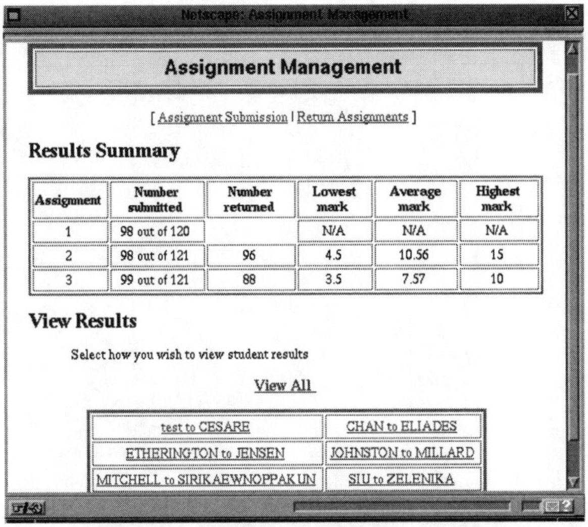

Figure 8.20 The assignment management page.

CONCLUSION

Class management tasks, due to their mundane nature, often run a poor second to other, more interesting tasks. Any methods of increasing the effectiveness and reducing the cost of these tasks are welcome. Because most of these tasks can be

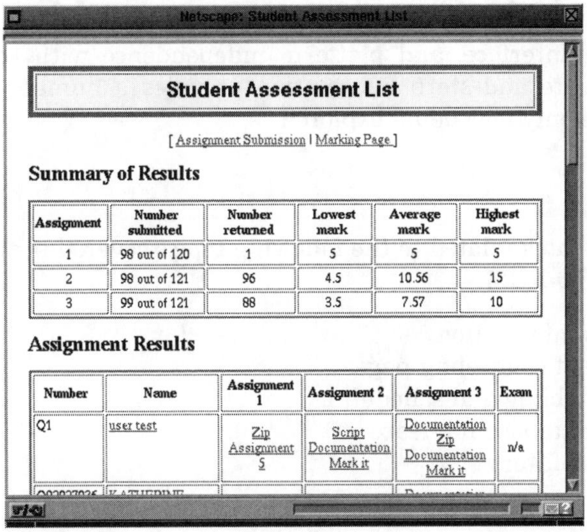

Figure 8.21 Group grading page.

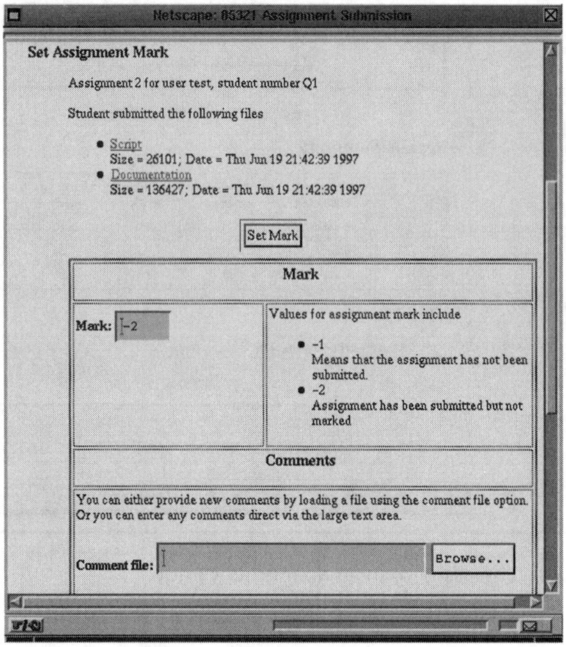

Figure 8.22 The individual grading page.

characterized as information management and distribution tasks or communication tasks, appropriate use of the Web can usually provide the desired outcome. In particular, the combination of the Web's information distribution advantages, familiar interface, and platform independence with the computer's ability to manipulate and store information provides a number of exciting possibilities that are only now being explored.

RESOURCES

A list of sites related to the following topics covered in this chapter can be found on the CD-ROM:

- Class information
- Student counseling pages
- Timetabling and scheduling
- Web/database interface
- E-mail filters

9

A Comparison of Web Classroom Builders

Without assistance from appropriate tools, building and maintaining a Web-based classroom can require significant effort, time, resources, and technical skills. This fact, combined with educators' increasing desire to use the Web in their teaching, has led to the development of a number of systems that help educators construct and maintain Web-based classrooms. Each of these systems help reduce the effort and skill necessary to build a Web-based classroom and provide support for the same basic tasks. The question for many educators is, which of these tools should I use? There is no one correct answer to this question, and this chapter is not about attempting to provide that answer. Instead, this chapter aims to provide you with a comparison of the features, capabilities, and requirements of three of these tools: WebCT, TopClass, and Webfuse.

In order to compare these tools, we built a Web-based classroom for one course using each of the three systems. The resulting Web-based classrooms are available on the book's Web site for further examination. Most of this chapter deals with an examination of each of the three systems, including a description of how the tool works, the process used to construct the example Web-based classroom, and the requirements for using the system. In closing, the chapter provides a comparison of the features of each system and pointers to where more information can be found about these and other systems.

CHOOSING THE TOOL

A wide selection of systems and tools is available to help educators build Web-based classrooms. Given time and resource constraints, it is simply not possible to compare all of the available tools in this chapter. Instead, we focus on three systems: WebCT, TopClass, and Webfuse. These tools were chosen for a number of reasons, including the following:

Offers a complete system. The purpose of this chapter is to compare systems that offer a complete, integrated set of tools that allow educators to perform each of the four major tasks: information distribution, communication, student assessment, and class management. This requirement rules out individual tools such as FirstClass or Majordomo.

Web-based structure. A number of network-based systems provide support for the four required tasks, but they are based on proprietary network software. Each of the chosen systems provides a Web-based interface for students, staff, and class designers.

Available for free. At the time this chapter was written, each of the chosen systems was either freely available (Webfuse and WebCT) or had an evaluation copy that was freely available (TopClass).

Under continuing development. Each of the chosen systems shows that it is still being supported and developed by the producers. In contrast, some tools have shown no development for more than a year.

UNIX versions are available. While student interaction must be Web based, most systems rely on some form of server software to work. Due to the resources available, we chose systems that have versions of the server that can be run on UNIX computers.

While performing the evaluations in this chapter, we made every effort to be impartial; the makers of the systems discussed were given the chance to examine and respond to the contents of this chapter while it was being written. Like the Web itself, the systems examined in this chapter are undergoing continual development and growth, so some observations and conclusions in this chapter may no longer be valid.

The Class

The example class in this process is a third-year computing class taught at the Department of Mathematics and Computing at Central Queensland University; the class is titled 85321, Systems Administration (referred to as 85321 for the remainder of the chapter).

The 85321 class has a number of characteristics that make it a prime candidate for a Web-based classroom. The majority of 85321 students are in the third year of a computing degree, so they are computer literate, have Web access (100% in 1997), and see the relevance to their career prospects of being able to use the Web. The course examines UNIX systems administration, so is able to draw on the large collection of Web-based material related to the topic.

Like all classes taught by the department, 85321 is taken by both on-campus and distance students. Students range from traditional, teenage, on-campus students to a middle-aged Australian federal policeman working with the United Nations peacekeeping force in Cyprus. All distance students have access to the Internet, but they pay for that access on the basis of how long they are connected. This means it is important to decrease the amount of time they must be online.

Given the characteristics of the class and the staff involved, it is not surprising that the class has twice been taught using a Web-based classroom as the primary learning medium. The first online offering of 85321 was in the first half of 1996; the second occurred a year later. This history of online offerings has helped create a large collection of locally produced, Web-based resources, including archives of mailing lists and a study guide (in HTML) of more than 300 pages.

The Design

A basic design of the 85321 Web-based classroom was created using the process outlined in Chapter 3. The resulting structure is shown in Figure 9.1. This design breaks all the Web-based information and tasks for 85321 into four main sections:

Information. Includes background and administrative information about 85321: prerequisites, a short class history, a suggested study schedule, and some previous student feedback.

Study material. Contains most of the class's learning materials: the online study guide, tutorial sheets, and previous versions of the class's Web-based classroom.

Assessment. All the details concerning student assessment: assessment requirements, assignment sheets, past exams and solutions, and rules for submitting assignments and viewing results.

Communication. Provides access to the communication methods available for students: details on the class mailing list, archives of both past and present mailing lists, and access to an interactive chat room.

Although the basic structure was retained for the Web-based classrooms built with each of the chosen systems, it was necessary to make some modification for each because each system, while providing the same basic functionality, does so with a different interface and components. The design of the Web-based classroom for each system must reflect the most appropriate use of its facilities.

Now let's examine each of the systems.

WEBCT

Web Course Tools (WebCT) grew out of a project to build a Web-based classroom for a third-year computer science course at the University of British Columbia. The

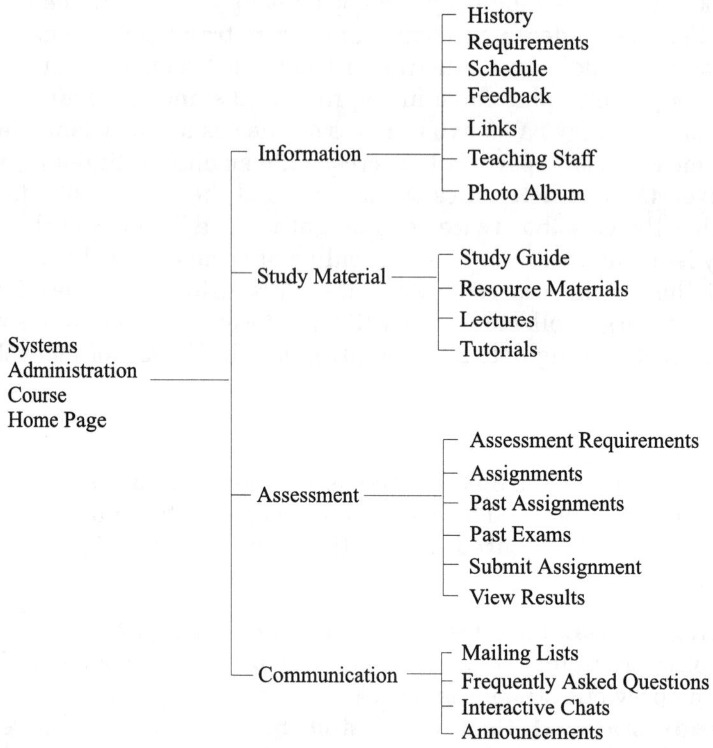

Figure 9.1 The graphical hierarchy of the 85321 site.

development of this Web-based classroom was time consuming, was expensive, and required a large amount of technical skill. Murray Goldberg, the designer of WebCT and the leader of the original project, recognized that the time, cost, and skill requirements for building a Web-based classroom put such development out of the reach of most educators. As a result, another project—to develop a system to help reduce these requirements—was begun. The result of this second project is WebCT.

Development on WebCT commenced in November 1995; the first beta version was released in August 1996, and the first official version is scheduled to be available commercially by September 1997. Due to the fact that the initial development of WebCT was funded by research grants, the initial beta releases of WebCT have been available for free.

How It Works

Simply put, WebCT is an integrated collection of CGI scripts, images, forms pages, and JavaScript and Java applets that work with a Web server to allow the creation, maintenance, and use of a Web-based classroom. This collection of tools and materials allows a class designer to build and maintain a Web-based classroom and students to use that classroom. Let's examine the features WebCT provides and how they appear to the system's users.

Accounts Each user of a WebCT classroom must have a valid user name and password (account) before being granted access. User accounts control the actions individual users can perform and allow the tracking of student use and participation in the class. There are four types of WebCT account:

Administrator. Each WebCT server has one administrator who is responsible for creating new classes, modifying the descriptions of existing classes, and changing the password of class designer accounts. The WebCT administrator account always has the user name admin.

Designer. Every WebCT class has one class designer who is responsible for designing and building the WebCT classroom, including tasks such as structuring the content, designing the "look and feel," and creating grader and student accounts.

Grader. Each WebCT class can have a number of graders who are responsible for marking student quizzes and possibly entering and managing grades in the student results database.

Students. Finally, each WebCT class can have a number of student accounts students use to gain access to the services of the WebCT classroom.

What the Student Sees Upon entering the WebCT version of the 85321 Web-based classroom, students see the home page shown in Figure 9.2. This page is an example of a WebCT tool page. The main purpose of a tool page is to organize a WebCT classroom into a hierarchy that is easy for students to navigate. The icons on the page shown in Figure 9.2 are a mixture of icons that were produced specifically for 85321 representing information, study material, assessment, and communication and icons provided with WebCT (resume session and change password).

The links on a WebCT page can point to five WebCT components:

Tool page. The links for information, communication, assessment, and study material all point to other WebCT tool pages, which in turn point to other pages and tools.

WebCT tool. WebCT provides a number of tools that provide a wide range of services. Tables 9.1 and 9.2 provide a complete list of these tools and their capabilities.

URL. A link can point to any standard URL and usually points to a Web page that is outside the current WebCT classroom.

Single page. As the name suggests, a single page is used to display a single Web page. However, a WebCT single page does not simply display the content

Figure 9.2 The WebCT home page for 85321.

of the page in the current browser window. Instead, selecting a WebCT single page (see Figure 9.3) opens up another browser window that is divided into two frames. The much larger bottom frame contains the single Web page to be displayed; the smaller top frame provides a simple navigation mechanism with the buttons Close, Back, and Forward. When students follow any links contained in the content of the page, the resulting pages appear in the bottom frame. This structure allows students to explore any links, but provides an obvious method for returning to the original page.

Path. A WebCT path allows students to navigate both sequentially and hierarchically through a collection of pages. Example uses of a WebCT path in the 85321 WebCT classroom include the chapters from the study guide, three assignments, past exams, and solutions.

WebCT Paths A WebCT path is the primary method for distributing learning material in a WebCT class. Students' first view of a WebCT path (see Figure 9.4) displays a hierarchical table of contents for the pages within the path. Using the arrows, students can view or hide sublevels of the path or jump straight to a particular page in the path by clicking on the appropriate link.

An individual page (see Figure 9.5) in a WebCT path is broken up into two frames, similar to a WebCT single page. The much larger bottom frame holds the content of the page; the smaller top frame provides access to various navigation

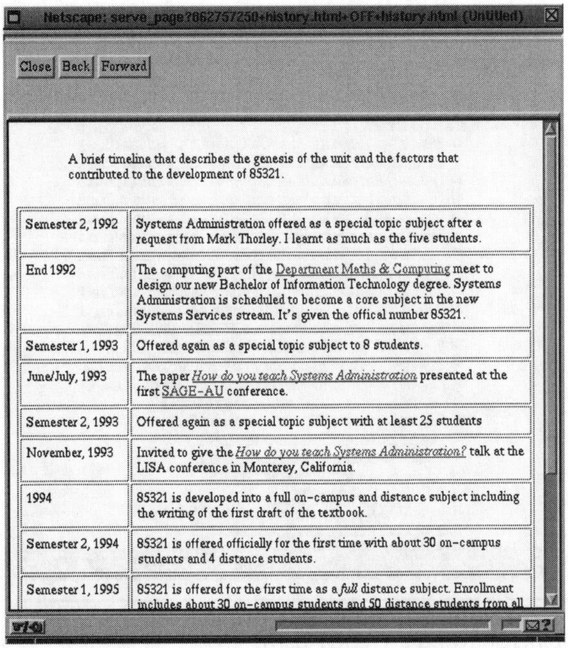
Close Back Forward

A brief timeline that describes the genesis of the unit and the factors that contributed to the development of 85321.

Semester 2, 1992	Systems Administration offered as a special topic subject after a request from Mark Thorley. I learnt as much as the five students.
End 1992	The computing part of the Department Maths & Computing meet to design our new Bachelor of Information Technology degree. Systems Administration is scheduled to become a core subject in the new Systems Services stream. It's given the offical number 85321.
Semester 1, 1993	Offered again as a special topic subject to 8 students.
June/July, 1993	The paper *How do you teach Systems Administration* presented at the first SAGE-AU conference.
Semester 2, 1993	Offered again as a special topic subject with at least 25 students
November, 1993	Invited to give the *How do you teach Systems Administration?* talk at the LISA conference in Monterey, California.
1994	85321 is developed into a full on-campus and distance subject including the writing of the first draft of the textbook.
Semester 2, 1994	85321 is offered officially for the first time with about 30 on-campus students and 4 distance students.
Semester 1, 1995	85321 is offered for the first time as a *full* distance subject. Enrollment includes about 30 on-campus students and 50 distance students from all

Figure 9.3 A WebCT single page.

and tool icons. Every page in a WebCT path has a navigation box that allows readers to traverse the path in the top frame. The top frame can also provide links to a number of WebCT tools.

WebCT Tools WebCT tools provide many of the useful features of WebCT and are divided into page-specific and global (or course) tools. Page-specific tools can be assigned only to a single page within a WebCT path; global tools can be linked to both a page in a WebCT path and from a WebCT tool page. Tables 9.1 and 9.2 provide a description of local and global tools and the facilities they provide.

What the Class Designer Sees The class designer is responsible for preparing and maintaining the structure, presentation, and content of a WebCT class as well as creating accounts for graders and students participating in the class. Each WebCT class has a single account for the class designer. The user name of this account is the same as the class name. For example, the account for the class designer of the 85321 Web-based classroom has the user name 85321.

To allow the class designer to complete these tasks, WebCT provides the designer with a view of the WebCT class that combines the look and feel of the actual WebCT class in one frame with a number of buttons in another frame, as shown in Figure 9.6. With this interface, the class designer can navigate around

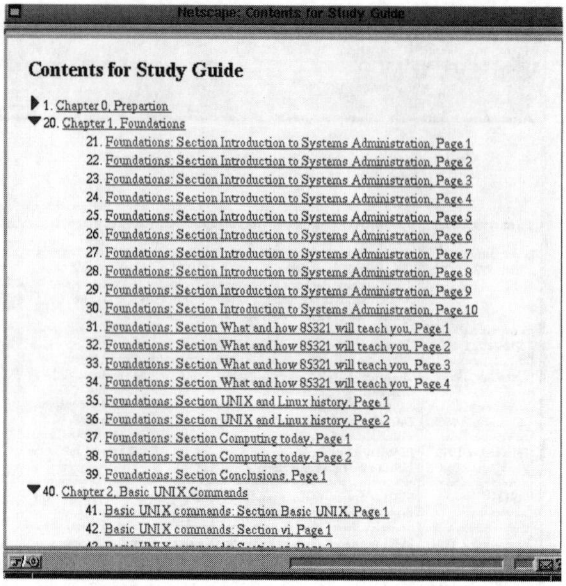

Figure 9.4 A table of contents showing a WebCT path.

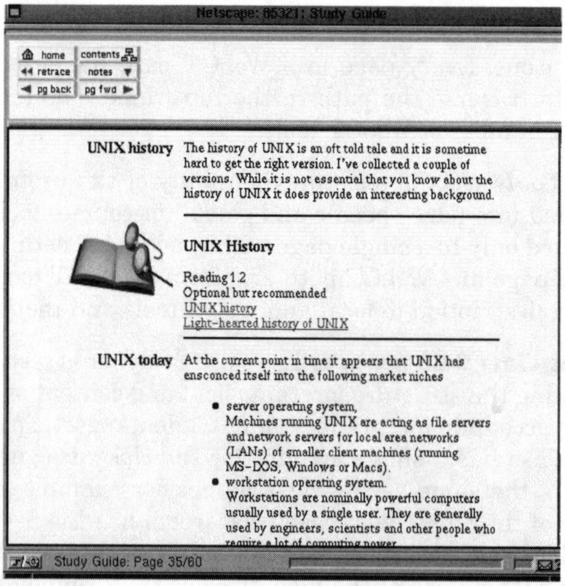

Figure 9.5 A page from a WebCT path.

Table 9.1 WebCT Global Tools

Tool Name	*Purpose*
Glossary	A list of terms and definitions common to the class
Text search	Perform a search of the class pages for a particular word or phrase
Course index	A list of the class's important terms and links to appropriate places in the course notes
Student tracking	Allows students to see how they have used the WebCT class
Student records	Provides students with access to their results
Image database	A searchable collection of images related to the class
Student presentations	Areas where students can place material on the WebCT server for access by other class participants
Real-time chat	A synchronous chat facility similar to IRC, implemented using a Java applet
Bulletin board	A Web-based bulletin-board system that can be used only within the WebCT class
Private e-mail	A Web-based e-mail system that can be used only within the WebCT class
Quizzes	Timed quizzes that are marked online by a grader
Password changing	Allows users to change their passwords
Compiling pages	Provides a system by which a number of pages from a WebCT path can be joined into a single Web page and then printed
Resuming a session	Takes students to the page they were on when the finished their last session in the class

Table 9.2 Page-Specific Tools

Tool Name	*Purpose*
Self-test	Multiple-choice questions that are automatically marked; intended to be used by students as self-tests, not for assessment
References	Provides pointers to supplementary resources such as textbooks and journal articles
Learning goals	Defines for students the learning goals for a particular page
Multimedia clips	Allows the linking of audio and video files to a particular page (links can also be placed into the HTML of the page content)

Figure 9.6 The WebCT class designer's interface.

the classroom in much the same way that students do and at any time can use WebCT's services to modify the class. Table 9.3 summarizes the facilities available to the class designer.

Table 9.3 WebCT Management Services

Facility	*Purpose*
File manager	Copies files onto the server (see Figure 9.9)
Course settings	Specifies the default look and feel for pages in the classroom, including the banner, colors, and the header and footer HTML
Path editor	Allows the designer to insert, delete, and move pages around within a WebCT path
Page editor	Enables the customization of individual pages within a WebCT path, including editing the HTML and adding tools
Class management	Provides the facilities to create and manage student accounts and results and allows the designer to generate graphs summarizing results and manage the class gradebook

What the Grader Sees A WebCT class grader is presented with the same interface as students, with one exception. The grader's interface (see Figure 9.7) includes a link to the WebCT tool that allows the grader to view and mark the timed quizzes that students have completed. WebCT automatically makes completed quizzes available to the grader and provides a facility where they can be marked online.

What the Administrator Sees The WebCT administrator account is a specialized account with a limited role that includes tasks such as creating new WebCT classes, modifying class descriptions, deleting WebCT classes, and changing class designers' passwords. Each of these tasks is straightforward and achieved through the interface shown in Figure 9.8.

Features

WebCT provides a large number of features that can help support the building of and teaching in a Web-based classroom. The following section examines these features by dividing them into the four major tasks we have discussed throughout this book: information distribution, communication, student assessment, and class management.

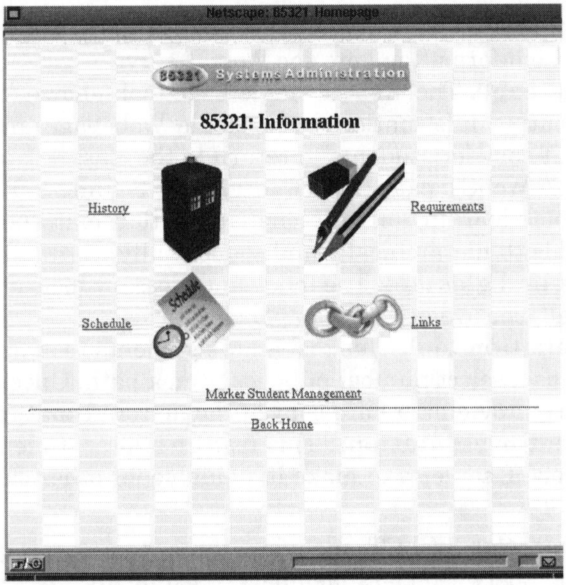

Figure 9.7 The WebCT grader's interface.

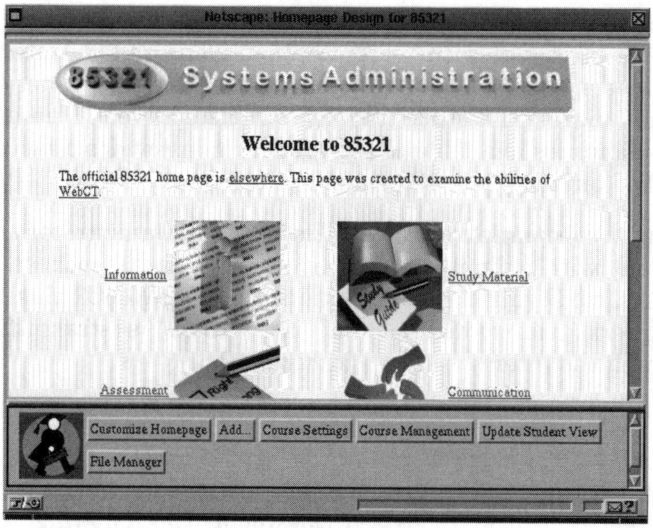

Figure 9.8 The WebCT administrator's interface.

Information Distribution Six WebCT components aid in the distribution of information:

- **File manager.** The WebCT file manager (see Figure 9.9) is used to place and organize information onto the WebCT server.
- **Single page.** The WebCT single page tool (shown in Figure 9.3) is means of distributing information via a single Web page and includes features that make it easy for students to return to the class.
- **Path.** A WebCT path (shown in Figures 9.4 and 9.5) is the major tool used to distribute learning material and allows that material to be organized and navigated both hierarchically and sequentially.
- **Index and glossary.** The index and glossary tools of WebCT provide students with alternative access to important terms.
- **Compilation tool.** This tool allows students to create a single Web page that contains a select number of pages from a path. Once created, that page can be printed, providing a hard copy of the material that can be read offline.
- **Student presentations.** This feature allows students to place material onto the WebCT server and make it available for other class participants.

Communication WebCT includes three communication facilities to enable interaction between class members. Each facility uses an integrated Web-based interface:

Class bulletin board. The class bulletin board provides an asynchronous group communication system that is open to the entire class. The class designer is able to delete messages from the bulletin board.

Class e-mail. WebCT's Web-based class e-mail facility allows participants to send e-mail to any other member of the class.

Interactive chat. The WebCT interactive chat facility uses a Java applet to provide a simple chat mechanism that groups of students can use for synchronous communication. The applet supports a number of "rooms" and keeps a record, or log, of each session in the chat room.

Currently, the WebCT communication facilities can be used only while connected to the WebCT class and to communicate with other class members.

Student Assessment WebCT provides four features that can be used in assessing student progress:

Self tests. Self-tests are simple multiple-choice questions that are automatically marked by WebCT.

Timed quizzes. Timed quizzes require students to complete a series of questions within a specified period of time. Once completed, students' answers are made available to a grader, who grades and returns them via the Web.

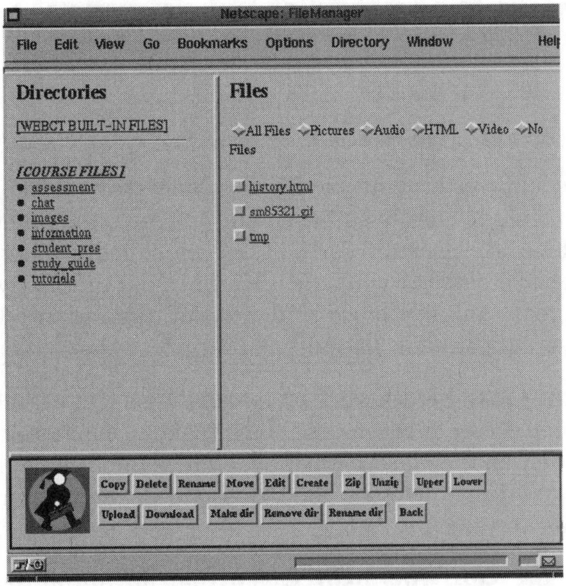

Figure 9.9 The WebCT file manager.

Student progress and participation tracking. WebCT's facility for tracking the number of pages students have read and the number of contributions to class discussions students have made could be used to ensure that students have fulfilled some minimum participation requirement.

Results management. WebCT provides a Web-based gradebook that can be used to record student results in both timed quizzes and other assessments. The gradebook also includes a number of facilities for manipulating and viewing student results, such as a Java applet that produces a distribution graph.

Class Management The class management facilities provided by WebCT deal mainly with the management of student lists and results:

Management of the student database. This includes facilities to add extra columns, batch registration, select entries on various criteria, and delete entries.

Release of student results. One of the features of the student database system is the ability to allow students to see particular columns from that database. This can be used to distribute results directly to students.

Online marking of timed quizzes. Once submitted by students, quizzes are available to graders for them to mark and comment on using a form.

Tracking student participation. WebCT provides a number of analysis methods in both graphical and tabular formats. (See Chapter 7 for a more detailed description of this facility.)

Implementing 85321 with WebCT

WebCT's features provide the freedom necessary to implement the structure and look and feel for most Web-based classrooms. This makes the implementation of the Web-based classroom for 85321 a reasonably straightforward process using seven steps: create the class, develop the class hierarchy, place the content on the server, create the structure and presentation, associate the structure with its content, create student accounts, and update the student's view.

Create the Class Before work on developing a class can begin, the WebCT administrator must create the course. This task uses a simple form that requests such information as the class identified, class name, a description, and the password for the class designer. Once done, this course description creates the class and the class designer account.

Develop the Class Hierarchy Given that an initial design for the 85321 Web-based classroom has already identified a rough hierarchy (Figure 9.1), this step involves identifying the modifications necessary due to the capabilities and features of WebCT. There were three major changes:

Asynchronous group communication. The original class design called for the use of mailing lists, which are not directly supported by WebCT. As a replacement, we'll use the WebCT bulletin-board facility for group communication. Because it is integrated into WebCT, the bulletin-board facility is easier to implement, maintain, and use.

Information distribution. WebCT's single pages and paths will be used for information distribution.

WebCT tools. WebCT provides a number of tools and features not originally available, so the design of the class hierarchy has been modified to include these tools.

A number of pages from the 85321 Web-based classroom were modified to include some of the WebCT tools. The 85321 home page had WebCT's resume session and change password features added to it. Access to WebCT's glossary, index, quiz, and compile tools were placed with the rest of the study material. Additions to the assessment page included the timed quiz and tools to allow students to check their records and participation in the class. The communications page was completely changed to make use of the WebCT communication tools, including the bulletin board, e-mail, student presentation, and interactive chat systems. Figure 9.10 shows the results of these modifications.

Place Content onto the WebCT Server WebCT is not designed to assist in the creation of the content for a Web-based classroom. Instead, it provides the tools to control the structure and presentation of a Web-based classroom as well as additional services such as communication and student assessment. The content for a WebCT classroom is created on the class designer's computer using traditional computer applications such as paint programs and HTML editors (as discussed in Chapter 4).

The raw material for the WebCT version of the 85321 Web-based classroom came primarily from the existing 85321 Web-based classroom. It was divided into four major groups:

Student details. The 1997 offering of 85321 has more than 100 students who each require accounts on the WebCT server. Student-related information, including student number and name, has been extracted from the existing student records system in a form that can be reused (a comma delimited file).

Icons. A number of icons were developed for the 1996 85321 Web-based classroom. Where possible, the WebCT version of the 85321 Web-based classroom uses these icons.

Study guide. The 85321 study guide is a 20-chapter introduction to UNIX systems administration and includes a large number of Web pages and associated sound and image files.

Miscellaneous Web pages. The remaining information for the 85321 class, including assignments, past exams, and tutorials, are also available as HTML files.

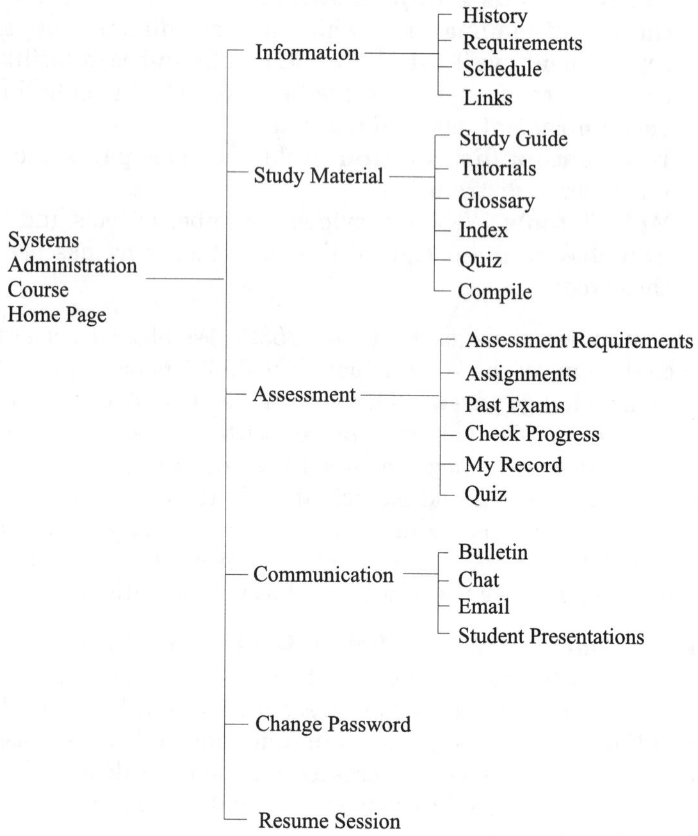

Figure 9.10 The structure diagram of the WebCT version of 85321.

The WebCT file manager shown in Figure 9.9 is used to place content onto the WebCT server. The file manager allows the class designer to upload single files and create directories as well as providing the ability to copy, rename, and delete files. The file manager uses the file upload ability supported by most modern Web browsers to allow one file at a time to be placed on the server.

To avoid the tedious task of placing a large number of files onto the WebCT server one at a time, WebCT supports the use of zip files. This allows the class designer to create a zip file containing a large number of files, load that single zip file onto the WebCT server, and then unzip it. Zip is a utility available on all platforms that combines multiple files into a single file and compresses them. The content for the 85321 Web-based classroom was placed onto the server using this zip file upload method. The files were then separated into logical categories and placed into directories created using the WebCT file manager.

Create the Structure and Presentation One of WebCT's advantages is the simple process by which the content for a Web-based classroom can be structured. With the content for the 85321 classroom now on the server, the next task is to create the structure and presentation of the 85321 classroom. There are three steps involved:

Specify the default presentation. Via WebCT's course settings tool, the class designer can specify the default look and feel of the Web-based classroom, including the page banner, default colors, and any additional HTML to place in the header and footer of every page.

Add appropriate links to the home page. When created, the home page for a WebCT class contains a number of default links. Usually these need to be replaced by the links appropriate to the class. WebCT provides facilities that allow links to be added to and deleted from the home page. In the case of the 85321 home page, six links were placed onto the home page: four links on the tool pages (information, communication, study material, and assessment) and two links on the WebCT tools page (change password and resume session).

Add appropriate links to the tool pages. WebCT tool pages provide the same functionality as a class home page and allow the class designer to structure a class into sections. Adding links to a tool page uses the same approach as adding links to a home page, so this process was repeated for each of 85321's four tool pages.

Associate Content and Structure Associating the content and structure involves making the necessary connections between the raw content on the WebCT server and the structure built in the previous step. In reality, building the structure and associating the content and structure overlap because the creation of some parts of the structure requires specification of the content.

For example, when adding a link to a tool page, you need to provide the type of link it will be—WebCT tool, tool page, single page, URL, or path. Creating each link type usually also requires some additional information that can include the icon to use, the name of the link, and the content. For example, when creating a link to URL, you are asked to supply the actual URL.

Create Student Accounts Each student who uses a WebCT class must have an account. Two methods can be used to create the necessary student accounts: by the class designer or by each student. Allowing students to create their own accounts requires using a WebCT facility that is normally used to allow "guests" to visit the class and create their own temporary accounts. Using this facility may not be advisable, because students could create multiple accounts and try quizzes many times.

WebCT offers the class designer two approaches to creating student accounts: individually or in a batch. Batch registration involves providing WebCT with a text file that contains student information, one student to a line. WebCT uses that information to create the necessary accounts for students. Creating an account one at a time is supported by a simple Web-based form.

Update the Student View The view of a WebCT classroom seen by the class designer is different from that seen by students. A class designer's view of the pages is generated on the fly from information stored in a database; the students' view is provided by static HTML files. These HTML pages are produced from the stored information when the class designer chooses to update the student view. Until this stage, students will not see any of the changes that have been made by the class designer.

Client and Server Requirements

To use a WebCT class as a student, grader, or class designer, it is necessary to have a Web browser, a WebCT account, and a connection to the server.

All interaction with a WebCT classroom, both as a student and a course designer, occurs via a Web browser. The WebCT team officially supports only Netscape (2.0 or higher) browsers due to WebCT's use of JavaScript and the fact that a number of browsers, in particular those from Microsoft, do not correctly implement the same version of JavaScript as the Netscape browser.

All WebCT classes require a valid account before access is granted. However, WebCT can be set up to allow anyone to create guest accounts. Four types of WebCT account, described in the "Drawbacks" section, are each allowed to perform a number of particular tasks.

WebCT is a server-based system, which means that students and course designers must be online and have a connection to the server via their Web browsers before they can participate in the class.

The WebCT server is currently available only for UNIX; a Windows NT version is due by September 1997. The WebCT server should be equivalent to a Pentium 90 with 32MB of RAM. Requirements for disk space include between 8MB and 10MB for the WebCT software, approximately 2MB for each class plus whatever space is consumed by the class content, and 30KB to 70KB for each student.

Support

Support for WebCT, as with the other two systems described in this chapter, is primarily via the Internet and includes mailing lists, online documentation, and a collection of papers.

Mailing Lists Two mailing lists are related to WebCT: webct-users and webct-announce. Webct-users is a reasonably active mailing list for discussion among the users of WebCT and the WebCT developers. Webct-announce is used by the WebCT development team to make announcements. To subscribe to the lists, send an e-mail message to majordomo@cs.ubc.ca with "subscribe webct-users" and "subscriber webct-announce" in the body of the messages. The archives for the webct-users mailing list are available by e-mailing majordomo@cs.ubc.ca and on the Web at **homebrew.cs.ubc.ca/webct/docs/mail/index.html**.

Online Documentation There is a collection of documentation about WebCT available online. It includes a FAQ, a "getting started" tutorial, online help, installation documentation, and a graphical overview of WebCT elements. Most of the documentation is available on the Web at **homebrew.cs.ubc.ca/webct/docs/**.

Papers A number of papers about WebCT and its origins have been presented at conferences and published in journals. They are also available online at **homebrew.cs.ubc.ca/webct/papers/**.

Getting It

As of May 1997, the third beta release of WebCT is available for free downloading from the WebCT home page (**homebrew.cs.ubc.ca/webct/**). However, the WebCT team plans to release the first commercial version in September 1997. Details about the commercial version of WebCT and its availability are available from the WebCT home page.

Drawbacks

No computer program is perfect, including WebCT, which has a number of drawbacks. All of the drawbacks are relatively minor in nature and do not detract greatly from the usefulness of WebCT as a tool for building Web-based classrooms. In addition, these drawbacks may be of importance only in particular situations, and solutions to many of them are being worked on by the WebCT development team. The drawbacks include these:

Compulsory accounts. Anyone who wants to access a WebCT class must have a valid WebCT account. This can add to the effort involved in setting up a WebCT class and in some cases may not be required. However, this feature does provide a number of benefits, including access control and student tracking, that are not possible without accounts.

Account sharing. The people responsible for creating the Web-based classroom with WebCT must share the same account. This could cause some small problems when a team of people is involved.

Browser limitations. Incompatibilities between Web browsers cause a number of problems for WebCT. These problems arise because WebCT uses browser functionality that the Netscape and Microsoft browsers implement differently, so it is not directly the fault of the WebCT developers. Examples of these limitations include the use of JavaScript, used quite extensively by

WebCT, and the file upload capability used by WebCT's file manager. Microsoft and Netscape implement different versions of JavaScript, and the version used by WebCT has problems with Internet Explorer. As for file management, Microsoft has recently announced support for the file upload capability.

Interface problems. The interface used by WebCT—especially the class design interface, its use of frames, JavaScript, and the lack of any consistent standard—is disconcerting at first, and it may take some people a while to become familiar with it (a fact borne out in survey responses discussed later). However, any person with some experience with graphical user interfaces and Web forms should be able to overcome this hurdle without too much difficulty.

Closed communication tools. The e-mail and bulletin-board system provided by WebCT can be accessed only from within WebCT and currently cannot interact with e-mail and other Internet communication systems. This means that students who already have Internet e-mail accounts must learn another tool and interface in order to check class e-mail and must regularly check another location for new messages rather than have all their e-mail arrive in the one location. This approach does provide some advantages, however; in particular, it separates class discussion from other e-mail discussions, which allows students and instructors to concentrate on the class material and minimizes the loss of class e-mail.

All online. All participation in a WebCT class must take place online, while students are connected to the WebCT server. This causes problems for students who pay for their Internet access on the basis of time connected. This problem is addressed somewhat by the program's capability that allows students to compile and print study material.

WEBFUSE

Webfuse is a general Web publishing tool that provides a number of tools and facilities that support the creation and maintenance of Web-based classrooms. Because Webfuse is a more general tool, it does not provide the same level of predefined structure as the other tools, in particular, TopClass. This lack of predefined structure is a double-edged sword that provides more freedom to shape a Web-based classroom but may require more skill and experience to do so effectively.

Like WebCT, the initial spark for the development of Webfuse came from the experience of creating a Web-based classroom with no available support tool. The effort, skill, and time required to create that classroom made obvious the need for appropriate tools to automate the procedure. It was also recognized that the same problems exist for the creation of any Web site, not just a Web-based classroom.

The result is a general Web publishing tool with a number of features designed to specifically support a Web-based classroom.

Evaluation of existing tools and the available resources led to a number of design guidelines for Webfuse:

Don't reinvent the wheel. The Webfuse development team was never large, so it wasn't possible for the team to develop such items as computer conferencing and interactive chat tools. Such an effort would be particularly wasteful because a large collection of freely available tools already fulfills these requirements.

Provide a standard management interface. Although a number of very good tools are available, each tool has its own management interface. This heterogeneity increases the effort and skill necessary to manage and use these tools. To solve this problem, Webfuse provides a standard interface that can be used to create and maintain all of the tools incorporated into Webfuse.

Separate content and presentation. One of the drawbacks with HTML is that both the content of a page and its presentation are specified in the same place. This makes it very difficult to modify one without adversely affecting the other. Webfuse, attempting to emulate a feature of Hyperwave (**www.iicm.edu/hyperg**), separates the look and feel of a page from the content of the page. This separation allows the look and feel for an entire site to be changed quickly and automatically without affecting the content.

Provide platform independence. Many Web publishing tools are available for a limited number of platforms. Dependence on a single or limited number of platforms restricts choice, limits the number of people that can use the system, and can influence future use of the system as platforms become dated.

Minimizes new skills. An increasing number of students in Web-based classrooms already have experience with computers and the Internet. Many also have e-mail addresses and are familiar with a particular e-mail program. Rather than force those people to learn new skills and tools, Webfuse provides tools that use these existing skills and minimize the need for new skills.

Provide the tools, not the rules. People want to perform different tasks using different methods. Some existing systems require the use of a particular structure or presentation that, although simple to use, prevents the designer from achieving his goals. Where possible, Webfuse provides the tools to assist in development of Web-based classrooms and not the rules governing how those tools are used.

Provide the necessary support services. Additional support services required in a complete Web site include access control, user management, HTML validation, link checking, and searching. Current versions of Webfuse provide most of these facilities.

Development on Webfuse commenced in the second half of 1996; the first alpha release for UNIX and Windows 95/NT became available in June 1997. The first official version of Webfuse to include support for the Macintosh is due for release at the end of 1997. Webfuse is available free of charge.

How It Works

Webfuse is a collection of Perl scripts that provides a standard management interface to a number of existing, freely available tools. These tools provide a number of features: an interactive chat facility, Web-based conferencing, page counters, database storage, validation of HTML, and conversion of Postscript files to images. Webfuse uses a metaphor to create and manage a Web site. In this metaphor, a site consists of a number of related pages. Each page is a combination of three components:

Template. A template defines the presentation format of a particular page, including the page's graphics, colors, and available links. The current version of Webfuse includes more than 10 templates that offer a range of presentation possibilities. A template is completely separate from content, which means that the template a page is using can be changed easily without affecting the content. Figure 9.11 provides an example of the same page created using a number of templates.

Content. Content is the raw information that the page displays. The type of content depends on the page type. For example, the content for an index page

Figure 9.11 Same Webfuse page, different templates.

type is a list of index elements; the content for an interactive chat room is the location of the chat server and the color of the interface.

Page type. Each page created by Webfuse serves a particular purpose—for example, displaying some HTML, pointing to a number of other Web pages, providing an interactive chat room, or allowing the submission of assignments.

Updating a Page When a page is created with Webfuse, it has no content, has the title "Under Construction," and is of a default page type and template. It also has, as does every page produced using Webfuse, a footer that contains administrative information about the page, including its URL, the date and time it was last modified, and the name of the person who modified it. The URL for the page not only provides an indication of the page's location, useful if someone prints the page; it also provides a link to the Webfuse page update system. Selecting this link and entering an appropriate user name and password provides access to the page update form for this particular page. The page update form for a page provides the ability to do the following:

Access Webfuse services. Webfuse provides a number of support services, including HTML validation, link checking, access control, file management, and adding a counter to the page.

Modify content. Each page type expects to receive different types of content; consequently each page type displays a different form interface by which the author provides the content.

Modify page characteristics. The characteristics of a page include the page's template, page type, title, colors, and a variety of other information.

The page update form contains a number of modify buttons. Pressing one of these buttons causes the information in the form to be sent back to Webfuse. Depending on the content, Webfuse then performs a number of operations, which normally include updating the current page. Once these operations are complete, Webfuse presents another page update form that includes some comments about the operations it performed.

Accounts Whether or not a valid user name or password is required to view the pages in a Webfuse classroom is left to the discretion of the course designer. Currently, most Webfuse classrooms do not require an account to gain access. Even though they are not necessary for participating in a class, Webfuse does use user accounts to restrict access to the page update facility.

The Webfuse access control system does not make any distinction between types of accounts; there is no concept of a course designer, administrator, or student account in Webfuse. Instead, each user account belongs to one or more groups. Each group is assigned a list of access permissions that specify objects the group members can access and the operations they can perform on those objects.

An object is anything Webfuse manages; objects include files, users, and scripts. Each object is identified by a unique identifier, which currently takes the form of a directory path. For example, the identifier for the 85321 home page on the machine science.cqu.edu.au is mc/Academic_Programs/Units/85321_Systems_Administration. The identifier of the script used to create users and groups is webfuse/s-cgi-bin/adin.cgi.

Each object Webfuse manages has a valid set of operations that can be performed with that object. There are three valid operations for a Web page:

Access. The ability to access and view the Web page. By default, Webfuse allows everyone with or without a Webfuse account to access a page.

Update. The access operation allows the modification of the page using Webfuse's page update system. By default, only the person who created the page has permission to update a page.

All. Having the "all" permission means that the user can perform any valid operation with the page.

Particular page types inherit these basic operations and add to new ones. For example, the assignment management page adds a "mark assignment" operation that allows markers to view and mark a student assignment.

A typical Webfuse classroom might include a class designer's group, a group that includes all students and a unique group for each student. The designer's group would include the accounts for each of the course designers and would be given access and update permission on the class Web-based classroom. If access to the Web pages for the class were restricted to students who were enrolled in the class, it could be done by restricting access to the pages and creating a student group with relevant access permission that contains all the student accounts. If each student is to have his or her own presentation area where he or she can place material on the Web, a unique page would be created for each student, creating a group for each student, and giving each student group update permission on his or her particular page.

What the Student Sees What students see when they visit a Web-based classroom built using Webfuse depends on how the class designer structured the pages and the page types that were used. Typically, students see a Web page with a particular look and feel that provides pointers to other pages with a similar look and feel (as illustrated in Figure 9.11). A Webfuse classroom generally uses a hierarchical structure to organize the information and tasks it contains. In the case of 85321, the structure of the Webfuse classroom matches almost identically to the structure shown in Figure 9.1.

What the Designer Sees The class designer's view of a Webfuse classroom is exactly the same as that of students. The only difference is that the class designer's account has update permission for all the pages in the Web-based classroom and thus can modify the pages.

Features

Webfuse provides a number of page types that are useful for a Web-based classroom. This section looks at the possibilities by examining the four major tasks required of a Web-based classroom: information distribution, communication, student assessment, and class management.

Information Distribution Webfuse currently provides eight page types designed specifically for information distribution:

> **Lecture.** The lecture page type allows the author to manage and create an online lecture that includes a number of lecture slides. The individual lecture slides are implemented by the lecture slide page type. Creating a lecture can be done either by individually creating each lecture slide or by providing a PostScript file. The lecture page type converts each page from the PostScript file into an individual lecture slide. This is one mechanism by which a Powerpoint presentation can be placed onto the Web.
>
> **Lecture slide.** A lecture slide is an individual slide from an online lecture (see Figure 9.12). A slide can be created either by hand or automatically by the lecture page type when it converts a PostScript file. Each slide can also be accompanied by an audio clip in a variety of formats, including RealAudio. The audio clip can be provided in any of four sound formats, and the page type automatically converts it to the other formats.

Figure 9.12 A Webfuse lecture slide.

Study guide. The study guide page type is used to manage a collection of study guide chapters. It provides support for adding, deleting, and moving study guide chapters as well as creating an index.

Study guide chapter. The study guide chapter page type accepts a single HTML file that contains a number of special tags. These special tags break the HTML file into a number of sections, which in turn contain a number of pages. The tags can also be used to indicate terms that should be placed into the study guide index. The study guide page type converts the file into a two formats: a print version that allows students to print the entire chapter and an online version that consists of a number of small pages that can be navigated sequentially. It also produces a table of contents (see Figure 9.13) and an online index with hyperlinks to the various chapters.

FAQ. The FAQ page type supports the creation and maintenance of lists of frequently asked questions (and answers). The FAQ list can be divided into a number of categories, including a most frequently asked category that is automatically maintained by the page type based on how many times questions are viewed. This page type provides mechanisms by which people can ask and answer questions.

Content. The content page type is a simple page used to display any section of HTML.

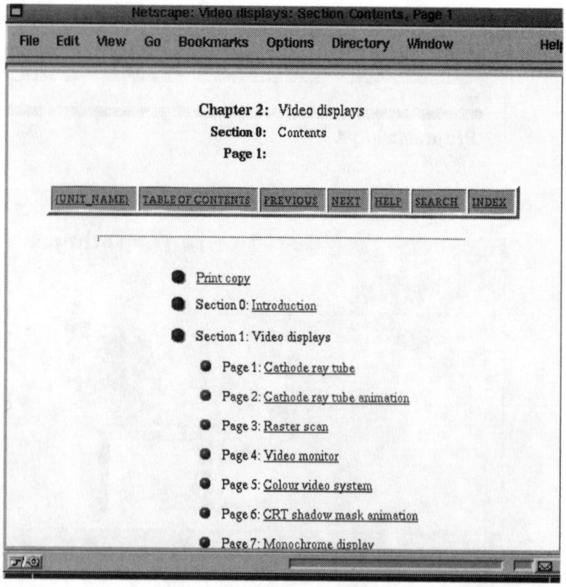

Figure 9.13 A study guide chapter table of contents.

Table list. Primarily used to separate and organize a collection of pages, the table list page type presents multiple lists in table form. The elements of the lists are words or phrases that become links to other pages.

Index. The index page types (there are two: graphical index and text index) serve a purpose similar to that of the table list page type and provide a mechanism to organize a collection of pages.

Webfuse also provides an archive and download feature that allows students to obtain compressed copies of the Web-based classroom, which they can install onto their hard drives and view offline. The problem with offline use is that Webfuse features that require a connection to the server—for example, the interactive chat and WWWBoard page types—are not useable when the user is not connected to the server.

Communication Webfuse currently provides three page types that can be used to facilitate communication in a Web-based classroom:

Ewgie chat. This page type uses Ewgie, a Java-based chat client and server, to provide a synchronous group communication mechanism. As well as an interactive chat facility, Ewgie also provides a shared whiteboard and the ability to offer guided tours of a Web page.

WWWBoard. The WWWBoard page type (see Figure 9.14) uses a CGI script written by Matt Wright to provide a simple Web-based bulletin board. By

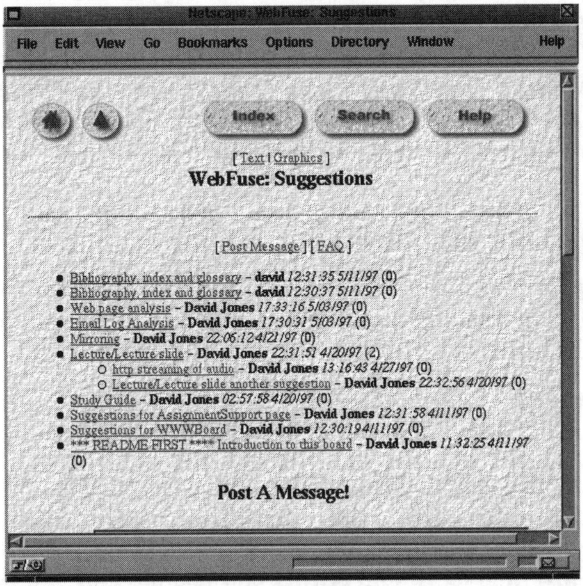

Figure 9.14 A WWWBoard page.

default, anyone can post a message to a WWWBoard, but using Webfuse's access control features, it is possible to restrict access to the WWWBoard to a group or a single person. For example, a simple method to implement a class announcement facility is to provide only the instructor with permission to post to a WWWBoard.

Email2WWW. The Email2WWW page type uses a collection of e-mail messages to produce a sequence of Web pages. A common use of this page type is to provide a Web-based interface to the archives of mailing lists.

Student Assessment Webfuse currently provides two page types that can assist in student assessment:

Online quiz. Enables the creation, taking, and marking of online quizzes that work in both online and offline modes.

Assignment submission. The assignment submission system for Webfuse, discussed in more detail in Chapter 8, provides support for the submission, management, marking, and distribution of marked assignments via the Web.

Class Management Webfuse supports a number of class management tasks:

Results management. The assignment submission page type provides a system by which student results can be shared among a group of graders and modified via the Web.

Student tracking. Webfuse uses Follow, introduced in Chapter 8, to analyze user sessions with a Webfuse classroom.

HTML validation. Webfuse can check the validity of the HTML used in a Web-based classroom and generate reports identifying problem areas.

Link checking. Webfuse can also check if any of the links within a Web-based classroom are not pointing to a valid URL.

Implementing 85321 with Webfuse

Building the Webfuse classroom for 85321 involved the following steps: set up the class; identify the structure, page types, and template; produce the content; and create the pages.

Set Up the Class The administrator of the Webfuse server must perform the initial setup of the class by completing the following two steps:

Create the initial page. Usually achieved by adding a link to an existing index or table list page that contains pointers to a list of Webfuse classes. This empty page is the initial building block of the class.

Allocate access permission. The people who will create the Webfuse class must have Webfuse accounts with permission to modify the initial page and all of its descendants.

Identify Structure, Page Types, and Template Figure 9.1 specifies the structure for the 85321 Web-based classroom. The first step in implementing the Webfuse version of this class is to identify which Webfuse page types will provide the necessary functionality for each page in that structure. Figure 9.15 is a modification of Figure 9.1 that includes a description of the Webfuse page type that will be used to implement each page.

The next step is to choose the template that will be used to provide the look and feel for the 85321 Web-based classroom. The simplest approach is to choose one of the existing Webfuse templates. If none are suitable, you can create your own template. Figure 9.11 shows the 85321 home page implemented with a number of templates. The top left page in the figure is the template currently being used for the 85321 Web-based classroom. This template was designed specifically for classes taught by the Department of Mathematics and Computing at Central Queensland University.

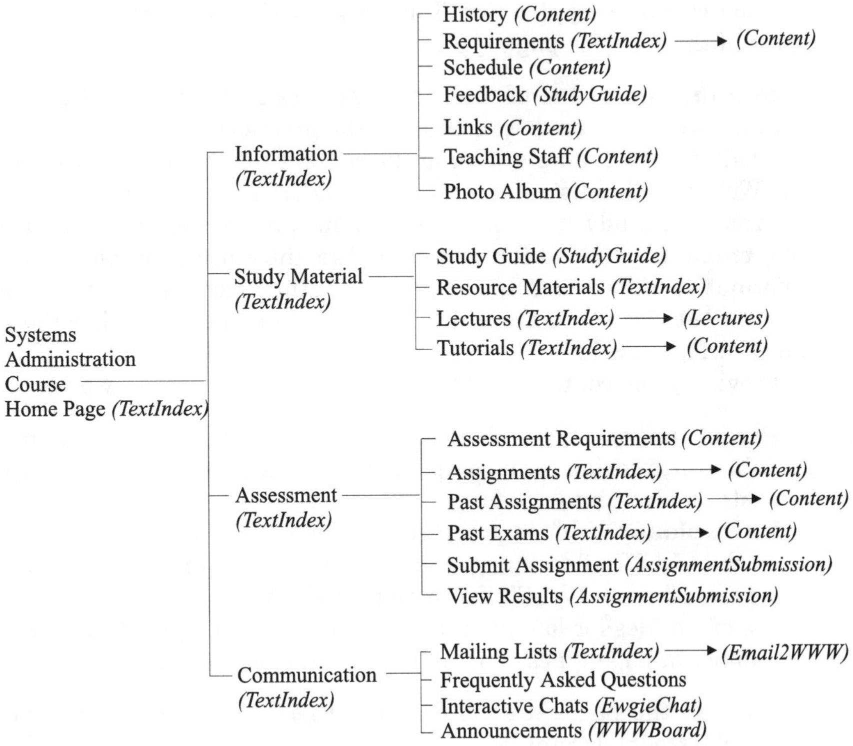

Figure 9.15 Modified 85321 structure.

Table 9.4 Content Format for Webfuse Page Types

Page Type	*Expected Content*
Text index	A list of words or phrases and optionally associated URLs
Content	A section of HTML, usually created by a familiar HTML editor
Email2WWW	A collection of mail messages in the standard folder format
Lecture	Either no content or a PostScript file
Lecture slide	HTML, an image or sound file in .au, .wav, .aiff, or RealAudio format

Produce the Content Like WebCT, Webfuse provides little support for actually creating the content for the Web-based classroom. Each Webfuse page type expects to receive content in a particular format, which is usually created by another computer application. Table 9.4 describes the type of content expected by some of the Webfuse page types.

Create the Pages One of the characteristics of Webfuse is that the structure of the site is built automatically during the process of creating pages and providing the content. For example, adding the content to the 85321 home page, created by the Webfuse administrator, automatically creates the four descendant pages for information, study material, assessment, and communication. Therefore, once the content is provided for the home page, the author can move onto the page for information. Providing the content for this page also creates any required descendant pages. The structure that is evolving here matches the structure outlined in Figure 9.15.

Providing the content for these pages is done in one of two ways:

Direct entry. A number of page types, including Content, Index, and TableList, provide form components that allow the author to type (or cut and paste) content into the form.

File upload. Webfuse provides a file manager that serves the same purpose as the WebCT file manager and allows people to place files on the Webfuse server. Like the WebCT file manager, the Webfuse file manager supports the use of zip files for loading multiple files. The file upload facility is built in to a number of page types that could use a file as content.

Once all the pages are created and their content provided, the 85321 Web-based classroom is complete.

Client and Server Requirements

To access the services of a Webfuse classroom, you must have access to a Web browser. For most Webfuse services, a Web browser that supports HTML forms, tables, and file upload is sufficient. Accessing the interactive chat system requires a Java-capable browser. Due to Microsoft not implementing the file upload facility correctly in its Internet Explorer (up to and including version 3.1), Netscape Navigator 2.0 or higher is the safest choice.

In most cases, access to a Webfuse classroom also requires a network connection, especially for interactive features such as the WWWBoard and EwgieChatRoom page types. However, Webfuse does provide an archival service that can be used to archive an entire Web-based classroom, download it, and view it from a hard drive.

The Webfuse server needs to be either a UNIX or Windows 95/NT machine; a Macintosh version is planned by the end of 1997. The power of the server, especially the speed of the CPU and the amount of RAM required, depend on how busy the server will be, the number of classes, and the complexity of the features used. During development of our system, a small Webfuse server ran on a small Windows 95 computer with a 486-DX266 CPU and 8MB of RAM. A computer of this size is not suitable if a reasonable amount of page modification is planned. A Pentium 90 with 32 MB of RAM should be able to act as the server for quite a busy Webfuse site.

The Webfuse server needs at least 20MB of disk space to store the Webfuse software and templates. Some of this space includes a Web server that may not be needed if you already have one installed. Additional space is required to store the actual content and pages for the Web pages produced using Webfuse.

Support

Webfuse is not a commercial product, so phone support is not available. However, a number of online forums include mailing lists, WWWBoards, and Ewgie chat rooms in which assistance can be obtained. Details on these forums are available from the Webfuse Web site, **webfuse.cqu.edu.au/**.

Getting It

Webfuse is available for free, and copies of it are included on the CD-ROM that accompanies this book. The most recent versions can be obtained from the Webfuse Web site (**webfuse.cqu.edu.au/**).

Drawbacks

Webfuse has a number of drawbacks:

Relative youth. In comparison to the other systems described in this chapter, Webfuse is in an early stage of development and so lacks the polish of these systems. However, the use of existing, free tools means that Webfuse is very close to these systems in terms of functionality.

Lack of quality documentation. A symptom of Webfuse's youth is the lack of quality documentation explaining how to use it.

Too much freedom. The high level of freedom provided by Webfuse in the structure and design of the Web-based classroom may also be a drawback in that it provides users with too much choice in how they build their Web-based classrooms. This variety of choice increases the possibility of mistakes or the development of poorly designed Web-based classrooms and makes it more difficult to learn how to use the system.

TOPCLASS

TopClass, with its origins in 1995 as WEST, appears to have been the first education and training product to support Web-based classrooms. The developers of TopClass have a history in the use of technology in distance and distributed education, which comes through in TopClass's design and features. The fundamental concept behind the product's design is to combine the collaborative aspects of face-to-face learning and the self-paced, flexible aspects of distance education. To achieve this combination, TopClass provides three components:

Integrated learning environment. All interaction in TopClass occurs via the Web browser and includes such features as tracking individual student progress, standard navigation components, and collaboration tools.

Content management. TopClass provides an environment that simplifies the process of placing content into the system by providing automatic link management, the ability to add and remove learning units at will, a facility to create personalized courseware for individual students, and automated testing.

Class management. Provides security, student tracking, and student management features.

TopClass is a commercial product available for the Macintosh, Windows, and UNIX platforms, with more than 1,400 licenses in 40 countries. TopClass is undergoing continual development, with at least four releases a year.

How It Works

The TopClass server is built on an object-oriented database from Neologic (**www.neologic.com**) that provides fast, efficient, and controlled access to all the data associated with a class, including its content, exercises, student information, and instructor details. The Web pages presented by TopClass to students and instructors are generated on the fly using the information stored within the database. The dynamic generation of the Web pages allows TopClass to customize each page that visitors see based on information stored about them in the database.

Accounts Like WebCT, TopClass requires every user to have an account in order to be able to access a class. Unlike WebCT, a single TopClass user account can access multiple classes. For example, under WebCT, if a student is a member of three classes—85321, 85349, and 85343—the student must have three accounts, one for each of the classes. Under TopClass, the student has one account that permits access all three classes.

TopClass recognizes three types of user account:

Student. Student accounts are used to access course material and discussion forums. A student account can be allocated to many different classes.

Instructor. A TopClass instructor account can be used to create and edit course material and classes, mark student assessments, and respond to student queries. The exact privileges assigned to an instructor account are decided when the account is created.

Administrator. Administrator accounts are able to create and manage instructor and student accounts. Common tasks include creating a new class and allocating instructors (and possibly students) to that class. Administrator accounts can also allocate privileges to the other accounts—in particular, the instructor accounts.

What the User Sees TopClass presents the same interface, with some slight changes, to all users, regardless of whether they are students or instructors. After logging in with a valid TopClass user name and password, users are presented with their personal home page, an example of which is shown in Figure 9.16. The home page provides access to all the information and services a TopClass user will need, including these:

Coursework. The coursework link, present only for students, provides them with access to all the course material for all of the TopClass classes they are enrolled in. The interface to the course material is shown in Figure 9.17.

Exercises. A collection of questions to be completed by students and that can be automatically marked by TopClass or sent to an instructor for marking and comments.

Messages. The read and send messages links provide the student access to TopClass's internal e-mail system, which allows them to send e-mail to any other TopClass user. A useful feature of TopClass, which employs the dynamic creation of the pages TopClass presents, is that when there are new messages in a user's mailbox or class discussion lists, the appropriate icon displays a flashing "NEW" message.

Discussion lists. Both discussion lists and class announcements use an asynchronous, group bulletin-board system. Class announcements are just one thread that appears in the class discussion list; only the class instructors can post to the announcements thread.

Utilities. Provides access to any additional utilities the user needs. For students, the list of utilities is usually limited to viewing their online photo and viewing a list of users. For instructors, the list of utilities includes tools to create and edit coursework and classes, import and export classes, and manage user accounts.

Logout. Before leaving a TopClass class, users must log out—in other words, they must select a link that indicates that they are finished using the system. Because TopClass licenses are based on the number of users using the system, neglecting to log out may prevent another user logging in.

The TopClass home page for an instructor or administrator has the same look and feel as a student home page. The major difference is the presence of some extra tools the instructor and administrator use to create learning material, mark student submissions, and manage a class list.

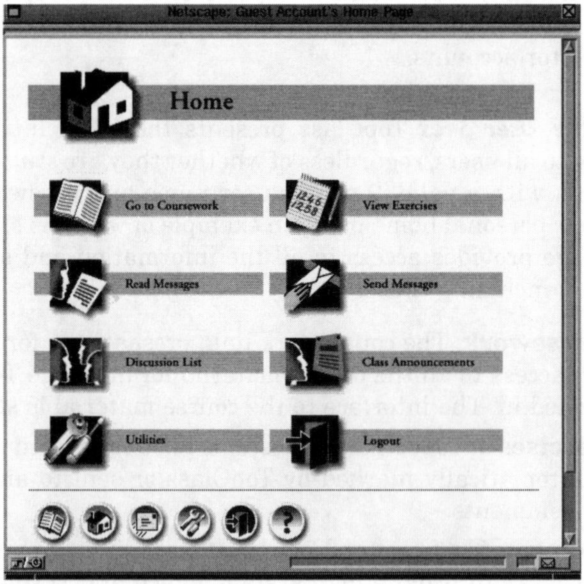

Figure 9.16 The TopClass user screen.

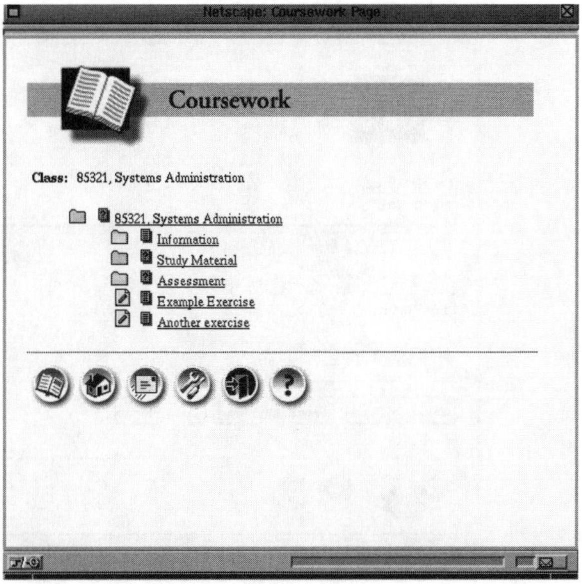

Figure 9.17 The TopClass coursework interface.

Features

Through its standard interface, TopClass provides a number of features that aid in the development and maintenance of a Web-based classroom. The following section describes each of these features by breaking them into the four major tasks: information distribution, communication, student assessment, and class management.

Information Distribution A link on a student's home page provides him or her with access to assigned coursework via a hierarchical folder interface (as shown in Figure 9.17). This interface provides access to all of a student's coursework for all of classes. Students are able to select and move through the material both sequentially and hierarchically.

In TopClass, coursework consists of units of learning material (ULMs), which in turn are made up of HTML pages and exercises. ULMs can be shared between courses and allocated to students in response to certain events. For example, if a student successfully completes an exercise, TopClass can automatically add a particular ULM to that student's coursework based on the student's results.

ULMs are created by instructors and then assigned to a particular course or student. It is not until a ULM is assigned that it is available to the participants. Creating a ULM is done using a simple Web-based interface, shown in Figure 9.18,

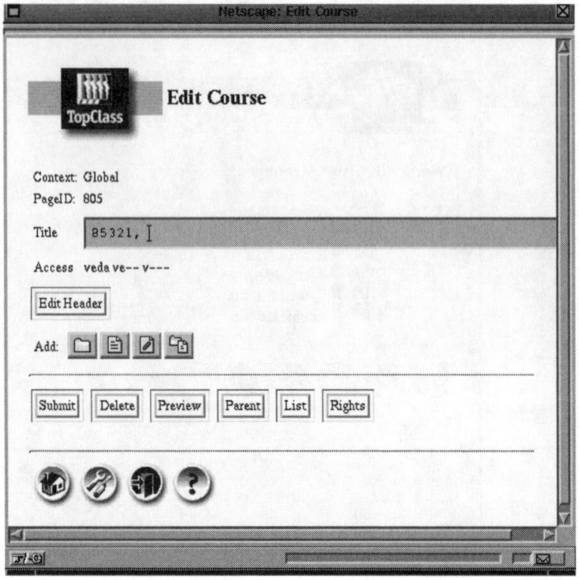

Figure 9.18 Creating a TopClass ULM.

that can structure, organize, and create pages and exercises. To increase the simplicity of creating ULMs, TopClass automatically generates the links that allow students to sequentially navigate through a ULM.

Communication TopClass provides both private and group asynchronous communication facilities using the same interface, shown in Figure 9.19. TopClass e-

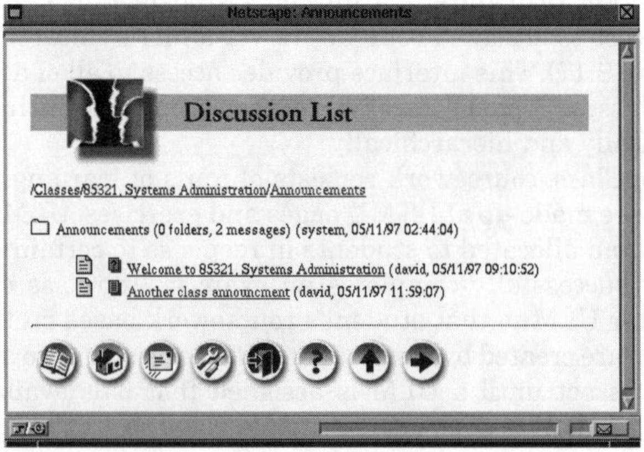

Figure 9.19 The TopClass communication interface.

mail provides a method for sending private communication to other TopClass users. The TopClass discussion list provides a group communication mechanism based on a concept of separate topics. For example, each class discussion list includes a class announcements topic to which only the class's instructors can post, but which all class participants can read.

Student Assessment TopClass provides a forms interface that allows the creation, marking, and taking of online quizzes. A TopClass exercise is a combination of the following:

Questions. An exercise question can either be a short-answer question, for which students must enter some text, or a multiple-choice question, for which students pick one answer from a selection.

Marking method. TopClass provides two methods for marking exercises: TopClass can mark the exercise automatically or it can send the submitted exercise to an instructor for marking. Automatic marking works best for multiple-choice questions.

Actions. You can tell TopClass to perform a specific action in response to a student completing or achieving a particular grade from an exercise. The two possible actions are to add coursework or to notify an instructor. The add-coursework action can be used to assign an additional ULM to students or send them to a particular ULM. Notifying an instructor causes TopClass to inform an instructor that a student has just completed the exercise.

Class Management TopClass support for class management tasks includes the following:

Account management. TopClass provides mechanisms to add, delete, and modify accounts for students, instructors, and administrators. It also includes a batch registration process that generates user names and passwords for students from a file of student details.

Student tracking. TopClass provides a student tracking system that allows the instructor discover what students have read (using the same interface students use to read the course material) and a history of student submissions.

Assessment management. The student exercises are delivered automatically to the appropriate instructor, who can mark them online and return them. Records of the submission are made available for students and the instructor.

TopClass does not currently provide a gradebook-style application to manage student results.

Implementing 85321 with TopClass

Creating a Web-based classroom for 85321 using TopClass is a relatively straightforward process due to a number of factors: TopClass's standard interface and the structuring system for information distribution. Creating the classroom includes the following steps: create accounts for the instructors, create the class, place the course material onto the server, and assign the course material to the class.

Create the Instructor Accounts Instructor accounts are created one at a time by filling out a forms page (the same page can be used to create student and administrator accounts) and providing information that includes the following:

Instructor personal information. This includes instructor's names (first, middle, last, and user names) and initial password.
Assigned classes. An instructor can be assigned responsibility for a number of TopClass classes.
TopClass privileges. Instructors can be allocated a number of privileges to perform various tasks: create/edit units, user accounts, and announcements; delete discussion items; customize student course material; create/edit and import/export classes; and directly access the database that underlies TopClass.

Create the Class In TopClass, a class is a collection of course material, students, and instructors. Creating a class can be done using TopClass administrator accounts or by instructors who have been granted the appropriate permission. Creating a course involves filling out a forms page and providing the following information:

Identification. Each class has a unique class ID, used by instructors and the administrator to access the course via some of the modification pages, and a more descriptive class name.

Instructors. Each class normally has one or more instructors assigned to it who are responsible for tasks such as marking student assessments, responding to queries, and possibly adding course material.

Default course material. The TopClass administrator can add material to the class from the material already on the TopClass server as default course material. If granted the appropriate permissions, class instructors can also add material.

Students. TopClass provides a batch registration facility; TopClass automatically generates user names and passwords using a scheme chosen by the course administrator from the several available. Students can also be created one at a time via the same form used to create instructor accounts.

Create the Course Material A TopClass course consists of information, in the form of Web pages, and exercises that provide the instructional experience for students. Course material, which TopClass calls ULM, is created by instructors, then assigned to particular classes or students. A ULM can be assigned by the TopClass administrators, instructors, or by TopClass itself in response to a student completing a particular exercise. The interface students use to interact with the course material is shown in Figure 9.17.

All material to be distributed via a TopClass class must be placed into a ULM, and students must use the interface shown in Figure 9.17 to interact with it. The metaphor used, a hierarchical collection of folders and documents, is familiar to most people and so is relatively easy to understand and makes the creation of this material straightforward, particularly because the instructor does not need to pay attention to the task of linking documents.

Creating course material is performed using a forms page (shown in Figure 9.18). The page lists the title of the current ULM and a list of the ULMs contained by this ULM. Using the supplied buttons, the instructor can edit or remove existing ULMs. The four icons near the bottom allow the instructor to perform the following tasks:

Add a page. Allows the instructor to add a Web page to the existing ULM. The HTML for this page is entered via another forms page.

Add an exercise. Provides access to a forms page in which an automated or instructor-marked quiz can be added to the current ULM.

Add another ULM. A ULM is a collection of pages and exercises, so the ability to add another ULM to the existing ULM is how a hierarchical structure, in which one ULM contains another, is constructed.

The page also provides access to services that allow the instructor to delete the current ULM, reorder the contents of the ULM, preview the contents, change the access rights on the current ULM, and obtain a list of the currently available courses. Which of these services are available depends on the privileges assigned to the instructor's account when it was created.

The interface that TopClass presents students, including the standard home page and the course material interface (shown in Figure 9.17), makes the TopClass 85321 Web-based classroom somewhat different from the WebCT and Webfuse versions. The main differences are that there is no communication section and all the information has been placed into a number of ULMs.

The home page for each instructor and student provides direct access to personal e-mail, class discussion lists, and class announcements for all the classes in which a student is enrolled. The remaining sections—information, study material, and assessment—are created as separate ULMs that belong to the 85321 course. Each of these ULMs in turn contains pages and exercises.

Creating the necessary ULMs is a fairly simple task that involves adding a page to a ULM and then adding the content to the page. Adding a page to a ULM is simply a matter or clicking on the appropriate button on the ULM editing form (shown in Figure 9.18). This brings up another form page in which the content for the page can be added either by directly typing text into a text area (cut and paste works, too) or by using the file upload facility.

Although this task is straightforward, creating a large collection of pages can take some time.

Assign Course Material to a Class Generally, TopClass course material, in the form of ULMs, is created independently of any particular class. Once created, the course material is assigned to a particular class. The modularity provided by this approach means you can reuse the same course material in a number of classes. Assigning course material to a class is performed by the TopClass administrators, instructors with appropriate permissions, or automatically by TopClass.

Client and Server Requirements

To use TopClass, instructors, administrators, and students require a Web browser that supports tables and a network connection to the TopClass server.

The TopClass server is available on the MacOS, Windows 95/NT, and UNIX platforms. Table 9.5 summarizes the requirements for the various platforms. The suggestions for hardware are minimum recommendations.

Support

Support for users of TopClass comes in a number of forms: traditional e-mail and telephone support, online documentation, and two mailing lists. The collection of online documentation, available from the TopClass Web site, includes

Table 9.5 TopClass Server Requirements

Platform	*Hardware*	*Software*
MacOS	Power Macintosh or 68020+ processor, 16MB RAM	N/A
Windows 95	486+ processor, 16MB RAM	Microsoft Personal Web Server or Netscape FastTrack 2.0 for Windows 95
Windows NT Server 3.51+	486+ processor, 16MB RAM	Microsoft IIS 1.0+ or Netscape FastTrack 2.0 servers
Windows NT Workstation 4.0	486+ processor, 16MB RAM	Microsoft Peer Web Services or Netscape FastTrack 2.0 or Enterprise servers
UNIX (Solaris, Linux also)	Sparc or UltraSparc processors	Solaris 2.5+ and a Web server that supports CGI

a white paper describing TopClass, an instructor's guide, an administrator's guide, and a collection of FAQs. Subscribing to both lists can be done via the Web at **www.wbtsystems.com/support/lists.html**. Both lists are hosted by a mailing list manager at the address **listserve@mail.wbtsystems.com**, and the archives for both lists are available and make interesting reading. Sending an e-mail message to **listserv@mail.wbtsystems.com** with the word "Help" as the body of the message will result in an e-mail message explaining how to obtain the archives.

Getting It

TopClass is a commercial product. It is available under three pricing schemes:

- **Annual.** As the name suggests, this pricing scheme allows you to use the software for 12 months, at which time the software expires and cannot be used. During those 12 months you are entitled to full technical support and to any upgrades that occur.
- **Purchase.** A once-off scheme that provides you with the current version of the software that you can use indefinitely. With this scheme, you receive technical support for only 90 days. Additional technical support and upgrades cost extra.
- **Subscription.** A combination of the annual and purchase schemes, this scheme provides the current version of the software and all upgrades and technical support for the following 12 months. Technical support and free upgrades end after that 12 months.

Educational prices for TopClass range from $750 for a 25-user license to $2,495 for 200 users. These prices are for the annual pricing scheme; the other schemes are a few hundred dollars more.

TopClass Lite is a free evaluation version of TopClass that provides all the functionality of the full version but is limited so that only four people can use it at any one time. TopClass Lite is available from the TopClass Web site free of charge.

Drawbacks

TopClass suffers from a number of minor drawbacks:

Unlabelled icons. Many of the navigation bars and services provided by TopClass are indicated by graphic icons with little or no textual hints. In other words, unless you can associate the graphic image with the intended purpose, it can be difficult to use the system initially.

Dynamic generation. Every page seen by a student or instructor is generated from a database when the page is requested. This process requires that the computer running the TopClass server performs more work than a normal Web server, which simply passes the document to the requesting browser.

No offline facility. Both WebCT and Webfuse provide facilities for students to print large sections of course material so that they can read material offline. The pages within a ULM are generally kept quite small; to print an entire ULM would require printing each individual page.

Compulsory account. Like WebCT, TopClass requires that all students have an account on the system. However, unlike WebCT, TopClass does not require students to have an account for every class they are enrolled in. Requiring every student to have an account does provide additional management overhead, which some of TopClass's support systems address.

All online. All interaction with the system for both students and instructors must be performed online. This can be expensive under some situations.

Limited interface. Creating and accessing course material under TopClass is very simple, mainly due to the characteristics of the interface. It is not possible to provide ad hoc links between the pages of a ULM. Although this decreases the cognitive load on instructors, it places severe limitations on the paths that students can take and it removes the ability to use the hypertext structure of the Web. A similar limitation is that every TopClass Web-based classroom must use the same set of icons.

Closed communication tools. Like WebCT, the TopClass communication facilities do not integrate with existing Internet communication facilities, so existing student knowledge and practice cannot be used.

Many of the characteristics of TopClass that cause these drawbacks also provide benefits. For example, the lack of links between course material makes it easy to create and access that material. Whether the benefits outweigh the disadvantages depends on the particular situation in which the tool is used.

SIMILARITIES AND DIFFERENCES

At the lowest level, all three systems provide the same basic services, but do so using different methods, interfaces, metaphors, functionality, and complexities. It is possible to examine these basic tasks and compare how each of the systems provide support for these tasks. Tables 9.6, 9.7, 9.8, and 9.9 provide brief comparisons of the three systems based on the four major tasks in a Web-based classroom: information distribution, communication, student assessment, and class management.

As time progresses and these tools develop further, the contents of these tables will change drastically. The book's Web site contains an updated copy of these tables.

OTHER VIEWS

So far this chapter has been a collection of experiences and opinions of one or two people. In comparing these tools, it is essential that you hear the opinions

Table 9.6 Comparison of Information Distribution Support Facilities

Product	*Content Preparation*
WebCT	Limited to nonexistent
TopClass	Limited to nonexistent
Webfuse	Limited to nonexistent
Product	Content Management
WebCT	File upload (including zip files); ability to copy, delete, edit files on the server
TopClass	File upload
Webfuse	File upload (including zip files); ability to copy, delete, edit files on the server
Product	Modifying Presentation
WebCT	Good, change icons and colors
TopClass	Limited
Webfuse	Good, change icons and colors
Product	Content Structuring
WebCT	Somewhat restrictive
TopClass	More restrictive than the other two
Webfuse	Less restrictive than the other two
Product	Content Validation
WebCT	None
TopClass	HTML validation (doesn't support links, so need for link checking)
Webfuse	HTML validation and link checking
Product	Content Viewing
WebCT	Online viewing, tool to collate pages from a path for printing
TopClass	Online viewing only
Webfuse	Online viewing, offline viewing*, study guide page type provides a print copy
Product	Student Provision of Content
WebCT	Student presentation areas allow students to place content on server
TopClass	Could be simulated by giving students instructor accounts
Webfuse	Most flexible access control system which allows students to be given control of any part of the Web-based classroom

* Offline viewing means pages can be downloaded onto students' computers and viewed from the local hard drive without being connected to the Internet.

Table 9.7 Comparison of Communication Facilities

Product	*E-Mail*
WebCT	Support for attachments, no integration with Internet e-mail
TopClass	Support for attachments, no integration with Internet e-mail
Webfuse	No special support, supports standard Internet e-mail
Product	***Group Discussion***
WebCT	WebCT-specific tool, no support for other Internet tools
TopClass	TopClass-specific tool, no support for other Internet tools
Webfuse	Simple Web-based bulletin board, e-mail archive
Product	***Interactive Chat***
WebCT	Java applet, text based
TopClass	None
Webfuse	Java applet, text based, shared whiteboard, and support of guided tours of the Web
Product	***Anonymous Communication***
WebCT	None
TopClass	None
Webfuse	Web-based bulletin board can be anonymous, support for anonymous forms-based surveys

Table 9.8 Comparison of Student Assessment Facilities

Product	*Quizzes*
WebCT	Multiple choice, short answer, and essay, auto-marked and distribution to grader
TopClass	Multiple choice, short answer, and essay, auto-marked and distribution to grader
Webfuse	Multiple choice, missing word, auto-marked
Product	***Assignment Submission***
WebCT	Limited support provided by student presentation areas
TopClass	None
Webfuse	Support for submission, online marking, gradebook management

Table 9.9 Comparison of Class Management Facilities

Product	*Account Management*
WebCT	Creation, deletion, including batch registration
TopClass	Creation, deletion, including batch registration
Webfuse	Creation, deletion
Product	***Online Marking***
WebCT	Marking of quizzes
TopClass	Marking of quizzes
Webfuse	Marking of assignments
Product	***Results Management***
WebCT	Most features and control over calculation and distribution of results
TopClass	Some features, not as good as WebCT
Webfuse	Limited features
Product	***Student Tracking***
WebCT	Summaries of participation of all class members, including graphs
TopClass	Some limited ability
Webfuse	Still under development

of others—in particular, the people who are using these systems to build and teach in Web-based classrooms. This section provides you with the results of a survey of these users and provides pointers to other online locations where they and their opinions can be found.

The Survey

In late May 1997, a message announcing a survey was sent to a number of mailing lists dealing with the use of the Web in education. The aim of this survey was to gain some feedback from Web-based classroom designers and implementers about the systems they were using to create and manage their Web-based classrooms. The following is a summary of the results of that survey. A more complete and up to date record of the survey responses and a copy of the survey itself can be found on the accompanying CD-ROM and on the book's Web site.

As of June 3, 1997, 28 people had completed the survey, including 15 users of WebCT and 9 users of TopClass. The remaining respondents were using a variety of other methods to create their Web-based classrooms, including Nicenet, Frontpage, and a plain editor. Because Webfuse had not been released at that time, there were no responses from users of that product.

Type of Course The type of course in which the Web was being used by the survey respondents included information systems, courses in an MBA, engineering, computer applications in agriculture, biology, elementary, middle and high school teachers, small business management, environmental ethics, human ecology, Western literature, quality management, inorganic chemistry, social work, wireless telecommunications and intelligent networks, telecommunications in special education and rehabilitation, education, law, and geography.

Tasks An important consideration when choosing one of these systems is the ease with which you can perform certain tasks with it. A series of questions on the survey asked people to rate the level of difficulty of the system they were using to perform the seven tasks outlined in Table 9.10.

The survey asked respondents to rank the difficulty of performing these seven tasks with their system using the following scale: very easy, straightforward, moderately difficult, and very difficult. Figure 9.20 provides a comparison of the mean scores for TopClass and WebCT. The results show that people find performing all tasks with both systems to be somewhere between very easy and straightforward. WebCT was reported to be slightly easier to use for most tasks except initially learning how to use it. This could be explained by WebCT's more flexible nature and lack of a standard interface for both students and course creators.

Respondents were also asked to rank their level of computer and Web knowledge on the scale of novice, capable, and advanced and whether or not this level of knowledge was sufficient to use the particular system they had chosen. All the TopClass users ranked themselves as either capable or advanced computer and Web users. Two of the WebCT users ranked themselves as novice computer users; only one ranked him/herself as a novice Web user. When asked if their knowledge

Table 9.10 Surveyed Tasks

Number	*Task*
1	Setting up
2	Learning how to use the system
3	Creating a class
4	Creating course material
5	Navigation
6	Tracking progress
7	Making a backup

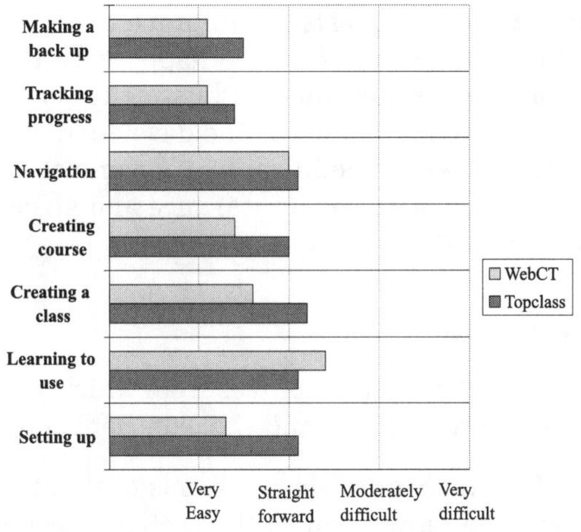

Figure 9.20 Difficulty level of seven tasks.

was sufficient to use their chosen systems, 11 of 14 WebCT users said yes; 8 of 9 TopClass users said yes.

Student Reaction For many of the survey participants, it was too early to predict student reaction, because they were still developing their courses. For most of those who could provide an indication of student reaction, it appears that students felt positively toward the use of either TopClass or WebCT when implemented appropriately, and there was some obvious benefit to the students. Positive student reaction was particularly obvious when the use of either Web-based system fulfilled an obvious need or provided a required service.

A major hurdle reported was the negative feelings of students who are intimidated by computers. This was a particular problem in classes in which computers are not traditionally used. Apart from fear of computers, the major negative response reported by users of both WebCT and TopClass were problems caused by the instability of the systems.

Best Features People using both WebCT and TopClass commented that one of the best features of both packages is the integration of all the necessary tools in one system. Another common theme was the quality of the support and responsiveness provided by the developers of each system.

The best features of WebCT that were mentioned by more than one person included the well-organized structure it provided for course material, the online quizzes, and, in particular, the ability for student self-evaluation and WebCT's abilities in tracking student progress.

As well as the integration of tools provided by TopClass, the most common theme from the TopClass users was the system's ease of use and simplicity. More general comments indicated that the use of TopClass provided an alternative delivery mechanism that offered a number of advantages over traditional methods.

Better Features Most requests for improvements in both WebCT and TopClass appear to come from people who are happy with the basic operation of the systems but who desire some minor adjustments or additional features. Many of these points are already known to the developers of these systems, and they are working on the necessary modifications. A common request for both systems is to provide more flexibility in the appearance and structure of the Web-based classrooms created with these systems.

Other Information Sources

There are at least three other sources from which you can gain information about the features of these systems and the experiences of the people using them:

Mailing list archives. Most systems of this type have mailing lists (pointers to these lists are given in the sections for each system) where the users of the system discuss the features, problems, and their use of the system. The discussion on these lists can sometimes be quite frank and provide real insight into the worth of the particular system. In particular, you will find going through the archives of these mailing lists a useful method for picking up the history of the system and the quality of the response from system makers.

Academic papers. All three systems have had conference and journal papers written about them and are sure to have more written in the future. Reading these papers and communicating directly with the authors are useful methods of gaining more information.

Other comparisons. A number of people have performed comparisons of the various systems that are available including Tools for Developing Interactive Academic Web Courses, University of Manitoba (**www.umanitoba.ca/ip/tools/courseware/**), Comparative Analysis of Online Educational Delivery Applications (**www.ctt.bc.ca/landon/**), and Web-Based Course Management Systems, University of Iowa (**adpsrv1.adp.uiowa.edu/ ITS/ ISDG.nsf/**).

CONCLUSIONS

All three systems examined in this chapter help reduce the effort involved in creating and managing a Web-based classroom and provide a number of services that lend additional functionality. All three perform the same basic tasks, but they are implemented using different applications, interfaces, and metaphors. It is these differences that make one system more appropriate than another for a given situation.

10

Setting Up and Maintaining a Web-Based Education System

This chapter is divided into two main sections. The first section looks at how to set up components of your system, such as the Web server and student accounts. The types of tasks you may need to perform when preparing your Web-based education system include setting up your operating system, setting up your Web server (including setting up accounts and limiting access to areas of the server), setting up your computer on your network, connecting to the Internet, ensuring security, setting up a mirror site, setting up MIME types on the server, setting up a resource center, and configuring students' browsers and setting up their personal space.

The second section examines what you need to do to maintain your system and the utilities you can use to do that. Maintenance involves looking after your system, making sure copies of your system are kept safe in case of accidents, and fixing problems. The maintenance tasks we look at are performing backups, checking server performance, searching and indexing your site's contents, reporting and managing problems, creating an emergency plan, and analyzing log files.

SETTING UP THE SYSTEM

This chapter is not intended as a definitive guide to setting up and maintaining all the technical aspects of your Web-based education system; the material is provided as a means to quick-start your Web classroom development. If you have a technical person at your institution, you should not hesitate to pass the tasks outlined in this chapter onto that person. In this event, you should read through this chapter to get an idea of what is feasible and useful so you know what to expect or request from your technical staff. Determined readers should consult other books or relevant Web sites (check out some of the sources for information mentioned in Chapter 4) for more in-depth details.

Setting Up Your Operating System

The first thing you need to do is select the computer that will act as your Web server. If you have a choice of candidates for a server, you can examine which operating system is the best to use for a Web server.

The question of which is the best is not a very straightforward one to answer; each operating system has its advantages and disadvantages. At the moment, the most popular operating system for Web servers is UNIX. If you use UNIX, you will have access to a wide range of available software, much of it free. However, software for computers comes in two forms: source code, which needs to be compiled on a computer and is generally usable on a wide range of computers, and binary (or machine code) form, which is usable only by the platform for which it was created. Some software requires specific versions of UNIX, so if you intend to use UNIX, make sure all the software that you want to use is compatible with the version of UNIX that you choose. If you want to convert your PC to use the UNIX operating system, there are two main choices, both of which are available to download at no cost:

> Linux (**www.linux.org/**) is available principally for Intel-based computers, but there is also a version in development for the Macintosh. All the forms of Linux that are available are relatively easy to install if you are new to UNIX.
>
> An alternative to Linux, BSD, is available in several distribution kits; NetBsd (**www.netbsd.org/**) and FreeBSD (**www.freebsd.com/**) are the main variants.

Both of these systems come with instructions on how to set them up and a program that helps automate the process for you. You will have to do some work yourself, though, and some familiarity with UNIX is advised.

One thing you should note is that both of these systems can consume a large amount of disk space on your computer, 100MB at least (not counting the space needed to hold the installation files). CD-ROMs with the installation files for the operating systems on them are available at low cost. Some CD-ROMs even allow you to install only a small part of the operating system and use the CD-ROM for the rest, thus negating the need to install the whole system on your hard disk. This is not a particularly good option if you are using the system as a Web server, because access to the CD-ROM is much slower than access to the hard disk.

The problem with UNIX is that it is by no means easy to learn to use, so if you are familiar with another operating system and you are expected to set up and maintain your own Web server, you may be wise to stick with what you know.

Windows 3.1 can be used as your server operating system; however, Windows 3.1 was not designed to be able to handle such a demanding job, so it will not be as stable nor as fast as the same machine running Linux or BSD under conditions of even moderate usage. Windows 95 is a better choice than Windows 3.1, but Windows 95 requires more resources just to run the basic operating system, so a basic machine running a Web server on top of Windows 95 may be strained a bit.

Windows NT is another option for a Windows-based Web server, but requires even more resources than Windows 95. There are two versions of NT: the workstation version and the server version; the workstation version is the cheaper. Most Web servers available for NT run on either version, but not all of them, so be careful which version you choose. If you use an NT workstation as a Web server, you should select the Foreground and Background Applications Equally Responsive option in the Tasking menu under the Control Panel to ensure that the Web server gets an acceptable share of the machine's CPU resources.

Macintoshes, both the older 68000 based and the PowerPC models, can also be used for Web servers and are, as is usual with the Macintosh platform, generally very easy to use.

Setting Up Your Web Server

Table 10.1 gives a partial list of Web servers that are available for the various platforms and some details about them. For a more comprehensive list of available Web servers, look at **webcompare.iworld.com/**, which provides a list of each server's features as well as links telling you where the servers can be obtained.

Table 10.1 Web Servers for Various Platforms

Name	*Location*	*Status*
UNIX-based servers		
Apache	www.apache.org/	Free
NCSA HTTPD	hoohoo.ncsa.uiuc.edu/docs/Overview.html	Free
CERN Server	www.w3.org/hypertext/WWW/Daemon/Status.html	Free
Plexus	bsdi.com/server/doc/plexus.html	Free
EIT Enhanced HTTPD	wsk.eit.com/wsk/doc/httpd/pacifica.html	Commercial
FastTrack SuiteSpot	home.netscape.com/	Commercial (evaluation copies are available)
BOA	www.boa.org/	Free
Open Market Web	www.openmarket.com/	Commercial

Continued

Table 10.1 Continued

Name	*Location*	*Status*
Windows servers		
Fnord (95/NT)	www.wpi.edu/~bmorin/fnord/	Free
Commerce Builder (95/NT)	www.ifact.com/	Commercial (evaluation copies are available)
Win-HTTPD (3.1)	www.city.net/win-httpd/	Free
HTTPS (NT)	emwac.ed.ac.uk/html/internet_toolchest/https/contents.htm	Free
Microsoft Internet Information Server (NT)	www.microsoft.com/	Commercial (evaluation copies are available)
Microsoft Personal Web server	www.microsoft.com/	Free
Netscape FastTrack (95/NT)	www.netscape.com/	Commercial (evaluation copies are available)
WebSite (NT/95)	website.ora.com/	Commercial
OS/2		
GoServe	www2.hursley.ibm.com/goserve/	Free
DOS		
BOA for DOS	ryoohki.res.cmu.edu/dosboa/	Free
Macintosh		
WebSTAR	www.starnine.com/	Commercial (evaluation copy is available)
NetPresenz	www.share.com/peterlewis/netpresenz/netpresenz.html	Shareware
QuidProQuo	www.slaphappy.com	Free
4D Web SmartServer	www.acius.com/	Commercial
Personal Web Server	www.microsoft.com/	Free
Java-based servers		
JigSaw	www.w3.org/pub/WWW/Jigsaw/	Free
Java Web Server	jeeves.javasoft.com/products/java-server/webserver/	Free

Which Is the Best Web Server? This is a difficult question to answer, because it depends so much on the circumstances in which you use the Web server. Usually, you look at such criteria as ease of installation and use, the platform it runs on, its price and its features. Features may be important if you want to use your Web server for more than just an information distribution system.

One feature to keep an eye out for is the ability to use your server as a proxy. A proxy is a computer that browsers must go through to connect to the Internet. With a proxy, you do not have to protect individual computers from "attack" if they want to connect to the Internet, and you can use settings on the proxy to control what computers are allowed to access the Internet. Other features that a Web server can have are security, the ability to run CGI programs and Server Side Includes, and a system for creating and managing user accounts.

The Netscape servers are some of the easiest to use, because they use Web pages as an interface to setting up and maintaining the server (as opposed to most other systems, which require you to alter settings in files and then restart the Web server). However, Netscape servers can be quite expensive.

The version of the Cern HTTPD given Table 10.1 is still popular but is an old one that is no longer being developed. The next generation of the Cern Web server, called Jigsaw, is exciting; it is written in Java and so is suitable for all-Java supporting platforms. You could write supporting CGI scripts in Java without having to use intermediate languages like Perl. It also means the Web server can consist of standard set of programs that will run on any platform that supports Java.

The NCSA HTTP server is getting old and has effectively been taken over by the Apache server project. The servers are almost identical in regard to configuration options, but NCSA is still popular because of its download procedure, which allows you to use forms to supply your local options (such as the root directory, the name of your machine, etc.) to a configuration program at the NCSA site, which then creates a ready-to-run HTTP server for you to download (**hoohoo.ncsa.uiuc.edu/docs/setup/OneStep.html**). This process saves you some effort; it's a pity other developers don't use such a system as well.

Before Starting the Installation Before you attempt to install a Web server, your computer should already be configured to run on a network. Setting up your computer on a network is dependent on the type of operating system that you have and the form of your network. You should consult your local system manager if you are unsure of the state of your machine. If your candidate server can connect to other computers on the network using a browser or Telnet, you are more than likely ready to go. You should collect the following pieces of information that you may need to set up your server (some Web servers will be able to figure these out for themselves or will be configured with default values you can get by with):

The root directory. What will the root directory be? Remember from Chapter 3 that this directory is where you put all your Web files.
Where the Web server is going. What directory will the Web server be placed in?
The machine name. What is the name of your computer? Sometimes the IP number will be required as well.
The e-mail address of the administrator. This is the e-mail address to which users are referred when they encounter a problem with the system.

Instructions for Installation First, download the relevant server. Most servers come in some sort of archived and compressed format. Unpack the server, using the relevant decompression and archival tool, into the directory it will occupy, and then start the relevant configuration process.

In this section, we look at installing three Web servers, one for each type of platform. The servers we look at are all available at no charge and are included on the CD-ROM in directory /setup/servers. They are Apache for UNIX, HTTPS for NT, and Fnord for Windows 95.

Most Web servers come with their own installation instructions. Another source of installation instructions for Web servers is available at **web66.coled.umn.edu/Cookbook/**.

Apache The Apache setup instructions are pretty much identical to the instructions necessary to install the NCSA server, so this server can be used instead if desired.

First, go into the directory that will contain the HTTP server (usually /usr/local/etc). To install and run the HTTP server, you need to have root privileges (the ability to log in as user root). If you have not got root privileges, ask your system manager to give them to you or to perform the installation and start the server for you.

In the discussion, we show you how to set up a server that has already been compiled for your platform. If your type of UNIX does not have a binary, you need to compile the source code on your platform yourself (see **www.apache.org/docs/install.html** for further instructions).

The server package is either compressed using the UNIX compress utility (available on all UNIX platforms) or the gzip utility. (Note that the names of these files may be different as newer versions of the program become available.)

For the file

```
apache_1.2b7.tar.gz          apache_1.2b7.tar.Z
```

do

```
gunzip apache_1.2b7.tar.gz   uncompress apache_1.2b7.tar.gz
```

Then

```
tar -xvf apache_1.2b7.tar          tar -xvf apache_1.2b7.tar
```

This will create a directory tree apache_1.2b7 under the directory you are currently in.

Change the name of this directory to HTTPD (i.e., mv apache_1.2b7 httpd); this is the standard name for an HTTP server directory.

Go into the directory httpd/conf (which holds all the configuration files). In this directory are three example configuration files named access.conf-dist, httpd.conf-dist, and srm.conf-dist. Copy these files to remove the dist extension:

```
cp access.conf-dist access.conf
cp httpd.conf-dist httpd.conf
cp srm.conf-dist srm.conf
```

You can now alter the configuration files.

The first file to alter is the main HTTPD configuration file. Edit the file called httpd.conf. Below we describe some of the options you may need to change; the configuration file contains many more options that can be left alone for the moment:

ServerAdmin. The e-mail address of the server's administrator. This will be given to users who encounter a problem with the server as the person to contact to report the fault or the problem. Set this to your e-mail address or the address of the person maintaining the system.

ServerName. The name of your server computer. Set this to the full name of your computer—for instance, courseserver.orgname.orgtype.

ServerRoot. The path to your server directory (where the HTTP program is located). If you followed the guidelines above, this should be /usr/local/etc/httpd.

The next file to edit is the srm.conf file. It specifies the location of some of the resources used by the server. You will need to alter the following:

DocumentRoot. Set this to the path of the Web root directory, such as /usr/local/www. Make sure this Web root directory exists. Calling the server with a URL now translates this into the Web root directory; for instance, **courseserver/main/index.html** will look for the file index.html in /usr/local/www/main/index.html.

ScriptAlias. This refers to the location of the CGI scripts on your system and how their URLs will appear. For example, if you put ScriptAlias /cgi-bin/ /usr/local/etc/httpd/cgi-bin/, any time you want to use a script—for example,print-time.pl—you put the script in the /usr/local/etc/httpd/cgi-bin/ directory and call it using the /cgi-bin/ extension: courseserver/cgi-bin/print-time.pl.

You may also want to add a line similar to the following to the end of the srm.conf file:

```
ErrorDocument 404 /notfound.html
```

This code sends a user who has requested a document that the server cannot find a file called notfound.html, which is located in the root directory. This file can contain an explanation of the common reasons the server cannot find the file, such as the user misspelled the URL or the file has been moved. (See the training and reference materials on the CD-ROM for a more thorough discussion.) The file notfound.html can also contain a link to a search utility (see later in this chapter) to enable users to search for the information they were looking for.

Finally, we look at the access.conf file. This file controls access privileges, including what users are allowed to access the server, what directories particular users can access, and the computers that can be used to access your server. You may need to alter the entry

```
<Directory /usr/local/etc/httpd/htdocs>
```

It will need to be altered to the directory name you specified as being your root, so, following our example (where the root was directory /usr/local/www), you change the Directory entry to

```
<Directory /usr/local/www>
```

This Directory entry marks the start of the access configuration settings for each directory; the end of the particular entry is </Directory>.

NOTE

Any time you change any entry in the configuration files, you must "kill," or stop, the HTTP server and restart it. ■

Now that you have completed the configuration process, you can start the server. Place an HTML file in the root directory that you specified in the srm.conf file.

Our discussion assumes that you put the server in /usr/local/etc/httpd. Start the server by typing

```
/usr/local/etc/httpd/httpd -d /usr/local/etc/httpd
```

Then you can use a Web browser to access the page you put in the root directory. If the page was index.html, for example, and the server's name is courseserver, you access the URL

```
http://courseserver/index.html
```

If this doesn't work, go through the set of steps again and ensure that all your directory names and paths were typed in correctly, that your machine has network access, and that you are currently the root user.

Once you have established that the HTTP server works, you can add it to the system startup. Then, every time the computer is restarted, the HTTP server will also start. Details on how to do this vary from UNIX system to system, so you should consult your documentation or local system manager to find out how it is done.

HTTPS Part of the appeal of HTTPS is that it is free and that it is easy to install. Unfortunately, it lacks a lot in terms of features, but is suitable as a basic Web server.

HTTPS can be found at **emwac.ed.ac.uk/html/ internet_toolchest/ https/ contents.htm**. It is available in zip format, meaning that you must get WinZip or PKUNZIP to unpack it. Once you have uncompressed it, move the files https.exe, https.cpl, and https.hlp to the \winnt\system32 directory.

Next, type

```
https -ipaddress
```

If this reports the wrong host name or IP number for your computer, you need to fix your TCP/IP setup. Type

```
https -install
```

to install the server. To check that this worked, start the Services item in the control panel and see if the HTTP server is listed. Next, you need to configure the system by starting HTTPS from the control panel (it should be under "Services"). In the dialog screen that appears, there is a Data Directory field. Type in the root directory.

Finally, you need an account the program can use. Create a new account using the General User privileges. Go back to the Services menu of the control panel, highlight HTTP server, and click Startup. A dialog box will appear in which you enter the account you created for the server in the Account field. Enter the password and click OK. Your server should now be running. You can place an HTML file in the root directory and access the server using a browser to test it.

Fnord Setting up Fnord is a relatively straightforward process. Unpack the distribution, making sure you maintain the correct directory structure of the archive. The best place to unpack it is in the c:\ directory, because this is the default directory for the server distribution. Then run the file FnordCtl.exe. This program brings up a control panel.

You can set the IP number of your server by selecting the General section. If you leave this blank, the server will try to establish the IP number on its own.

If you want to change your root directory, select the Paths section and insert the new root along with the path used for URL references to your server. For example, if you wanted to put your files into c:\www, you would create the entry

```
\      c:\www
```

Once this is finished, exit FnordCtl.exe and run Fnord.exe. If the server did not start (its icon will appear on the bottom left of the screen), check the error.txt file in the Fnord home directory for an indication of the problem. You should add the Fnord program to your list of startup files so that it starts when the computer does.

Fnord allows you to set MIME types, create groups, and protect areas of your course. To access these services, bring up the server control by placing the mouse over the server icon and double-clicking.

Setting Up Server Side Includes Server Side Includes are tags you can include in your HTML pages that the Web server uses to perform some operation, like inserting a file or supplying the date the file was last altered. You saw some of the uses of Server Side Includes in Chapter 4. Not all Web servers allow the use of these tags; however, NCSA and Apache do. (Note that, for other Web servers, the process for switching on Server Side Includes may be different from that shown here.)

To enable Server Side Includes for these Web servers, you need to alter the srm.conf file. The line

```
AddType application/x-server-parsed-html shtml
```

is usually commented out by default (it has # in front of it), so to activate, remove the # .

You also need to alter the access.conf file. One of the entries in the access.conf file contains an entry for the root directory. Add the word "Includes" to the existing options:

```
<Directory /usr/local/www>
Options {existing options} Includes
</Directory>
```

When you restart the server, any file with the extension .shtml will be examined by the server to see if it contains any Server Side Includes. For example, if an HTML file test.shtml contained

```
<!--#echo var="LAST_MODIFIED"-->
```

the server would remove it from the file and replace it with the date the file was last modified, which would be displayed in the browser window.

You could have altered the shtml in the AddType declaration to html so that every file with the extension .html is examined for Server Side Includes. However, this can be hard on the server, which now has to examine every file with .html as its extension as opposed to simply transmitting the file.

Protecting Areas of the Course You may need to limit students' access to material, such as tests or specific segments of the course. You may also want to limit who can access the course material to prevent people who are not students from viewing your resources or limit the computers that your students can use to gain access. There are several methods of protecting your course. We look at how to protect the course using the NCSA/Apache server, but a number of other servers have security facilities that can be configured using the same general principles.

You can do two main things to protect your course materials on the Web:

Limit access to directories on your server (access can be limited to individuals or to certain groups).

Limit access to certain computers.

If you set up such a system of protecting your server, you should give students an explanation of how it works and a person to contact if they have problems. The best way to do this is to leave your course home page unprotected; a link to a help page (also unprotected) can be made available from this page, where students can read how to access protected areas of the system or how to register for permission to access these areas and what to do if they are having problems.

Another way of helping users who have trouble with the system is to set up the server so that if users fail to log in properly to a protected area, they are automatically brought to a specific page that can contain details about registration. This can be done for the Apache server by placing the line

```
ErrorDocument 401 /refused.html
```

at the end of the srm.conf file. The HTML file refused.html should be placed in the root directory and is called when the user fails to receive permission to log in to a protected area.

The disadvantage of any security system is that it requires extra work to set up and monitor. People also invariably forget their passwords or have trouble with the login procedure in general, which can lead to a degree of frustration with the system.

Limiting Access to Certain Areas Limiting students' access to certain areas means that you must create an account for them using a utility supplied with the HTTP server. The account a student has on the HTTP server differs from an account on the server's operating system. Students have user names and passwords they will be asked for when they attempt to access protected areas. (See Figure 10.1 for an example of the window that will appear when students click on a link or select a URL that is protected.) If they have no account or supply an incorrect password or user name, an error message appears and they are invited to try again. (Figure 10.2 presents an example of the type of error message that appears when they fail to gain access.).

Using the Apache Web server, there are two ways of limiting access to certain directories. The first way is to alter the main access.conf file. Create a Directory entry for the directory you want to protect. In our example, we want to protect the directory /usr/local/etc/www/tutorial:

```
<Directory /usr/local/www/tutorial>
```

You should give users a message if they try to access this directory. This message will appear in the window that asks them for their name and password:

```
    AuthName English 101 Tutorial - Dr. Fischer
```

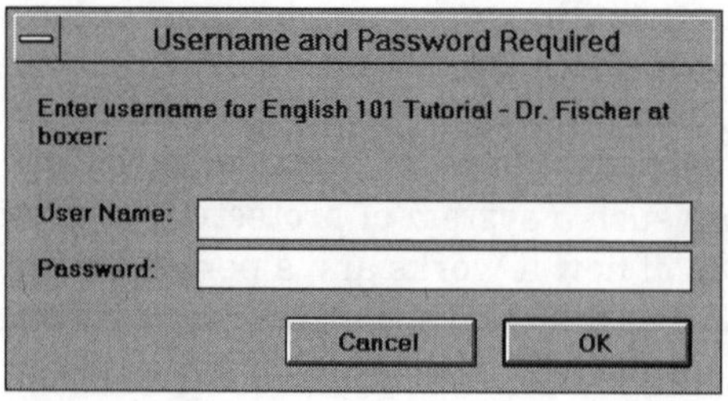

Figure 10.1 A login window.

This message tells students that they are being asked for a password to enter Dr. Fischer's English 101 tutorial.

On the next line, tell the server where to find the file that contains the list of passwords and account holders so it can check if the person trying to access this section is an authorized user:

```
AuthUserFile /usr/local/etc/httpd/conf/passwd
```

In our example, we gave the name of the password file as passwd. You can create multiple password files—for instance, one for each course stored on the server—and use this directive to associate the correct password file with the relevant directory.

Next, place an entry that denotes the level of protection you are giving to the password:

```
    AuthType Basic
```

It is possible to encrypt passwords and user names by changing the entry, but to do this you would have to install other security packages.

Next comes the section that indicates what the user is allowed to do in the directory:

```
<Limit GET>
```

Figure 10.2 An access refused message.

This limits users to getting files from the directory. If you want to allow users to send information to scripts in the directory (known as "posting" information), you type

```
<Limit GET POST>
```

Next, supply a list of names of users who are allowed to access this directory (how to create accounts will be shown later). These user names are stored in the password file. The names are preceded by the words "require user," indicating that the user is required to be one of the following in order to access the information:

```
require user fred andy mary
```

This entry says that the only users permitted to access the directory /usr/local/www/tutorial are Fred, Andy, and Mary.

You can write out all the account names of the class here, or you could make it easier by including all the account names of the students in a separate file, called a group file, and specifying the name of the group file here. (We look at group files in a later section.)

Finally, indicate that the configuration for this directory is ended by closing the Limit and Directory entries:

```
</Limit>
</Directory>
```

The complete entry in the access.conf file will now look like this:

```
<Directory /usr/local/www/tutorial>
AuthName English 101 Tutorial - Dr. Fischer
AuthUserFile /usr/local/etc/httpd/conf/passwd
AuthType Basic
<Limit GET>
require user fred andy mary
</Limit>
</Directory>
```

The method we just examined requires you to alter the access.conf file every time you want to protect (or unprotect) a directory. You can protect directories on a directory-by-directory basis by placing a file with the name .htaccess (note the full stop before the directory name) in each directory you want to protect. To create an .htaccess file, you omit the Directory portion of the method for protecting a file in access.conf, so our configuration would look like this:

```
AuthName English 101 Tutorial - Dr. Fischer
AuthUserFile /usr/local/etc/httpd/conf/passwd
AuthType Basic
```

```
<Limit GET>
require user fred andy mary
</Limit>
```

and you place it in the directory you want to protect—for example, /usr/local/www/tutorial.

You can use .htaccess files or a central configuration file; however, you do not need to restart the server every time you make an alteration to the .htaccess file, whereas you should restart the server after each alteration to the srm.conf file.

Limiting Access to Certain Machines You might want to prevent your system being accessed from certain computers. To do this, use the configuration for an access file that we looked at above. You use two new entries:

deny from. Indicates that users who try to access from these computers are denied access.

allow from. Indicates that only users who access from these computers are allowed to connect.

A third entry, order, denotes the order in which the allow and deny directives are processed.

This system can be added to your password protection system or used on its own. For example, say you altered the access.conf file to look like the one below:

```
<Directory /usr/local/www/tutorial>
<Limit GET>
order deny,allow
allow from .myuni.edu, local-isp.com
deny from all
</Limit>
</Directory>
```

In this case, only users connecting from computers that end in the name .myuni.edu and the name of the local Internet service provider (local-isp.com) are allowed access to the directory indicated. So, a student using a computer called pc1.lab2.myuni.edu would be allowed access to the directory. Users accessing from other computers would be refused access.

The big problem with this scheme is that people can often forge computers' addresses to break into sites. The only way to be absolutely sure that people outside your institution are not accessing your course is to remove the server from the Internet. This is an extreme measure because it will prevent users from accessing the course from home, as in the example above, where you allowed students to access the course from the local Internet service provider. You can combine the method above with individual accounts or a common account (every student using the same account) to make your system a little more secure from unwelcome "students."

Creating Student Accounts The password file you reference in the access control entries you saw above contains the account information for each student. Each file looks something like this:

```
tom:Xr3242V4
jane:3gh43FH1
```

which corresponds to the name of the account and the encrypted password, separated by a colon. This file can be edited manually, and the account names can be altered. Deleting the line an account name is on effectively removes the user's account.

The information is a subset of that contained in a UNIX password file commonly located in /etc/passwd. Indeed, if your students have accounts on a UNIX system, you can just add their account names and passwords to the Web server password file that you are creating.

The Apache and NCSA servers come with a program that can be used to create a password file and add entries to it. It is located in the support directory of the main HTTPD directory (/usr/local/etc/httpd/support if you are following the example we used at the start).

The program is called htpasswd. On some systems, it does not come in executable form, so you may need to type "make" in the support directory in order to compile it. (If this doesn't work, try "cp Makefile.tmpl Makefile" and then type "make.")

You can create a password file called passwd by typing the following:

```
htpasswd -c passwd administrator
```

This code creates a password file called passwd and asks you for the password for the user called administrator. Any time you want to add a new user to the password file called passwd, type

```
htpasswd passwd username
```

where username is the name of the user you want to add. If the user name already exists, you will be asked for a new password for that name.

You can create as many password files as you want, one for each class, for example, just as long as you use different names for each one. Make sure you remember which password file to use when writing the directives that will limit access to sections of the server.

A common cause of security problems is not hardware or software inadequacies, but users who do not realize how important a password is and how easy it

Note

For security reasons, make sure your password file is in an area that people cannot view using a browser; ensure that it is not in the root directory or its subdirectories. ■

is to guess someone else's passwords. Here is a list of guidelines that you can offer students for choosing their passwords:

- Pick a password that cannot be found in a dictionary or whose derivative cannot be guessed.
- Do not use a small password of fewer than eight characters.
- Make sure nobody can watch you typing your password.
- Do not choose a name or any other word that can be guessed by those who know you, such as the name of a family pet, your address, or your phone number.
- Choose a mix of alphanumeric and upper- and lowercase letters, such as NotEZ2Guess.
- Do not use the same password for all the machines you have access to.
- Do not write down the password. If it is not possible to avoid making a note of the password, store it in a secure place.

Creating Groups If you want to restrict access to a directory on your server to a list of people in a particular group, add the following directive to the protection directive we looked at above:

```
AuthGroupFile /usr/local/etc/http/conf/classes
```

This code indicates that the group file that contains the list of names of students in your class is called classes.

With the Limit section of the directive, state the name of the group that is allowed to access the directory:

```
require group english101
```

This code indicates that only members of the group called english101 that is contained in the file classes are allowed to access this directory.

The file named classes contains the names of various groups and the names of the users who belong in each group. For example, the file classes could contain the following:

```
english101: fred andy mary
history201: susan pat nadine
```

This file indicates that the members of english101 are the users Fred, Andy, and Mary; history201's users are Susan, Pat, and Nadine. This is the format of a group file: the name of the group, followed by a semicolon, followed by the names of the accounts of the users in the group (separated by spaces). You need to create this group file manually.

So, the access.conf entry to limit admittance to the directory to the members of English 101 would look like this:

```
<Directory /usr/local/etc/www/tutorial>
AuthName English 101 Tutorial - Dr. Fischer
AuthUserFile /usr/local/etc/httpd/conf/passwd
AuthGroupFile /usr/local/etc/http/conf/classes
AuthType Basic
<Limit GET>
require group english101
</Limit>
</Directory>
```

Setting Up Your Web Server on the Network

In most organizations, you cannot simply set up your Web server without telling anyone. Usually, a specific person is in charge of the local network and in charge of setting up computers to access the network. You will have to work with this person in order to obtain permission to set up your server on the local network. Usually, what this involves is getting a number for your computer, called an IP number. Each computer has its own unique IP number so that it can be identified.

Naming your Computer As well as a unique IP number, each computer on a network also has a name. If your computer already has been set up, it will have been given a name. You can change this name if nobody else objects or get the person in charge of your network to add another name for your server computer (called an alias).

Why are we concerned about the computer's name? You and your students will use this computer a lot, so it makes sense to give it a name that is easily remembered when you want to load a page or add a link. For example, a name like qe12.tr.xyz5.rtp.edu is a bit difficult to remember off the top of your head, so consider changing it to something simpler, like webcourse.rtp.edu.

Some parts of the name cannot be changed because they denote the organization you belong to. For instance, in the previous example, you cannot change the rtp.edu part of the name because it is like a city or a country part of an address. You should be careful about choosing your name, because someone else may want to set up a Web course and you have taken the name for your own computer. To avoid conflict, give the computer a more descriptive name like webcourse-english.rtp.edu, which denotes that the machine is the server for the English Web course.

Subnetworks If you are in a large institution, you are likely to have a main network (called a backbone) and separate networks that are branches off the main network. These branches are called subnetworks, and in this arrangement, a computer in the subnetwork that needs to send information to another computer in the subnetwork requires no part of the network outside the subnetwork to send the information. Communication between computers on the same subnetwork is usually faster than communications between computers on different subnetworks or between computers on the backbone and a subnetwork.

What this implies for your system is that if the majority of your students will access the system from one particular laboratory, you should try to have your Web server connected to the subnetwork that serves that particular laboratory. This will increase the speed at which information can be transferred from your server computer to students' computers.

Setting Up on a File Server Some computer laboratories that work on a subnetwork still use a system whereby a computer's operating system or applications are kept on a central computer, called a file server. On occasion, installing the browser on the server and having the students run it from there can result in the server becoming overloaded and crashing. Check that this cannot happen if you have such a setup in your institution by starting the browser on all the computers in the laboratory simultaneously and observing the reaction of the server.

Connecting to the Internet

You may not need to get connected to the Internet; the course may be confined to local campus-based students only. If you want your students to be able to access the course from outside your local network, though, you need permission for your server to be accessible from the Internet. This permission is usually obtained from your local system manager. If you do not have a local system manager, you may need to engage an Internet service provider to set up and maintain your Web server on the Internet. (See the guidelines on choosing an Internet service provider on the CD-ROM.)

Security

Security should always be a consideration when setting up a system. Most systems allow you to implement various levels of security, from so secure that it makes life difficult for even authorized users, to so insecure that it becomes an easy target for electronic vandals. Getting the security level right is a delicate balancing act.

Checking Your Server's Security How do you check your server to see if it cannot be tampered with? Unfortunately, as any good book on computer security will tell you, no system connected to a network is completely secure. However, you can perform a number of checks to ensure that your server is as secure as can reasonably be expected.

The Satan program (**www.fish.com/satan/**) probes your server for security weaknesses and reports these weaknesses as well as providing a tutorial on them, in some cases. This is the best set of free utilities for checking out your system; you should use them to secure your system before someone else uses them to try and break in.

The most common area of weakness is not faults in the software, but simple password breaking. If your password is not well chosen, it can be guessed easily. A list of guidelines for creating passwords was given earlier, ostensibly for students' use, but you should stick to those guidelines as well.

Password Checkers Utilities such as Crack (**ftp://ftp.cert.org/pub/tools/crack**, for UNIX systems) can be used to attempt to break, or crack, a password file. Once the Crack program guesses a password, it reports the name of any user whose password was guessed. This user can then be told to choose a better password.

Auditing Packages You can use an auditing package to check for holes in your system's security. Some of the more popular packages can be found at these sites: **ftp://ftp.cert.org/pub/tools/cops/** and **ftp://net.tamu.edu/pub/security/TAMU/**.

File Alteration Checkers A program like Tripwire (**ftp://coast.cs.purdue.edu/edu/pub/COAST/ Tripwire/**) can be used to check if any files have been altered since the last time the program was run. This will enable you to see if anyone has been tampering with files.

Screening Sites Many organizations are worried about allowing their students access to the Internet because of the presence of inappropriate material on some Web sites. If you are planning to use Internet resources in your content, you have to do one of the following: convince the administrators of the system that there is no real risk, implement a system of screening material students are attempting to access, or educate students about the consequences of undesirable conduct (perhaps using sanctions as a threat).

The idea of screening is that a program on the computer the student uses to access the Internet examines the URL references that the student is attempting to access and compares them to a list of references that are known to contain inappropriate material. Users can also be prevented from using certain words to perform searches on search engines such as Alta Vista.

There are two ways of doing this. The first way is to install software on each machine used by the student that will perform the screening task. This is prone to problems because students can tamper with the configuration files on their local computers or disable the software. Also working against it is the fact that software must be purchased for each student's computer.

Some of the software available for this purpose can be found at the following sites: CyberPatrol forWindows (**www.cyberpatrol.com/**), CyberSitter for Windows (**www.solidak.com/**), SurfWatch for Macintosh and Windows (**www.surfwatch.com/**), andNetNanny for Windows (**www.netnanny.com/**).

Most of these products need to be upgraded frequently to keep pace with new sites and new pages that become available on the Internet. All of the software manufacturers offer periodic upgrades to their list of banned sites and pages. This introduces an added overhead for screening in that you must upgrade the software on students' computers at regular intervals. Another point to consider is that not all of the upgrades are provided free of charge, so you may incur maintenance costs keeping your list up to date.

The second way of screening is to have the students' browsers send their requests for URLs through another computer that checks them to see if they are appropriate. This is known as using a proxy system. The computer (or proxy) that handles students' browser requests also contains a list of banned sites or words that cannot be tampered with by students because they are located on a computer to which they have no direct access. Some companies are starting to provide proxy-based services, where administrators can supply a list of undesirable material to be screened out. The students' browsers are then configured to go through the company's site. For an example, see the **www.bess.net/** site.

A method of screening that uses a voluntary rating systems for sites or pages has been proposed. Called the PICS system (**www.w3.org/pub/WWW/PICS/**), this system operates like a movie rating system. Each site sends its rating to the browser that accesses it. The browser is configured with a specific rating limit and decides whether to block access to the site based on the site's reported rating. If sites do not provide their own ratings, you can subscribe to a service that will rate the site for you (see **www.shepherd.net**).

Secure Server Communication Most of the current Web traffic is unencrypted. That is, it is like the telephone system, where if someone can tap into the line connecting two people, they can listen in on the conversation. There are a number of systems around which will encrypt, or scramble, communication between browsers and servers so that it cannot be read by an unauthorized third party. If you want to ensure that the communications between your students' browsers and the server are completely confidential, you need to install a secure Web server.

The main system in use is Secure Socket Layer (SSL), which was developed by Netscape (see **home.netscape.com/newsref/std** for details). Because it is widely used by most browser and server producers, it's pretty much the standard. To use this system, you need to obtain one of the HTTP servers that support it: Netscape's Commerce Server for NT/UNIX (**www.netscape.com/**) or Commerce Builder (**www.ifact.com/**) for Windows 95/NT. The Apache server also has extensions that implement the SSL. Your choice of extension depends on your geographic location. This is due to patent restrictions and U.S. rules about the exporting of encryption technology.

Inside the United States, you can use Stronghold (**www.us.apache-ssl.com/**). Outside the United States, try Apache-SSL, available at **www.algroup.co.uk/Apache-SSL**. Both these implementations use software called SSLeay, which is available at **www.psy.uq.oz.au/~ftp/Crypto/**. Both of these systems work only if both the browser and the server support the security system and the security features are enabled. Remember, all that these systems do is make the traffic between the browser and the server unreadable; they do not improve the security of the server. There will always be a security risk, so it is inadvisable to store sensitive information such as exam papers, memos, and the like on a server. Before you place any material on your server, assume that students will be able to get to it if they are determined enough.

Directory Lists In Chapter 4 we said that if you specify a URL where the directory does not contain an index.html file, the contents of that directory will be displayed. This may not be desirable if you are keeping data files from quizzes and other important information in directories users can access.

There are two ways around this problem. One is to make sure that you have put an index.html file in each directory. (You can create a general-purpose index.html file that contains a link to the main page and place in each subdirectory.) The other method is to alter the configuration of the HTTP program to prevent users looking at a list of files in a directory. If you use the second option, it will be awkward to provide an easy means of distributing files, because you must give an absolute URL for each file as opposed to supplying the directory or branch it is located in. The best way to implement the second option is use .htaccess.

Scripts If users are allowed to run scripts on a server, they can sometimes be used to circumvent security precautions on UNIX systems. Users could create scripts that would allow them to perform tasks that exceeded their privileges, such as copying other users' files.

Viruses Viruses are programs that attach themselves to other program and data files and can have a negative effect on the computer. The effect varies depending on the virus, but it can range in severity from a harmless message to the deletion of the contents of your hard disk. If a file is infected with a virus, it can usually be cleaned using utilities accompanying the virus check you use. Viruses can be found on most major operating systems and can even occur in word-processed documents.

To avoid acquiring viruses, always use a virus-checking program (for example, visit **www.mcafee.com/**) to verify that applications are virus free before allowing students to download them. To avoid the Word virus, you can store word processor files in RTF format, which the virus cannot infect. You can also make sure that you perform regular backups of your system so that if you are infected by a virus that erases the contents of your hard drive, you have something to fall back on.

Education is an important weapon in the fight against viruses. Ensure that your students know what sort of behavior is acceptable and how they can avoid contracting a virus or infecting other computers. Virus myths can spread panic among students unfamiliar with the mechanism of a virus, so students should be given an idea of the difference between a threat and a hoax. (See **www.kumite.com/myths** for more details.)

Setting Up a Mirror Site

You don't have to have a large, powerful server to support your Web-based education system. You can spread the load placed on your server by using mirror sites. A mirror site is simply another server that contains an exact copy of all the information stored on your main server. You could have a single mirror site or multiple mirror sites available in different geographic locations. The idea of having a mirror site is that it will reduce the load placed on the main server when people access it, speeding up the rate at which students will be able to download files and information. Your server computers can be relatively slow on their own, but by sharing the load among them, they may approach the performance of an expensive purpose-built server. Another advantage of a mirror site is that if one server breaks down, users will not be stopped from accessing the system; the server's mirrors will provide alternative access.

If you want to set up a mirror system, you need to do two things. First, you need to set up the mirror servers; second, you need a method by which the mirror computers can maintain an exact copy of the content kept on the main course server. There are a number of ways to set up a mirror site; they vary in complexity and effectiveness. Let's look at a couple.

DNS Change This method must be set up by your local system manager. It involves altering the data that a computer, known as the domain name server (DNS), uses to match a computer's name with its IP number. Most computers on the Internet have a name, which makes it easier for people to remember them. Computers cannot use each other's names directly, so they must translate the name into a number. It works like a phone system: If you have a person's name, you need to obtain his phone number before you call him. In the same manner, before a computer communicates with another computer, it must know its number. The DNS contains a list of names and their corresponding numbers, just like a phone directory. You can alter this computer phone directory so that a name can have more than one number associated with it. This means that when the DNS computer is given a name and asked for the number of a computer, it has a choice of numbers.

For example, the entry below

```
webcourse.eg.edu  134.56.7.1   134.56.78.9   134.56.7.90
```

shows that the computer with the name webcourse has three numbers associated with it. Each of these numbers represents an individual computer (every computer on the Internet has its own unique number). When you ask your browser to open a page **webcourse.eg.edu**, you might be brought to the computer with the number 134.56.78.9, or you might be brought to the computer with the number 134.56.7.90, and so on. In other words, if three people ask for a page on webcourse, they could be connected to three different computers.

This method is effective but a little crude because it takes no account of the relative capabilities and current load of the servers involved in the mirroring system. Alternative methods of mirroring are being developed with this in mind (see **www.nsrc.nus.sg/STAFF/edward/pweb.html** for an example).

Server per Section Another option to help ease the load on your server is to split up the facilities of your course among different servers. For example, one server could handle the communications facilities, another could handle the information distribution resources, and a third could store and process all the quizzes. This way, the load will be shared among a number of computers, but you have to go to extra trouble to set up and maintain the computers that will handle each section. Another disadvantage is that the setup of the system may not match usage patterns. For example, if a class of students all log on at the same time and start a quiz, you are back to where you started.

Voluntary System A voluntary system is one that relies on users to choose a particular mirror computer. For example, you could ask students whose names begin with the letters "a" to "j" to use the computer named webclass1.rtp.edu and students with names that begin with "k" through "z" to use the computer webclass2.rtp.edu. This is not as satisfactory an arrangement as altering the DNS, however, because students are still totally reliant on one server—so, for example, if lab sessions are conducted with students attending in alphabetical order, you're back to square one.

Machine Selector Software Another idea is to allow students to access a central server that then automatically sends them to a mirror computer. Users would open a page or a CGI script that then loads the real starting page from one of the mirror computers it randomly selects.

A JavaScript program to do this is shown here. The names of the mirror computers are alpha.xyz.edu, beta.xyz.edu, and delta.xyz.edu. When students load the HTML page containing this code, they are randomly brought to one of the machines. To specify which server they are brought to, you should put the name of each mirror server in one of the Servers variables. You must also set the home page that you want the users to be given. In our example, the page to be loaded is main/first.html. So, for example, if the randomizer selected the mirror machine alpha.xyz.edu, the page /alpha.xyz.edu/main/first.html would be loaded. If the page variable is left empty, users are brought to the Web root of the mirror machine. You can specify up to 10 mirror computers; just be sure that each entry is in a form similar to the examples and that the variable NumberofMirrors contains the number of mirror computers that you have.

```
<script>
var time=new Date();
var Random;
```

```
var NumberOfMirrors=3;
page = "main/first.html";
Servers = new Array(NumberOfMirrors);
Servers [0] = "http://alpha.xyz.edu/";
Servers [1] = "http://beta.xyz.edu/";
Servers [2] = "http://delta.xyz.edu/";

Random=(time.getSeconds())%10;
location=Servers[Random%NumberOfMirrors]+page;
</script>
```

Maintaining Your Mirror Machine When preparing material to be used on a mirror system, it is important that all your links are relative. If each of the links is absolute, users will always be brought to the machine associated with that link. (See Chapter 4 for a discussion of relative and absolute links.)

Once you have set up a system for using your mirror computer, you must then set up a system to ensure that your mirror computers always have the exact same contents— that the mirror machines are indeed exact copies of each other. If the content of your server never changes, you can simply copy all the files on the server to the mirror computer at the start of the year using FTP, NFS, or one of the downloading utilities such as MGET, discussed in Chapter 4.

If your content is liable to change, you can copy the changes on a phased basis (every hour, day, or week) or you can use software that will automatically decide what has changed and copy the relevant files. Such a software package is the mirror package found at **src.doc.ic.ac.uk/packages/mirror/**. This software can be set up to run automatically by creating a batch file or setting the mirroring software to run at preset intervals in UNIX using a cron job. This means that you can set the interval at which the software will make sure that all the servers have the same copy of the material to be a convenient time, such as at weekends or late at night, when the number of students accessing the system is low. A Windows 95/NT package called File Dog does the same thing (**www.edgepub.com/fd/**).

One thing that is very tricky to manage with mirroring is discussion group software such as WebBoard (see Chapter 6), which is liable to have new messages added to it every minute. In this situation, it may be best to create a separate server specifically to manage your communications facilities as opposed to having your mirroring software try to keep up with the constant changes in content of your discussion.

Setting Up MIME Types on the Server

We talked about configuring the browser to start various applications to cope with files of different types in Chapter 4. In that chapter, we mentioned that you must configure the Web server to recognize files with a certain extension and tell the browser that it was sending it those files. In this section, we show you how to do this with the Apache Web server. Most servers require you to supply the following:

The MIME type, which indicates the general contents of the file. For example, a picture file in GIF format has the MIME type image, so any file that requires a program to use it will have the type application (i.e., a word processor).

The MIME name, which you assign to files of this particular MIME type. For example, the image type JPEG is assigned the name JPEG. We saw in Chapter 4 that there is a standard set of names agreed on, so you can use any name you want, provided you do not use a name that is already taken. If on the other hand a name already exists for the file type you are dealing with, you should use that name. If you are making up a new name, put the letter "x" before it to indicate that it is nonstandard.

The file extension– the name the file will end with, such as .doc, .exe, or .txt. Any file for which the Web server has an extension listed is given the MIME name you define for it, and this name is sent to the browser asking for the file.

Apache/NCSA For this Web server, you must add a line like the following to the srm.conf file:

```
AddType application/x-msppt ppt
```

This line indicates that all files ending with the extension .ppt are of type x-msppt. The message that the file is of this type will be sent to any browser that requests a file ending with .ppt.

Setting Up a Resource Center

Depending on the information you make available to your students—videos, sound files, and so on— they may need certain plug-ins and helper accessories to be able to use it. You can create a page that contains a list of what students will require and where they can obtain the material. This list will change as sites move and new plug-ins are made available, so an up-to-date version of this file will be kept at the book's Web site. Most browsers now have an ability to automatically contact their home site about plug-ins that can handle the file they are attempting to download. This ability enables users to obtain the necessary plug-ins much more easily.

Setting Up Students' Web Browsers

As you saw in previous chapters, you may need to configure Web browsers to handle such things as helper applications and sending e-mail. You have a number of ways to ensure that students' browsers are set up uniformly.

One way is to set up a page of instructions that tells students how to set up their browsers. A second way is to set up one browser for a system identical to the one students will use, then distribute the configuration file for that browser to students and tell them to replace their computers' current configuration files with yours. For example, for Windows systems, the configuration files for the Netscape browser are netscape.ini (for the settings such as news server and helper applications) and bookmarks.html (for the file that contains a list of bookmarked locations). For both of these methods, you need students to have already installed the browsers on their computers.

Another method is the development of browser configuring software (known as administration kits) by companies such as Netscape and Microsoft. These kits allow you to create your own customized browser with your own configuration files in a form that can be sent to students so that when they set up their browsers, they will contain all the settings that you require.

Browser Settings You may want to configure the settings of the students' browsers to the following:

Set the course Web server as the home page. Then, whenever the browser starts, it immediately accesses the course server.

Configure the helper applications. Add the locations of the helper applications and their MIME types.

Set the news server. Give the location of the news server and the directory in which news articles are to be stored.

Set up the mail facility. If you want students to be able to send you mail using a form, you need to enter the location of the computer that will handle this mail. (Such mail servers were discussed in Chapter 6.) Most UNIX systems have a mail server built in and automatically enabled, so if your course server is a UNIX machine, you can set the outgoing mail server preference to your server computer.

Setting Up Students' Personal Space

In Chapter 5, we discussed giving students personal home spaces where they can place their own pages. You have a number of ways of doing this. You could give them an FTP location in which to place their files. You could give them access to the server or you could allow them to upload files to a location on the server. Note that all these methods involve a security risk to your server, so you should ensure that a close eye is kept on the system to prevent breaches of security by students.

Giving Students FTP Access We discussed giving students FTP access in Chapter 4. If your server also supports FTP, you can create FTP accounts for students.

Each student who has an account will be able to use FTP to log into the server and upload files into his or her directory.

Giving Students a Server Account If students can be given accounts on your UNIX-based server, they can place their Web files in their home directories. Most Web servers allow the use of paths to act as a guide to users' directories. For example, if you access an Apache server with the URL **courseserver/~fred**, the server will look in the home directory for the user with the name fred for a directory called public_html. Therefore, you can give each student a UNIX account and have students create or place their files in a directory called public_html (this is the default setting for many servers; others may vary), which can then be accessed using URLs. This way, students have complete control over their accounts, and you can keep your root directory off limits.

Allowing Students to Upload to the Server There are two ways of allowing students to upload to the server. One way is to see if your server will support the put protocol for uploading information (it should indicate if it does in its documentation). If your server does support put, you can turn it on, create accounts for the students (or create a common account for all the students), and allow students to use a browser like Netscape Navigator Gold, which has an option for uploading (or publishing) to servers that support put. Netscape servers support this method of file uploading.

The other way is to place an upload script in directories assigned to students. (We saw such an upload script in Chapter 4.) Once the script is in the directories, you need to make it executable by students who own the directories. For the Apache server, you need to alter the srm.conf to allow students to execute the upload script. Add the following MIME type to srm.conf:

```
AddType application/x-httpd-cgi cgi
```

You also need to alter access.conf as follows:

```
<Directory /usr/local/www>
Options {existing options} ExecCGI
</Directory>
```

where /usr/local/www is the root for your server. The upload script must have the extension .cgi for students to be able to execute it.

MAINTAINING THE SYSTEM

Performing Backups

Backups are important; they provide you with a snapshot of your system at some particular point in time. If something goes wrong and you lose information stored on your system, you can retrieve it from the backup.

The usual way to perform a backup is to use a utility, called an archiver, that will place the contents of your directories all in one file. This file, called an archive, can then be reduced in size using a compression utility. (We looked at some of these utilities in Chapter 4.)

Backup Devices Not many disks have enough storage space to accommodate a full backup of a system, but a number of devices on the market can be used to store your backup:

Zip drives. Mainly used for the PC and Macintosh, these are a form of disk drive that uses a special type of disk to store much more data than a normal floppy disk (20MB to100MB). A good, cheap method of performing a backup.

Tape drives. Common on UNIX workstations, they use a digital audio tape to store information.

Magneto-optical disks. A cross between a CD-ROM and an ordinary disk, these are another way of storing a large amount of information.

Be careful of the medium you use. For example, if your institution has only one tape drive, what happens if it breaks down when you want to retrieve something from the backup? Try to use media that can be read on machines that are readily available in your institution.

Backup Utilities You saw some of the archival form and utilities available in Chapter 4. Tar is the most common backup format on a UNIX system. Each tar file is usually compressed to reduce its size. Tar can also be used on the Macintosh (see **hyperarchive.lcs.mit.edu/HyperArchive/Abstracts/cmp/HyperArchive.html** for sources of tar programs, such as tar and suntar) and Windows machines (see **www.winzip.com** or **people.darmstadt.netsurf.de/tst/tar.htm**).

Tar backups can be compressed using the compress program available on most UNIX systems or the gzip program available for UNIX platforms (**ftp.sunet.se/pub/gnu/**) and PCs (**people.darmstadt.netsurf.de/tst/tar.htm**).

Again, like selecting your media, it is best to use a backup format that is widely used and for which you have machines available that can interpret it if your server breaks down. A number of commercial backup utilities are available to manage your backups for you. A list of commercial backup resources can be found at **www.yahoo.com/Business_and_Economy/Companies/Computers/Software/System_Utilities/Backup/.**

Backup Policy You should get into the habit of performing a backup and ensure that each backup you do is effective and thorough. Develop a backup policy for your system. This policy could incorporate the following:

Scheduling policy. Try to time your backup to avoid inconveniencing people using your system during your backup because a backup usually takes a large amount of system resources to perform. During a backup, access to the server is usually cut off to prevent users from interfering with files as the files are being backed up.

What to back up. Identify directories/information that need regular backup.

Frequency of backup. How often should you perform the backup—every day, week, month? Some information needs to be backed up very often, other information may not change for months at a time. You can create lists of information to back up and when each should be backed up.

Media used. What sort of media is used to hold the backup? Should you create a backup file and transfer it to another system? Or should you put your backup on a removable media, like a tape?

Storage. Where is the backup stored? If the backup is stored on the same system, any damage to the system will also damage the backup, so it is necessary to store the backup at least on a different system and preferably on a removable media that can be stored in a different building in case of fire or other damage.

Checking Server Performance

Assessing your server performance enables you to be satisfied that it can cope with the demands placed on it. You can do a number of things to check your server's performance. Let's examine a few.

Benchmarking Software You can use a benchmarking system to measure the speed of your server and the Web server software. The main benchmark system used at the moment is WebStone (**www.sgi.com/Products/WebFORCE/WebStone/**). Other benchmarking systems available are SpecWeb96 (**www.specbench.org/osg/ web96/runrules.html**) and WebBench (**ftp://ftp.zdnet.com/pub/zdbop/ webbench/webdoc.exe**).

You can also do your own benchmark test. For example, you could start 20 browsers and have them access a page full of large images. You could include a refresh tag (see Chapter 4) in the page header that would cause the page to reload at regular intervals and watch how your server handles the load.

Improving Performance How can you improve the server's performance? You could buy a server with a faster processor or with a better network card, but the two most common ways of improving a server's performance are increasing the amount of memory in the server and using a subnetwork. You can also alter your HTTP server to improve the speed at which it processes requests. Things you can do to it are as follows:

Switch off logging. This eliminates the effort needed to open and add to logs.

Disable accounts. If you require users to have a user name and password, switching this off reduces the time that the server must spend checking the user.

You can improve your server hardware by getting a faster CPU and a faster disk drive, but these usually lead to only marginal performance increases. Other performance improving hints can be found at **louvx.biap.com/performancetalk/slideframe.html**.

Searching and Indexing Your Site

One of the problems we looked at in previous chapters was how to set up your pages so that users can find the information they are looking for easily. We looked at creating index pages and navigation pages to help users get an idea of where the information would most likely be located. However, if users have only a few keywords to go on, you need to implement a more advanced system for searching the information you have available. We looked at methods for searching the Internet for information in Chapter 4; here we look at how you can set up your own searching system.

The way the majority of searching systems work is that they use two separate programs. One program examines all the files that you want to include in the search and notes information like the location of the file, the words contained in the file, and the time the file was last altered. This program is called an indexer because it creates an index of all the files and their contents. This index file is usually in a special format that can be read by the search program. The search program is used by someone searching for information. As you saw in Chapter 4, to do a search, you supply a list of keywords and start the search by sending these words to the search program. The search program then looks through the index file for the words you have specified and prints out all matching files. There are a number of indexing and search programs, each of which can index various types of files—for example, the Alta Vista indexer can index Microsoft Office and Eudora files as well as HTML files.

One thing to note about indexing is that an indexing program creates an index file that is about 5 percent of the size of the files it has indexed (assuming the files consist primarily of text). For example, if 100MB of files are on a system, the index for these files could occupy 5MB. This can also mean that a search could take some time and would be a fairly intensive task for the server to handle because the index must be loaded and checked a word at a time for each search term.

Table 10.2 shows some of the searching packages that are available.

We look at a number of indexing and search utilities, two of which (ICE and WWWWais-Swish) are included on the accompanying CD-ROM in the directory /setup/search. Each has its own particular features and limitations.

Table 10.2 Searching Packages

Name	*Platform*	*Location*	*Status*
Alta Vista	NT	altavista.software .digital.com	Commercial (demo available)
ICE	Written in Perl	www.informatik .th-darmstadt.de/ ~neuss/ice/ice.html	Free
Excite	NT and some UNIX platforms	www.excite.com/ navigate/prodinfo .html	Commercial, (demo available)
Topic	NT and some UNIX platforms	www.verity.com/	Commercial
glimpse	UNIX	glimpse.cs.arizona .edu:1994/	Free
Swish	Written in C	www.eit.com/ software/swish/ swish.html	Free (indexing program)
wwwwais	Written in C	www.eit.com/ software/wwwwais/ wwwwais.html	Free (Web interface for Swish and FreeWais)
SFGate	UNIX	ls6-www.informatik .uni-dortmund.de/ir/ projects/SFgate/	Free (Web interface for Free Wais)
Free WAIS-sf	UNIX	ls6-www.informatik .uni-dortmund.de/ir/ projects/SFgate/	Free (indexing program)

ICE ICE, written by Christian Neuss for the CERN HTTP server, consists of a set of two Perl scripts. The script ice2-idx.pl creates the index file; ice2-frm.pl searches this index file.

Indexing with ICE First, you must configure the ice2-idx.pl file. Edit the file and change the following entries:

```
@SEARCHDIRS =( 'whatever' );
```

This entry should be altered so the directories you want to index are placed within quotes. For example, to index the entire example Web site, you could change it to

```
@SEARCHDIRS =( '/usr/local/www' );
```

You should use the path format that is particular to your computer; the above is fine for UNIX, but for Windows you might use \usr\local\www, whereas for the Macintosh you may have to use usr:local:www or \\usr\\local\\www.

Next, you need to specify where the index file is going and what its name will be:

```
$INDEXFILE='WHATEVER';
```

For example, you could put the index file in /usr/local/etc/httpd/ice-index:

```
$INDEXFILE='/usr/local/etc/httpd/ice-index';
```

You will need to remember this location later on when you set up the search script.

You then set the type of the system you are currently on:

```
$TYPE="UNIX";
```

For example, if you were on a Windows machine, you could change this to $TYPE="PC"; if you were on a Macintosh, you could say $TYPE="MAC". Now run the script. It indexes the files in the specified directories.

The Thesaurus Once this is done, you can add a thesaurus. A thesaurus is very useful because some of the terms you use in your documents may have several meanings. For example, the words "computer" and "machine" could be taken to mean the same thing.

The thesaurus file for ICE can take two types of entry:

AB. Abbreviations.

EQ. Equality or a synonym.

For example, if you created a file called thesaurus, the contents of which were

```
Photo EQ Picture
URL AB Uniform Resource Locator
```

then, if the search program receives a request to search for the word "Photo," it would also search for the word "Picture" (but not vice versa; if you wanted it to search for "Photo" when given "Picture," you should put in the line Picture EQ Photo). The second line of the thesaurus file indicates that if the program receives a search request for "URL," it should also look for references to "Uniform Resource Locator."

Configuring ice2-frm.pl The second script is the one used to perform the search. You should put this in your cgi-bin directory (/usr/local/etc/httpd/cgi-bin) and perform the following alterations:

```
$title ="ICE Indexing Gateway";
```

which is the title which will appear on the search page. You could change it to your own title, such as

```
$title="English 101 Search";
```

Next, indicate where the index file is to be found. In our example, we put the index file in /usr/local/etc/httpd/ice-index, so you set the indexfile variable to indicate this:

```
$indexfile ="/usr/local/etc/httpd/ice-index";
```

If you created a thesaurus file, you need to indicate the location of that:

```
$thesfile ="/usr/local/etc/httpd/thesaurus";
```

Finally, you need to specify how to translate from the path on your disk to the path from the root. You do this by altering the root (in this case /usr/local/www) urltopath entry thus:

```
%urltopath = ( '/' , '/usr/local/www' );
```

This means that if the program finds a document called data.html in /usr/local/www, it will print out a link for the URL for that document as machine/data.html (which is correct from the point of view of accessing the system). If you get this entry wrong, any link that is returned as the result of a search will be inaccessible to someone clicking on the result, because it relates to a path that does not exist.

When ice2-frm.pl is called, it displays a form like the one shown in Figure 10.3. You can fill in the words you are looking for (or a list of words separated by "or" or "and"). You can also specify how old you wish the document to be, whether to

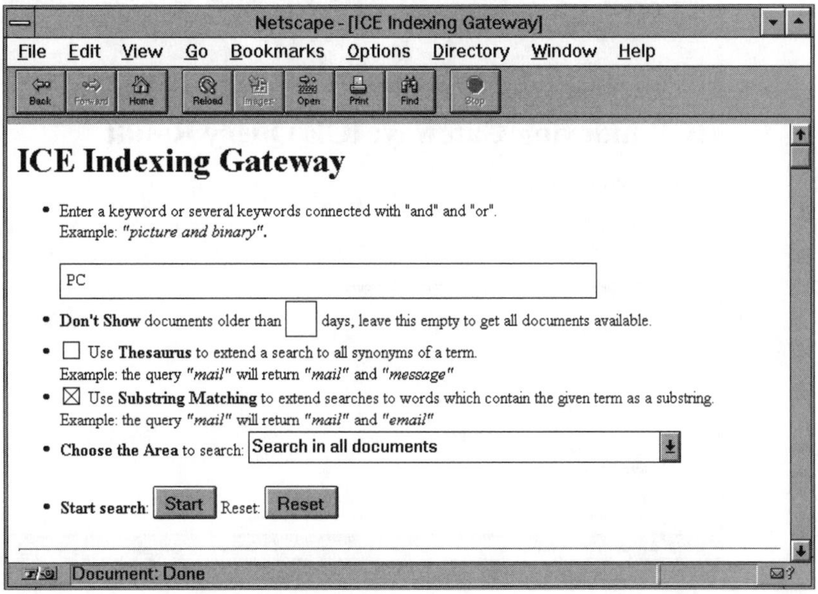

Figure 10.3 An ICE search page.

use the thesaurus, and whether to search for strings that contain the word you are looking for. Pressing the Start button begins the search. The result of an example search is shown in Figure 10.4.

The name of the document that contained the search term is shown first. This is also a link, so clicking on it loads that document in the browser window. The last modification date for that document is also shown. Following that is the path for the document. At the end of each entry is the name of the term searched for and the number of times it was found in the document. The documents are shown in order of most "hits"—that is, the document that contains the most occurrences of the search term is shown first.

Swish-WWWWais

Simple Web Indexing System for Humans (Swish) was developed by Kevin Hughes of Enterprise Integration Technologies as an indexing program. It is written in C and, like ICE, is a single program. The archive that contains the source code (swish.11.tar.Z) can be obtained from **ftp://ftp.eit.com/pub/eit/web.software/swish**. Also in this archive is a sample configuration file, swish.conf, which you need to alter.

Swish needs a C compiler to create an executable file. On a UNIX system, simply type "make" to produce the executable swish.

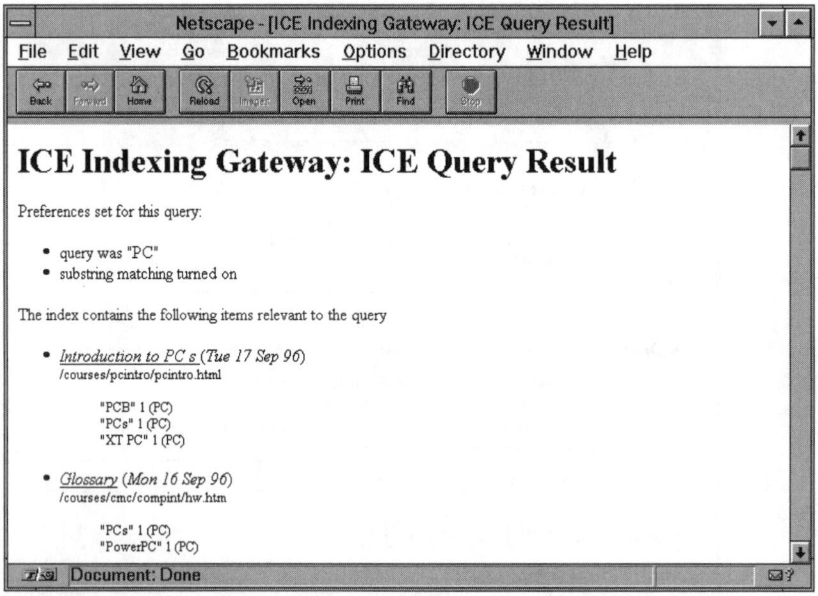

Figure 10.4 Result of an ICE search.

The Swish program uses its configuration file to create an index, so this must be edited to insert local information. First, IndexDir, the www root directory, must be edited. So, for the example, we would have

```
IndexDir /usr/local/www
```

Next, IndexFile, where the index file is to be kept, is changed to

```
IndexFile /usr/local/etc/httpd/cgi-bin/index.swish
```

ReplaceRules replaces the path of a file by the reference needed to turn it into a valid URL. For the example setup, we use

```
ReplaceRules replace /usr/local/www/      /
```

Other values to be altered include these:

IndexOnly. Tells the program which file extensions to add to the index.

NoContents. Tells the program not to look inside files with these extensions.

Filename contains. Swish will not index these files.

Pathname contains. Swish will not index files with directories that contain these names.

To run Swish, go into the directory with the executable and type:

```
swish -c /usr/local/swish/swish.conf
```

where /usr/local/swish/swish.conf is the configuration file. This creates the Swish index. You can search this index using the Swish program like this:

```
swish -f /usr/local/etc/httpd/cgi-bin/index.swish -w midterm
and result
```

This code searches the index you have created for files that contain the terms "midterm" and "result."

Be careful if some of your directories contain .htaccess files, because Swish will not index files in these directories or their subdirectories. You should remove the line

```
FileRules directory contains .htaccess
```

from the swish.conf file to index these directories. This prohibition is set up to prevent information in protected directories from compromise by an indexing program.

Creating the Swish index is one thing, but we would like to be able to search it using a Web-based interface. Such a program is available courtesy of the author of Swish; it is called WWWWais. It can be downloaded from **ftp://ftp.eit.com/pub/eit/web.software/wwwwais**. The last release was called wwwwais.25.c. You can also find a number of other files in the same directory, such as icons.tar and the WWWWais configuration file wwwwais.conf, which you should also download. Information about Swish and WWWWais can be found at **www.eit.com/software/wwwwais/wwwwais.html**.

Like Swish, WWWWais must be compiled before you use it. Before compiling it, edit the wwwwais.c file and change the #define value to indicate the location of the configuration file for wwwwais. For example, you could have

```
#define CONFFILE "/usr/local/etc/httpd/cgi-bin/wwwwais.conf"
```

Now compile it:

```
cc -o wwwwais wwwais.25.c
```

Move the executable file, wwwwais, to the cgi-bin directory and untar the icons.tar file you downloaded into an icons directory in your root. You now need to adjust the configuration file wwwwais.conf. Alter the following:

PageTitle. This holds the title of the search page.

SelfURL. The URL for the wwwwais program. In the example setup, it would be **courseserver/cgi-bin/wwwwais**.

MaxHits. The maximum number of results of the search to return. This prevents an excessively long response to a search term.

SortType. How to sort the results of a search. They can be sorted in order of score, where the score is the number of times the search term will appear in the file; lines, which is the number of lines in the file; or bytes, which is the size of the file. So, if you set sort type to score (the customary setting), the search results will be output in order of files containing the most hits.

SwishBin. The path to the Swish executable (the Swish program you created in the previous section).

SwishSource. The path to the Swish index file and a phrase describing it (e.g., English 101).

UseIcons. Whether icons should be used to denote the types of file.

IconUrl. The URL to be used for the icons. In our example, if you placed the icons contained in the icons.tar file in the directory /usr/local/www/icons, the IconUrl would be /icons.

Once this is set up, you can call WWWWais by opening its URL in a browser—for example, **courseserver/cgi-bin/wwwwais**. A screen like that in Figure 10.5 should appear into which you can input your search terms. When you click on the Search button, it returns a list of the documents containing your search term in the order you specified in the configuration file (see Figure 10.6).

If you have problem, make sure all your path names are correct and that the Swish index file is valid by running a test search using Swish.

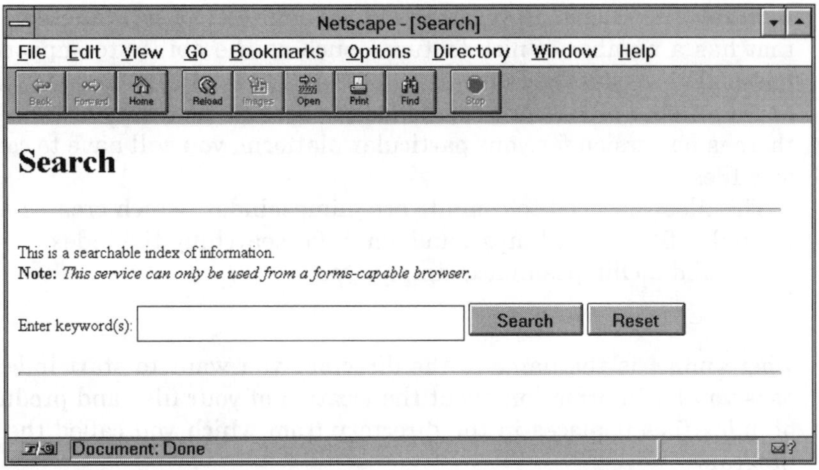

Figure 10.5 A WWWWais search page.

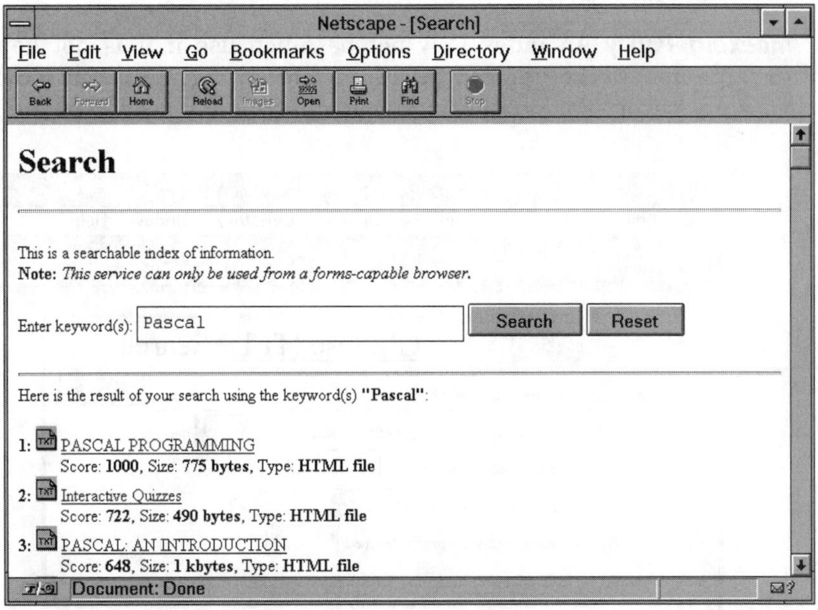

Figure 10.6 Result of a WWWWais search.

Glimpse The Global Implicit Search (Glimpse) tool is a another search utility that has a number of nice features, such as the ability to support searches for misspelled words. The home page for Glimpse is **glimpse.cs.arizona.edu:1994/** and a number of versions can be found there for a variety of UNIX platforms. If there is no version for your particular platform, you will have to compile the various files.

The files you need to compile are glimpseindex, which creates and maintains the index files and Glimpse, and agrep for searching the index.

To build a Glimpse index, simply type

```
glimpseindex name
```

where name is the name of the directory you want to start indexing. Glimpse asks you for information about the location of your files and produces a number of index files it places in the directory from which you called the glimpseindex program.

The Glimpse program can act as a search program, but for a Web page interface to the Glimpse program, you need to download the GlimpseHTTP program, also available from **glimpse.cs.arizona.edu:1994/**. When run, this program asks for the location of the Glimpse package and uses it to create indexes and a CGI searching program. An example of the Glimpse search program screen is shown in Figure 10.7.

Indexing Policy An index may not be much use if it is not kept up to date. Imagine how well organized your local library would be if it indexed its collections once every six months. However, indexing can be a very intensive task for

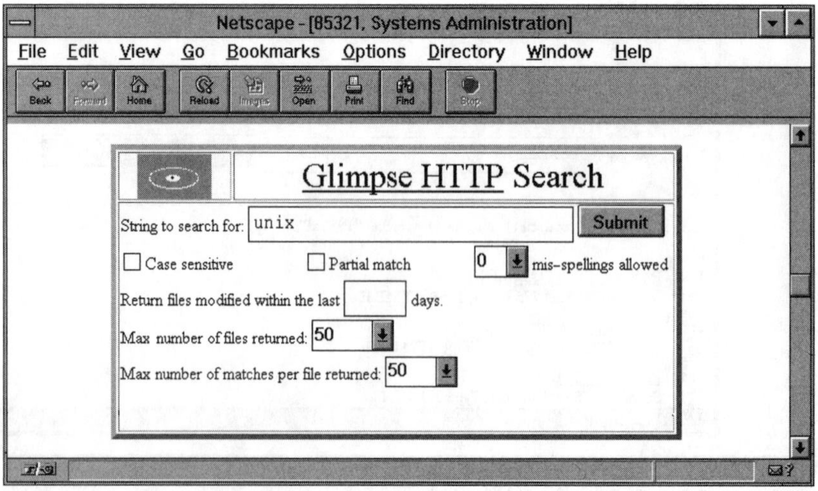

Figure 10.7 A Glimpse search page.

the computer to perform, so try and index at off-peak times. A good policy to adopt is to update the index when making a backup of the system.

Simple Search Simple Search (**www.worldwidemart.com/scripts/search.shtml**) is a Perl script that allows searching a site without having to create an index file. This means that you are saved the trouble of updating your index file at regular intervals. However, it also means that the script must search every file when it is called to look for the search term. This can be particularly time consuming for your server, so if you anticipate that your users will be doing a lot of searches, you may be wise to stick to one of the search utilities discussed above.

Another point about Simple Search is that it returns the results of its search in no particular order. This makes it more difficult to find the documents that are most relevant to you.

Setting Up a Problem-Reporting Facility

A number of problems can occur with any system. You can break down the problems into five main types: software, hardware, configuration (when there are problems with configuration settings), logistical (nonequipment or nonsoftware problems), and educational (when users don't know what they're doing).

You can implement a number of systems to ensure that people can notify you about their problems. You can use a simple e-mail link via which users can send messages regarding problems, such as a feedback method like the one discussed in Chapter 6.

Alternatively, you could implement a more complicated system based on a form that allows users to indicate the problem specifically and provide more detail (severity and frequency, perhaps). This can be implemented using the quiz-making programs shown in Chapter 7. Your form could contain the following questions:

- Please enter the URL where the problem occurred.
- Please summarize the problem in one line.
- Please enter your e-mail address.
- How frequently does the problem occur?
- If the problem is intermittent, can you say what you do before the problem appears?
- What is the severity of the problem? minor __ annoying __ prevents you working __

If you are managing a large system, you can implement a more complete error-reporting and management package that allows you to store your error reports in a database and query it to find out the status of an error (fixed, being examined, etc.). This type of package is ideal for a large system in which tutors or students need to report errors; your maintenance team can use it to help provide a list of what needs to be fixed and what sort of priority each error has.

One system for doing this is the free product Gnats/PRMS (Problem Report Management System). The Gnats page can be found at **alumni.caltech.edu/ ~dank/gnats.html**. This is quite a complicated system, but has a Web interface that can be found at **alumni.caltech.edu/ ~dank/wwwgnats/README.html**. It not only provides you with a facility to report and manage problems, but also to allocate problems to members of your maintenance team and watch the progress of the solution. It also allows you to keep a record of all problems that occurred for reference and use in updating and evaluating the system or planning new procedures and services.

If a problem-reporting system like Gnats is too cumbersome, you could set up a Web interface to a database that can be used as an error-reporting and management system. Details about Web-to-database interface gateways can be found at **gdbdoc.gdb.org/letovsky/genera/dbgw.html** and **cscsun1.larc.nasa.gov/ ~beowulf/db/existing_products.html**. You should also see Chapter 8's discussion of installing a Web-based database.

An Emergency Plan

It is important to make a contingency plan in the event of something happening to the system. How important this is depends on the importance of a system—if students are totally dependent on the system for their education, it is important to reconnect them as soon as possible. It's usually a good idea to prepare an estimation of anything that can go wrong with the system and to have a contingency or emergency plan available.

To formulate an emergency plan, you need to make a list of all that could go wrong, how likely it is to go wrong, how easy it is to ascertain whether the component has gone wrong (and whether built-in checks can be implemented), what sort of effect it could have on the course (so it can be assigned a priority for fixing), and how easy it is to put right. It is also in order to consider the steps you could take to prevent any mishaps and what sort of a procedure you can put in place for monitoring your system. For example, you could analyze the possibility of power interruptions and install an uniterruptible power system to cope with this. You could monitor the system by writing a page your browser continuously loads from the server. (See the CD-ROM discussion of benchmarking for details and an example of such a scheme.)

Log File Analyzers

To get an idea of how the system is being used, you can look at the log files your server keeps. There are a number of log files: error log files, which report the errors experienced by the server (can't find a certain page, for instance) and access log files, which are usually the most interesting. Most server access log files contain entries like the one below that show the name of the computer accessing the Web page, the name of the user who accessed (if you have enabled an access protection scheme), the time accessed, the name of the page, and the amount of data transported:

```
odyssey.ucc.ie - 91000000 [14/Sep/1997:17:16:05 +0100] "GET
/index.html HTTP/1.0" 304 0
```

Keeping log files is an option that is usually switched on by default when you install your Web server. The configuration file for a Web server usually gives the location for these log files. For our example server, the log files are found in /usr/local/etc/httpd/logs. You can view the logs in their raw form, but it makes more sense to have the logs summarized according to certain preferences. A large number of utilities are available to produce various types of log file summaries. A list of some log file analyzers is given in Table 10.3.

Most of the log analyzers produce the following details:

- A summary of the amount of times pages were accessed, usually in order of most frequently accessed first.
- A summary of the amount of traffic for each hour of the day.
- A summary of the amount of traffic per computer.

These details represent summaries of the traffic on your server. If you want to track access by user, you need to use a utility such as Follow.

You may set an interval at which you analyze the log files— once a week, once a month—to prevent being overwhelmed by the amount of traffic that can occur on your server. Note that log files can get quite large, so after analyzing them, you may do well to compress the current log file and create a new one to save space.

CONCLUSION

In this chapter, we looked at many of the procedures and utilities useful for setting up your Web-based classroom. Many servers now come standard with many facilities built in and with an easy-to-use interface. In the future, setting up and maintaining a classroom will be a reasonably easy task. However, no piece of software does *everything* you want, so it is a good idea to use a server and a platform to which you can add various components that other Web users have developed. This may not be possible with some commercial Web servers, so check out your requirements carefully.

RESOURCES

The following resources are explored in more depth on the CD-ROM:

- Newsgroups for troubleshooting problems
- Utilities
- Search engines

A

Using the CD-ROM

The accompanying CD-ROM contains programs and source code for the following platforms: UNIX, Windows 95/3.1/NT, and Macintosh. Instructions regarding the installation of individual programs can be found in their relevant directories on the CD-ROM. You can find the directories using the main index file located in the first directory of the CD-ROM.

You will need a browser to view the files on the CD-ROM. For a list of all browsers currently available, check **www.browserwatch.com**. The most popular browser, Netscape Navigator, can be obtained from **www.netscape.com/**.

LINKS

So that you don't need to type every HTTP reference that interests you, the CD-ROM contains a list of links referenced in the book. These links are ordered by chapter. Use the main index file on the CD-ROM to move to the file that contains the links. Clicking on a link brings you to that link's location. Remember, links can change quickly on the Web, so if a link mentioned in the book is no longer valid, please consult the book's Web site to check for changes.

USING THE CD-ROM

The main index file on the CD-ROM consists of a set of links to the files available on the CD-ROM and to related sites. To use the CD-ROM, proceed as follows:

1. Insert the CD-ROM into your CD-ROM drive.
2. In Netscape, choose the File option from the list of options. Choose the Open option from the menu displayed.

3. Change the directory displayed in the resulting list to that of the top-level CD-ROM directory (for example, f:\).
4. Highlight the file index.htm, which is located at the first directory on the CD-ROM.
5. Select OK.

THE BOOK'S WEB SITE

For the latest information and updates to files contained on the CD-ROM, visit the book's Web site at **www.wiley.com/compbooks/mccormack**. This site also contains discussion groups and a facility for reporting errors you might find in the book.

Index

N

O

Q

R

S

X

Y

Z